SYZYGY
Crossing the Bridge to Self

To Dee-Dee
Love,
Barb

BARBARA ANN JENNINGS
© 2016 All Rights Reserved

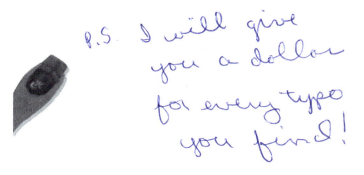

P.S. I will give you a dollar for every typo you find!

Cover Art

Joyce Mae Wilson
©2016 All Rights Reserved

*(**PLEASE NOTE**: My mother followed my naïve instructions in the painting of this cover art, but—while I love each and every stroke— I later found it to be more suitable for the syzygy website, which is great considering at the time I had no idea I was going to build a website. However, I did derive great joy out of incorporating various elements of her work in the design of the book cover and its interior.)*

Mom & Dad

In your honor, with gratitude,
compassion, and great love.

With our souls in sacred contract, one
with the other for the expansion of each
and, thus, the expansion of our Divine Source,
our reunion in other dimensions shall be enlightening.

Credits

Cropped fire and water images
from Free Images, www.freeimages.co.uk/.
See the story behind my creation of the syzygy logo
below the vertical navigation bar at http://bit.ly/1HVMSFp.

For further information on all footnotes,
please visit http://bit.ly/1T97t9G.

QUOTE FROM THE FRONT COVER[1]
"The syzygy seems to be an essential part of [Self],
or like two halves of totality represented by the royal brother-
sister pair, and hence the tension of opposites from which
the divine child is born of the symbol of unity."

Violet de Laszlo, ed.
*Psyche and Symbol: A Collection of Selected Works
from the Writings of C. G. Jung*
[http://bit.ly/1Mw72V6]

QUOTE FROM THE BACK COVER[2]
"Jung himself did not see the purpose of life as being the victory
of light over dark. Rather his own vision was one of wholeness, of
all elements of the Self moving in a complicated dance, in and out
of balance, in an endless, unfolding creative drama of growth."

Notable Names Database
[http://bit.ly/1I4FTKa]

My Alchemical Symbols of Self

Of my collection, I selected these stones to symbolize my four phases of Self-discovery, which may vary from one person to another. For me, they represent (clockwise) nigredo, the dark night of the soul; albedo, the enlightenment of the soul

(which also depicts the image of my soul in my mind's eye as a child); citrinitas, the new dawn (matter infused with spirit); and rubedo, or gold (a symbol of the soul's highest achievement, that is, individuation).

Who I Am

I WOULD LOVE TO TELL YOU WHO I AM in a nice, tidy little paragraph. But as much as I roll my eyes at the hackneyed phrase, "It's complicated." Yes, I know my name, although my character uses an alias. And it's true I rest my head on a pillow in Tennessee as of this editing. But I can hear Virginia Beach calling me, not with human words, but with whistles. More like a dolphin calling its mate. I swear, I would tell you who I am—if I only knew. But my surroundings often obscure my identity. Find Waldo if you can.

Nonetheless, no matter where I am or how far I travel, my roots twist and turn in the depths of a ghetto on the West Side of Syracuse. Dumpster flies and rubber bands aside, I was born to be a writer. Like Hershey kisses, words have been melting in my mouth since spelling bees in grade school. And to this day I salivate every time I walk into a library or smell the fresh ink hot off the press in a newsroom. When diagramming sentences, dissecting clauses, and juxtaposing and analyzing words, I feel like a forensic scientist raising words from the dead. I revel in metaphors that add new dimensions to reality. And similes that are full of surprises delight me. But if you really want to get a good laugh out of me, just dangle a participle.

Throughout much of my 20s, my kaleidoscopic eyes blossomed with Ferris wheels and fireworks and pampered pageantry. God and I huddled every day, and I gushed from room to room about the impossibilities—whether His answer was yes or no. With my childhood defects scuffed up like the etchings on a wind-battered tombstone, I had become best friends with my parents. And my husband, my best friend of all, cherished me. Together, we nurtured our chirpy little family in a cozy little village in a cheery little pink house, with perky tulips on both sides of the front walk waving at potential visitors. And in the backyard, modest marigolds tap danced along the perimeter of a six-foot privacy fence that assured them that one would have to climb a tree to see them. And my ocean of black and blue ink welled with waves of words, at first.

So much to see, so much to do, but my wanderlust words were shipwrecked. Sure, I could write eloquent, persuasive letters to anyone who outwitted me in an oral argument. But as I scribbled away my life, it occurred to me that I didn't know what I didn't know, and I damn sure didn't know how to write it. So I began taking night classes at University College. But I got smacked down by Therasia, my English 101 teacher, and by my sociology professor, who could have been my father's doppelgänger. I went on to defy them, or tried to anyway. But *summa cum laude* was knocked out of my reach when their grades came back to bite me at graduation.

Other than that crap, my little world was a candy land with cupcakes and peppermint stripes—until the day the doctors handed down death sentences for both my mother and my husband. I knew that prayer had saved my mother's life, but why hadn't it saved my husband's life? His death knocked the born again Christian right out of me.

I moved to Virginia Beach a year later and followed the White Rabbit down the hole, where I lost myself for the next three years in the masterpieces of English, American, and world lit, marveling at the wit, the literary devices, the genius. Everything intrigued me, from Plato and Aristotle to Emerson and Thoreau, from *Sir Gawain and the Green Knight* to Chaucer's *Canterbury Tales*. And Herman Melville's *Moby Dick* overwhelmed me with an impossible number of thoughts for me to process in one short semester. Meanwhile Ralph Ellison's *Invisible Man* and Toni Morrison's *Sula* touched my heart, and Emily Dickinson's poetry touched my soul. And, of course, I was star-struck by everything Shakespeare.

But it was through my in-depth analysis of Walt Whitman's poem "Out of the Cradle, Endlessly Rocking" that I first saw the pattern, that I realized that all religions are one. The only difference was how various cultures interpreted the Great One— the devil was in the details. However, I had no time to milk that cow, any more than I had time to lap up Moby Dick's ocean, as much as I wanted to. I had 10 short fiction stories to write for two independent research projects, and I needed an 'A' on both to graduate *summa*. Piece of cake—the masterpieces were chomping at the bit. Although my professor slapped 'A's on both projects at the end of the semester, I knew they were shoo-ins. I saw my fiction wipe out, as if thrown from a horse at full gallop. Confounded, I drove deep the dread that I had misunderstood my destiny and that Therasia 101 and Professor Doppelgänger were right: I would not be a talented writer.

I had maxed out on English credits by the last semester of my senior year—and I wanted nothing more than to just be done with it—when I discovered Edward C. Whitmont's *The Symbolic Quest* and Carl G. Jung's *Man and His Symbols*. They took my "Out of the Cradle, Endlessly Rocking" revelation to a whole new level. If only I had discovered the symbolic life sooner I lamented, I would have changed my major pronto. Stupid life. Even a shirt comes with a tag.

Ten years later, I found myself writing puffery for a trade association and married to someone who kept missing the elevator in my dreams. And there were loads of other detours since then, too, like that job editing and designing a daily newspaper for three years and working at a publishing company for seven years, proofreading transcripts, and editing and rewriting outlines for college-level courses in literature, art, photography, music, science, history, math, philosophy, religion, psychology, and economics, not to mention all those stints at various companies, providing technical support for one and payroll services for another, updating and maintaining websites and databases at others, and writing SOPs, RFPs, and mission statements, and—yikes! As I thought about all this wasted time, as I wrote it in my head while I was stirring the rice for dinner one late afternoon—a little ghost jumped out of my blind spot and yelled, "Boo!"

As I scanned my life in my rearview mirror, I realized that all of those detours equipped me with the exact tools I would need to write my Truth and to build the syzygy website. I realized that the 60 credit hours in literature required to graduate as an English major built a sturdy structure of bricks and mortar, but those three credit hours in philosophy established the cornerstone of my life.

Mastering clever literary devices to pen witty prose was not my destiny but just another tool to help me to get from point A to point B, like a very cool state-of-the-art satellite slash drone in my driveway, to help me to record and to interpret the endless data—but with a bum GPS. But first I had to get out of the house and behind the wheel. I was driven to be a writer. But I had misunderstood it as my destiny. It seems so obvious now. It's not about the destiny but about the journey, that space between leaving my driveway and arriving to my destination—the en dash on a tombstone—that is, not writing in and of itself but the message my writing hopes to convey.

Disclaimer

MY MEMOIR IS MY TRUTH, but I changed the names of most people to protect their identities. I also altered a few dates, sometimes creating composites of events, but only to avoid redundancy and/or identification. And where memory failed, artistry created dialogue, transitional details, and backdrops, but always in an effort to capture my Truth. I hope that for every quibbler, open minds and hearts will prevail and won't miss the deeper truth expressed between the lines. As part of this disclaimer, I quote Emily Dickinson and McKay and Fanning, who best illustrate my point.

> Tell all the truth, but tell it slant—
> Success in Circuit lies
> Too bright for our infirm Delight
> The Truth's superb surprise
>
> As Lightning to the Children eased
> With explanation kind
> The Truth must dazzle gradually
> Or every man be blind—[1]

"Tell all the truth, but tell it slant—" [http://bit.ly/1PSVJKB]
By Emily Dickinson [http://bit.ly/1NKcGkb]

This work is licensed under the Creative Commons Attribution-ShareAlike 3.0 Unported License. [http://bit.ly/1PSVJKB]

To view a copy of this license, visit http://creativecommons.org/licenses/by-sa/3.0/ [http://bit.ly/1Olbl8c]

Or send a letter to Creative Commons, PO Box 1866, Mountain View, CA 94042, USA.

I paraphrase the following from the work of Matthew McKay, Ph.D., and Patrick Fanning:

> We rarely perceive reality with 100 percent accuracy and objectivity. Most often we filter and edit, as if our eyes and ears were a TV camera and we were seeing reality on a screen in our head. Sometimes the screen is not in focus. Sometimes it zooms in on certain details and omits others. Sometimes it magnifies or minimizes. Sometimes the colors are off or the picture shifts to black and white. Sometimes when we are remembering the past, the screen shows us old film clips and we see no 'live' reality at all.[2]

Matthew McKay [http://bit.ly/21bQZn2]
Patrick Fanning [http://bit.ly/1Om9I8h]
Self Esteem [http://bit.ly/1lcGFKI]

Table of Contents

WHO I AM ~ i
DISCLAIMER ~ v
SYZYGY DEFINED ~ x
PREFACE ~ xi

PART I ~ 1

Introduction
1. Woodman quote about God as the Dreamgiver—Jung calls it the Self.
2. Woodman quote about crumbling foundations.

    Chapter 1:   the red Jell-O [January 5, 2000] ~ 2
    Chapter 2:   the frying pan [March 7, 2000] ~ 7
    Chapter 3:   the art of dying [March 8, 2000] ~ 14
    Chapter 4:   the first day of spring [March 20, 2000] ~ 24

PART II ~ 35

Introduction
    Woodman quote about a child's projection of "King/Queen" onto their parents.

    Chapter 5:   the human bean [1959] ~ 36
    Chapter 6:   the dumpster riddle [Fall 1961] ~ 47
    Chapter 7:   the storks [Fall 1962] ~ 56
    Chapter 8:   the color of blood
                    [Fall 1963 to Summer 1964] ~ 69
    Chapter 9:   the string that broke
                    [Fall 1964 to Summer 1966] ~ 75
    Chapter 10: the first bite [1966] ~ 83
    Chapter 11: the fine line [1967] ~ 91
    Chapter 12: the curse [1969] ~ 107

PART III ~ 117
Introduction
  Woodman quote about how when a child grows up they will seek a partner like their parent.
  Chapter 13: the color of my world [1970] ~ 118
  Chapter 14: the trooper [1971] ~ 125
  Chapter 15: the American pie [Winter 1971 to Fall 1972] ~ 130
  Chapter 16: the rape (well, not a real one)
              [Winter 1972 to Spring 1975] ~ 146

PART IV ~ 165
Introduction
  Woodman quote about a mother not wanting the baby.
  Chapter 17: the secret delivery [Fall 1975] ~ 166

PART V ~ 175
Introduction
  Woodman quote about the bird who has lived in a cage.
  Chapter 18: the golden dream
              [Winter 1975 to the Early 1980s] ~ 176
  Chapter 19: the blockage [Early 1980s to Fall 1985] ~ 193
  Chapter 20: the praying hands [December 1985] ~ 205
  Chapter 21: the athlete [Spring 1986] ~ 214
  Chapter 22: the vulture [June 1986] ~ 222

PART VI ~ 233
Introduction
Jacobi quote on four as an age-old symbol.
  Chapter 23: the dead babies awaken [1990] ~ 235

♂ SYZYGY ~ viii ♀

PART VII ~ 247
Introduction
1. Hall quote on anima/animus projection when 'falling in love.'
2. Woodman quote on projecting God onto your partner.
    Chapter 24: the crack in everything [Early 1990s] ~ 249
    Chapter 25: the repeat offender [Summer 1994] ~ 267
    Chapter 26: the lie [End of Summer 1994 to Winter 1997] ~ 269
    Chapter 27: the banana peels [Late 1998 to Early 1999] ~ 277
    Chapter 28: the little rag doll [Summer 1999] ~ 283
    Chapter 29: the brick in the head [Fall 1999] ~ 290

PART VIII ~ 301
Introduction
Woodman quote about return to the garden as coming full circle.
    Chapter 30: the magical smile [Spring 2000, Part 1] ~ 303
    Chapter 31: the mess I created [Spring 2000, Part 2] ~ 309
    Chapter 32: the unexpected storm [Spring 2000, Part 3] ~ 316
    Chapter 33: growing pains [Spring 2000, Part 4] ~ 325
    Chapter 34: the healing mother [Spring 2001] ~ 336

PART IX ~ 345
Conclusion
Woodman quote about women dreaming about beautiful little boys as their inner masculinity is healing; how too, by finding their soul, they discover the soul of the Universe at its core.
    Chapter 35: the pond beyond [Fall 2001] ~ 346

IN RETROSPECT ~ 355
SYZYGY WEBSITE & SITEMAP ~ 359
EPILOGUE ~ 362
DEDICATION ~ 364
AFTERWORD ~ 366
SOURCE NOTES ~ 367
SOURCES & RESOURCES ~ 383

Syzygy Defined

♂ ♀

sĭ'-zə-jē

LATIN: CONJUNCTION
GREEK: YOKED TOGETHER

Yin and Yang and Shiva and Shakti are just two embodiments that represent sacred duos, the Divine inner marriage—or the syzygy—of the masculine and the feminine.

> "The syzygy seems to be an essential part of [Self], or like two halves of totality represented by the royal brother-sister pair, and hence the tension of opposites from which the divine child is born of the symbol of unity."[1]
>
> Violet de Laszlo
> *Psyche and Symbol* [http://bit.ly/1Mw72V6]

"The special structures of the personal psyche, both conscious and unconscious, are four: the ego, the persona, the shadow and the syzygy (paired grouping) of animus/anima."[2]

"Anima (Latin, "soul"): The unconscious feminine side of a man's personality."[3]

"Animus (Latin, "spirit"): The unconscious masculine side of a woman's personality."[4]

James A. Hall
Excerpts from *Jungian Dream Interpretation* [http://bit.ly/1NlTnDH]

Preface

I BEGAN TO WRITE THIS BOOK IN MY MOTHER'S WOMB, kicking and screaming every inch of the way. The magical green frost of March christened the union that bore my soul, but that was it. Reality slapped me right on the butt in the early hours of December 17, 1955. I could almost hear the bartender say, "Drink 'em up." As Daddy lifted his beer mug, Mommy pushed her hardest.

As Mars slaved away in the depths of Scorpio trying to satiate his glut for food and sex, Venus's heart hardened under Capricorn's dominion.[1] Torn between two worlds like a rope in a cosmic game of tug of war, I was schlepped from the other side of knowing to here. In those few seconds I forgot some important stuff, like where I came from and why.

So I wandered for 40 years in the wilderness before I actually sat down to write a word of it. Uprooted in birth like a child of Israel, I had lost my way to the Promised Land. But as the child who once clasped hands with little Lucy in the school courtyard long ago, I would keep searching for home, for mama, for truth, for something, I didn't know what.

I didn't know Lucy that first day of first grade, when I found her crying in the courtyard because she couldn't find her mother.

"I'm sure this is where she said to wait," Lucy had said.

The next thing I remember, I was marching her through the streets like a trophy. Yummy smells, like pork chops and brownies, took their turns up my nose as my stomach growled. I had no clue which way to turn, but I kept on a brave face for Lucy. Just as I turned the next corner, sniffing the air for Mommy's burnt macaroni and cheese, I spotted the bar where Daddy sometimes pissed away his money.

"Hey, I got a great idea! How about coming home with me? My mommy's real nice, and she can file a missing person report."

"Call the cops? Are you crazy? Mama would kill me!"

I led Lucy toward the curb to cross the street, knowing my mother would kill me if she knew I was anywhere near that bar. I shrieked when the barroom door swung open behind us. Lucy turned to look.

"Mama!"

I handed over my charge, and ran home, barging through the back door to tell Mommy about my adventure, rendering every detail, as to how this good little Samaritan, little ol' me, had saved the day. But Mommy and Daddy were not amused. Before I could finish my story, Daddy yanked me by my collar and hauled me up the stairs to give me the belt because he loved me, Mommy said later, because I worried them.

"Daddy wouldn't have spanked you, you know," Mommy said after supper, when Daddy was in watching the six o'clock news.

"But we never know when to believe you. You're always making up stories."

I stomped my foot, my hands on my hips.

"I'm telling the truth. I swear on a stack of Bibles."

"There you go, Gabrielle, lying again. And blaspheming too! When are you ever going to learn? Repeat after me, I'm a liar!! Say it!"

"I'm a liar. I'm a liar. I'm a liar, a liar, a liar, a liar—" When I couldn't stop blubbering, she clamped her hand over my mouth, pressed her knuckles up against my nostrils, and pushed my head into the chair rail.

"Now let that be a lesson to you," she said when I stopped squirming, her finger pointing at me, her other hand on her hip.

Mommy was my queen and Daddy was my king, but if even they didn't believe me, if everything I thought was just in my imagination, then what was real? What was true? Am I real? Am I just in my imagination? I don't get it! Who am I if I am not me?

Eventually, I learned to shut up and repeat after them. But I learned a few lessons from Hansel and Gretel, too. Like Hansel, I had a hope, a shred of courage, a little genius, and enough common sense to leave behind a trail of shiny white pebbles. Someday I would remember once upon a time. Like Gretel, I would trick the wicked old witch into climbing into the oven.

Then I'd slam shut the oven door, eat and run. I'd find my way back to that path of moonlit pebbles, and follow them all the way back home[2] [http://bit.ly/1Lv7NtB].

But after stuffing myself on a sugarcoated house, I looked around and realized that I had left behind breadcrumbs instead. And I was pissed, really pissed, so pissed I would sooner pop your head off than look at you. I tried to think back. I tried to remember what made me so angry. I remembered trying to tell anyone who would listen what I witnessed, what I experienced, and how it made me feel—and all I could hear was my mother and father wisecracking: "When you grow up, you should write fiction!"

Well, here it is, Mom and Dad, to the best of my fictitious memory—in my efforts to figure out who the hell I am and why the fuck I'm so pissed off all the time—I'm about to tell the biggest story of my life.

PART I

"If you think of God as the Dreamgiver ... [you understand that] it is the Divine that guides the dream process ... keeps us in touch with our own path and therefore the path of the entire universe."

"What's not brought to consciousness is brought to us in fate. In other words, if you don't realize it consciously, it will keep happening, and you'll think God is cruel... . If you are not working on your dreams, you are living them.... If you don't dream, analyze what happened at the breakfast table this morning."

"Once it happens in the unconscious, it's just a matter of time until it happens in consciousness."

"The intuition will pick it up in the unconscious months before it happens. And then it will gradually work its way up to consciousness, and then it will explode."[1]

Marion Woodman [http://bit.ly/1PoTLrw]
Excerpts from Sitting by the Well [http://bit.ly/1OagpMK]

"If life is to be lived in a healthy, holy way, the archetypes that nourish the imagination must be pouring their energy into the ego. The dialogue must go on between consciousness and unconsciousness if we are to live creatively. It is therefore crucial to recognize when we have lost touch with our archetypal ground. When that happens we dream of crumbling foundations and flooded basements, collapsing underground parking lots, disintegrating retaining walls, cellars that have caved in. It is then our task to go down and do something about the chaos below."[2]

Marion Woodman [http://bit.ly/1PoTLrw]
Addiction to Perfection [http://bit.ly/1X6OqTQ]

1
the red Jell-O

THE BLACK XS
"Fuck you!"
"No! Fuck you!"
Griffin and I shove each other toward the edge of the scaffolding, an unfinished addition to the back of his parents' house, which overlooks a golf course. The tribal dance at the Indian reservation is about to begin. Griffin jumps off the ledge, lands on a motorcycle in the yard below, and motions for me to hop on the back.

"It's not fair. I want to drive, too." I say.
"To hell with it." He revs the engine and peels out, leaving me in the dust, not even a kiss good-bye, which is unlike him.

I'm roaming the house from room to room when Griffin pops back in, his hazel eyes slipping around under a coating of thin ice.

"Where, um, why—"
"It's none of your damn business where I went or why I didn't kiss you good-bye. Just shut the fuck up."

"Okay, honey. Please, just relax," I say, inching toward him. "Let me rub your shoulders, baby. It's all good."

He shirks my touch, and pulls out a pistol, which he points at me, then aims at the wall, then points back at me.

"Holy shit!" I back off, scanning the room for an escape. "You didn't fucking load that thing, did you?"

He lunges at me, like how dare I ask. We're struggling again on the edge of the scaffolding.

Then he stops, and lets me go.

"Of course I won't shoot you," he says, still pointing the gun at me.

I look from the gun to his eyes to the gun, then, click, it occurs to him.

"Yes. I might as well kill you. Because if I don't, you might try to kill me, considering all that's—"

The sun creeps out from behind the clouds as Griffin's voice trails off. As I shrink back, the ice melts, dimming his eyes. He takes my hand and leads me to the kitchen, where we sit at the table near the front door. I surrender as he fondles my breasts.

"Go ahead, baby, eat. I made them for you."

But soon his caressing tongue strikes out in hunger, and his hands can't seem to get enough of my breasts, which I had sculptured into funnels of red Jell-O. He stops, looks up at me, scopes out the room.

No one is looking.

Then he proceeds, growling and biting.

That's when it hits me. Oh my god. What if he eats all the Jell-O and discovers that I had hacked off my breasts, that there's nothing left but scars—two black Xs. He'll kill me for sure.

Dream Journal Entry
January 5, 2000

January 5, 2000

MORE LIKE IN A TRANCE THAN IN A DREAM, I snapped to, as if someone had said I will awaken on the count of three. One, two, three! I jumped out of bed, and backed away. As my eyes adjusted to the dark, it occurred to me.

He's not snoring!

His arm jerked up, just one arm, and it stunned me. It was as if he was there, for real, in my dream, and now he was toying with me.

I bolted from our bedroom to my office across the hall.

Images flashed through my mind of a man stabbing a woman to death in the shower at the Bates Motel and a dead mother sitting in the attic in a rocking chair.

I booted up my computer and flinched when it beeped at me. I fought the urge to vomit as I opened my electronic dream journal and searched for words like 'murder' and 'kill' and 'death.'

It's impossible. I would've remembered. But there it was, in my own journal. Griffin had been stalking me, trying to kill me for almost two years. In a dream dated February 2, 1999, almost a year ago, he had succeeded.

I'm floating on a raft on the flood waters of a familiar city. As I drift into unknown territory, I think it's fun, but I know I'm in danger. When I realize I'm back where I started, I'm somehow catapulted back on dry ground, where Griffin is stalking me, trying to kill me. He busts through two doors with several deadbolts on them, then swoops down on me with a huge frying pan, bigger than Big Ben's pendulum. I'm in a daze and about to lose consciousness, when it occurs to me, "Now I know what it's like to be murdered." [Uncut and unedited dream journal entry available at http://bit.ly/1ZyhNMA.]

I remember now. More than 20 years had passed since I'd read *Looking for Mr. Goodbar*, but the image of Theresa Dunn flashed through my mind that morning. I knew from the start that she would be murdered. Yet I was stunned when the phone was ripped from the wall, and the lamp rose above her head.

Is Griffin just going to flip out one day like Gary did on Theresa? Or is he killing me on a symbolic level?

"You just have an overactive imagination."

I could hear Griffin, and my dad, too, laughing.

Fuck them!

At least Della gets me. We meet for happy hour on Tuesdays to discuss our dreams. She's Freud and I'm Jung, and we love to dabble, to debate, to analyze, and to theorize about hypnosis, reincarnation, soul mates, astrology, past life regression, yoga, healing with stones, and meditation. We read tarot cards and shop at New Age stores, which tout lectures on shamanism and auras and chakras, oh my.

Every Tuesday's like finding a brand new yellow brick road. But even so, my journey was taunted by the idea that Griffin didn't care which phenomenon preoccupied me that week so long as I didn't interrupt his movie or his video game or his high by dragging him into it.

Well, he could have at it on Tuesdays.

Instead of sitting at the bar with our friends like usual, Della and I would sit at a table, our dream journals, books, and pens out, ready to thumb through, ready to share. At first our friends steered clear, but one by one, they pulled up a chair, some who were curious and others who just wanted to chat. But I didn't care. I felt like a crusader, and I hoped the nonbelievers would see the light and come into our fold.

One of them would recount a dream and then look at us, as if we were psychic, their bugged eyes implying that if this was a legitimate "Dream Circle," as Della and I liked to call it, then we should have a clue.

"If this were my dream," Della would say in the voice of Robert Moss [http://bit.ly/1Se2Cnz], who autographed our copies of *Conscious Dreaming* at a lecture in Virginia in October of 1999. Then she'd pick the dream apart, extrapolating on various interpretations, at least according to her experience. When she would finish, I would recite the answer I had rehearsed for just such occasions.

"Well, like Robert Moss says, it's difficult to interpret one dream without referring to a collection of dreams and then searching for patterns and recurring symbols. Imagine a rooster, for example, how differently a city boy who eats cornflakes every morning would interpret it compared to a farm boy whose family raises roosters."

But as much as I preached to others, I hadn't paid much attention to the patterns in my own dream journal—other than the dead babies, of course—until the death scare of the Jell-O breasts, that is.

Nonetheless, like a pebble lodged in tire treads, I went round and round, beating my head into the pavement, unable, or unwilling, to change course as my nightmares exploded into daylight.

2
the frying pan

CIRCUIT BREAKER
Griffin and I are at home, arguing nonstop. Just as it occurs to me that something awful will have to happen before we remember how much we love each other, I find myself at my mother's house, where pipes beneath the floor had burst, spurting water up through the floorboards.

If the water converges on the electrical wires bunched up in a corner, I will be electrocuted. I scream and run around the room, searching for the circuit breaker. Damn! I used to know where it was. I scream for my mother to come and show me where it is.

Just as the water swells up to the wires, my mother appears, spots the circuit breaker, and pulls the lever. I'm sitting in silence in a puddle in the middle of the floor with the plug in my lap. I sigh as a red glow recedes from the plug down the length of the cord.

Much time has passed when Griffin and I cross paths again. We speak and kiss with affection, then move on. I'm thinking that it's too bad we had to go through what we did but, on the bright side, the experience helped us to overcome our anger.

Dream Journal Entry
July 12, 1999

WHERE WILL THE NEXT BOMB GO OFF?
There is someone pursuing me. I run around the house locking up everything to prevent him from breaking in. Every time I think I have it under control, he finds some ingenious way of getting in. Then he tells me something about the two bombs

he has planted. One has exploded already, and I can see that it has maimed and killed my dog Tasia. I am horrified. The guy will not tell me for sure where he planted the other bomb.

He hints, "It might go off and kill Dakota, or it might go off in Chernobyl."

Dream Journal Entry
November 17, 1999

Acquainted with the Dead

Griffin and I are driving up a highway, going home, when traffic comes to a halt because of a huge crash up ahead. I can see that the accident was fatal, and somehow I am informed that I am apt to know several of the dead people.

Dream Journal Entry
December 14, 1999

At the Crossroads

Griffin and I are on some kind of long journey, and we make it two legs of the trip, but get stranded on the third, at some kind of station, where I find myself alone. Through the windows, I see people on sleds sliding down a huge hill. It looks like a lot of fun, but Griffin and I are short of money and must get home today because we now have two babies to take care of, which amazes me, considering I had a hysterectomy when I was in my early 20s.

I see a tram of people pass by and wonder how far it takes them, if it would take us home or if it is just for tourists and stays on this property. I meet a couple of ladies there, like caretakers of the place. One says this is where we would catch the subway home, but that it was Monday. The trains don't run on Mondays.

But I insist we must go home today. The ladies suggest I call a cab, which I do. The dispatcher says I'm out of the company's district. But he will make an exception. I begin packing up our stuff, which is strewn everywhere. I have stuff that goes into numerous little bags that then go into bigger bags, and I'm having great difficulty getting it together. The place is filthy, and I'm overwhelmed by the mess. Then, somehow, I burn the back of my left hand on something, like black tar. When I try to wipe it off, it spreads into a bigger and bigger circle, making it worse—

I'm in a shadowy underground facility at a crossroad, which I need to pass through to find my way back to Griffin and the babies. Two lady crossing guards, who look more like ghosts in the fog, are standing on the corners motioning to the other spirits as to when and how to cross over, like they can read minds. I speak to one crossing guard, who tells me telepathically when to cross, but I can't seem to get across. It occurs to me that it's silly, having crossing guards there. There's not even any traffic. It's a parking lot—

Back where I began, my mother, instead of Griffin, is holding one of the babies. I look down the stairs, and see the other baby slipping out the back door. I'm in a daze, and the danger doesn't occur to me for a minute. But when it does, I run down the stairs after it. Meanwhile the cab arrives. My mother is already in the cab holding the one baby by the time I return with the other baby. As I climb into the cab, it's weird, like descending into a basement with about six steps.

I set the baby down and turn to go back for my stuff. But my mother urges someone to—quick—shut the door. I'm very angry and want to get out to get my suitcases. I explain to her that I must at least have my toiletry bag. And there are other things I will need. But she says there is no room for my stuff.

Dream Journal Entry
January 30, 2000

March 7, 2000

"YOU'RE A DREAMER, FOR CHRISSAKE!"

"Well, you're an asshole!"

Tasia and Dakota, their heads hung and their tails between their hind legs, sulked down the hallway to our bedroom, where they would cower under the bed.

"I will get my Ph.D. I will finish my book. It just takes time. Wait and see. One day, I'll be on Oprah."

"Earth to Planet Gabby. I just can't picture you as a shrink. And you're not exactly famous. What makes you think anyone's going to publish your book? There's a ton of books out there. What are you going to write about that hasn't been written before? Be real. At least I know my limits. I don't try to be someone I'm not."

"But that's the point. I don't know who I am."

"You're 44 years old, for Chrissake. How can you not know who you are?"

"I don't know who the hell you are anymore. You always used to be so supportive of me. Now you fight me on everything I try to do."

"I liked things the way they were."

"Bullshit. You hated me being angry all the time. That's why I'm doing all this."

Griffin rolled his eyes, and for the first time I saw the scary man from my dreams standing right in front of me.

"You think by reading all this spiritual crap and by writing some book about your childhood, you're going to make some great discovery that's going to solve all your problems. Who cares? Shit happens. Just get over it!"

He slammed my journal on the table.

"Yeah, I read what you wrote when you were pissed off the other night, threatening to cram the dogs' hairballs down my throat when I'm sleeping. You're reading all this healing crap one minute, and threatening to cut off my balls the next. You're a hypocrite."

"You're an asshole! Yeah, I wrote that. But that's none of your damn business. You can't expect me to heal my anger overnight.

So when you piss me off, I write it rather than blow my temper at you. Joan told me to try it. And it's been working."

I stood up knocking my chair into the wall, then bent over and ran my fingers along the baseboard, scooping up a handful of dog hair, holding it up for him to see.

"I'd like to cram this down your throat right now," I said, fighting the urge to try it. "Tasia was fine. But you just had to have another dog. But now you won't even clean up after them. I'm sick of dog hairs all over everything, and you know it."

"And you know I've been under a lot of pressure at work. When I get home, I just want to chill. But, no! I gotta listen to your bitching, to your endless chitchat about some psychic fair or your session with Joan—"

"You're so full of shit. You haven't even noticed that I've made it a point for the last three weeks not to say a word to you about money, my dreams, my school, my interests—or dog hair. I was trying to give you your space. But where did it get me? Your perception of me hasn't changed one iota, but the house is now three inches thick in dog hair."

I flung the fur ball up in the air and plunked back in my chair.

"So little Miss Perfect is sick of dog hair. Well let me just tell you what I'm sick of. I'm sick of you analyzing everything I do. I'm an ISFP and you're an INFJ. Nothing but alphabet soup to me. It is what it is. But you're always trying to find some deeper meaning. I'm a simple person. I don't even dream, and I get along just fine. I work. I make money. I relax. It's that simple. Work. It's something you ought to try."

"Oh, fuck you! I'm still making the same amount of money temping and tending bar at the golf club. We would have plenty to pay the bills if we didn't spend 300 freaking dollars a week at the bar. That's $1200 a month. That's the mortgage payment right there with 200 dollars left over for chump change."

"You quit your job, and you have the nerve to sit there and tell me how I should spend my money? Who do you think you are, my mother? Always telling me what I should watch on TV, when I should do my chores, what I should wear."

"Oh! Now that you're half in the bag, why don't you tell me how you really feel! I always thought you wanted my opinion."

"If I had told you how I really felt, it would have turned into a fight just like it is now. I was just trying to keep the peace. But what do you care? You don't care what I think. If you did, you wouldn't have quit your job to go off on your own little tangent. And now you expect me to give up my lifestyle to accommodate you?"

"Face it, Griffin. I was bringing in $50,000 a year for the last two years. We were still always fighting and always struggling to pay the bills. A 'real' job or not we are still in the same boat. You're just using me as an excuse."

"I'm just saying that you're unpredictable, Gabby. I never know from one day to the next — from one minute to the next—what you're going to do. You're like Jekyll and Hyde. One minute you say you love me, and the next minute you're screaming so close to my face I have to wipe off your spit. I can't trust you."

"Can't you see how much I've improved? I used to get angry at every little thing, sometimes several times a day. But I've been keeping track. It's been three weeks today since I lost my temper."

"You can go six months without losing your temper, but you can't erase the picture in my mind with your face all twisted in anger telling me to go fuck myself."

"Go fuck yourself!" I screamed, my face twisted in anger.

"And you wonder why we don't have sex. How can I make love to you when all I see is that face when I close my eyes."

"Hah! Now use me as your scapegoat for that, too, you impotent little bastard! Did it ever occur to you that your lack of sex drive might have something to do with that half a bottle of Jack you suck down every night? That's why we couldn't even consummate our vows on our wedding night."

"Jack had nothing to do with that. It was you. Your bitching. Complaining that I forgot to light the fireplace. I forgot to light the candles. I forgot to dance with you when one of our songs played."

"You didn't forget those things. You knew the plan. But you said it was too warm that day. And it was. But I just wanted the ambience. To appease me, you promised to light the fireplace and the candles while I was getting dressed. If I had known you had no intention of lighting them, I would have asked someone else to do it. Someone I could rely on. But no! You promised to do it. Then you didn't. Then you want to know what the hell is wrong with me. Admit it. You were doing what the fuck you wanted to do."

Griffin's chair scraped the floor.

As I followed him to the bedroom, I was beside myself, my hands and voice shaking, my head swimming in alcohol.

"If you can't tell me you love me—if you can't understand where I'm coming from, it's over. The house is in my name. The truck's in your name. You can take your precious truck and get the fuck out of my house."

He packed his shit.

Twenty minutes later, when he finished loading the truck, he came back to the kitchen where I sat, my eyes already swollen. He stood by the counter and hesitated, as if he was trying to open a door, or at least not shut it all the way.

"Look," I said.

"What?" he asked, his ears already plugged.

"I'm sorry. I love you. I'm not trying to hurt you. I don't really want you to go. I just want you to hold me, to tell me you love me. That's all I've ever wanted."

"You're too fucking needy, Gabby."

When he slammed the front door behind him, a huge frying pan, the size of Big Ben's pendulum, came crashing down.

A new day would not dawn.

3
the art of dying

Dying
Is an art, like everything else.
I do it exceptionally well.

I do it so it feels like hell.
I do it so it feels real.
I guess you could say I've a call.[1]

> Excerpt from "Lady Lazarus " [http://bit.ly/1X6OSBz]
> By Sylvia Plath [http://bit.ly/1I4PJMd]

March 8, 2000

"OH, GOD! WHAT HAVE I DONE?"
Not that I expected an answer. I had washed my hands of God 14 years ago, the cursed month of March, as a matter of fact. Like lemon drops, unshed tears puckered in the hinges of my jaws. I rested my chin on my palms as my finger tips kneaded out the prickles.

I refuse to cry another tear over that bastard.

I sat back in the kitchen chair to admire the airbrush paint job on my fingernails, where stars studded with sequins twinkled and crescent moons dangled in a midnight-blue sky beneath the smoky wings of birds, hovering in shadows, mirroring my soul.

"How much did you pay to have that done?"

That's all Griffin had to say.

"Fuck you."

I scanned the bookcase, where I had assembled my collection to mimic arrangements in magazines, intended to impart peace.

Yeah, right.

Three weeks ago, when I was dusting, I had dropped my favorite piece, a crystal ball, shattering the crystal stars that hung from its pewter base, shaped like two half moons back to back, a priceless treasure Griffin had bought for me in Key West during the holidays.

"Come here, Gabby. You're going to love this," he had said, leading me into the shop next door. Then he bought it for me, a gift for our third anniversary, he had said, a gesture I had hoped indicated he accepted the 'New Age' me.

He strolled ahead, smiling, the gift bag swaying at his side.

We will make it after all.

"Mother fucking, son of a bitching bastard. I can't fucking believe I did that."

"What? What happened?"

Griffin flew into the kitchen as if he expected to find the walls covered in blood.

"I knew it was going to happen. Damn it! Why the fuck didn't I pay attention to what I was doing?"

Griffin scrambled around on the floor picking up the pieces.

"I can fix it, glue it."

"Fucking shit! It can't be fixed. The best part of the crystal ball is broken."

Even that morning, though Griffin stood right in front of it, he didn't see it, not until that night, when I lit the candles.

"What's this?" he had asked, eyeing the column of shelves once cluttered with phone books and cookie jars. "An altar?"

His eyes followed the smoke trickling from vents shaped like stars and moons of the little potbelly incense vessel. He looked from shelf to shelf where I had arranged precious stones and ordinary rocks, musical glitter domes that encased angel figurines, and ceramic praying hands, ashen with age, a pyramid candle, an Egyptian fountain, and the crystal ball that once had stars dangling from its base, until the day I dropped it.

Fucking dumb ass.

That night, Griffin tended to the candles and kept the incense burning as if he understood what it meant to me, as if he understood what I have to do, that is, fulfill the prophecy written on the little gray magnet of the glowing moon, a gift from Della, which reads, "Shoot for the moon, and even if you miss, you'll end up among the stars."

But blood rushed to my face when I remembered Griffin's tone, his shrug, his eyes rolling as he mocked my dreams, my search for meaning, which didn't end up among the stars, but in a world of hurt. I had begun my search almost two years ago with a few simple questions: Why am I so angry all the time? What's really wracking my soul? What is it I sense missing? Who am I?

The more I searched for answers, the more confused and frustrated I became, like a dog with worms chasing its tail. In my search for Self, I lost myself—and Griffin.

"I liked things the way they were," Griffin's words flat-lined through my thoughts.

Marion Woodman's voice responded.

"The old Mother, that old dragon that sits in the bottom of the unconscious and doesn't want anything to change. It's static. It likes it the way it is. And if the little ego tries to do anything, she just puts out her tongue and just goes—cluck—that's the end of that. You try to do something, and that voice just says, what's the use? Why bother? It's all been done before. Much better than you'll ever do it. You know, get up and look in the mirror, and see who you think you are."[2]

I stood up and dragged myself to the bathroom mirror.

It was almost daylight, and I had downed enough beers and a bottle of Naprosyn marked, "Warning: Do not take with alcohol." I flipped the bathroom light switch off and went to bed, my eyes dry, my heart clouded over. The dogs stepped aside. Steeped in their sadness, I fumbled with the bedding, crawled under the blankets, flattened the pillows. To know what it's like to be murdered is one thing, but to know death, ah.

My bones and muscles melded into the absence of light as disjointed images of my life fumbled around in my head. A clear voice uttered the words of a poem I had memorized for a speech project my freshman year in college.

"Dying is an art. . . ."

Like a zombie, I awoke at noon, wondering if I, too, was a Lady Lazarus, who Sylvia Plath named after Lazarus, Mary and Martha's brother, who Jesus raised from the dead in John 11. I don't know why God couldn't just mind his own business. Alas, I decided that if God insisted on mocking me, as did Griffin, I would need a housemate to share the bills. I called my temp job and took off the rest of the week citing a personal crisis, put a cold pack on my eyes, then did my chores, and Griffin's too.

I sucked up wads of dog hair from the hardwood floors with the vacuum cleaner hose, then mopped. But the oil soap couldn't cut the layers of dirt, which streaked as I swirled the mop, spreading into bigger and bigger circles of grime. I tossed the mop out the door with the dogs, then vacuumed the once-beige carpet. But the machine had no effect on Dakota's dried up piss.

As I slumped to the floor, the walls and furniture receded into shades of gray.

Ping. Ping. P-ping.

One by one, the rubber bands that secured me to Earth snapped. My head became detached, then my shoulders, then my arms. Anxiety oozed from my gut. Reality slipped from my reach. The abyss invited me in.

Ping, ping.

My feet were free.

My last rubber band was hooked like an anchor to the base of my spine. It stretched to the breaking point.

Boing.

Tasia nudged my elbow and whimpered, and Dakota licked my hand.

I called the suicide hotline. I called a mental health hotline. But no one wanted me. Dejected, I pounded down lots of beers.

I woke up Monday morning, son of a bitch! At work, in my cube, I couldn't keep track of my pen. The red light on my phone flashed, but I couldn't remember how to retrieve messages. I kept looking for something, but kept forgetting what. Then to complicate matters, the phone rang.

"Um, you, this is, um—Gabby. Hi, I mean, Hello?"

"Ditzzz—" said the dial tone.

I hung up.

The power of positive thinking.

"Attention is what you focus on and for how long," my psyche 201 instructor had told the class. "Remember it. It'll be worth 10 points on your midterm."

But I didn't get it.

"You MUST main-tain FO-cus," I repeated in Arnold Schwarzenegger's voice every time I peered over the edge of a skyscraper.

The power of positive thinking.

The phone rang again.

"Hello. You have reached the technical support line at Energy Software. This is Gabrielle. Can I have your serial number please?"

Between calls, I went to a search engine and typed in 'the power of positive thinking,' which directed me to a site for a free e-book [http://bit.ly/1NmLvSo] on the power of positive thinking, by Norman Vincent Peale [http://bit.ly/1OntMXY]. Interesting. I had no idea he founded *Guideposts*, the magazine Grandma Williams had been subscribing for me for Christmas for years, but like the old *Readers Digests*, they soon gathered dust in a stack on a bookcase.

I began to read something about how our minds are not just in our brains as some tend to think. Our minds permeate every cell in our bodies. And whether real or imagined, our bodies react to every positive—and negative—thought. What we think creates our reality.[3]

It doesn't make any sense. It's backward. I think the way I do because of what happened!

I didn't get it, but it was worth a try. I began to train my thoughts to create a new reality.

Yes, Griffin will return, and we will rebuild our marriage. Yes, I will excel at my temp job and be hired permanently. Yes, I will drop my crazy idea of getting a Ph.D. at my age. Yes, I will give up therapy. Give up my book. Yes, things will be better then, back to the way Griffin likes them.

That night, when Griffin came to the house to pick up some of his stuff, he said that during the weekend he had read, *This Much Is True I Know*, the book I had asked him to read months earlier.[4]

But I know this much is true: It's too late.

"Too bad all the people in Dominick's life died by the time he got over his anger," Griffin said.

Too bad you waited until our marriage died before you got around to reading it.

"And it really hit home when, what's her name?"

"Dessa," I said, rolling my eyes. He knew damn well what her name was. "It hit home when Dessa told Dominick his anger consumed all her air when he was in the room, and that's why she had to leave him."

"Yeah," he said.

I knew out of the 900-plus pages of that book that Griffin would cling to that one sentence and miss the point of the rest of the book. Joan, my Jungian analyst, had suggested I read it. She thought I might learn by Dominick's struggle with anger, how to learn to deal with my anger. I read it in three days, then gave it to Griffin to read, which he said he would. I wanted us to talk about it at the end of each chapter, so that we could discuss the parallels between my journey and Dominick's, to show him how Dominick healed his anger, and I would too, so our marriage could avoid the same fate.

But the book turned yellow sitting on the back of his commode. Now that he finally read it, he identified with Dessa. He clung to my anger like a Frisbee that landed beyond the No-Trespassing sign in his backyard, a weapon he could boomerang back at me to justify himself later. He believed that he personified the perfect little angel Wally Lamb projected through Dessa. He didn't get it, and nothing I could say would change that.

He hugged me hard. Packed more of his stuff. Before he left again, he said we'd get back together, but he needed some time.

"I'll call you at the end of the week," he had said.

On St. Patrick's Day, I grieved in dry silence. March 17. Once upon a time, my wedding day with Teddy, who also died in March, on Easter Sunday.

March. I hate March. Now March and Griffin is gone. March sucks.

The phone never rang that night or that weekend. But I rejected every angry thought, amazed at how easy it was to play this little trick on my mind.

Sunday night, I went out to the other bar, the one Griffin boycotted after he said they had ripped him off. I drank a few beers and talked with the patrons about nothing that really mattered. I hadn't told anyone that Griffin didn't come home nights anymore, that he slept at his best man's house.

George came in from the bar across the street, the bar where Griffin and I usually hung out together and played darts until closing.

"What's up? How come you're here and Griffin's across the street?"

"We've got a few issues," I said.

"Issues you can work out, I hope?"

"I hope."

"Give the man a hug, and it'll all work out," he said. "You're a very beautiful woman."

Hah, beautiful! Little do you know.

I gulped down my beer, paid my tab, and walked to the bar on the adjacent shopping strip. I approached Griffin from behind, between his turns at the dartboard, and touched his back. He turned around in surprise, then pecked me on the lips. We talked about his promotion and his dart game. By last call, his darts wouldn't stick, and he began to bump into tables. But I loved him. I drove us home in his truck, and we spent the night in our king-size bed, holding each other in a way that I had wanted for so long. The next morning he dropped me off at my car.

"I'll call you tonight after work," he had said. "We can have dinner and figure out the bills." Then he kissed me, a peck, as if it were an ordinary day.

I should have rippled with excitement, knowing that we would snuggle in the same bed tonight. But a commotion in my stomach tormented me all day, like butterflies, like when one first falls in love. But these were sick butterflies.

"You MUST main-tain FO-cus."

Of all the days to feel so negative. Cripe! I wanted to show Griffin how much I've changed. But my old self had crept in, and I couldn't shake the bad vibes. I guarded my words as I wrote them, expecting the phone or doorbell to ring any minute.

7 p.m. Not unusual.

8 p.m. Probably wrapping things up.

9 p.m. Probably on his way.

10 p.m.

10:03 p.m.

10:07 p.m.

I couldn't take it any longer. I dialed his work number.

"Griffin, here."

"What's up? I thought you were going to call."

"I've been busy."

Unaware of anger ticking, I blew up.

"Too busy to at least call your wife and say you can't make it?"

"Gabby, I'm busy. I don't have time to go into this with you right now."

"That's the problem. You keep blaming me. But it's you who can't deal with a family. You can't even take two minutes to call me to say you can't make it. You just leave me sitting here like an idiot while the food gets cold. And when I get mad, you say I'm too needy. How the fuck do you expect me to react?"

"Look, I gotta go."

I tried to hold on. I tried not to cry.

"Gab, I don't see us getting back together."

"We've got to at least talk," I said. "So much has happened the past few weeks, that I've learned, that I want to share."

"Write it!"

The clock stopped ticking as Griffin's two words banged around in my head.

"How can you be so stupid, you fucking moron!" I yelled at myself, slamming down the phone. As I stood up, I flipped the kitchen table over on its side. Ashtrays and cigarette butts and beer cans went flying.

I grabbed another beer and sat on the floor amid the mess and cried between guzzles. There is a bottle of pills calling out for me, and this time I will not fail. This time I will not kill myself over him. I will kill me for me, for screwing up my life, for not becoming the writer of my destiny, for being stupid enough to think anyone would believe in me enough to hang in there not only through the good times, but through the bad times.

"Fuck it. All this time I've been searching for meaning, and all I did was waste my fucking life," I screamed at God, as I stood up and plucked the cassettes on the power of prayer from the bookcase and threw them on the floor.

Meep, meep, meep, meep.

"What kind of God are you?" I yelled at the ceiling.

The same God who took Teddy from you.

"It's the sins of your past catching up with you," I could hear Grandma Williams say.

My buttocks prickled. My face reddened.

"I hate you, God! I hate you, Griffin!"

I climbed up on a chair to reach the top of the hutch, where I had hidden Teddy's machete, which was once part of his medieval collection, and I fell on it. I jumped off the top of the house and splattered on the cement sidewalk below. My Mercury Topaz careened off a bridge. I remembered a high-school girlfriend, whose brother hanged himself in a ravine. I remembered my cousin who hanged himself from a tree on the edge of a vacant parking lot and my uncle who shot himself in the head. I slumped over in a puddle of blood, my brains all over the cement. I remembered the maintenance people who had to scrape my uncle's brains off the wood floor.

"Dying is an art," Sylvia had said.

"It's so fucking simple. A blow dryer in a tub of water or turn on the gas."

I hate you, you fucking little coward.

Just as I popped off the childproof cap, the stupid phone rang. The caller ID—yes, even in the throes of death, one must look. 'Out of Area.' A telemarketer, no doubt. I seized the moment. I would hang up one last time on someone trying to switch me from one long distance carrier to another. I'd tell them if they can fix the loose connection between God and me, I might consider changing services. But my jaw dropped when my mom and dad's voices chimed in together on their speakerphone 1,600 miles away.

"Hello, Gabrielle."

"Hello, Gabby-doll."

Overcome by the sounds of their voices, I began babbling. I told them everything, about Griffin, about me, about the pills, about the ledge I dangled from, and the fact that I was about to let go.

"We knew something was wrong. Your father and I were just sitting here looking at each other. But I could read his mind. Call her, I told him. Eight kids, but he knew who I was talking about. Without another word, he dialed your number. And you know him, the way he worries about long-distance fees."

"Yeah, I don't know how I knew it. But I've been worrying about you for the last month."

"Hop on a plane, Gabrielle," Ma said. "We have a spare bedroom, plenty of food, everything you need. Take all the time you want to sort things out."

"Yeah," Dad said. "And while you're here you can show us how to use that stupid computer Mariah gave us."

"Plus, you can use it to write your book," Ma said.

"Maybe I should. But I can't fly. I don't know where it came from but I'm suddenly afraid of heights."

"Well, you can't drive. That's too far by yourself!" Ma said.

"I'll be okay. I think I would have a stroke if I tried to board a plane."

"Hear that, Gabby," Dad said, chuckling, as his multitude of clocks chimed in the background. "It's midnight. And today's the first day of spring."

4
the first day of spring

"The duckling is led to within an inch of his life. He has felt lonely, cold, frozen, harassed, chased, shot at, given up on, unnourished, out there way out of bounds, at the edge of life and death and not knowing what will come next. And now comes the most important part of the story: spring comes, new life comes, a new turn, a new try comes. The most important thing is to hold on, hold out, for your creative life, for your solitude, for your time to be and do, for your very life; hold on, for the promise from the wild nature is this: after winter, spring always comes."[1]

"The insistence of keeping a thing private is poison. In reality, it means that a woman has no support around her to deal with the issues that cause her pain."[2]

Clarissa Pinkola Estés [http://bit.ly/1lcHVNN]
Excerpts from Women Who Run With the Wolves
[http://bit.ly/1Sd2y7B]

PACKING STONES

I'm packing an array of stones and figurines in a box, but they won't fit. I work at this for some time and end up filling something like a display case, each piece wrapped in paper in different compartments. My old boss, Aleisha, comes in, and I am glad because I want to explain to her that I can't do one of the jobs because something has changed since she had assigned it to me, making it impossible to complete.

She looks at the case of stuff I had wrapped.

"That's why," she says. "By the time you finished getting all those things put in their places you forgot what you were doing."

She tries to take over the job and realizes that I'm right. The job can no longer be performed with the original specs.

Dream Journal Entry
January 30, 2000

GIFTS

A heavyset woman wearing a yellow floral-print dress is choking back the urge to cry. She and her husband are breaking up, and she is leaving. There are many gifts in wrapped packages that she's picking up and taking with her. A voice says she's very rich, that she doesn't need these packages. But I figure she is taking them with her to ease her pain.

Dream Journal Entry
March 1, 2000

March 20, 2000

THE NEXT MORNING I FELT LIKE SHIT. I looked like shit, too. As my tiny, crusty eyes peeked out over mounds of cheek, I noticed the tips of my bra crinkled without enough flesh to fill them. I must have finally lost a pound.

Whoop-de-doo.

As I looked at my reflection in the mirror I played back the quote I had read on the power of positive thinking website.

What you think permeates every cell of your body.

"You create your own reality," I announced to the mirror.

That's fucking scary!

I laughed at myself.

"You are safe in the arms of the Universe," I chanted, as I rummaged through my dresser drawers, and dirty laundry, and the washer and dryer, stuffing my clothes in trash bags.

When the phone rang, it freaked me out for a second.

"Ah! Della. What's up?"

"Happy spring," she said. "How about our dream circle tonight instead of tomorrow night?"

"Um. Sure. But the earlier, the better. Okay?"

Fucking computer!

I ransacked the house, the dogs underfoot, packing my toiletry bag and wrapping knick-knacks and ornaments in towels and sticking them in nooks and crannies in the passenger seat and back seat and trunk, all the while my heart and brain racing against each other as if I were cleaning up a crime scene.

I can see them all gloating, especially the jealous ones.

"Stop it! Your thoughts create your reality," I said, as I shoved some of my favorite books under the car seat.

"Good-bye, Tasia. Good-bye, Dakota."

I gave them doggie cookies and kisses. They wagged their tails and licked my neck. But I could hear what they were really thinking.

It's just as well. Now you won't scare the crap out of us every time something goes bump in the night.

I fought back the urge to barf as I backed out of the driveway.

Hold on to your oatmeal.

I watched my back as I popped the rear gate of the Durango with the remote and retrieved my golf clubs and my tennis bag. And let's not forget the sterling moon with a crystal star hanging from the rearview mirror. I fidgeted with the chain, my eyes flickering back and forth from the charm to the rearview mirror. But my breath soon fogged up the windows.

"Mother fucker!"

I backhanded the sweat from my eyes.

At last, I got it. I held it tight as I slid out of the driver's seat, and took stock of the parking lot and the fifth-floor windows.

All clear.

From there, I drove around the corner to the bank.

You little thief!

"Would you like that in small bills or large?"

It's just a thousand bucks.

"Large bills are fine."

Thief!

"Have a nice day," the teller said.

Half the money's mine anyway!

"You too," I said, as I sped out of the drive-thru as if I had just robbed a bank. Zipping in and out of traffic with my eyes fixed more on the rearview mirror than on the traffic in front of me, I rushed to the bar.

As I was reaching for the doorknob, I saw a strange reflection in the tavern window, and an old tune began to play.

Those were the days [http://bit.ly/1N7oSMC].[3]

"Hey," I said, seating myself on the stool next to Della.

The bartender held up a Coors Light bottle, and I nodded.

"Hello to spring, to butterflies. Woo-hoo." Della said, saluting me with her rum and coke.

"To new beginnings," I said. "Good-bye, Griffin. Hello, Texas."

"What!?"

"I'm done with that fuck wad. The asshole promises to call me, then he doesn't. Then he acts like he can't understand why I'm so pissed off. He says he hates it when I'm pissed off, but he does everything he can to piss me off."

"Hey, slow down. Back up. I'm sure he meant to call. I mean people get busy and forget."

"He didn't fucking forget three times in a row, especially when he saw how much it upset me the first two times."

"Don't you think you might be overreacting?"

"Oh, for god's sake, Della. I'm telling you, he's pushing my buttons on purpose. He said he didn't like me angry all the time so I've been working on that, now he says he doesn't want things to change. He wants them the way they were. I can't fucking win!"

"Try looking at it from his point of view," she said, walking her fingers across the bar, showing the two of us walking side by side. "You both had your careers and shared financial goals. And then you suddenly quit your job and go back to school," she said, as her fingers representing me veered down another path. "You've changed paths, and he needs time to adjust."

"Oh, my, god, Della. Duh-ditty-do, Underdog! No matter what I'm upset about—as if I'm the villain—you always take anyone's side but mine. You never see it from my point of view."

"Never say never."

"You're fucking killing me. I swear, you're almost as bad as Griffin when it comes to pushing my buttons."

"I'm just playing the devil's advocate. I think you two can work it out. I don't think you should make such a major decision when you're so upset."

With my eyes stinging, I shook my head.

"You need to ask your guardian angel for guidance," she said, referring to the talk we had had earlier that week about Mamaw, her grandmother, who watched over her.

"Fuck that," I said. "Griffin was my angel."

"Okay. I'm sorry. Maybe you do need a little break from each other. But you shouldn't drive all the way to Texas by yourself in your frame of mind. Have you thought about flying? You could have your car shipped later."

"I did call American Airlines last night. My mother insisted on it. But it'll cost almost $1,200 for a flight next week. I can't afford that, and I can't wait that long. Besides, I have my whole life packed in that car. Hell, I would already be on the road if it weren't for my freaking computer. Of all days, I got some strange reboot errors when I tried to log in. It's ridiculous that I don't even know how to get out of Dodge without MapQuest."

"We'll figure out something," she said, laughing. "But I hope you have a backup of your book."

"Yep. Several. Anyway," I said, continuing my rant. "Remember how I just had to go back to Key West from Marathon—and how everyone just groaned, not that I'm blaming anyone that the lighthouse closed before we got back from the bar. But Griffin was a good sport. I'll never forget that day. We got lost in some local neighborhood, and then we sat in a parking garage and drank beers, laughing, like teenagers playing hooky, wondering what our next move would be so the locals didn't get us. It was like magic—"

"See? You're getting teary eyed just thinking about that day. You and Griffin have something special. It's worth working on."

"I don't know. Maybe, you're right. Maybe if I just go to Texas for a couple of months. See what happens. Anyway, back to flying. We finally got to the lighthouse, and on like the fifth or sixth step, I chickened out. I had no freaking idea that I was afraid of heights until that moment! If I can't climb the stairs of a lighthouse, I sure as hell won't get the nerve to board an airplane!"

"Una mas, amigo, and our tabs," Della called down to the bartender.

As we talked for another half hour, I kept looking at my watch and over my shoulder, imagining Griffin barging through the door any minute, with a huge frying pan in his hands. I was so nervous, I was going to the bathroom every five minutes. When I came back from the bathroom the last time, Della was on her cell talking to Regina.

"I'll be over in a little bit," she was saying. "I won't stay too long."

My chest tightened. The thought of Della leaving me alone scared the shit out of me.

Did she forget I was going to her house? That we were going to do some research on the net?

"Let's stop by Regina's on the way to my house," Della said. "She's real levelheaded when it comes to these things."

Whew. Della just wants Regina to help her talk some sense into me.

I somehow unloaded all my troubles onto Regina, someone who I had never confided in before. And all this unloading was really amazing me, since it was so unlike me. I usually reserved all my unloading for Griffin.

Della found a flight for $306 leaving Thursday at 5:40 a.m. out of Reagan National. I would just need Valium or something before I boarded.

When I awoke the next morning on Regina's couch, my brain felt like a Mexican jumping bean and my guts were trying to crawl out through my throat.

"I need to take a personal day," I heard Della say on the phone, as if she knew how I felt.

That morning she drove me to my house to get my suitcases. Then to the temp agency, who agreed to cut my paycheck early, given the circumstances. Then she drove me to the Loudoun campus so I could withdraw from my classes without a grade penalty, then to pick up my airline tickets. By then it was lunch time so she pulled into a Burger King. I gagged on the third bite.

Back at Della's that afternoon, once I guzzled about six beers, I felt fine again, and I managed to eat some chili without puking. The next day, Della dropped me off at Regina's, where my car was parked. As if my mind and body understood the task before them, they switched to low gear as I double wrapped in newspaper all the little pieces of my life to fill a small box.

Shit, it won't all fit.

I unpacked and repacked and unpacked, picking and choosing what could go and what had to stay. You might have thought the angels lost, and most did, except for the musical glitter globe, which Alton had bought for me. By the time I finished sifting through all the bags in the car to fill two suitcases, two bags, and the box, it was happy hour.

Della picked me up, and we went to the bar to meet Regina. Della and I told her all that we had accomplished that day and the day before, and Regina told us about a job interview she had had that day. Everything was cool. She put my car key on her chain and promised to move it up in the driveway until I could send for it. And Della held onto my house key, just in case Griffin refused to take out the dogs, which I doubted.

That Wednesday night though, my knuckles turned white trying to hold onto the rails of my imaginary roller coaster. I worried that I might not have the guts to get on the plane, so I stayed awake all night and drank beer and talked on the phone and hoped by the time I got on the plane I would already be high enough not to care, and too tired to stay awake.

I left a message on Griffin's voicemail, telling him I was taking off for a few months, and that if he wanted, he could move back into the house—so long as he didn't let the house go into foreclosure or let the auto insurance lapse. I was sure he'd agree to that.

The next morning, Della drove me to the airport, but we couldn't find the terminal to save our asses. When we did find the terminal I had only 10 minutes to get to the gate. Della motioned to a porter, and he helped me get my luggage on a cart and led the way to the gate. By the time the porter and I arrived at Gate 7E, the plane had taken off without me. I was furious with the porter. It was all his fault, and I damned well wasn't going to tip him.

The lady at the ticket counter said I could catch the next flight at 9:30 a.m., which would connect to a flight to Dallas/Fort Worth in Detroit instead of Memphis.

Fucking shit.

I checked my bags and walked the airport. All the bars were closed so I found a coffee stand, bought a tall cup, and went outside for a smoke, where I saw the porter who had led me to my gate, talking in the pit with his coworkers.

I had told myself, so what, it's not like he was ever going to see me again, or me, him. Then I remembered what Alton said the other night on the phone about my recent attempts at suicide.

"Mom, how could you think we would just get over it in a day if you killed yourself?" he had asked. "Look, to this day, you're not over Daddy's death. And he died 14 years ago. Don't you think if you killed yourself, we would suffer and miss you the rest of our lives, too?"

"Well, I don't know. I lived with Daddy, saw him every day. He was my husband. But I only see you and Grandma and Grandpa every few years. That's different."

"Mom, I think of you every day. And I want to go on thinking about you every day, not dead, but alive, knowing I will see you again."

I knew I was running late this morning, but I just had to shave my legs!

"Excuse me, sir. Your tip," I said, as I handed him $5. He smiled, like it made a difference in his life, a genuine smile. And I smiled.

I went to the restroom, but no amount of makeup was going to make my face look less distorted. Even though I hadn't cried since Sunday night, my eyes were still red and puffy. But by the time I placed my carry-ons on the X-ray machine, I was sober. As I walked the ramp to the plane, the hollow sounds of footsteps in the tunnel reminded me of the herding of Jews like cattle into the gas showers.

"This is a fine time to realize that you are also claustrophobic," I mumbled, keeping my head down as I walked to the back of the Northwest medium-sized jet.

Counting down the seats, I could hear myself yelling at the lady at the ticket counter that morning, telling her I didn't give a shit if I had a window seat or a seat on the wing. Out of spite, she probably squeezed me in between a window and an aisle seat, and I would suffocate for sure. When I found my seat, a window seat, I swung my bags up into the overhead compartment and whispered a little apology to her.

As I stared out the window, I wondered what I might do when the plane lifted off, if I would crack up like my little cousin did at Bobby's funeral when she tried to climb into her brother's coffin as they were about to close it. Would I jump up and begin scratching out someone's eyes, lunging on their backs and biting them, like I used to do to my brother Zach whenever a dog or a bee freaked me out? Or would I panic and pull the emergency cord and demand they let me out?

"You MUST main-tain FO-cus," I whispered, catching myself just as it seemed my brain was about to slip on a banana peel.

Shut up. If you keep talking to yourself, the flight attendant might refuse to serve you alcohol.

Everything that had happened in the last few weeks began to spin around in my head, and I wondered how I had made such a mess of my life. Here I was 44 years old, and I had no keys on my key chain. Everything I owned that meant anything to me fit in a 1991 Mercury Topaz.

As the plane began to rumble, I looked on the bright side.

Hey, what's the worst that can happen? The plane crashes and we all die?

"Hah! At least no one can blame me."
What is wrong with you!

As the plane's piercing shrill after liftoff intensified to the point where it felt like it might blow up—or I might crack up—images of Marcy, Bertha, and the bad girl who showed her underpants flashed through my mind.

Like one in the basement runs upstairs to get something only to forget by the time they get to the top step what they went up for, I too forgot what I came for. Just as one must return to the basement to jar their memory, I too must descend to the basement of my life to recall what I was looking for and why.

> I go down . . .
> I came to explore the wreck . . .
> I came to see the damage that was done . . .[4]

Excerpt from "Diving into the Wreck" [http://bit.ly/1PI920a]
By Adrienne Rich [http://bit.ly/1NKbMUM]

PART II

"If you are the child of parents who could not see you, could not really hear you, were very narcissistic, used you to mirror them—ordinarily a parent would mirror a child. . . . the child cannot develop his imagination because of the danger of not knowing what or who the parent is."

"By nature, a child projects King/Queen onto the parents . . . It's natural for that projection to take place. If the parents accept that projection and think of themselves as King/Queen, there is no boundary at all. The child has no way of distinguishing between reality and the imagination."

"Father has accepted Kingdom. And if father has done that, he accepts the fact that he can take control over the child in whatever way he pleases. So the child is bound into this psychic incest with the parent."

"They think that they are god and goddess, and they think that they have that power over their child, their child, not the child of God. . . . And some parents just violate—physically and spiritually—both the body and the soul of the child because they take on that power."[1]

Marion Woodman [http://bit.ly/1PoTLrw]
Excerpts from *Sitting by the Well* [http://bit.ly/1OagpMK]

5
the human bean

Childhood is not from birth to a certain age
and at a certain age
The child is grown, and puts away childish things.
Childhood is the kingdom where nobody dies.

Nobody that matters, that is. Distant relatives of course
Die, whom one never has seen or has seen for an hour,
And they gave one candy in a pink-and-green stripéd bag, or a Jack-knife,

And went away, and cannot really be said to have lived at all.[1]

> Excerpt from "Childhood Is the Kingdom Where Nobody Dies"
> [http://bit.ly/1XjheDb]
> By Edna St. Vincent Millay [http://bit.ly/1Sd3Tv8]

1959

I FIRST SAW THE REAL WORLD through the window of a Greyhound bus when I was three and a half, going on four. Living in a housing project on Syracuse's West Side, I was used to flies and dumpsters and holes in my socks. But as I waved good-bye to Mommy through the window, I held my chin up, looked down my nose as I had seen others look down at me, and pretended I was a rich girl on her way to some important event halfway around the world.

I didn't know my way around the block yet, true, but I'm sure I saw black cows roaming green fields outside little red farm houses somewhere. I swallowed my Adam's apple, though, when the bus driver cranked into high gear outside the city limits, because all I saw was a pack of lies around every bend.

Last night I posed as Mommy cut and sewed and fitted some pink fabric to my size. When she was satisfied with the bows and ruffles, she turned me to look in the mirror. I squealed and hugged her neck. But she shushed me. The other kids were sleeping. Then she trimmed my socks with pink lace and rubbed some white polish on my grimy shoes until they looked brand new. I waved my arms and grinned a lot.

"You're the greatest mommy in the world!" I told her. "Wait till the other kids see me."

As she scrubbed my hair, she said I was to leave this filthy city in the morning and see for myself that there was a great big world out there, a better world, a much brighter world.

So my heart drooped like a wilted dandelion at the sight of crumbling silos, worn farmhouses with boarded up windows, and endless piles of rusty fenders and old tires. Mommy will be so sad to see what had become of the rest of the world since she'd last seen it. Just as I was about to sink into my seat, a flock of geese passed my window, and a pond, and a field of cows, and horses, and another pond, this one with ducks. I sat tall. We had arrived at last!

"Pee-yew! Daddy," I said loud enough for everyone on the bus to hear. "What's that smell?"

I pinched my nose and craned my neck to look at the people sitting across the aisle, as if I wasn't used to bad smells. I especially didn't want anyone to think it was me. The nice man in the Army uniform, the one who winked at me as Daddy and I walked by, took a deep whiff, as if he could smell chocolate-chip cookies baking somewhere, and he sighed.

Daddy reached into his pocket and pulled out his hanky, which Mommy starched and ironed.

"That's the fresh air your silly mother's always saying you kids are so deprived of," he said, using the hanky to block the smell from getting into his nostrils, nostrils much larger than most I'd seen.

"There's a whole great big world out there," Mommy told me and Daddy this morning, as she ripped the brush through my hair. "Just because you grew up in the city, Zach, doesn't mean we have to live here the rest of our lives."

"What the fuck are you talking about, stupid? We don't have money to move. And even if we did, what am I supposed to do, drive a fucking jackass to work? Your mother's silly. Don't pay any attention to her."

Mommy sighed.

As the bus rounded the next bend, and Daddy's attention shifted from his hanky to his Timex, I unplugged my nose.

If Mommy likes that smell then—fuck you, Daddy—so do I.

He slipped his hanky back into his pocket, butted his cigarette in the ashtray, adjusted his daddy long legs for the umpteenth time, put his head back against the head rest, and shut his eyes. After a few minutes, his lips parted. I couldn't understand how he could sleep at a time like this. But good! Because his nagging about how long the ride was and how bumpy distracted me from my adventure.

I looked back out the window and saw my reflection skip across the glass, my thumb in my mouth. I spit the stupid thing out and wiped it on the inside of my hem. Not because Daddy might say I was a slob or a pig or smack me. He never did those things in front of people outside our family. But because I was a big girl now, and I was off to see the world, or Rochester, anyway, to my great-grandmother's house.

"Grandma Moses!"

I didn't suppose that was her real name, but that's what Aunt Velma called her. She often tells Mommy and Daddy about some crazy thing Grandma Moses did, the humor of it over my head. Then she'd say, "Grandma Moses!" I knew by the way Mommy and Daddy chuckled that Grandma Moses must be a wonderful but wacky character.

When we arrived at Grandma's house, it was like Easter or Thanksgiving, with everyone talking at once, laughing and kissing. They all shook hands and hugged as they tried to remember the last time they saw one another.

"What's your name, sweetie?" asked the lady in a pink and white frilly apron. The only people I know who wear aprons are Lucy and the Beaver's mom. Mommy never wore them. And she only had three dresses, which she made herself.

Why doesn't she make herself an apron?

I decided that when I grow up, I would wear a pink and white frilly apron, too.

"Gabrielle Hayes," I said, standing up tall.

"She looks like a Hayes, all right," she said, smiling, squeezing Daddy's arm.

Daddy's mother, Grandma Louise, was there, too. We called her husband Jerold, not Grandpa, because he wasn't our real grandfather. Our real grandfather died in the good old days, before I was born. Grandma Louise and Jerold always visit us on Sundays, which is the best day of the week because they always bring us candy, a whole bag of it. But this past Sunday when they stepped off the bus, I spotted something different as us kids ran up the street screaming, "They're here. They're here!"

Grandma Louise had the shiny bag with pink and green stripes on it instead of the usual brown paper bag. I knocked over everybody in my path to get to it. Of course, God saw me and tripped me, and I scraped my elbow and my knee. But even God couldn't tear my eyes from that bag of candy, kind of like now with those brownies.

"Come sit," said one of the old ladies, who was pleasantly plump, according to Aunt Velma. One step closer to the brownies, I climbed up on the stool and sat at the counter, which was cluttered with pill bottles and matchbooks.

"She's got your olive skin color, Zach, and your thick brown hair, but those eyes! Are they blue or green? She must have got those from her mother."

One of Daddy's uncles slapped him on the back. "Damn, time flies, Speedy. Last time we saw you she was just a twinkle in your eye."

I turned my head like I was shy, but I just wanted to roll my eyes. The only thing that twinkled at me was his shiny belt buckle, and word on the street was people with brown eyes were full of shit. Daddy's aunt winked at me as I washed my brownies down with milk. When I licked the last crumb from my fingers, I sat on my hands so as not to forget and suck my thumb. Surely they thought me mature for my age as I looked with earnest from one speaker to the next. But my mind soon wandered to the skirted subject behind the ruffled curtain. I scooted off the stool and slipped into the other room, where Grandma Moses was sound asleep in her coffin, her gray hair clasped with pins, her lips tucked in, her hands wrapped in black rosary beads. A fly walked across her nose, and she didn't even bat an eyelash.

"Mommy, Mommy," I screamed, partly in excitement, and partly in fear, as I ran through the back door. I would never forget the day I came running in the backdoor and called her Mommy, and she said I must be lost, because she didn't recognize me. She was not my mommy, and she would not relent until I was sobbing and had put on my coat, and had headed out the backdoor to go find a nice policeman to help me find my real home.

But this day she recognized me, thank goodness, and she clutched my arm, pinched her lips together, and turned the key.

"Tiptoe up to your bedroom and change into your play clothes," she whispered. "Then you can go out and play—if you don't wake anybody up."

I did as she said, and by the time I tiptoed back out into the hall, Mommy and Daddy were in their bedroom with the door shut. I bent down and listened under the door.

"Squeak. Moan. Squeak. Moan. Squeak."

I liked it when those sounds came from their room.

Down the stairs and out the back door, I searched for someone I could tell that I had seen a real live dead person and that farmers didn't look anything like Mr. Green Jeans. But all the little kids must still be napping. And all the big kids were still in school, lucky ducks.

I dragged my feet down to the other end of our housing row and gazed up in awe at the big shiny red complex across the street. St. Agnes's! I sat on the grass between the sidewalk and the curb and dreamed of the day I could get a taste of it, as if it were a giant candied apple, and thought it must smell like cinnamon toast inside.

I glimpsed into the past as pairs of horses drew elegant carriages through the majestic archway. One pulled up by the green lamppost, and a handsome young lad wearing a cape held out his arm for the young lady wearing white laced gloves. When he held wide the big red door, she stepped through. I knew at that very moment that wondrous mysteries were unfolding behind the great red-brick walls, where my brother, Zachary, was gobbling up big helpings of everything I wanted to know.

That night in bed, I told my little sister all about Rochester and Grandma Moses down to the finest details. She was almost two and I was almost four, and we giggled at the sound of our own voices.

"Get to sleep up there," Daddy yelled. So I whispered for a few minutes. But then I forgot, until the door burst open.

"I said get to sleep," he hollered, as he snapped his belt. We screamed and cried, and he left when he was done.

"Don't cry, Mariah," I whispered. "It only hurts for a few minutes. It'll be okay." I could see that he only patted her butt, but she cried as if her world had come undone.

"I bet it don't hurt no more. You're just sad. See me? I'm not crying. It didn't really hurt. I only pretended to cry so Daddy would stop—"

Daddy punched the door open, slamming the doorknob into the wall.

"It didn't hurt, huh?" he said, hiking up my nightgown. Then he bore down on me, his face twisted, his teeth clenched, his brown bedroom eyes, the ones most people had never seen, looked red with the night light shining in them, like the devil's eyes. I squirmed and screamed and cried. But this time he didn't stop until he crumpled me up into a sniveling little ball. By the time Mommy yelled for him to stop, I had nothing left. I tried to pretend I was dead, that my name was Grandma Moses, but the trembles and sighs that wracked my body said otherwise.

Just fuck you, Daddy. Just fuck you. Just fuck you, Daddy. Just fuck you.

That's how I prayed myself to sleep that night.

As the days passed, they still told their Grandma Moses stories as if she had always been or had never been. I could only say for sure that she was dead. And my newfound knowledge of death earned me the right to the knowledge of life. And if it meant resorting to blackmail, so be it. What could they do if they caught me? Beat me? Hah!

I cornered Zachary, who turned six that year in the summertime. We were playing hide-and-go-seek after supper one night when I followed him to his hiding place behind the green dumpster in the parking lot, where we weren't allowed to play.

A kid chanted in the distance: ". . . eighty-five, ninety, ninety-five, a hundred. Apples, peaches, pumpkin pie, who's not ready, holler I."

"I!" I screamed, and Zachary spun around.

"What the heck are you doing here? Go find your own hiding place."

He didn't realize yet the full gravity of the situation.

"Tell me about the birds and the bees. Or I'll tell Daddy you were running in the parking lot."

"You promise to scram if I tell?"

"Cross my heart and hope to die."

"The birds and the bees is how they make babies. The man puts his pee-pee in the woman's pee-pee."

"Yuck! You're pulling my leg!"

"It's the truth, I swear. That whole thing about the stork is baloney. Now, scram!"

So that's what Mommy and Daddy were doing when we got back from Grandma Moses's house. Making a new baby? A person dies, so you make a new one? But what did any of it have to do with the birds and the bees?

Sure enough, it was true, though, because the next day Mommy told us we had to move to a bigger housing unit, two courtyards away, because she was going to have another baby. Up to my ears with babies, I decided it was time I got out into the world.

For the next year, I had one thing to say, "I wanna go to school." I said it every morning when Zachary put on his coat. I said it every afternoon when he got home.

"Don't be silly," Daddy said. "Look at you. You can't even put your shoes on the right feet. Now, shut up! The commercial's over."

I said it at the supper table every night, when the whole family sat as stones while Daddy sat there with one ear cocked, the volume on the television in the living room turned up.

"I wanna go to school!"

"You don't even know how to tie your shoes, dummy," Daddy said, flicking my head with his fingers.

I had so much to learn. So every morning when the big hand was on the 12 and the little hand was on the nine, I sat front and center of the television. But I wasn't stupid like Mariah, who turned the magic key to the magic door to the wonderful magic toy shop—ta-dah! a smile—to see Miss Merrily and Eddie Flum Dum.

"Television is make-believe," I yelled at her. "You dummy!"

Or so I thought, until one day, my luckiest day ever, Miss Merrily from *The Magic Toy Shop* invited me to be on her show. That's right. I got to go on television, believe it or not! Me! A real live person in *The Magic Toy Shop* audience. If you don't believe me, I understand. Most people didn't. But I was there all right, waving into the camera at Mommy and all the little kids who watched from home. That was my claim to fame. And I told everyone I met. And if they didn't believe me, I'd ask Mommy to prove it. And she would vouch for me.

"It's true. I saw her on television. I saw her wave."

And that satisfied me a lot.

But most days, I couldn't find anyone to tell. After lunch, when all the daddies were still sleeping and all the mommies were watching the world turn, I'd wander around our housing project looking for Bazooka bubblegum wrappers that still had comics in them. I'd look for old shoe heels and for rocks you could write with. But a penny was the best find. I'd brush off the dirt, unsnap my pink purse, its status long since downgraded from an Easter accessory to a toy, and drop it in. Then I'd wait for the big kids to get out of school, especially for Maureen, who taught me the most that year.

I'd hide behind a tree, picking its bark until I saw the big kids coming around the corner. Then I'd run to my back porch, which was just a few doors down from Maureen's back porch. I'd sit on the step, my purse lodged between my ankles, and wait. As the kids walked across the commons, sometimes they'd look at me, much like one looks at a bump on a log. But I was patient. I'd wait until they all turned and waved good-bye. Then I'd wait some more until Maureen was halfway up the walk.

"Psst. Maureen. Can I come over? I'll help you with your chores."

She'd turn around to ensure all the big kids had turned the next corner and nod. Then she'd let herself in with her very own house key, leaving the door ajar for me. When I was sure no one was looking, I'd grab up my purse and follow her in. The first thing she'd do is switch my shoes and show me how to tie them. Day after day, I tried, but every time I took a few steps, they'd come undone. When I'd get frustrated, she'd tie them for me, nice and snug, and then together we'd do the dishes and laundry. She'd wash and I'd dry. I'd sort socks and she'd fold.

Then we'd drink root beer and eat potato chips while I dumped the contents of my purse on her kitchen table. She'd read the Bazooka comics to me. And when I didn't get the joke, she'd explain it. That's where I learned my sense of humor, from Maureen Johnson, who was 12 and had freckles and hair the color of pumpkin pie, my favorite.

She taught me the strategy of tic-tac-toe so the cat always wins. And she taught me how to sing rhymes while we clapped each other's hands and how to build houses of cards and how to make patterns by crossing large rubber bands over our fingers. It sure beat playing patty-cake and peek-a-boo and drinking Kool-Aid at my house. But Maureen wasn't all fun and games. Sometimes she was dead serious. Sometimes she told me secrets like the one about her daddy, and how he died.

"You know why I never let you sit there," she asked me one day, pointing to the captain's chair.

I shook my head.

"Because Pop used to sit in that chair, sometimes all night, and drink whiskey. He wouldn't eat or talk much, except sometimes he muttered stuff to himself. Ma said he was sick, and she was always telling him to get off his ass and go to the doctor's.

But he said no. Said he'd be fine if she would just leave him the hell alone. Then one night, when we were sleeping—"

Maureen stopped and looked around to make sure her brother, Jake, wasn't listening.

Jake, he's the one who taught me how to play hide-and-go-seek in the house when Maureen wasn't home. It tickled me to no end that we could turn off the lights, pull down the shades, and play in the house. Plus, imagine, a boy 10 years old taking time to play with little ol' me. My importance as a human bean skyrocketed.

Jake said we had to play in our socks. Of course, otherwise you could hear the other running to hide. And when we got found, we had to take off our socks, then unbutton our shirts, and then undo our pants . . .

"You hear me?" Maureen's voice was hoarse and urgent.

I snapped to.

Pointing at her head, she pressed down her thumb.

"Bang!"

"Holy cow!" I said. "Do you suppose he went to heaven?"

I hated my daddy, had since I could remember. I hated the way he called Mommy and us kids stupid. And I don't know if I feared for us or for him, but I sure hoped he didn't have a gun.

"For sure," she said. "Can't prove it. No one believes me. But I was standing at my bedroom window that night when the ambulance drove off. My eyes were blurry, for sure, I was crying. But honest, swear to God, I saw Pop standing on the front walk that night. I started to open the window, to call for him. But I froze when I saw two angels glowing in the dark. They lifted Pop up into the air with them, and they floated away. I swear."

The secret was too big for me to contain, so I told Mommy. But never again.

"Maureen's a liar," she said. "She's filling your head with nonsense. I'll just have to have a little chat with her mother."

"No, you can't," I begged her.

"Why not?"

"Because I made it up, I swear. I was just bored."

"You lie to me again, little missy, I'll wash your mouth out with soap. Now go play. And don't leave our courtyard. I feel like an idiot every time the police have to bring you home."

That's how I learned to keep secrets, and by school registration day the next summer, Mommy and I had a secret, too. After I hounded her and Daddy for a whole year, she had two options: Take Daddy's advice and tape my mouth shut or, her alternative, erase the seven on my birth certificate.

"If anyone asks," she said. "Don't forget! Your birthday is December 1. If they find out you lied, they'll kick you out."

"It's our little secret," I said, then I pinched my lips and turned the key.

St. Agnes's didn't have kindergarten, so I had to start school at Sherwood, which wasn't my idea of real school. But it was so much fun singing "High-ho the derry-o, the farmer in the dell" and playing "I'm tall, I'm very tall." But my favorite part of each day was the milk and graham cracker breaks, followed by story time. We'd sit in a half circle on the floor around Miss Dollar, who sat in a chair, and she'd read us stories like *Curious George* and *The Little Red Train That Could* and *Green Eggs and Ham*. Before turning each page, she'd turn the book around to face us and move it from side to side so we could all see the pictures.

Even naptime wasn't so bad because Miss Dollar knew that I had outgrown naps a long time ago. I told her so. Plus, she was the nicest lady I had ever known. So I played along with her and the nap game, taking off my shoes along with the other kids, rolling out my nap towel, lying down and closing my eyes, pretending to sleep to humor the other kids because Miss Dollar said they weren't as mature as me. After naptime, I'd slip my shoes onto the right feet and tie them nice and snug. Then I'd help Miss Dollar tie the other kids' shoes. I was very, very tall.

Still, I couldn't wait to go to real school, where the nuns would put away all this silly nonsense. But little did I know that we would read real stories, true stories about the devil, and murderers, and thieves, and liars, and that I would find out I was one of them, one of the evil ones.

6
the dumpster riddle

They shut me up in Prose—
As when a little Girl
They put me in the Closet—
Because they liked me "still"—

Still! Could themself have peeped—
And seen my Brain—go round—
They might as wise have lodged a Bird
For Treason—in the Pound—

Himself has but to will
And easy as a Star
Look down upon Captivity—
And laugh—No more have I—[1]

"They shut me up in Prose—" [http://bit.ly/1MJsPJ3]
By Emily Dickinson [http://bit.ly/1NKcGkb]

This work is licensed under the Creative Commons
Attribution-ShareAlike 3.0 Unported License.
[http://bit.ly/1MJsPJ3]

To view a copy of this license,
visit http://creativecommons.org/licenses/by-sa/3.0/
[http://bit.ly/1Olbl8c]

Or send a letter to Creative Commons,
PO Box 1866, Mountain View, CA 94042, USA.

Fall 1961

EASY AS TIC-TAC-TOE, I crossed off kindergarten and traded in my finger paints and crayons for a fat green pencil and a thick yellow tablet with lines. I had waited my entire life for this moment. At last, five going on six (on December 1st, of course), I was going to real school, to the big kids' school, to the big mouth-watering red school.

As I stood in the courtyard that morning, my eyes darted from one girl to another, thinking how much fun it was the way we all matched, our white blouses under our blue pinafores. All the nuns looked alike, too, as they whisked back and forth across the courtyard, their thick black rosary beads jingling against their black skirts, with only the tips of their black shoes showing, as they sorted us out and lined us up in neat little rows, two rows to a nun, one of boys and one of girls.

"My favorite color is red," I whispered to the girl in front of me.

"Quiet!"

Heat rushed to my face as the first word a nun ever spoke to me echoed in my head.

"Stand still and fold your hands behind your back," she said. "And no talking!"

When the bell rang, my mouth filled with juice. But the nuns did not budge. My aching back, plus the anticipation, was wearing me out. I couldn't wait to step through those doors, to sit at my own desk, to smell the brand new pages of my very own books, and to run through this courtyard at recess and play tag around the flagpole as I had envied so many other kids before me. And to think, now I was one of them!

"There will be no talking as you follow me into the school," said another nun with a softer voice.

Lucky me!

As we followed her into the building, the smell burned my nose, like the smell in the bathroom after Mommy cleaned it. As I followed the girl in front of me, I felt like the little lamb that followed Mary to school one day.

"Halt!" said the nun, her voice more stern, her back a little straighter, as she stopped in front of a big wooden door, Room 102, and knocked.

"Excuse me, Sister St. Helen, these are your pupils." She curtsied and fled, leaving us standing there in a lineup against the wall.

After seating us alphabetically, Sister St. Helen stood in front of the blackboard and wrote all the rules in chalk. I was paying attention for the longest time, but then I began to wonder why they call sister 'sister' when she isn't our sister? Why do they call it a blackboard when the slate is really green? Why are the curly wrought iron legs of my desk bolted to the floor? What in the world is that hole for in my desk—

"Gabrielle Hayes! What did I just say?"

"Um."

"Um, what," she snapped.

"Um, Sister St. Helen."

"Are you mocking me?"

"Goodness, no."

I didn't hear what she said next, but I'm sure it was something like, "I've got you my little pretty, and your little dog, too," because I could see her pinched face and costume looked a lot like the Wicked Witch of the West, her long pointy nose, her black dress, her pointer stick a broom.

I tried really hard to be good, but I just can't explain it. Just like I pissed off Daddy at home, I made Sister St. Helen madder than a wet hen. Daddy would hit me in the head with his knuckles, and Sister St. Helen would beat my knuckles with the ruler. They'd grab me by my pissy hair, as they called it, and drag me to my bedroom or to the cloakroom and lock me in. But neither of them could make me. Daddy could make me go to bed and close my eyes, but he could not make me sleep. And Sister St. Helen could make me close my eyes and repeat the prayers after her. But neither of them could make me think as they wished for I was a lot like Curious George, except I didn't have a Man with a Yellow Hat.

Someone might have told you that they nailed Jesus to the cross because Eve talked Adam into eating the apple. Not so. He was crucified because of my talking, my bedwetting, my daydreaming, my thumb sucking, my Kool-Aid spilling, and my evil questions. And it was their duty to see to it that I atoned for the blood of Christ.

I would remind myself of kindergarten and stand very, very tall, except at recess when Sister St. Helen would stand me by the dumpster. The flies would whizz into my face and hair, and I'd screech and twirl and smack myself. Then I'd look around at the kids chasing each other through the courtyard, hoping no one saw me, and for a second I was grateful to be invisible. But I still felt like an idiot, just like Daddy said I was.

From the dumpster, I could see my old housing project—and the patch of grass where I used to sit. And I would remember how silly I was back then, squandering away my childhood.

Then one day, as I was twiddling away at the dumpster, I began to think that I was searching for the mysteries of the Universe in the wrong place. Yes. Sister taught us how to count to higher numbers and to read bigger words than did Captain Kangaroo. And the prayers she taught us, the Captain never mentioned them. But with Mommy being pregnant again, the possibility of twins or triplets—though not likely, she said—got me thinking.

I remembered how two of a kind used to delight me, and how I loved playing Go Fish. But in first grade, things in threes added a whole new dimension. I found them catchy. Dick and Jane and Spot. The Our Father, the Hail Mary, and the Glory Be. Tom, Dick, and Harry. And to the red, white, and blue, we pledged our allegiance. But it was the Father, the Son, and the Holy Ghost that stumped me.

With my dumpster riddle in mind, I would lie on the cold linoleum on my belly, with my nose under the crack of the cloakroom door, and I would think long and hard. In the name of the Father, the Son, and the Holy Ghost. That's three. Yet when saying the sign of the cross we touch four spots: forehead, chest, left shoulder, and right shoulder. It just didn't add up. Why would some great prophet or ancient wise man—whoever invented the sign of the cross—not make it three, like touching the forehead, the chest, and the bellybutton, for example. But then it wouldn't be a cross!

I'd roll over on my back and try to make the sign of the cross touching just three points, but alas only triangles. When Daddy or Sister St. Helen thought I was locked up begging for forgiveness, I would work on this problem, until one day, ah-hah, I figured out a solution.

"In the name of God, who is the Father, the Son, and the Holy Ghost, Amen!" I felt like I had solved the greatest riddle facing mankind—but the nagging sensation that something was missing soon returned. The four made sense. It matched the four points of the cross. But it boggled my mind that a perfect God who knew all things would use four points to represent three things! I was right back where I started.

Is there a fourth thing, but it's a secret? Is it something only grownups are allowed to know? Does that fourth thing lurk about our classroom when we pray? Is that why the nuns make us shut our eyes? That doesn't make sense either. If the Father, the Son, and the Holy Ghost are all invisible—heck, even the devil is invisible—what difference does it make if we open our eyes? And to top that off, considering they are all invisible, how did we get pictures of them? It was as if that fourth thing had cast a magic spell on me. And I just knew that if I could figure it out, the doors of the Universe would open for me.

The next time we prayed in class, I peeked.

But I never saw a thing.

God struck me in the face with His rod, or so it seemed, until I realized Sister St. Helen was towering above me with her pointer stick, my eye burning, and my glasses on the floor two aisles over.

"How dare you open your eyes during prayer!" she yelled.

"But you must've been praying with your eyes open, too!"

Yank! Back to the cloakroom.

As Sister St. Helen shoved me in and slammed the door, I just stood there, stunned, not from her reaction but because a new riddle had occurred to me. They say God is good, and the devil is evil. So you'd think God would be the nice one and the devil would be the mean one. But it was the other way around!

"I thought Sister St. Helen was very nice about Gabrielle's glasses," Mommy said to Daddy at the supper table that night. "She explained how it was an accident, and even offered to pay for them. Much younger and prettier than I expected for a nun."

Hopes that Sister St. Helen would lead me into uncharted territory faded, as did my uniforms, which I thought odd since most of the other girls' dresses still looked like new. And I could smell their ravioli or chicken noodle soup or grilled cheese sandwiches as I walked by their doors on my way home for lunch.

"Lunch is ready," their mothers would croon. "What do you want to drink?"

The kids would jump up from playing with their little puppies or kitty cats. As they ran into the house, they'd pipe back, "Chocolate milk."

"Little fuckin' babies!"

When I got home, I'd climb up on a chair and pull out the peanut butter and jelly from the cupboard and make myself a sandwich on day-old bread, which was more than a day old. Then I'd pour myself a cup of Kool-Aid. Mommy would be busy yelling at one of the little kids to sit still because she was trying to blow their noses or clean out the wax from their ears. I had four little sisters born in a row and, like I said, Mommy was pregnant again.

Daddy worked the night shift and the unborn baby tired Mommy out. At least that's what they said as they claimed exemption from the fate of a mortal sin. Truth is, I could not remember a single time that either of them went to church. They would still be snoring when Zachary and I left for church, which I hated—kneeling and sitting and kneeling and standing and kneeling. I prayed all the while the priest recited the Mass in Latin that it would end soon because my back hurt, and I wanted to run home, change clothes, and go out and play.

But I had no choice. If us kids missed church, a mortal sin marked our souls, and we'd burn in hell, plus, the nun would spank us with the heavy wooden paddle on Monday mornings unless we had a written excuse from our parents.

On the way to church, I'd watch the cars pass us by with one classmate or another in the back seat. We didn't have a car, so riding in a car was a special occasion. At first I'd wave, hoping they might stop and offer us a ride. Or at least wave back. But they never did. They'd look at me, then turn away, as if they could see the black Xs on my soul. In time, I trained myself not to look when cars approached. Instead, I'd search the ground for pennies.

But I hung my head most when we entered the classroom on collection day. Sister would give us yellow envelopes to take home to our parents to collect money to buy new hymnals or to rebuild the church steps.

"We're lucky we can put food on the table," Mommy would say. "That church has more money than we'll ever have."

After slinking into the classroom empty-handed enough times, I got an idea. Instead of giving Mommy the envelopes, I cut up green construction paper the size of dollar bills and put them in the envelope. When we filed into the classroom the morning they were due, I felt very, very tall as I walked by Sister St. Helen's desk along with the rest of the kids and dropped my envelope in the stack with theirs. Sister would never know because one of the big kids always collected them before recess.

I never got caught, but I still got in more trouble than any of the other kids, I think because they only raised their hands to answer questions, not ask them, or to go to the bathroom. But I just never learned. Plus, I had to go to the bathroom more than most.

"You can hold it," Sister said when I raised my hand to go. "You must learn to discipline yourself."

But one day the warm pee seeped out between my pinched thighs and knees. I stared straight ahead at the map of America on the easel in the front of the classroom, where Sister stood pointing with her stick, hoping I didn't pee enough to show. But she saw it, and she made damn sure the whole class saw my wet dress and the puddle under my desk.

"You're worse than a puppy," she said, yanking me out of my chair by my hair.

"I gave you a note from my mother about my infection."

"What note, you little liar! You never gave me a note. You must have lost it. Now stand right there till the janitor comes."

The wheels on the janitor's bucket squeaked as he steered it up the aisle. He squeezed the string mop in the wringer and began to lap up the puddle. With his back to Sister St. Helen, he smiled at me, but I could see the pity in his eyes. I shivered with goose bumps as I stood there in my wet uniform, rubbing my sore head, loose hair falling from my sweater. I shook it off. I was a pretty good fighter, but the janitor's eyes! I wanted to run home and burrow into Mommy's warm flesh, where no one could see me, and suck my thumb. I wanted Daddy to pat my head and sing a song. I wanted to scamper with Curious George. I wanted to jump out of my world and into his. In all my thinking, I didn't see the janitor leave. I didn't see Sister St. Helen in my face until she grabbed me and began shaking me and cursing me because I had committed yet another sin. I was sucking my thumb.

As bad as I wanted to, I knew running home to Mommy was pointless because, if I did, Sister St. Helen would make me regret it more. And I was already regretting every day as it was. Besides, Mommy said I have a vivid imagination. She'd think I imagined giving Sister St. Helen the note. And telling Daddy, well, that would be like asking for it. So as much as I regretted it, Sister St. Helen and I had a secret, too. Only my classmates knew I was one of the bad kids at school. They avoided me like the plague because they were afraid the evil in me would rub off on them, except for Chrissy Prescott, that is.

Her family was about as poor as mine, but we didn't become blood sisters until the day she committed a sin worse than mine. She committed a mortal sin. She was not in our assigned pew at Sunday Mass the day before, yet she had the nerve to come to school Monday morning without a note.

Sister St. Helen summoned another nun to help deliver Chrissy's punishment. She pulled her chair out to the side of her desk and sat in it, and the other nun stood against the wall, her hands behind her back, as she directed Chrissy to lie across Sister St. Helen's lap. Chrissy was bold. I admired her for that. All by herself, she walked up and stretched herself across Sister St. Helen's lap. Then Sister drew up the paddle way over her head and swatted Chrissy hard, real hard, again and again. Chrissy was screaming and squirming when the most terrible thing happened. The giant rosary beads that hung around Sister St. Helen's waist broke, and the cross that hung from them fell to the floor.

"Look what you've done," she screamed at Chrissy, pushing her off her lap and standing up. "You broke something sacred. Put her up against the blackboard," she yelled at the other nun.

As the one nun pinned Chrissy to the blackboard, Sister St. Helen spanked her harder than she had ever spanked me. I turned away. Every time I heard the whack of the paddle, my butt puckered. I stared at the little faded heart someone had carved in my desk, trying to concentrate. I knew I was next in line if my oatmeal came up.

Chrissy and I had become best friends by the summer break, and we defended each other to the death. When someone made fun of a hole in the armpit of her shirt or laughed at me because I wore rubber bands to hold up my knee highs, I would unpin the waistband of my shorts. We'd prick our fingers and press them together, and then we'd pick up sticks and rocks and chase the mockers all the way home, pelting them as much as we could along the way.

I didn't know I had been branded like a calf until summer was over, and I discovered that Sister St. Helen had passed her appointment to scrub the black Xs from my soul to Sister Annetta, my second-grade nun. And I would not know until later that autumn that other people can die. They didn't have to be old or someone you didn't know. Death could visit babies, even mothers, people you know, people you love.

7
the storks

"I know the pond in which all the little mortals lie till the stork comes and brings them to their parents. The pretty little babies lie there and dream so sweetly as they never dream afterwards. All parents are glad to have such a child, and all children want to have a sister or a brother. Now we will fly to the pond, and bring one for each of the children who have not sung the naughty song and laughed at the Storks.

"But he who began to sing—that naughty, ugly boy!" screamed the young storks; "What shall we do with him?"

"There is a dead child in the pond, one that has dreamed itself to death; we will bring that for him."[1]

Mother Stork

"The Storks," *Tales. Harvard Classics* [http://bit.ly/1YooJs2]
By Hans Christian Andersen [http://bit.ly/1ML7eoxz]

Fall 1962

LIKE A SILLY GOOSE, I STOOD IN LINE with high hopes in the courtyard at St. Agnes's, sure that second grade would be much better than the first, my uniform as blue as the next kid's, my socks snug, and my black patent leather shoes so shiny I could see my foolish grin in them. But Sister Annetta wiped that grin off my face before I could scuff my shoes.

It had been ages since I wet my pants or sucked my thumb in public. And after praying with the lights on and my eyes wide open, I still didn't have a clue. At last diverted from the imperfect Trinity that added up to four in my book, I had more time to focus on something far more intriguing, something that had not yet lent itself to words, that is, the whitish, murky sphere, like a full moon on a foggy night, that had always just hovered there in the back left-hand side of my mind.

"I can see it right here," I said to Chrissy, touching my head.

"You're silly," she said. "Nobody can see their soul."

"You think our souls are in our heads? I always thought our souls were in our butts."

Chrissy laughed so hard I thought she was going to pee her pants.

I had to laugh, too, but the idea that Chrissy couldn't see the moon-like image in her head fascinated me. Am I the only one who can see their soul? Maybe I'm special or something. I wanted to ask a grownup. But Mommy would call my imagination wild—she had promoted me from vivid over the summer. Daddy would call me crazy and predict my stint in the nuthouse one day. And Sister Annetta would say it was proof I was evil. So I locked up this little marvel in my imaginary vault of secrets. Whenever I waited to be let out, I'd ponder all the unsolved mysteries taking refuge in my mind. Mommy didn't mind much. She chalked it up to daydreaming. But it drove Daddy and Sister Annetta insane.

"You're not paying attention," they yelled day after day. "That is your biggest problem."

"You're my biggest problem," the voice in my head would yell back at them.

As if they heard me, they'd shake me until I rattled.

"Pay attention, dammit! Pay attention."

Then one morning I was so rapt in a bird sitting outside on the window ledge, my pencil dropped and rolled across the floor. I flinched and looked up, as did everyone, including Sister Annetta.

"You've distracted the whole class," she yelled, as she marched me up to the front of the room.

"Apologize this instant, to me and to the class, for disturbing us while we are trying to do our work."

I looked at her, then at the class, then at the cup of pencils on her desk. I bolted past her and knocked the cup over. As the pencils rolled across the floor, every little kid in the room gasped, even Chrissy.

"How dare you!" Sister Annetta hissed as she lunged for me, grabbing me by my hair and slamming my head against the blackboard. When the banging stopped, I walked in a daze back to my desk. As I sat down, the bell rang.

I looked at Sister, who had sat at her desk, looking dazed too. Her favorite little pupil, Mary, broke the silence.

"Sister, may we go?"

Sister waved her hand without looking up. One by one we fled the room, being careful not to step on the pencils.

Walking home that day, I vowed to tell Mommy about Sister Annetta. But when I got home, Mommy was up to her elbows in beet juice, and Daddy was complaining that if she didn't finish canning soon, supper would be late. Kali was on the potty hollering that she was done. And the baby was wrapped around Mommy's ankle crying to be picked up.

"Hurry up, Gabrielle. Get your play clothes on. I need your help here."

"I swear! I'll tell her after supper, when Daddy's watching the news," I mumbled under my breath as I changed my clothes.

But by the time I finished drying the supper dishes and jumped off the footstool, the president of the United States had interrupted the regularly scheduled program—which gave me goose bumps.

> "Good evening, my fellow citizens: This Government, as promised, has maintained the closest surveillance of the Soviet military buildup on the island of Cuba. Within

the past week, unmistakable evidence has established the fact that a series of offensive missile sites is now in preparation on that imprisoned island. The purposes of these bases can be none other than to provide a nuclear strike capability against the Western Hemisphere."

That night and for the next day and night, Daddy and Mommy seemed to forget our bedtimes or notice that we were helping ourselves to their popcorn as they speculated about missiles, about nuclear warheads, about the Soviet Union taking over the world, about World War III. This could be it, they shook their heads. The names of Fidel Castro, Khrushchev, and JFK hung in the air as they analyzed each and tried to predict their next moves.

By the time I got home from school the next day, Mommy and Daddy were taking a break from the end of the world. It seemed the potential doom had painted them in a corner, and now they could only wait for the paint to dry.

With the babies down for a nap, Daddy sang along to the records on his phonograph and Mariah and Lizbet were sprawled out on their bellies coloring in their coloring books.

"Remember, Jolly," Daddy said, as I stood by her elbow helping her to sort the flat sides of a jigsaw puzzle.

"Remember the first time I sang this song to you? 'I'm yours. All the world knows, I'm yours. Can't you see it in my eyes? Can't you hear it in my sighs? I'm yours.'"

Mommy chimed in.

"I'm yours. Take my lips and take my arms. I'm a victim of your charms. I'm yours. I'll take your hard-on in my hands."

Mommy giggled and Daddy chuckled.

"I'm yours," they sang.

That night as Mommy blew out the candles on her birthday cake, yum, I vowed to be a perfect little girl at school from now on. And I held my tongue pretty good for the longest time, I think for like two whole weeks. But one afternoon, after raising my hand again and again with the answer to every question without being called on, I said fuck it.

"1942!" I called out, like yelling bingo.

To shut me up once and for all, Sister Annetta did something even Daddy had never done. She stuffed the corner of a dust rag in my mouth. I started to gag, but she warned me.

"You gag and I'll shove that whole rag down your throat. Now stand in that corner and don't move."

When Sister Annetta dismissed us, I ran home. Even without the rag in my mouth, I fought back the urge to gag. I swallowed hard not to cry. But as I pictured Mommy pulling me up on her lap and cradling me, telling me that everything would be all right, I choked. I cried. This was the day I would tell Mommy everything.

But when I swung open the back door, Mommy and Daddy's chairs were empty. Instead, Maureen's mother hovered in a corner in the kitchen on our phone, whispering.

Mommy's little baby wasn't born pink like little girls should be. She was born blue, with water on the brain. I remembered how Mommy kept telling everyone that she had a bad feeling. She said the baby didn't kick much. But Marcy and Maureen's mother and Mrs. Bertram had all told Mommy not to worry. If something was wrong, the doctors would know it. And I didn't worry because God created people. What would be the point in Him bringing us a dead baby?

But God did, and it made no sense. The image of a dead blue baby, detached and nameless, filled my head. I didn't know the baby, but I wanted to touch its head, to say I was sorry. A question mark hit me right between the eyes. But unlike most of my questions, this one had no words attached to it. It was unthinkable, like peanut butter without jelly or Oreos without milk.

As I sat on the kitchen floor peeling off my galoshes, my neck prickled, like someone was watching me. I turned around and looked up. No one was there. I sat very still. Then I felt it. The baby's spirit hovered above me, in limbo, in the kitchen that day. The baby must be scared. She was supposed to live here, but now she can't. She must be confused. Will she be lost now? Would she know how to find her way back to God?

"Why would you be so mean, God?"

Maybe He sees how bad you are turning out and changed His mind. Or maybe the baby died because you didn't believe in the storks.

I tried to think back. Had I ever made fun of the storks? Zachary said the story about the storks was a bunch of baloney. And you believed him, and repeated him. So, yes, you are guilty.

"Oh, God. Please forgive me. It's not the baby's fault. Please send your angels to guide her back to heaven."

God must've heard me because the baby drifted outward then, beyond my senses.

When Mommy came home from the hospital, us kids were sitting at the table cutting and pasting construction paper and making turkeys and pilgrim hats to tape in the windows, to surprise her. But she didn't notice.

"Be thankful. One less mouth to feed," a neighbor said.

Mommy said nothing.

One afternoon after school, after I charged through the back door bearing good news, I found Mommy sitting at the kitchen table putting on her glasses. I could tell that she had just wiped the tears from her eyes. Daddy had nicknamed her Jolly because when she laughed the whole room laughed. Until now, her cheeks had always matched the pink semi-gloss paint on the kitchen walls and the pink speckles in the Formica table top, which displayed the little black and white cow creamer and sugar bowl, with pink dotted collars and pink ears and little cowbells strung around their necks with twine, which Daddy was quite proud of the year he bought them for Mommy for Christmas. Daddy's favorite color was pink and every place we moved they would paint the kitchen pink. He dreamed that someday we'd live in a pink house with a white picket fence and he'd have a pink Cadillac in the driveway.

Mommy smiled at the 'A' on my spelling test the way I smiled at Daddy when he tried to cheer me up after tickling me so hard he made me cry. Instead of bustling around the house cleaning and yelling at us to hang up our coats and put away our toys, she poured another cup of coffee, and sat at the table watching the steam rise from it.

The phone rang, and when she didn't budge, I climbed up on a chair and answered it.

"Who is it?" I asked, but she snatched the receiver from me clearing her throat.

"Hello?"

"Yak-yak."

"Oh, hi, Margie. Sorry. I was daydreaming."

Sitting next to Mommy, I could hear Margie's voice squawking, but I couldn't make out the words. I picked at the dirt under my fingernails while I waited for them to hang up.

"Oh, I'm fine," Mommy said. "Thank you. That's nice of you to offer. But, really. I'm fine."

"Yak-yak-yak."

"Mm-hmmm. Mm-hmmm." Mommy said, rolling her eyes.

"Yak-yak-yak. Yak-yak-yak-yak-yak."

"That's a crock of bull!"

I looked up from my fingernails.

"If that's the case, then none of my kids should've been born. We couldn't afford any of them."

"Yak-yak-yak."

"Pope or no Pope. Zach and I have used every kind of birth control method under the sun. It wasn't my idea to have six kids for crying out loud. But there's not one of them I'd give back for all the money in the world."

Mommy stood up and slammed the phone back into its cradle on the wall.

"The nerve of her," she said, as she sat back down, the tears welling up in her eyes.

I put my arm around her, grateful for a chance to comfort her. But she composed herself.

"Everything's okay," she said. "Why don't you go out and play."

When I got home from school in the days that followed, Mommy wouldn't be watching her soaps or cleaning the kitchen or yelling at the kids. She'd be lying on the couch. Daddy yelled at her every minute to get her lazy ass up because she had not washed the dishes or swept the kitchen floor or boiled hotdogs and macaroni and cheese for supper yet.

"Look at this place. It's a pigsty. And all you can do is sleep all day."

"I'm sick for crying out loud, Zach. Can't you see that?"

"It can't be so fucking bad that you can't even get supper on the table. What are we supposed to do? There's not even a clean dish in the house, and the laundry's piled up to the fucking ceiling."

Mommy moaned and closed her eyes.

Daddy yelled and yelled but she stopped answering him. She stopped talking to us kids, too. She wouldn't even talk to her best friend, Marcy.

"Come on, Rose. Please. Try to sit up."

Marcy was beautiful, her long hair dark and shiny as a penguin's slick coat. When she got excited, her pupils darted around like little black fish in light green pools of crystal. I had watched her many times walk back and forth across the courtyard, stopping to talk to this neighbor and that neighbor, her back arched, her chest pulled taut, her cleavage showing, just a little. Every inch of her body said she didn't belong with the rest of us lowlifes. I liked her and sensed something in common with her.

The little black fish in her eyes searched Mommy's face, but Mommy didn't budge.

"Rose, are you okay? Can you hear me? Let's sit up, Rose. Do you need a doctor?"

Mommy nodded.

Marcy called a doctor, who came to the house. He examined Mommy while Marcy and Daddy filled him in on the details of the blue baby.

"She's depressed over the loss of the baby," he concluded. "That's not uncommon. She just needs some time to get over it. You'll see. She'll be fine. In time," he said as he left.

Marcy wasn't satisfied. She begged Daddy to call an ambulance.

"I can't believe that doctor. Can't he see how pale her face is? Anybody can see she's sick for Pete's sake. What the hell's the matter with doctors these days? I can't tell you what to do, Zach. But if I were you I'd call an ambulance. There's no way she's going to miraculously recover just lying there. Something's wrong with her. I promise you. Even if it is in her head, even if she's having a breakdown. She still needs help. Call an ambulance. Will you please? Before it's too late?"

"Maybe," Daddy said. "Maybe." That was his answer for everything. "Maybe."

Daddy pretended to listen to Marcy. But all the words she said followed her out the door when she left.

"Blah-blah-blah. Blah-blah-blah. Blah-blah-blah." he mumbled to himself. "She never knows when to shut up."

Then he went back to the living room.

"I know you're upset about losing the baby," he said, kneeling by the couch and stroking Mommy's long hair. But you've got six other kids and a husband to take care of."

Mommy didn't answer, and Daddy didn't have a lot of patience.

"This is fucking ridiculous," he said, standing up. "When are you going to grow up and get over it? You can't stop living for crying out loud."

That afternoon after Daddy ran out of energy for yelling, Mommy began trembling and gurgling and turning blue.

"Get Marcy," he yelled at Zachary. "Get Marcy!"

Marcy came running over, and this time Daddy didn't put her off. She called an ambulance, which came and took Mommy and Daddy away. Marcy packed our clothes and divided us up among Mommy's friends. The Bertrams, who lived in back, took Zachary and me. That night, after Zachary and the Bertram kids fell asleep, I heard someone knock on the door. I sat on the top step sucking my thumb.

"How is she, Zach?" Mrs. Bertram asked. "Here, have a seat. Can I get you something to drink, a beer, coffee, soda?"

"Naw."

The couch creaked, so I knew it must be serious.

"It doesn't look good."

I strained to hear.

"She has blood poisoning. No one knew."

I pulled my thumb out from my mouth so I could hear better.

"Oh, Zach, we're so sorry," she said.

"Is there anything we can do?" Mr. Bertram asked.

"No. We just have to wait and pray, the doctor said."

His voice cracked like he was going to cry.

I couldn't remember ever seeing Daddy cry before, or pray. He was nothing but a mean old bastard, and Mommy might die because of him.

I cannot live without my Mommy.

I ran back to my bunk, and for the first time since I had learned how to say my prayers, I said them like I meant them.

I prayed and I cried so hard that I got a bellyache.

When Mrs. Bertram checked in on us after Daddy left, she heard me crying. She gave me Pepto-Bismol, which was a real treat, as she tried to calm me down. But when my lips were licked clean, I burst into tears all over again. She called Daddy to come back over.

"She has a temperature of 103. It wouldn't be that high just from crying, I don't think."

I expected Daddy to holler at me for being sick and call me a faker. Maybe he couldn't in front of the Bertrams. But he might give me a dirty look if they weren't looking, so I avoided his gaze. My eyes widened, though, and my heart pounded as he picked me up, smoothed my sticky hair, and carried me out to Mr. Bertram's car.

"Does that hurt?" the doctor asked pressing down on my stomach. It didn't hurt until he let go, then I shrieked.

"A sure sign of appendicitis," he said.

I woke up in a hospital bed that had bars on it like a crib, and a bandage on my tummy. I thought about my bellyache the night before, and it reminded me of a song we sang on hayrides at summer camp. I sang it over and over in my mind.

"Found a peanut, found a peanut, found a peanut just now. . . cracked it open, cracked it open, just now...It was rotten . . . ate it anyway, ate it anyway, ate it anyway, just now. Got a stomach ache. . . Called the doctor just now... operation, operation, had an operation just now. . . . Died anyway, died anyway, died anyway, just now. Went to heaven, went to heaven just now. Met St. Peter at the gate....Found a peanut, found a peanut..."² [http://bit.ly/1YpoGMw].

I asked the nice nurse if Mommy and I were going to die anyway, and if the blue baby would be at the gate with St. Peter. She assured me we would both be fine, and she let me eat as much Jell-O as I wanted and, in that sense, it seemed like I did die and go to heaven.

Every afternoon I sat at the window watching for Daddy to get off the bus. When I spotted him, I'd jump back into my bed, get myself primed for pitiful, and await his arrival. As he stood by my bedside, I begged him to take me to see Mommy. But he said no. Children weren't allowed in her hospital. Besides I had to stay in the hospital until my operation healed.

Ten days after my surgery, the doctor said I could go home, but Daddy and I knew I couldn't because Mommy was still in the hospital. I started crying, holding my stomach.

"What do you say we call your Mommy," the doctor said, raising his eyebrows at Daddy.

"I didn't think of that," Daddy said. "I guess we could."

As soon as Daddy handed me the phone, I began to cry again. "Please, Mommy. Can I come see you? Please? Pretty please? I promise to be good. Please?"

Mommy always did have a hard time saying no to me. So Daddy and I took the bus to her hospital, and she met us in the lobby in a wheelchair. The minute I saw her smile, I knew she would be good as new one day. A hug and a kiss, and it was time to go. But I was satisfied to see her alive. Plus, I had bragging rights. I was the only kid who got to see her since she went to the hospital. It made my operation worth every stitch.

It was still weeks before Mommy came home from the hospital, before we were all united again, the whole family. I never saw Daddy so happy as he helped Mommy into the house. He fetched her housecoat and ice water and anything she asked for. It was the first time I'd ever seen him wait on her. I didn't know that it would be the last time for many years to come, until the next time death knocked on her door.

When Daddy was at the store buying her some ginger ale and ice cream, I curled up next to her on the couch and put my thumb in my mouth. Other people said Mommy was fat like that was a bad thing, but I liked it because it made her soft and cushy, like a giant teddy bear. As I wrapped my fingers over my nose, she held me close to her breasts, and I forgot all about Sister Annetta and the bruise she left on my arm when she grabbed me that afternoon. I told anyone who asked I got it from bumping into the doorway. I rathered they think I was clumsy than evil. Besides, the nuns taught me how to pray. I was grateful for that knowledge for without it Mommy would have surely died.

Day after day in the months that followed, I learned to ignore the silhouette of my soul that had always lingered in my mind as I kneeled down on my sore knees in the cloakroom where Sister Annetta had cast me off. And I believed.

I believed in one God, the Father Almighty, maker of heaven and earth, and all things visible and invisible. I believed in one Lord Jesus Christ, the only begotten Son of God, God of God, Light of Light, true God of true God, who was born of the Virgin Mary, and who was crucified under Pontius Pilate. I believed He suffered and was buried, and arose again on the third day and ascended into heaven, and that He now sitteth on the right hand of the Father. And I believed in the Holy Ghost, the Lord and giver of life, who proceedeth from the Father, who with the Father and the Son together we worship and glorify[3] [http://bit.ly/1NKVPxR].

Whether a venial or mortal sin I'm not sure, but between my prayers I fantasized about the day I'd do what Toto did to the Wizard of Oz. And on that day, God would throw Sister St. Helen and Sister Annetta into hell and, like the Wicked Witch of the West, they would cry out, "I'm melting. Help me. I'm melting."

But for now, as the snow melted into mud puddles, whenever Mommy asked me how school was going, I'd say fine. And when she asked if I liked Sister Annetta, I'd say Sister Annetta is nice. But the new girl in class, she didn't know any better. She told her mother, who had just met my mother the other day when they were out hanging clothes.

"Why didn't you tell me?" Mommy asked me, and I could see the pain and shock in her eyes as if Sister Annetta had just banged her head into the blackboard.

My lips quivered somewhere between aghast and a smile, while Mommy went crazy.

"Who does she think she is! What gives her the right to slam your head against a blackboard or lock you in a closet like you're an animal?"

When she returned from my school she was huffing and puffing.

"Those self-righteous bastards. I don't care if you did anything wrong or not. That's not the point. She had no fucking right! Just because we're poor doesn't mean we're ignorant."

I had heard Mommy swear before. Daddy even laughed about it because when I was a toddler I sounded just like her, walking around the house, declaring "Some of my beets!"

But the 'F' word? I had never heard her say that before. The next day, she registered me at the public school, where my new teacher, Mrs. Shenanigans, treated me just like she treated all the other kids, like a regular human being.

Just as the Cuban missile crisis had passed, the pain of the blue baby began to fade. Mommy's cheeks had become rosier than ever, and she was busy, and she put her foot down. And for the first time in my life, we were moving out from under the towering shadow of St. Agnes's steeple to a brand new housing project. But just like "Pig-Pen," I would be followed by a cloud of dust wherever I went.

8
the color of blood

"Now is the time to make real the promises of democracy. Now is the time to rise from the dark and desolate valley of segregation to the sunlit path of racial justice. Now is the time to lift our nation from the quicksands of racial injustice to the solid rock of brotherhood. Now is the time to make justice a reality for all of God's children.

"It would be fatal for the nation to overlook the urgency of the moment. This sweltering summer of the Negro's legitimate discontent will not pass until there is an invigorating autumn of freedom and equality. Nineteen sixty-three is not an end, but a beginning. Those who hope that the Negro needed to blow off steam and will now be content will have a rude awakening if the nation returns to business as usual. There will be neither rest nor tranquility in America until the Negro is granted his citizenship rights. The whirlwinds of revolt will continue to shake the foundations of our nation until the bright day of justice emerges."[1]

Martin Luther King, Jr. [http://bit.ly/1QCneYJ]
"I Have A Dream" speech [http://abcn.ws/1N6mWHf]

Fall 1963 to Summer 1964

NO ONE TOLD ME, BUT MODEL CITIES designed Central Village to integrate Negroes and Caucasians fifty-fifty, like we were lab rats. We were still unpacking boxes when Martin Luther King, Jr., marched on Washington, D.C., where he told the world he had a dream. And this little white girl didn't know it yet, but she was part of it.

As Daddy turned up the volume, Mommy said she would have given her right arm to be in Washington, D.C., that day.

"Let us not seek to satisfy our thirst for freedom by drinking from the cup of bitterness and hatred," Rev. King said, as I took a big gulp of my cherry Kool-Aid.

But the project filled up with mostly colored people, I mean negro people. I mean black people. Mommy said they didn't like being called 'colored.' She said 'Negroes' would be fine when comparing them to 'Caucasians'. But the coloreds she knew preferred to be called 'Blacks.'

"It's not the skin color that counts anyway," she said. "All men are created equal. What matters is what's on the inside."

But the black kids who had crossed my path since we had moved in didn't seem very nice on the inside or the outside. And I was scared to death of them. For months and months, I ran and they chased. I hid and they hunted—except for that one Friday in November, I'll never forget.

We were right in the middle of a history quiz when an office aide tapped on our classroom door, let herself in, and whispered in our teacher's ear.

"Oh, my God! It can't be true," Mrs. Jockey cried out.

But it was. Someone had shot John F. Kennedy, the president of the United States, in the head.

The bell rang, and the teachers said not to dawdle, to go straight home to our families. It was so goose-bumpy to see grownups crying in the hallways while all the kids scattered from Croton Elementary in silence like church mice when the bells ring and the doors open.

Skin color made no difference that night as horror gripped the minds and hearts of everyone in our neighborhood and across the country. Poor little John-John and Carolyn. I thought they were the luckiest kids in the whole wide world, but now—please, I begged Walter Cronkite, please say it's all a big mistake. I held onto hope for two days despite the television's incessant declaration that John F. Kennedy was dead. But when I saw those horses pulling the president's casket up the street, my heart sank to its deepest.

If the president of the United States isn't safe, who is?

The holidays came and went, as did the unspoken ceasefire in our neighborhood.

"Why don't you take your ugly white ass back to Honky Town where you belong," taunted one of the black girls after she and her friends had cornered me.

"Yeah! We don't need no white trash here," said another.

I ducked and darted out of reach and ran like hell till I caught up with Zachary. As I gasped for air, he spread his arms to prevent the girls from getting any closer to me.

"Go find someone your own size to pick on," he said.

Just then some boys walked out from between the housing rows. As they moved in on Zachary, the girls backed off, like it was a trap. My hand dropped from my hip.

"Look," Zachary said. "I don't want any trouble. Just leave my sister alone."

Without saying a word, they closed in on him, grabbed his wrists, and began twirling him around and around and into the air, closer and closer to a tree. Then they let go. Zachary's body hit the tree, crunched, and then crumpled to the ground. They spat on him, then ran off laughing.

As Zachary hobbled around on crutches, all I could see was my hero twirling around and around in my head. Turn the other cheek my ass. I didn't know the boys who jumped Zachary, and if Zachary knew who they were, he wasn't talking. Either way, it wouldn't have happened if it weren't for me. But somehow, someday, one way or another, I would get even.

One day, a few weeks later, the other white girl in my class gasped, and we all turned to look.

"Oh, no! My diamond ring! It's missing!"

Yeah, right, diamond ring.

The other kids, of course, all banded together.

"Gabrielle must've stolen it," said one.

"I saw her take it," said another.

I stood up and turned the pockets of my sweater inside out. "Did not!"

"She must've hid it," someone said.

"Calm down, children," Mrs. Jockey said. "I'm sure it'll turn up."

That afternoon after school, more black girls than usual were waiting for me, like now they were justified because I was a thief.

I'm very, very tall.

I walked up to Cassandra, the tallest of them all, and put out my chin.

She knocked me to the ground and kicked dirt in my face.

My life flashed before my eyes. A fly. A sister crying. A bump on a log. Shoes on the wrong feet. A little pink purse. Pop. The little red train that could. A rotten apple. The blue baby. A horse-drawn casket. Bones crunching against a tree.

I sat up and spit on Cassandra's shoe. She lunged to tackle me but I rolled and jumped to my feet. She fell face-down in the dirt, and I laughed.

"When are they ever going to plant the damn grass around here?" I asked, echoing my mother, who often swears she can hear the dirt laughing at her.

Cassandra lunged for me again. She wasn't expecting it when I bopped her right in the nose. The next thing I knew, the principal was marching me back into the school, and the black girls followed, recounting how I stole a ring and how I should be kicked out of school.

While the principal talked to my mother on the telephone, Cassandra blotted her nose with tissue.

"I'll get you back," she said, scowling and kicking me under the table.

But as I sat there, mesmerized by the blood on my shaking hands, I realized I wasn't afraid anymore.

"Baloney!" Mommy said, when she walked in. "If you suspend Gabrielle, you have to suspend all of them, which is too ridiculous at this point, anyway. School's out in a week."

She stopped and looked at us.

"This little game has been going on long enough. Hasn't it girls?"

We squirmed.

"Don't you girls watch television? Haven't you seen the riots, with grownups throwing rocks through windows and setting fires?"

We had.

"Is that what you want in our neighborhood?"

We looked at each other.

"Well, I don't want to see you kids fighting either. So let's say you girls shake hands and make friends."

We shook hands, and the principal smiled.

Outside of that last week of school, I didn't see Cassandra for a month. And when I did see her coming up the street, my first impulse was to run the other way. I had to remind myself that I wasn't afraid of her anymore.

"Your mother's nice," Cassandra said, stopping to chat!

As if God was shocked too, a summer wind buckled us, and an onslaught of rain drenched us in seconds.

We clasped hands and ran.

I have a dream!

A little black girl and a little white girl joined hands on a summer day in 1964, and ran up the street together, shrieking and laughing as they tripped and fell on top of each other. It wasn't Alabama, but Martin Luther King, Jr.'s, dream came true in a Syracuse ghetto that day.

As Mommy frosted Zachary's birthday cake, and I counted out 11 candles, we could hear Rev. King talking on the television that blared in the living room.

"I call upon all Negro and white citizens of good will to continue to struggle unrelentingly but nonviolently against the racial and economic oppression—"

In the days that followed, the grownups repeated rumors that busloads of blacks were coming in from Rochester on the New York State Thruway to instigate more riots.

"Don't worry," one of our neighbors said as Mommy poured another round of coffee. "We won't let no harm come to your family. We've spread the word that you all are good folks."

When Walther Cronkite announced that the police had staked out the thruway and had turned the buses back around, everyone sighed in relief and slapped each other on the back and hugged one another—celebrating yet another victory since

President Johnson had signed the Civil Rights Act at the beginning of July.

I thought it was a done deal. I didn't realize I was living in epic times, and that I was witnessing just the beginning of a decades-long string of violent race riots that would continue on the very streets and even in the very hallways of my junior and senior high schools. And not one teacher ever mentioned Rosa Parks and how I was born just a few weeks after she was arrested.

9
the string that broke

"King, look into your heart. You know you are a complete fraud and a great liability to all of us Negroes... . You are no clergyman and you know it. I repeat you are a colossal fraud and an evil, vicious one at that. You could not believe in God and act as you do. Clearly you don't believe in any personal moral principles. ..."

"King, there is only one thing left for you to do. You know what it is. You have just 34 days in which to do [it] ... . You are done. There is but one way out for you. And you know what it is. You better take it before your filthy, abnormal, fraudulent self is bared to the nation."

Excerpts from the "suicide letter"
[http://nyti.ms/1lCKfy2]
to Martin Luther King, Jr., later proved to have been
sent from the FBI, then led by J. Edgar Hoover.

Fall 1964 to Summer 1966

D ADDY'S EYES WIDENED AS HE STOPPED and looked around our great big brand new pink kitchen like he thought the place might be bugged.

"I don't trust him. He's got too much power," Daddy almost whispered every time he spoke of J. Edgar Hoover. "Even our presidents are afraid to fire him, with his extensive dossiers on anyone with power to hang over their heads. He's shrewd. But that's not the worst of it. Now that idiot is saying Martin Luther King, Jr., is a communist!"

While the National Guard was restoring public order in Rochester over the summer, we were packing up boxes and moving out of public housing into a pink house, to an upstairs flat. But just because we moved out of the projects didn't mean Mommy would give up her crusade against racism and poverty, even though Daddy fought her every step of the way.

"You've got another fucking meeting tonight?" he yelled at her. "You're ridiculous."

"It's for a good cause, Zach. You know that."

"What about my damn cause? What am I supposed to do when you're gone all night?"

"I'll be home by ten o'clock. It's no big deal."

"Tell the weirdoes that. It's no big deal. Last time Jack picked you up for a Model Cities meeting, some weirdo called me up threatening to torch our house. The time before that, some other nut claimed you were pregnant with a black baby. Probably one of our own neighbors. They see you leaving the house all the time with black men. What are they supposed to think?"

"They might just think I don't have a car. How else am I supposed to get to the meetings? And you know this baby's yours. But if you're so worried what the neighbors think, then why don't you go with me?"

"I don't want to go to no stupid meeting."

"Fine. But I already committed myself, and I'm going. Let the nosey neighbors talk."

"Yeah, you need to be committed all right. Like you don't have enough to do around here. You're going out trying to take on the world's problems instead of staying home and taking care of your own."

"What are you talking about? Everybody's eaten and had baths and are ready for bed. The house is clean. The laundry's done. What more do you want?"

"I want you to stay the fuck home where you belong," he yelled.

"Well, I'm sorry. But there are some things more important in the world than sitting around on our behinds watching television every night."

"You keep this shit up, you know," Daddy said. "They'll be locking you up. Even the newspapers are linking Model Cities to communism. That'll be fucking cute, me stuck here with all these freaking kids while you're behind bars."

"That communism stuff is a bunch of bull, and you know it," she said.

"Yeah, I know it, stupid. But I'm not the one who's going to lock you up."

"You can fight me all you want, but I'm going."

The next morning Mommy and her Model Cities friends marched downtown and had a sit-in at City Hall to demand a winter clothing allowance. The cops arrested her and took her to jail, along with the other protesters, most of them black, because they refused to vacate government property.

"I told you so," Daddy said the next day, waving the newspaper at her. "Look at this! Here you are. It says you're all nothing but a bunch of communists."

"Yeah, yeah, yeah," Mommy said. "But you read the paper inside and out. Most people don't. No one's going to see that tiny little article on page 32!"

"You can't fight City Hall," he said.

Mommy stormed out to the enclosed back porch, and loaded up the washer.

I had heard enough myself and slipped past her, down the stairs, and out the back door. The landlord, Mr. Perici, had poured a concrete patio in the backyard and had mortared together cinder blocks three high, leaving out one cinder block in the center of every third column. I invented my sanctuary in this marvelous little castle in which I would sit and play by myself for hours, gazing out windows just my size at the vineyard and the vegetable garden where Mr. Perici weeded every day. I was the queen, and he was my servant. My husband, the king, was out ruling the kingdom. We had one boy and one girl, the perfect size family, and we were living happily ever after.

"Meow!" I heard a cat screech.

"Son of a bitch. I hate cats."

That was the voice of the lady upstairs, the lady wearing the yellow floral-print housedress. The first time she grabbed the cat by the scruff of the neck and threw it down the back stairs for pissing in one of her baskets of clean laundry, I shrieked.

"Mommy, you're going to kill it!"

"Damn cat," she said. "Next time I'll wring its neck!"

I gasped.

"Don't worry, Gabrielle. Cats always land on their feet." Then she laughed. "Dammit."

Mr. Perici's cat landed on its feet at the bottom of the stairway that day, too. It shook itself off, arched its back, then slunk toward my castle. Terror struck me. It might lunge at me, scratch out my eyes. Like Mommy, I hated cats, too.

I scooped up my bag of marbles, fled from my little palace to the front of the house, and wandered up the street, where I happened to meet another girl just my size, who also had a bag of marbles.

"Hi. You're new around here, aren't you?" she asked.

"Yeah. We just moved into the pink house next door to the yellow house."

"I live five houses down in the green house."

That fall, Martin Luther King, Jr., won the Nobel Peace Prize, and for the next two years the world was puddle-luscious as Katie and I played marbles and climbed trees and gathered chestnuts and threw snowballs and jumped rope and played hopscotch and ate ice cream.

For fourth and fifth grades I went to Clinton School, just up the street, and it was hard to believe but my teachers didn't even seem to notice that I was different from everybody else. Mrs. McLaughlin in fourth grade had her favorites, and I wasn't one of them, of course, but she didn't single me out, either. And I could see Miss Golia, my fifth-grade teacher tried her best not to show favoritism, and I appreciated it very much.

The only challenge I faced every day was trying to figure out how to lose my sister Mariah, because she was a goody two shoes—and a tattletale.

"Go home, Daddy's precious little Sugar-Dot," I mocked her one day, climbing up Katie's back fence until I reached high enough to climb up on her shed.

"I'm going to tell," Mariah said.

"No skin off my butt," I said, as she ran home crying.

Just then I lost my footing and slid halfway down the shed roof scraping my chest across a nail. Katie and I ran into her house, into her bathroom. Her parents were out, and her big brother wasn't paying any attention. I lifted my blood-drenched shirt as Katie wiped my chest with a towel. The huge gash just to the left of my right nipple looked much worse in the mirror than it felt, so much blood, like I had been shot in the chest.

"Oh my god. Did the nail puncture my heart," I cried out.

"Shhh! You're fine, silly. Your heart's on the other side."

When the bleeding stopped, she bandaged me up and gave me one of her shirts. By the time Mommy discovered my wound, she said it was too late to get stitches.

"Why didn't you tell me? Look at you. You're scarred for life! Do you understand? You're disfigured before you even begin to develop."

In that moment a black X marked my right chest, as if God was playing his own little game of tic-tac-toe.

Seating herself with a big sigh, Mommy looked on the bright side. "At least you had a tetanus shot when you stepped on that nail last month."

The day my breast was disfigured, it was once again clear that God had taken over as the head of the punishment department when Daddy wasn't looking, which didn't seem to be that often.

"What the hell are you doing, you knucklehead," he yelled.

"I've gotta pee," I said, not realizing that I was sitting on a kitchen chair.

"You idiot! Go to the bathroom."

"Zach! You're not supposed to startle a sleepwalker like that. C'mon. Gabrielle," Mom said, guiding me to the bathroom.

"I didn't mean to pee my pants," I told her.

"I know. I know. It's okay," she said.

"We can't have her roaming the house at night pissing wherever she wants for Chrissake," Daddy was yelling in the kitchen. "You and your bright ideas. You didn't want me to put a lock on their bedroom door when we moved in. But we've always had locks on the kids' doors. And we had good reasons for it. And this is a perfect example."

"Zach, it's not a big deal. Look, I've already cleaned it up."

"Yeah, but what if we were already in bed. What if I hadn't caught her? What if she sat on the couch and pissed herself."

"Zach, if she had, I would've cleaned it."

"Oh bullshit, like how would you have even known?"

As I sat on the toilet waiting for Mommy to return with dry pajamas, Daddy hammered holes in our bedroom door for a new lock. Tears fell in a puddle of shame on the cold linoleum that night as I tried to fall back to sleep, lying on my belly with my nose pressed up against the opening under my bedroom door. I could hear Daddy still bitching.

"She's nine years old for crying out loud and still wetting the bed!"

It was humiliating enough at home, especially since even Mariah didn't wet the bed anymore. But that summer, as Mommy packed our bags for summer camp, which I loved, I was mortified at the thought of wetting the bed there.

But I was rest assured when I sat on the cot that my cabin leader assigned to me: It crunched. I knew Mommy must have told them to be discrete, and they were. In the middle of the night, one of my cabin leaders shook me awake and guided me to the outhouse. And the next morning, the other leader woke me up first to change my bedding. But the bed and my night gown were both dry. Amazing! Just like that, overnight, I was cured of bedwetting.

That afternoon, just like I told Miss Dollar back in kindergarten, I told my cabin leader that I was too mature to take naps. So every day, when the assistant counselors monitored our cabins during naptime, I'd lie down like the other kids did, ha, ha, with one eye open. As the other kids settled down, I'd watch, until one of the counselors winked at me. Then I'd pretend I had to go to the bathroom, and sneak down the path instead to meet Nathan, the lifeguard with shiny black hair, who all the teenage girls swooned about. He took me out in the motorboat and taught me how to water-ski!

Boy, I loved camp: the meals at the mess hall, the games, the hayrides, the contests, the canteen full of candy on the other side of the lake, and the songs and scary stories around the campfire late at night. There was only one thing that troubled me, now that I didn't wet the bed anymore, and it was the same thing that tortured me every summer no matter where I went.

Bees!

Later that summer, my brother Zachary and I and Katie and her brother had trekked to Thornden Park to go swimming. It was overcast but we clung to the hope that the sun would come out by the time we walked almost an hour to get there. But that morning was weird. Not even one barking dog or buzzing bee made me scream and jump on Zach's back. It was especially ominous when even the old balloon man was absent from the corner of Oak Street and Burnet Avenue, where he whistled as he handed out balloons for two pennies apiece. Daddy always suspected the balloon man was really Howard Hughes because most homeless people wouldn't be entrepreneurial like that. Plus, he would appear and disappear on that corner but no one ever saw how he got there or how he left.

Just as we dipped our toes into the water, lightning cracked the sky, and the lifeguard blew his whistle. Trying to beat the storm home, the boys cut through the swamp, with Katie and I lagging behind, until one of them yelled.

"Look out! A bees nest!"

I didn't look up or down or across. I just ran smack into the nest and froze. As yellow jackets swarmed over my body, I screamed with my eyes wide open. A red car stopped on the road above. A man ran down the embankment, snapped off a switch and began whacking me. He then plucked me out of the nest, picked me up in his arms and ran, carrying me up to the lifeguards, who called an ambulance.

When Mommy bustled in with blueberry stains up to her elbows, I was still lying on a bed with wheels in a hallway. Several sets of pitiful eyes had walked by and looked down on me, like they knew I was going to die. And I almost did. The story was so big, my Aunt Sylvia read about it in her newspaper in Toledo, Ohio! First, *The Magic Toy Shop*. Now this!

A new kid moved into Katie's old house a few weeks later, and I bragged to him about my fame, but he said I was full of it. I marched him to my mother, who was sweeping down the stairs in the back hallway.

"I was in the newspapers across the country, wasn't I, Mommy?" I asked.

"Yes. It's true. Aunt Sylvia did read about you walking in a bees nest in Toledo, Ohio."

"And isn't it true I was on television, on *The Magic Toy Shop*?"

"Well, yeah. You were on the show. But, well, you were so excited, I didn't have the heart to tell you. But they must've sat you in the back. And you were so short. Truth is, I never actually saw you on the television."

I had been clinging to the image of a plain little girl with straight brown hair, who had debuted on television at age three, or was I four? Anyway, who could say what the future might hold for such a child? But that day, the string broke. The balloon disappeared. And I never mentioned *The Magic Toy Shop* again.

10
the first bite

Eden is that old-fashioned House
We dwell in every day
Without suspecting our abode
Until we drive away.

How fair on looking back, the Day
We sauntered from the Door—
Unconscious our returning,
But discover it no more.[1]

"Eden is that old-fashioned House" [http://bit.ly/1Tcgv5J]
By Emily Dickinson [http://bit.ly/1NKcGkb]

This work is licensed under the Creative Commons
Attribution-ShareAlike 3.0 Unported
License[http://bit.ly/1Tcgv5J]

To view a copy of this license,
visit http://creativecommons.org/licenses/by-sa/3.0/
[http://bit.ly/1Olbl8c]

Or send a letter to Creative Commons,
PO Box 1866, Mountain View, CA 94042, USA.

1966

A S I WAITED FOR DAD TO LIGHT A CIGARETTE, I finished scrubbing the meatloaf pan and strategically stacked it on the other dishes, since my sister, who is supposed to be drying, is otherwise entertained.

"Ain't you done eating yet?" I wailed at Dad.

"Ain't? What are you, ignorant?"

Then he looked at Mariah.

"Sing it again, Daddy," she cooed, like she was a freaking 4-year-old.

Fucking phony! Anything to get out of your chores.

"The itsy bitsy spider went up the water spout," Dad sang as his fingers climbed an imaginary wall.

"It ain't fair," I said, barging into the bathroom where Ma was giving the little kids their after-supper bath.

"Isn't," she said.

"Ain't! Isn't! Who cares? I always have to clean up the kitchen for Mariah in order to do the dishes before it gets dark. Plus, on top of it, I have to sit here and wait for Dad's plate while they do their idiotic spider song."

"You're just jealous," Ma said. "There's room on your father's lap for both of you, you know. If you weren't so angry all the time!"

"I'm not jealous," I yelled at her. "And I'm not angry. I wouldn't sit on his lap if you paid me. I hate him. I hate them both."

"Go play," she sighed. "I'll take care of your father's plate."

"And don't go more than a block away, idiot," Dad said. "I can see right through those bullshit tears. You'll do anything for an ice-cream cone. Dumb cops fall for it every time."

I skipped down the back hall steps two at a time and slammed the back door behind me before Ma had a chance to ask me to get a towel or a diaper.

Let the Sugar-Dot get it for her!

I ran two doors down to the vacant lot and then meandered into the view of the kids, who happened to be playing kickball there, and watched them play. I didn't know anyone in the neighborhood yet because we had just moved out of the pink house earlier this summer to a bigger house, a green house, a house that could fit all 10 of us, a house just six blocks from St. Agnes's, its once majestic steeple now crumbling, its red paint peeling.

Our new house was a downstairs flat, where Mrs. Dixon, our new landlady, had been living. She said the flat had gotten too big for her so she moved upstairs to the back apartment. I hadn't seen many black people since we left the Central Village housing project, but in our new place, a nice black couple lived in the upstairs front apartment, and right across the street from us lived a whole family of nice black people, living in a regular house: Mr. and Mrs. Cook and their daughter Olive, Mariah's age, and their son Derrick, my age. Mrs. Dixon introduced us to them, and it was so weird, the way they treated us, as if we were all the same color.

"Our team's short one," said Derrick, who was waiting his turn to kick. "Want to play?"

I fell in line behind the last kicker.

"If you want to play tomorrow, be here by six o'clock. That's when we pick teams," Derrick said, when we lost the game by two runs.

I was excited, but Derrick might as well have put gum on the bottom of my shoe when he asked me a few weeks later to be his girlfriend as we were leaving the field.

"Lemme think about it," I said.

I was excited, for sure. No boy had ever asked me out before. It was like I had matured at that very moment. And I had a grownup problem to prove it. Me, a boyfriend? I had never considered such a thing. I mean, of course, I knew that I'd grow up someday and have a husband. Ma said. And children, too. But I hadn't thought about the time in between. Plus, a black boyfriend? It seemed absurd. But he's so nice, and he invited me to play. Crap! I didn't know what to do.

But Ma made it sound so simple.

"Just tell him you are flattered, but your mother said you are too young to go steady."

And that was that.

It felt awkward to see Derrick after that, and I hadn't met anyone my age yet so I ticked off Mariah by horning in on her friends: Tanya, Rayna, and Bonnie. I was ten and Tanya and Rayna, the twins, were eight, and Bonnie was almost nine. I was older, and I could teach them things, like the multiplication table. But one rainy afternoon, a few week before school began, they taught me a thing or two.

We were playing in my little sisters' bedroom, which had two sets of bunk beds for the four of them, from the oldest to the youngest: Mariah, Lizbet, Kali, and Leanne. I voted to play school. It made sense that I would be the teacher since I was the oldest, but they voted to play house instead.

Playing house was stupid!

But they called it: who was married to who, and who was the wife and who was the husband, and whose kids were whose, and how old each was, and knee socks drew a divider between one house and the other, and you could tell if it was day or night if the overhead light was on or off.

Mariah called it first, to be Tanya's wife, and they changed their names to John and Heather, and they selected Leanne to be their baby girl, who they renamed Susie. And they taught Susie how to say goo-goo and gaga and mama and dada. Mariah appointed Bonnie to be my husband, and Bonnie changed her name to Michael and she named me Michelle. Michael said he adopted Kali from an orphanage and named her Jenny. Jenny was four, and she said a swear word so Michael said she would have to send Jenny to bed early.

When we finished supper, we tucked the little kids in the lower bunks and told them to get to sleep or else. Then the lights went out, and all the grownups went to bed in the top bunks, fully clothed, of course, but under the covers. As we shimmied down under the covers in the top bunk, Bonnie pulled me tight to her and pressed her pelvic bone into mine, rotating gently. I looked over at the other house and saw that John and Heather were moving under their covers too.

We're just playing house, for crying out loud. What could be wrong with that?

I began sixth grade that fall at Delaware Elementary, and I was reeling, that's how high with life I was. Sixth grade was the highest grade in the school, and after two weeks in Mrs. Dunbar's 'B' class they moved me to Miss Hawley's 'A' class, the highest of the high. I knew my multiplication table backward and forward and getting 100 percent correct on every spelling test, was like, of course. Miss Hawley was the nicest teacher ever. Plus, I had a really great outlet for my anger by kicking the crap out of this boy nicknamed Tuffy every night after school because he called my mother fat.

But that was short-lived.

I had to give up my fighting career in order to become a crossing guard. It just didn't sit well with those in charge: crossing kids to safety and then taking off my white belt and silver badge and chasing them home and beating them up. On a roll, I turned in my blue Camp Fire Girls cap and red kerchief to the Camp Fire leader (my mother, since Bluebirds) and joined Girl Scouts, and began earning badges for my new green sash.

Just when I thought things couldn't get any better, the music director selected me to sing a solo in the Christmas program. Now nothing could top that! (Well, it does if your name is Brook and the music director selects you to play Mary in the play and sing "Silent Night.") But no amount of milk could make my Wheaties soggy. I sang "The Holly and the Ivy" to a packed auditorium without even the aid of a microphone, my new claim to fame. Dad laughed at me, said it proved I had a big mouth.

Ha, ha, ha! He's so funny.

It was a time of hippies and peace signs and miniskirts. Race riots continued, but not in my backyard, not at the moment anyway. And while the Vietnam War was eating up most of the headlines, I sang along with Peter, Paul, and Mary, "Where have all the flowers gone?" [http://bit.ly/1kZwytf]

Meanwhile, Dad mostly grumbled about how much he hated his job and how convenient it was that Jack Ruby got cancer and how ridiculous it was that people would elect someone from Hollywood to be a governor.

Well, the good times rolled, and the next thing I knew, I was in junior high, in 7th grade. But I still didn't get it. The girl who sat in front of me told me that the cutest boy in my history class liked me.

Really? Guy Westfall likes me? He's the cutest boy in the class? And he likes me? I peeked at him out of the corner of my eyes. Well, I hadn't really noticed him before, but I can see now how you might call him cute. But he showed more interest in the rubber band he twirled around his pencil than in me.

The next day, the girl behind me passed me a note.

"Guy wants you to meet him at the park after school."

I turned to look at her.

She smiled big and wiggled her eyebrows.

"He wants to ask you out, but he's too shy," the girl behind me whispered. "Yes or no?"

I nodded.

After school, I walked the perimeter of the park, which took up a whole city block, but I never saw Wesley.

I guess he really is shy.

"Just as well," I shrugged it off and went home.

Here I was 11 years old, but I still didn't get it, girls swooning over boys and boys tripping over each other over girls—and kissing! It was like I was in between something. Maybe because I started school a year early? Maybe when I turn 12 in December I'll get it. Or maybe it will kick in when I start puberty and get my period. I knew I didn't fit in. I just hoped the kids in my school didn't know it yet. To avoid being discovered, I ignored them first, buried my nose in books, pretended I didn't notice them or their pea shooters one bit.

Little infantiles.

In the meantime, I thanked my lucky stars for my Uncle Mack.

"And then, and then," I'd say, as he waited with bated breath.

And when I told him my surprise endings, he would clutch his heart and drop to the floor. Delighted like a pig in shit, I'd pounce on him, and giggle, and mess up his hair. His rugged eyes and grin were warm from the sun, and he smelled like grease from his welding shop.

Uncle Mack and Aunt Velma visited every Saturday night to play poker. While phony Aunt Velma adored the dainty little Sugar-Dot and her naturally curly hair, I'd wait for Uncle Mack to park the car. As soon as he opened the front door, I'd squeal, then charge him. When he'd fall down and play dead, I'd growl and bark, jumping on top of him on all fours, laughing and screeching.

I didn't feel any older from one day to the next, the day my other uncle, my Uncle Carmen, stopped by for a haircut. But that day my mother decided I had crossed the fine line from childhood to puberty.

"Gabrielle! What's wrong with you? You're getting too big to climb all over every man who comes through that door. Now sit down! Your underpants are showing."

I backed off, my ears prickling, my butt puckering. I hung my head and ran to my room.

The following Saturday morning, I was making some tea, when someone knocked on the front door.

"I'll get it," I yelled at Ma, who was scrubbing tobacco stains off the kitchen walls with a rag doused in pine cleaner.

When I opened the door, Uncle Mack clutched his chest and grinned. My muscles tightened as I stepped back and pushed my hair behind my ears, then tugged at my pedal pushers.

"Please, come in," I said, and ushered him to the kitchen.

"I'm heading out to the farmers' market for Velma. You want anything, Rose?"

"Yeah, actually, Mack, that would be nice. I've been thinking about canning some tomato sauce," she said, as she pushed her hair behind her ears and tugged on her dress.

"Can I go? Can I go?"

"Gabrielle!"

"That's all right. She can keep me company."

"Fine, but don't talk his ear off," Ma said.

As Uncle Mack drove, I told him about the lunatic in Mr. Rochester's attic, but I could tell he wasn't listening. I chewed my lips and stared out the window. Between reading billboards and counting mile markers, my brain wouldn't stop.

He's pissed, probably hates your guts. Didn't you see the way his eyes flinched when you backed away from him at the front door? Then why did he invite you? So he could get even, ignore you back?

My stomach churned as cows grazed in the green pastures.

"What are you doing way over there," Uncle Mack asked as we passed yet another mile marker. "Come on, scoot over. Keep me company."

I scooted over, and then he asked me something unbelievable.

"Want to drive?"

"No way, José!"

"Why not! You're practically a young lady now. C'mon. I'll help you steer."

He took his right hand off the steering wheel and wrapped it around my shoulder.

While we were steering together, Uncle Mack's hand fell upon my chest. One of his fingers brushed across the forbidden X.

Doesn't he realize where he's touching? Of course not! Don't be silly. How would he know? Ma won't even let you wear a training bra because she said you don't even show yet, just little buds.

My forehead began to sweat. If you say something, he'll think you have a dirty mind. And if you scoot back over, he'll think you're mad at him.

Stop being so stupid! I'm positive he didn't mean it. Even Dad would say it's all in your imagination. And of course it is. Uncle Mack would never—

"Does it feel good?" he asked.

Feeling dirty like a whore, I slid back to the passenger seat, rolled the window all the way down and stuck out my head. Blinking and swallowing in quick succession, and choking back the tears, I hoped a telephone pole would come along and knock my stupid head off.

"You set yourself up for situations like this Gabrielle," Ma said, her back to me, as she stirred the spaghetti in the boiling water. "The way you're always clamoring to sit on men's laps. You're getting too big for that. And no more horseplay. You're almost 12 years old for crying out loud! It's time you started acting like a young—"

She didn't notice that I had slid into my room and shut and locked my door. I could still hear her, so I put my hands over my ears and sat on my closet floor and bit my lips, determined not to cry. But I broke down anyway, and once I got started, I couldn't stop. I was wailing from the depths of my soul by the time Ma had pushed through my lock. She pulled me up to my feet and prodded me from my closet to my bed, where she laid me back and stroked my hair.

"Just let it all out," she said. "Your soul rains today, but the sun'll come out tomorrow."

11
the fine line

"In the deep shade, at the farther end of the room, a figure ran backwards and forwards. What it was, whether beast or human being, one could not, at first sight tell: It groveled, seemingly, on all fours; it snatched and growled like some strange wild animal: but it was covered with clothing, and a quantity of dark, grizzled hair, wild as a mane, hid its head and face."[1]

Bertha, Mr. Rochester's lunatic wife

Jane Eyre [http://bit.ly/1Yo2Ls4]
By Charlotte Brontë [http://bit.ly/1NlgPRs]

1967

EVEN BEFORE MY FLOWERS HAD BEEN PLUCKED, I had exiled myself to my bedroom. Of course, in the meantime, I still had to come out and eat supper and wash the dishes.

"I'm talking to you," Dad yelled one night, poking me in the head.

What the fuck!

He slapped the pork chop out of my hands.

"Don't you have any manners? You're eating like a pig! Go wash your hands and face and get the fuck out of my sight. Now!"

My pleasure!

I shrugged my shoulders and moseyed on over to the kitchen sink, where I made a bubble bath out of dish liquid, soaked my fingernails, and cleaned under each one. When I finished, I dried my fingers on a dishtowel, one by one. Then I walked past him holding my chin up. I was very, very tall. He stood up, slamming his chair against the wall, and followed me, yelling at me more for not eating like a civilized human being, poking me in the head for not paying attention, shoving me onto my bed.

When he touched his belt, I began hissing and spitting and ripping the rubber bands out of my hair. I jumped from my bed and hunched like an ape and growled, my long hair sticking to the spit on my face. I ran from one corner of the room to the other, knocking over the card table and nightstand, jumping on the bed and off again. He lunged toward me several times, and when he almost seized my arm, I threw myself back against the wall and slammed my head and slapped myself and then bit my arm.

He backed away, and slammed the door behind him.

I ran to the door and listened.

"Your daughter's a lunatic," he said to Ma. "Now my damn food's cold."

I had to be careful because there was a fine line between devils and lunatics. The Bible said so. I knew because Uncle Ben, Ma's oldest brother, had read the passage to me when I told him the terrible news about Marcy, Ma's friend, who somehow managed to move to within a few blocks of us every time we moved.

> And when they were come to the multitude, there came to him a certain man, kneeling down to him, and saying, Lord, have mercy on my son: for he is lunatick, and sore vexed: for ofttimes he falleth into the fire, and oft into the water. And I brought him to thy disciples, and they could not cure him. Then Jesus answered and said, O faithless and perverse generation, how long shall I be with you? how long shall I suffer you? bring him hither to me. And Jesus rebuked the devil; and he departed out of him: and the child was cured from that very hour,"[2] Matthew 17:15–18 [http://bit.ly/1N8pODH].

Lunatic or possessed by a devil, who could say, the day I went into the pantry to get Ma a couple of onions. There she was, rolls of skin and a hairline, sitting on the floor, next to the potato bin, scolding the potatoes, gouging out their eyes with her long red fingernails.

I ran back to the dining room.

"Ma, quick. It's Marcy. Something's wrong."

Ma ran to the pantry, with me right behind her.

"What on earth?"

"I told them to stop," Marcy said, "But they won't—"

Ma swung around to me.

"Get a dollar from my purse and take the kids for candy or ice cream while I take care of her."

I walked the kids up the street to the corner bakery and set them loose at the day-old counter where donuts cost a nickel a piece. Chomping into peanut sticks and licking chocolate glaze, my sisters didn't notice the red flashing lights a block up. We sat on the curb eating as I watched the ambulance come and go.

As I swept up the neat little mounds of potato eyes from the pantry floor later that afternoon, they seemed to cry out to me, "If only we hadn't looked!"

I heard Ma repeat the story in my head again and again, how I found Marcy, how she dressed her and brushed her hair, and how she called the ambulance. How they took her to the hospital, then sent her to Marcy. Marcy was in Marcy. Marcy was in an insane asylum, like Dad said I would be one day. Everyone had theories, but no one knew for sure what made her crack. Dad said it was too bad, such a beautiful woman going off her rocker like that, but at least he could get a word in edgewise now.

"She probably drove herself crazy from talking too much," he said.

I took it as an omen considering how much I loved to talk. And the fact that I was already seeing a speech therapist because I talked too fast was not a good sign. But, then again, Dad should talk! He's the one who's always running his mouth and won't let me get a word in edgewise.

It was always the same.

"Dad! Guess what happened? I was walking to—"

"You were walking to the store. Or was it to school? To the library? You were walking or were you really running? Did you step on any cracks in the sidewalks on the way? Did you break your mother's back—"

"Dad! Let me finish. I was walking to the store, and I saw—"

"Let me guess. You saw a man parachute down from an airplane? No? You saw a pink elephant? Did it have blue polka dots?"

"No, Dad. I saw this guy and he was—"

"He was riding a cow? He was carrying a cow? No, let me guess. He was milking a cow?"

"Isawthisguywholookedlikehehadaguninhispocketlookingaroundsuspicious."

"What did you say? Gobble-de-gook?"

"Itwashotbutheworealongcoatandahat. Hetalkedtoawoman walking theotherway. Andsheturnedandwalkedwithhim. Shelookedscared."

"Oh, Gabby. You have such a wild imagination. When you grow up you should write fiction."

"Zach!" Ma hollered at him. "You promised not to call her Gabby! And you have to let her talk. All you're doing is undoing her speech therapy. Gabrielle, tell us again, but say it slowly."

"Never mind," I'd say, bitching at myself for getting caught in that syndrome with my ignorant father.

I will write a book one day, ha ha, and won't he be surprised.

Lucky for me, when we had moved into the green house, we had a family of 10 to divide into four bedrooms: Ma and Dad in the front, my three brothers in the bedroom off the living room, my four little sisters in the bedroom off the dining room, and me, little ol' me, in the bedroom off the kitchen. Of course, Zach was furious. After all, he was the oldest, and the youngest boys were babies. But Ma said you can't sleep boys with girls. That's the law.

I remember how Ma helped me to arrange the furniture: a single bed, a footstool for a nightstand, an old chest of drawers, a card table with a folding chair, and a vanity, which was my favorite piece. And that was it. I had packed all my toys and dolls and games in boxes at the pink house and had tossed them into my sisters' new bedroom for them to fight over.

The head of my bed fit beneath my window, and there was just enough room to open the door to the kitchen at the foot of the bed. And the vanity, with its three beveled mirrors, was just the right width to fit against the wall between the door to the kitchen and the door to the closet, a closet with no door, mind you, but a closet that would one day hide my darkest secrets.

I grabbed a fitted sheet and pillowcase and the least frayed blanket I could find from the wardrobe in the back hall and made my bed. Then I sifted through the junk drawer and fished out two hooks and two eyelets, one for the inside of my door and one for the outside.

I locked my door and pulled down the vinyl window shade and admired the little tassel and strings that ribbed its seams.

This is no ordinary shade!

I then hung my aquamarine silver-trimmed rosary beads in the center mirror of the vanity and stood back to admire my new room. It was so me. And all mine!

But Ma had other ideas.

She went to Ben Franklin's on Geddes Street and bought lots of fabric. In one night flat on her sewing machine, she conjured up a flowery three-layered bed cover, solid green curtains for my window and closet doorway, a matching pillow sham, and three pleated skirts, one she hung on the card table to hide its legs, one to hide the fact that the nightstand was a footstool, and the other to hide the marred legs of the vanity, all of which she adorned with shiny gold upholstery tacks.

Just when I thought the whir of the sewing machine had ceased for the night, she ran a piece of fabric up and down and over and across and, like magic, out came a table runner for the vanity that matched the bed cover—she even sewed green tassels on each end. As if that wasn't enough, she laid down a green carpet remnant to cover the worn linoleum in front of my bed. And as a final touch, she stood a large yellowed Bible on my vanity, the one that used to collect nicotine in the dining room. As she stood back with her hands on her hips admiring her work, I looked around and thought it looked like some other lucky girl's room. I hugged and kissed her and told her that she was the greatest mother ever.

"Now, what about pictures," she said. "You need stuff on your walls."

I shrugged.

"Here's $20. Walk up to Ben Franklin's tomorrow and pick out any pictures you like."

The next day, I looked through every picture in the store and passed on ballerinas and cats and horses and sunsets and hot rods. I rolled my eyes at posters of Elvis and the Beatles and the Smothers Brothers and Twiggy. All my heroes were dead. But giving $20 back to Ma was out of the question.

There must be something here I want.

I wandered away from the poster section and began walking the aisles when I stumbled across a gold mine: paperbacks, three for a dollar. I spent the next two hours ransacking shelf after shelf, reading back covers, and stacking the keepers. I brought stack after stack to the front for the gentleman to hold for me, titles like *The Tell-Tale Heart*; *The Strange Case of Dr. Jekyll and Mr. Hyde and Other Tales of Terror*; Andersen's *Fairy Tales*; *Frankenstein*; *The Diary of a Young Girl*; *Jane Eyre*, wow, my very own copy; and *The Scarlet Letter*. I think I was the only customer in the store for the most part, yet I had this fear that someone would come along and take one of my stacks. The old man eyed me warily, like he knew I couldn't possibly have enough money for all these books.

"That's 14 dollars so far," he said at one point, sure that I was making a mess of his book aisle for nothing.

"Let me know when I get to $19," I said, smiling, holding up my 20-dollar bill, after all I had to save enough for a Dr Pepper and a couple of Reese's peanut butter cups—and don't forget the sales tax.

"I'm starting my own library," I announced, as I dumped the two large paper bags of books onto the kitchen table.

"It's your room," Ma said, shaking her head.

That first year in my own room, I loved to lie on my bed and chew on Tootsie Roll Pops as I escaped from one fantasy world into another. It was the best year of my life, that is, until I identified with Hester Prynne the day Uncle Mack's finger slipped. Now that I'm almost 12 years old (in three months), it's time to grow up. My bedroom became more like my prison, and my books no longer intrigued me. And since I'm practically an adult now, I took up stealing alcohol out of the china cabinet and two or three cigarettes at a time out of Ma's pack. And the heck with Charles Dickens! Mrs. Dixon's books were far more alluring.

I kept my bedroom door locked at all times, but I kept my bedroom window wide open, in winter, spring, summer, and fall. I needed air, lots of air, because I would freak out when I couldn't breathe. When I'd finish a book, I'd sit at the window at the head of the bed and smoke cigarettes, blowing smoke out the screen and torching bugs between drags as images of Bertha and Marcy danced in my head.

Like I said, thanks to Mrs. Dixon, I had a whole new library at my disposal, and I'm not talking about *Reader's Digest* books either. When Mrs. Dixon finished reading her books, she'd offer them to Ma and Dad, who, as good tenants, accepted with grace. But the paperbacks weren't like anything I'd read before. Some were UFO books and books on the supernatural, books called *Truth Is Stranger than Fiction* and *Fate*, books that recounted psychic phenomenon and reincarnation and ghosts and extraterrestrial life.

Ma and Dad would read her hand-me-downs from cover to cover. Then they'd toss them in the bookcase in the dining room and declare them nonsense. Not me. I believed every word and hungered for more. One night as I stood at the bookcase, I was horrified. I had already read every single book, every single magazine that was in the bookshelf. I had pulled ahead of Mrs. Dixon's reading!

"What are you looking for," Ma asked, as I rummaged again through every shelf.

"For something to read, that's all. I'll just go upstairs tomorrow and ask Mrs. Dixon if she has any more books she's finished. I've been wanting to visit her anyway."

"Oh, no, you won't, little missy! Those books are nonsense. They're evil," she said. Then lowering her voice, "They have séances up there. They summon dead people. You don't want to go up there."

Oh, but, I do.

"I have nothing else to read," I snapped at her.

"Read the Bible," she said, hissing at me.

That night, I sucked my thumb raw.

Read the Bible? What a curious idea.

I sat up and threw off the covers and turned on the light. I retrieved the Bible from my vanity and wiped it down with a sock. I pulled up the folding chair, sat at the card table, opened the Bible, and cleared my throat.

"In the beginning . . ."[3] [http://bit.ly/1N8pODH].

In Genesis, Chapter 1, on the sixth day, "God created man in his own image, in the image of God created he him; male and female created he them." After blessing them and sending them forth to be fruitful, to multiply, God rested on the seventh day.

But then in Genesis, Chapter 2, God decided it's not good for man to be alone! After He created all the beasts of the field and fowl of the air, after Adam named them all, *then* God decided that it was not good for Adam to be alone. To top it off, He caused a great sleep to fall upon Adam, and took one of Adam's ribs to create Woman, like she was an afterthought, like she was created to be in the service of the man!

I grabbed a blank composition notebook and a pen from my school supplies and wrote the title of my first book on the first page.

"What Is God?"

I could just see all the Bible scholars rushing to their desks to make sense of it, then to their pulpits to explain it away. Let them explain this, I'd mumble each day as I found another contradiction and added it to my notebook.

If the Bible is true, if God is a perfect God, then why didn't Adam die the day he ate the fruit of the forbidden tree?

"And the Lord God commanded the man, saying, Of every tree of the garden thou mayest freely eat: But of the tree of the knowledge of good and evil, thou shalt not eat of it: for in the day that thou eatest thereof thou shalt surely die"[4] [http://bit.ly/1N8pODH], Genesis 2:16-17.

Adam did eat, and then he lived for 930 years! Besides, why would God put such a tree in the garden anyway? Here little boy, here's a Reese's. I'm going to sit it right here amidst all the vegetables and fruit. But don't eat it. It's poison. It will kill you. What father would tempt his son like that and then kill him for taking the bait?

How could a loving God become so angry and full of regrets that He destroyed almost every living creature on the face of the earth except for Noah and a few select people and animals? Come on! Wouldn't God, all-powerful, all-knowing, come up with a better solution? Why would God create man in the first place, knowing full well that he also was creating humans who He would one day condemn as evil and destroy? Was it a game? He made us, good and bad, and made us all accountable for Adam and Eve's sin in the garden, yet God does not take responsibility for His own creation? No, He just wipes them off the face of the earth if they don't do it His way.

Or did men just make it all up to control women and children. After all, how the heck would they know anyway? God appeared to *man*? Hmm. Why didn't God appear to a woman?

Before I knew it I was reading Exodus.

Why does the Bible say God is a jealous God, yet it is a sin for us to be jealous? How come God claims He gave us free will to choose, but if we don't choose Him we go to hell and are punished for eternity? How is that free choice? How can He appear on Mount Sinai and say that He is so high and mighty above the rest of us that anyone who dares touch the ground He walks on He will destroy? How does that mentality project love? What kind of God wants His people to fear and to tremble? If this God created all of us, then why does He choose an elite group to be His people? How does this angry, prejudiced, destructive, power-hungry, murderous God differ from Hitler, or from my own father, for that matter, minus the murder part, of course.

One night, after writing, then hiding my book in my closet with my diaries, I punched my pillow and closed my eyes to think. As I relaxed, music ping-pinged in the distance. The sound of flutes drew nearer summoning cobras to uncurl their bodies and rise. A school desk replaced my pillow. And as my head rested on its cool surface, my body levitated in mid-air. Aware, intrigued, I went with the flow. The desk evaporated, the music dissipated. Suspended, I began to float around the room.

When it didn't get any more exciting than that, I decided to go back to bed. But to my shock, I couldn't move a muscle. It seemed simple: Just holler for Ma. She'll come running. I tried but I couldn't even peep if my life depended on it. I began to panic. What if! Each time I floated past my bedroom door—not that I could see it, but I sensed it—I strained with all my might. But I tell you I was paralyzed from head to toe, and it seemed my life depended on my ability to break this curse.

"Pray!" Uncle Ben's voice cried out. "Pray!"

Once every five years or so Uncle Ben appeared like an apparition on our door step, his soft brown hair, thick, wavy, uncut; his bare feet swollen, blistered, and callused; a folk guitar slung over his hefty shoulder; and his gruff hands holding a black Bible, its leather frayed, its pages tattered. His suntanned skin radiated as if he had just descended from Mount Sinai bearing the Ten Commandments, like Charlton Heston, but a couple hundred pounds heavier and no teeth.

He would always catch us off guard, living in our lair of lasciviousness, in need of redemption. Ma would feed him, and he would wash dishes and hang clothes in the backyard. After supper he would preach to us and tell us stories. Then he'd go down to Geddes Street and preach on the street corner. If someone didn't have shoes, he'd give away the sandals Ma bought him. She'd get mad that he gave away his sandals to some bum on a street corner, but then she'd buy him another pair. Low and behold, he'd find another bum who needed shoes, who happened to wear his size, and give them away.

The last time Uncle Ben bellowed at our front door, we were living in the pink house. So much had happened since then, but he need not know. They called Uncle Ben a Holy Roller, and his thunderous voice shook the whole house when he plucked the strings of his folk guitar. After supper, neighbors stopped what they were doing and gathered outside our house to listen as Uncle Ben sang "The Old Rugged Cross" and other requests, especially spiritual songs and country and western.

Ma said Uncle Ben was on his way to stardom in his 20s, until he said he heard the voice of God one night when he was working late.

"Wilt thou work as diligently for me?" God had asked, his voice somehow echoing through the pipes in the old building.

"Yea, Lord!" Uncle Ben answered.

After that night Ma said he threw away his career, gave up the bottle and his life as a bigamist, and followed God wherever He would lead.

Long after the guitar stood on end and long after everyone else excused themselves, I'd still be glued to his adventures about hitchhiking and truck drivers and preaching and living on Skid Row in Los Angeles, where he tried to convert the homeless to Christ.

"God has a special plan for you, too, Gabrielle," he said one night, spreading a loaf of bread with a jar of peanut butter, and then gumming it.

"No, I could never be a nun."

"There are other ways to serve the Lord," he said.

"Like what?"

"You can teach others about the Gospel," he said. "And bring souls to God."

"How? Girls aren't allowed to be altar boys much less priests."

"No. I mean just being you, Gabrielle. You can teach the Word of God to your friends. You can tell other people the stories I told you. You can teach them, make them believers. And God will reward you in heaven for every soul you bring to Him."

"Oh, I don't know," I said, smirking inside.

People don't believe what I say now. They'd think I was really crazy if I took up your crusade.

"You'll see. One day God will reveal to you the purpose of your life," he said. "In the meantime, remember this. If you ever get into a bad situation, and you think there's no way out, pray.

"But what would I pray?" I asked, considering we didn't even pray to the same god. He was Baptist or Methodist, or something. And I was Catholic.

"The main prayers we say are the *Our Father*, *Hail Mary*, and *Glory Be*. I don't know any Baptist prayers."

"Ah, but the *Our Father* is *The Lord's Prayer*. It's straight from the book of Matthew." He wet his forefinger and opened his Bible right to that page.

"Jesus spoke to the multitudes. Do not stand in the synagogues and pray as if you will be heard for your much speaking. God knows what ye have need of. Instead pray in silence in this manner. Our Father, who art in heaven, hallowed be thy name"[5] [http://bit.ly/1N8pODH], Matthew 6:9–13.

"I know scripture by heart and didn't even know it!"

Just as he suddenly appeared, he was gone. God would call Uncle Ben in the middle of the night, and he'd disappear for about another five years. Once out of sight, out of mind, until that night I was floating around my bedroom, that is, and couldn't get down.

"Just pray," he had said.

"Our Father, who art in heaven, hallowed be thy name. Thy kingdom come, thy will be done on Earth as it is in heaven. Give us this day our daily bread and forgive us our trespasses as we forgive those who trespass against us. Lead us not into temptation, but deliver us from evil. Amen. Our Father, who art in heaven... ."

I repeated the prayer much like I had repeated it most of my life, memorized words, with little thought to their meanings but this time with fervor. Again and again, I repeated the prayer faster and faster

"Forgive us our trespasses . . . lead us not . . . deliver us . . . Our Father . . ."

Then, wham! The energy released me, hurled me back into my bed.

I scrambled up on all fours, jumped over the foot of my bed, and yanked the hook out of my door. I ran to the dining room and banged on Ma and Dad's bedroom door, turning the doorknob left and right even though I knew they always slept with it locked. The door flung open, Dad in his boxer shorts and Ma in her nightgown.

"You're cracking up," Dad said. "You just had a silly dream. Go back to bed."

But Ma's eyes opened wide. She knew I had been reading the evil books.

She hustled me out into the living room, demanding that Dad unhook the big wooden cross that hung over the living room doorway.

"Be careful," she yelled. "Don't drop the palms."

Ma told me to lie on the couch while she retrieved a blanket, which she drew up to my neck.

Then she proceeded to open these little secret compartments in the cross: One contained a bottle of holy water and the other contained white candles, which she sat on the coffee table and lit.

"What are you doing, you idiot?" Dad asked her. Then he snickered and went back to bed. "You're both nuttier than a fruitcake."

Ma handed me the black rosary beads from the cross, then she blessed me and the beads with the holy water as if she were performing an exorcism. Then she blessed herself and told me her fears.

"There's something evil in this house," she said. "I can feel it. Could ever since we moved in. I can feel the evil in this room right now. And it's no wonder," she said, looking and gesturing at the ceiling.

"One of the evil spirits she conjured up is probably looking for a soul to possess. And we have to ward off the evil spirits. So I want you to stay put right here for the rest of the night and say the rosary beads. The spirits won't bother you if you're praying. Good thing Uncle Ben had warned you what to do."

She sat with me for a while as I mumbled, "Hail Mary, full of grace, blessed art thou."

"Okay," she said at last, as she blew out the candles. "I don't feel the evil presence anymore. I'm going back to bed. But you keep praying till you fall asleep."

I thought Ma must be right. She didn't know about the evil thoughts I had been writing in my book. But it all fit. I kept my book hidden in the closet, but after the night a demon tried to possess me, I didn't write down any more of my evil thoughts, though they still wandered through my mind quite often.

In the spring, Mrs. Dixon moved out, and we annexed her apartment to the downstairs, making it 15 rooms total, which we needed because Ma was pregnant again. She didn't have to ask me twice to move upstairs so the new baby could have my bedroom off the kitchen. But the thrill was short-lived when night after night, I came barreling down the stairs hysterical about a noise or something brushing against my feet.

"You're a fucking lunatic, Gabby," Dad said, as he turned the pages of his newspaper. "You're 13 years old. It's time you learned to separate reality from your imagination."

"It was probably a mouse," Ma said. "I'll set a trap."

When my record player started turning itself on, I began sleeping with the lights on, fully dressed in sweatshirts and stretch pants and socks and sneakers. One night, I was lying there trying to go to sleep—absolutely positive that my stereo was off—I know because I verified again and again that the power light was out. As soon as I became drowsy, click. My phonograph turned on, one of my Dad's 45s dropped down on the turnstile, and the arm lifted and slid over. The needle touched down.

"I've—got—a—tiger by the tail, it's plain to see."

I had been ignoring a lot, but this, no way. I flew out of bed and turned it off. And that's when I heard an owl in my closet hoot three times.

"Somebody is going to die. Somebody is going to die. Somebody is going to die," I screamed, until I heard someone approaching my bedroom door.

I held my breath, grabbed the pair of scissors off my dresser, and crouched behind my door.

"Gabby," Dad said. "Are you okay?"

I could just see the headlines: *She stabbed her father to death with a pair of scissors in a fit of insanity, brought on by evil spirits.*

"Drop the scissors, Gabby. I believe you," Dad said, holding out his hanky. "It's clean. Wipe your face, and come downstairs. Your mother wants to talk to you."

I dropped the scissors to the floor and ogled him as I took the hanky. Then I followed him down the stairs, and the three of us sat at the kitchen table and talked until two in the morning. Story after story, Dad told me about the haunted houses he had lived in when he was a boy, and how much the ghosts had scared the living crap out of him and his brothers and sisters.

"We had just moved into this great big old house on South McBride Street."

"Yeah, I know the one," Ma said. "Everyone whoever went near it thought that that house was haunted."

"One day, my brother, your Uncle Pierre, we called him Bobby back then. We were up in the playroom in the attic putting some toys on the shelves when we got goose bumps. We looked at each other then toward the door. A huge shadow fell across the doorway and bam! The door slammed. Mind you, there were no windows open or wind or draft, nothing that could explain it. We both ran like hell to the door and opened it and ran down the stairs trying to get ahead of each other, almost killing each other. I don't even think our feet hit the stairs. Ever since that day, I have believed in ghosts," Dad said.

"Why didn't you believe me then?"

"Well, we believe ghosts exist," Ma said. "But if we told you that, we were afraid we'd scare you even more. Thing is, there's a logical explanation for most things. Like when I was a kid. We had just moved into this house out on an old country road. And we could hear the weirdest humming coming from the walls at night. We thought for sure it was haunted. But then one night when we got home, I had reached to turn on the light, and for a split second, I thought I was being electrocuted. I screamed. But once the light turned on we could see that a bee had stung my thumb. Of course, bees don't usually come out at night so your grandfather began to investigate. Turned out the walls were filled with bees, not ghosts."

"But how do you explain the record player turning itself on?" I asked.

"Well, maybe it is a ghost. But it's probably more scared than you. Maybe it's a friend of Mrs. Dixon's who got left behind when she moved."

"How come I'm the only one it bothers?"

"Actually, you're not the only one," Dad said. "One night, everyone was in bed, even your mother." He pointed to the kitchen cupboard behind us. "I was standing right there pulling out some bread to make a sandwich."

"Dad, making his own sandwich?" I said, laughing.

Dad chuckled.

"Yeah, it was against my better judgment, but I'll do some crazy things sometimes. Actually though, I never did make that sandwich. I had just pulled out the bread when I swear someone touched my shoulder. I thought about all the crazy things you'd been saying about ghosts, and I panicked. I put the bread back and went straight to bed."

"Yeah, I'll never forget that night," Ma said. "He shook my leg and woke me up. When I turned on the light to see what was wrong, he stood there babbling. He was whiter than the sheets."

We all laughed.

"Matter of fact, we slept with our light on that night. But they're just spirits," Ma said. "Probably just trying to find their way home."

She looked around the kitchen and started talking to them.

"Look." she said. "Mrs. Dixon moved to Vine Street on the north side, 104 Vine Street. If you want to see her, go there. If you need directions, I'll draw you a map. But I'm sure you can find it. There's no sense in hanging around here scaring Gabrielle, because she's onto you now."

I don't think all the spirits left that night, but the one who kept turning on my stereo must have found its way to Mrs. Dixon's house. And the owl only hooted twice after that. No one was going to die after all. Or so I thought.

12
the curse

"Children have different needs, different 'thicknesses of skin, different capacities for perceiving pain.' The one with the least 'receivers' so to speak, will consciously feel the least effect of abuse. The child with the most sensors will consciously feel it all, and perhaps strongly sense the wounds of others as well. It is not a matter of truth or not truth, it is a matter of having the ability to receive the transmissions going on around one."[1]

Clarissa Pinkola Estés [http://bit.ly/1Oakalh]
Women Who Run With the Wolves [http://bit.ly/1Sd2y7B]

1969

WHEN ARMSTRONG TOOK HIS FIRST STEP ON THE MOON, I was sitting on the steps of our front porch weightlessly touching down on the ageless terrain of my own moon, the hazy gray sphere in my mind, singing quietly from the depths of my soul.

"Like a whirlpool, it never ends—"

Crack! Dad knuckled me in the head.

"You're dizzy all right," he yelled. "Man is literally walking on the moon this very moment. A man on the moon! And it's live—do you hear me—live on live television. And here you sit out in the dark singing some ridiculous song!"

"I was watching! But they've just been repeating themselves for the past two hours. All you had to do was say something was happening, and I would have come right back in. They landed six freaking hours ago. Cripe! How was I supposed to know?"

When he turned to go back in, I rubbed my head, gave him the bird, butted my cigarette, and followed him into the house and sat on the couch, after all I wasn't stupid. I knew it was an amazing event of astronomical proportions, but I didn't realize just how amazing until Dad handed me a bowl of popcorn and a glass of Pepsi with ice in it.

That marked the beginning of the magical summer of '69, when two of the prettiest, richest, most popular girls in the neighborhood—who were two grades ahead of me, no less—took me under their wings and transformed me from an ugly duckling into a beautiful swan!

We met at Valerie's house Friday afternoon to begin my makeover. I would debut at the dance pavilion that night at the Campus Inn at Suburban Park! I'd been to the amusement park before. The 'A's on my report cards earned me a free pass for a day at the park every summer. Last summer I rode the Tilt-A-Whirl by myself all day in a space faraway. Not so this year. I had friends now, and I was going to a dance, my first dance ever.

Valerie thumbed through the rows of blouses and skirts and dresses that hung in her walk-in closet.

"Here, try this on," she said again and again, as one item after another flew out of her closet.

Her best friend, Michelle, helped me in and out of various outfits, and then I modeled for them until they both agreed that I should wear the white and silver metallic blouse and black leather mini-skirt, which felt so soft and creamy.

Valerie led me to her bathroom. where she handed me a razor and shaving cream and explained how to shave my legs and my armpits without cutting myself.

Neat! Ma only let me use the electric razor.

"After you shower, Michelle will blow dry your hair and show you how to trim the split ends and how to iron it so it will look flawless. Then I'll show you how to apply leg makeup. We'll do your face last."

Just call me Cinderella!

I hoped the shoe would fit, and turns out Michelle's black high-strapped sandals did, but I kicked them off on the dance floor under the strobe lights, and shimmied under the black lights, where my blouse glowed, as did my legs.

"Who is that chick?" I had asked Valerie's mirror.

I remembered how excited I was the first day I spotted blood on my underwear just a few weeks before my 13th birthday—how I ran through the house calling for my mother, announcing it to everyone in earshot. My period said I was a woman, but I had no idea that there was really a woman underneath my clothes!

Valerie had snuck us a couple of drinks from her parents' bar, and we smoked a couple of joints, too, in case you were wondering where all my inhibitions went. Two older guys had picked us up and drove us to the dance. They were both 18, Sean for Valerie and Doug for me. Michelle had eyes for someone else, who she hoped would notice her at the dance that night.

"C'mon Gabby. We're going to get some air," Valerie said, pulling me from the dance floor. I grabbed my shoes and ran through the crowd after her.

Doug and I ducked under the railing as we followed Valerie and Sean to the Comet, an old rollercoaster that reeked of grease, yet creaked every inch we moved. We sat a few cars down from them, and chatted while they necked. Within a minute or two, for no explicable reason, I began to giggle. One giggle led to the next. I couldn't help myself. Out of nowhere a spotlight went on, and I could see the silhouette of a short stout sheriff, his hand on his gun, running toward us, yelling at us.

"Stop! Don't move. Put your hands up. Or I'll shoot!"

After haranguing us for a half hour for trespassing, the sheriff let us go with a warning. That night when the five of us got back to Valerie's house, we sat in the backyard laughing our asses off, repeating again and again every detail of the night, until Sean got the bright idea to aim the hose at us, and told us not to move, which sent us all hobbling from our chairs. Shrieking, we chased each other around in the yard, our makeup running, our outfits dripping, our chests pounding.

I slept on the couch in Val's bedroom that night, and the next morning she bagged all the clothes she had tossed out of her closet the night before and gave them to me. Just like that, I had a whole new wardrobe.

Of course, Rome wasn't built in a day, and Val and Michelle's protégé still needed some work. After all, they wouldn't be caught dead hanging out with a nerd.

No one could say for sure. Everyone had their theories, including Ma and Dad and Zach.

"Why would Valerie and Michelle take a girl two years younger than themselves and invest so much in her?"

"Hmm. Were they just bored? Was Gabby just their little laughing stock? Or did they reach out to her out of the goodness of their hearts when they saw this poor little ugly duckling with no friends?"

"Hmm. Or was it because Valerie had a crush on Zach, and this whole 'make-friends-with-Gabrielle' was a scam orchestrated as a means for Valerie to get closer to Zach."

"You're going to get hurt," Ma said. "I promise you, Valerie and Michelle have some ulterior motive."

But I didn't care. If there was anything that Val or Michelle wanted from me, anything at all, I would gladly accommodate them for they introduced me to a whole new world, to a whole new me.

By the time school began that fall, they taught me how to be cool. They taught me how to cross the street with my nose up in the air. They taught me how to dodge stray bullets and black fists in the midst of racial riots. No, we would not get blood on our pretty little faces.

Unlike my Dad, I couldn't wait for the new school year to begin.

I'll bet the kids from last year won't even recognize me!

But much like Dad lamented that John F. Kennedy didn't live long enough to see the moon landing, he lamented my mother's increased absence late that summer as she attended various meetings to prepare for the upcoming school year.

"What are you talking about, stupid? Another meeting tonight? You just had a meeting last night for Chrissake."

"You're worst than a little kid, Zach! Why do we have to go through this argument every time I get ready to go out the door?"

You tell him, Ma!

I was so proud of her. Delaware Elementary had elected her "Mother of the Year" last year, and this year they elected her president of the PTA.

"That's because every night it's something else, stupid! Last night and the night before that! Don't they know you have a life of your own?"

"Oh, for crying out loud! It's not every night."

"You could have fooled me, idiot. All I know is I never see you."

Idiot? You're the idiot. What idiot would want to stay home with a fucking idiot like you?

But Ma just sighed.

"Have you forgotten you're pregnant? What's everyone going to do without you when you have this baby? You sure as hell ain't leaving me home alone with a newborn."

Aren't! You ignoramus!

"Don't worry. Everything will be fine."

"You could deliver any fucking day now. And you don't even have the baby's room set up yet."

"Oh, stop being ridiculous. The only reason it's not set up yet is that we have more stuff than I know what to do with. There's nothing that baby will need."

"He might need a stupid mother home once in awhile."

Oh my god, Dad! Will you get off her fucking back?

When Ma got home from her meeting that night, I was in the kitchen putting some pieces of her jigsaw puzzle together while Dad sat in his recliner in the living room watching some corny variety show.

She made herself a cup of instant coffee and sat down to work the puzzle.

"How do you put up with him, Ma, with him nagging all the time?"

"Oh, I'm used to it. He doesn't mean anything by it. He just wants attention."

"He makes me sick," I said.

"You know, you've never really given him a chance. He had it pretty rough growing up. His mother kept him locked on the porch until he was eight years old. Didn't even send him to school until the truancy officer knocked on their door. He wasn't allowed to so much as make a sandwich for himself up to the age of 16. Then when his dad died, his mother threw him out on his ear. He was only in the eighth grade!"

I rolled my eyes. I had heard it all before.

"He had been rejected most of his life, and then here you come along, his firstborn daughter, and you reject him, too! Even when you were a little baby, you'd scream bloody murder whenever he tried to pick you up. I don't know what it was about you and him. I never understood it."

I shrugged.

Ma sighed.

She did touch on an interesting detail, though—me as a baby. She often told stories about the births of the other kids, like that Thanksgiving at Aunt Dottie's when she drank a whole bottle of wine and then went into labor for Mariah. She couldn't stop laughing between contractions.

"Why won't you tell me what happened the night I was born?"

"Oh, I don't remember," she said. "I had so many kids. I can't remember all their births."

"I'm your firstborn daughter. Yet you can't even remember the day I was born? All you can remember is that I rejected *him*!"

"You and your father don't get along because you're too much alike."

"I'm not anything like him!"

"You should start reading the newspaper and watching the news. Then you and your father might find something in common. You know how he likes to talk about the news, especially politics."

"I don't give a crap about politics. And he doesn't give a crap about me."

Ma sighed.

But I wished I had taken her advice because later that week I needed to think of something to say to my father as we walked to the big red funeral home on West Onondaga Avenue to make the arrangements.

Unlike the last baby Ma lost, this one had a name. Bobby. Like in Bobby Kennedy who was assassinated shortly after Martin Luther King, Jr., last year. Like in Bobby Hayes, Dad's brother who got shot in the head during a mysterious dispute with the cops at age 28. As in Bobby Hayes, Jr., his son, my cousin, who died at age 16 trying to get high sniffing aerosol hair spray in a bathroom just a few months ago.

That afternoon when I got home from school, Dad was sitting at the kitchen table with his head in his hands. Ma had been in critical condition over the weekend, but yesterday the doctors said her condition had stabilized.

"Ma's okay, ain't she?" I asked.

"Isn't."

"Whatever."

"Yeah. To think we almost lost her."

"I would rather die than lose her," I said, as I sat down next to him.

"God! We should have known. Something about the name Robert, it's like a bad omen."

"Yeah, well, who can know those things, Dad."

"I have to go up to the funeral home and make the arrangements. But I'm—"

His head shriveled into his shoulders as he closed his eyes.

"I'll go with you," I said.

He looked up at me, half-nodded with a wince, the finger tips and thumb of his right hand opening and closing over his chest. Then he clenched his other fist and hit the table with his knuckles.

It was a light jacket kind of day. But I shivered as the wind rattled the reddish-orange leaves on the trees that refused to let go. Rain clouds followed us for several blocks before Dad spoke.

"Such a shame. All those years we didn't have a pot to piss in. Now we can afford a bike and rides on the Ferris wheel. And this happens. Ten pounds, ten ounces. He would have been strong as an ox."

"Yeah, he'd have been something."

"Do you want a service?" the funeral director asked.

Dad shook his head.

"Do you want a coffin?"

Dad shook his head.

"Did you name the child?"

Dad shook his head.

It used to be funny, the story they told about the day Grandpa Williams met Dad. Grandpa had asked Dad a series of questions, to which Dad just shook his head.

"Is that all you can do is shake your head?" Grandpa had asked, turning red.

Dad shook his head.

So that day we made the arrangements for another nameless baby to be buried in an unmarked grave, in an unknown cemetery. Dad said he could afford this baby, yet he wouldn't even cough up enough money to give the child a decent burial.

Yeah, sure. Cheap bastard.

We had turned down our street before he spoke.

"Your mother told me to take care of the arrangements before she comes home. She said no service, no grave, no name. I just have to do what she asks because, right now, Gabby, I can't even get her to lift her head off the pillow."

He paused.

I backhanded the tears from my face.

"She wants us to get rid of everything in the baby's room before she gets home. She doesn't care where. I'm going to need your help, Gabby. And when your mother gets home, she's going to need help, too. They're going to assign a caregiver to help her bathe and to change her bandages and to feed her, someone who can also keep house and cook and watch the kids."

I burst into tears.

Dad put his arms around my shoulders and held me. And for the first time in years, I didn't cringe.

"We don't need no one," I said, pulling myself from him. "I'll change her bandage. I'll bathe her and feed her. I'll cook supper and clean the house. I'll watch after the kids."

"You're my little toughie, Gabby. But the hospital won't let her come home unless she has a caretaker."

The day Ma came home, Mrs. Garrett showed up, but after a couple of arguments, I realized she would rather do anything than care for a sick woman or cook or clean or look after my six little sisters and brothers. So I made a deal with her. If she would do the laundry, that is, the washing, drying, folding, and ironing—she could watch soaps all day if she wanted—I'd take care of everything else. Within six weeks, Ma bounced back, even driving and singing. But they were not songs of joy.

"How far is heaven?"[2] [http://bit.ly/21chaKt], she pleaded, as tears streamed down my face. As she sped down 690 East toward General Electric, where Dad now worked, I put in my request.

"'My Daddy's Only a Picture'"[3] [http://bit.ly/1Obf3RH], I said, handing her some tissue. And we both laughed and blew our noses.

It was one thing to help mend the cut across her abdomen by changing her dressing twice a day and rubbing ointment on the red scabs until they formed shiny scars. I had held her and blotted the occasional tear that escaped her will. But who knew how to measure, much less cure, the wounds on the inside? And who knew whose sin brought this tragedy on my family?

Every time I changed Ma's dressing, I felt that twinge, the one deep within my buttocks, the one that stirred up shame, prickled my temples. A few days before the hospital had discharged Ma, I went into the baby's bedroom to clean it out. I filled 10 trash bags with the gifts from three baby showers: one from friends, one from family, and one from the school. All the while I kept one eye on the closet doorway, where no curtains hung. I wondered if I had brought a curse on my mother, on baby Bobby. Maybe there was something evil in that room, left over from me, when I had asked questions I shouldn't have.

PART iii

"Father has accepted Kingdom. And if father has done that, he accepts the fact that he can take control over the child in whatever way he pleases."[1]

"Now as that child grows up, his concept of reality is what he has known in his home. We all experience reality as we have known it. So naturally, that child will seek a partner like the parent. Our first marriage, or our first relationship, is almost bound to be what it was in our home. We project out what we have inside, and that's what we brought out of our home.

"Some people have yearning for the archetype of reunion so they may get into a compulsive relationship, where they project the God onto the partner, or whoever it is they happen to choose, and then they project their soul out on someone else and, of course, then they are tied into that other person. And even if the other person is abusing them they cannot get out of the projection."[2]

Marion Woodman [http://bit.ly/1I8tNua]
Excerpts from *Sitting by the Well* [http://bit.ly/1OagpMK]

13
the color of my world

Having long attempted to maintain cohesiveness within the Beatles, McCartney secluded himself with his new family at his Scottish farm, distraught at Lennon's departure. After being tracked down by reporters from *Life* magazine in late October, McCartney publicly acknowledged that "the Beatle thing is over."

Wikipedia [http://bit.ly/1Yo5ztv]

HOLLYWOOD, Oct. 4 — Janis Joplin, the rock singer, was found dead in her Hollywood apartment tonight. She was 27 years old. The cause of death was not immediately determined, but the police said she apparently died of an overdose of drugs. They said she had been dead for about two hours when she was found shortly after 10 P.M. Miss Joplin was the second noted pop singer to die in less than three weeks. Jimi Hendrix, 27, died in London Sept. 18 after taking nine strong sleeping tablets.

Reuters/The New York Times [http://nyti.ms/1OOSFoU]

The twin towers knocked New York City's own Empire State Building off the top of the list of the world's tallest buildings.

Wikipedia [http://bit.ly/1Yo5ztv], December 23, 1970

1970

"**I**N-A-GADDA-DA-VIDA"¹ [http://bit.ly/1P12OII], I sang the words to Iron Butterfly's masterpiece as I drummed my fists into the air and shook my head as he chugged another beer. I had spent most of the night perched on the edge of the couch with a butterfly net hoping to swoop down at the right instant and catch that slight dimple that flitted now and then in the hollow of his lean cheek. His dark chocolate eyes behind his jet black hair lured me into the whites of his eyes. And when he laughed, his milky white teeth and tawny lips slurped me in. The white mosaic design in his khaki green sweater glowed under the black light, which also accentuated the muscles in his naturally tanned forearms, where he had folded up his sleeves just enough to tease me.

It was a Friday the 13th party at Zach's apartment, and I had just met an honest to goodness, full-blooded Native American Indian. Zach and I were into that. Last time Uncle Ben left town he said he would take a detour from his usual hitchhiking route to Skid Row in Los Angeles and pass through Arkansas to research our family tree, still preaching, of course, to everyone who picked him up.

He later wrote Zach documenting his suspicions. How convenient, he said. The town hall in Little Rock, that housed our ancestors' records, had burned to the ground years ago under suspicious circumstances. But one thing he did verify, which Grandpa always denied: Grandpa was a half-breed—the son of an Indian chief who married a white woman—making Zach and I one-eighth Cherokee, which prompted in us a spontaneous kinship to Indians.

"I live on the St. Regis Reservation, *Ahkwesáhsne*," Alton said, as the beating of drums conjured up visions of Indian chiefs passing a peace pipe around the campfire.

"My ol' lady is Oneida and my ol' man is Mohawk," he said, flashing his tribal ID card. "We don't have to pay taxes and cigarettes are a lot cheaper on the Res."

Every nook and cranny in my body was filled with music as he spoke, and my heart swelled.

"I bet I'm the oldest one here. Huh?" Alton said, looking around the room. "How old are you, Zach?"

"Seventeen in July."

"Candy ass," Alton said, with a mischievous glint in his eye. "I'm two months older than you. I'm a Taurus, the Bull."

"Yeah, bull (shitter)," Zach said, chuckling.

I searched Zach's face as he stood by picking the strings of his guitar while Alton carried on about quitting school and making big bucks. Zach smiled with approval, after all, I had just turned 14 a few months ago, and this was just for shits and grins. It's not like I was going to marry the guy.

We hadn't told anyone yet, except for family and Alton, of course, but Zach had been at the house teaching me a song to perform on stage at the next dance. I didn't think it was a big deal until Ma surprised me with a brand new black silky outfit sprinkled with silver glitter for my debut as a female vocalist for Zach's band, Headstone. I hadn't heard the song before, so I played it again and again on Dad's stereo. Then when Zach stopped by to practice with me, he would play it on his guitar, cue me, working on my timing. But it still bugged me, like when I had to sing "The Holly and the Ivy," in sixth grade, just about the only Christmas song I had never heard of. Plus Carole King was more my speed.

"I already know a million songs by heart," I said. "Why do you want me to sing the only song in the world I never heard of?"

"This is like a tryout," Zach said. "It's all about timing and voice control. If you can show the guys you can sing this, then you can officially try out for the band."

"Don't sweat it," Alton said. "I'll be there, and I'll cue her. She won't miss a beat."

But I was confused.

"What am I supposed to do the whole time before and after I sing the lyrics," I complained. "Just stand there and look stupid on the stage?"

"Just act natural. Listen to the music. Let it move you." he said, looking at the clock.

"Yeah, I look stupid naturally," I yelled after him as he went out the front door.

Alton set the needle into the groove, and placed his hands on my shoulders as he swayed to the music. After a few minutes, I melted into his arms.

"Right on," he said, as he pulled me in close, and planted a hickey on my neck.

"Ouch! What the fuck you doing? My mother's going to have a freaking cow."

"It's just a love bite," he said, grinning, as he clenched and unclenched his teeth.

When it was show time, Alton tried to come backstage, but a bouncer stopped him.

"Hey, dweeb. My girlfriend's in the band," he said, pushing back on the bouncer.

Rather than make a scene, I nodded to the bouncer to let him in.

The lights flickered about the darkened stage in such a way that you couldn't see Alton standing at the edge of the curtain, his hand on my back. As I held the microphone up to my lips, I looked at Zach, and he nodded.

"As time"—thump—I began, like a hiccup.

"And now"—thump.

"Promise"—thump.

"And dreams"[2] [http://bit.ly/1SN6KuX].

"Thump!"

As Mickey eked out the last few notes on a flute, the strobe lights brightened, and the lovebirds drew back from one another and began to clap. I curtsied, and fled the stage. By then, Alton had stepped out the back door for a smoke. I flew into his face and went ape-shit all over him. I slammed his chest again and again, pushing him further into the parking lot, and when his balance was off, I wrapped my leg around his, and yanked it forward, dropping him on his ass. I was still a nerd on the inside, so to protect myself I had been working out in the attic on Zach's dumbbells and bench press, and at drinking parties I could beat all the guys at leg wrestling, at least all the guys who were brave enough to accept my challenge.

"Fucking unreal!" I screamed. "How dare you sucker-punch me in the back, you punk."

"I was just trying to make sure you kept to the beat," he said, scooting back on one elbow and one leg, trying to block himself with his other arm, until he could get back far enough from me to scramble to his feet.

"Yeah, right! You were fucking punching me in the back," I screamed as I stalked off.

He reached out to grab my arm, and I back-handed him.

"Kiss off!"

But the freak followed me.

Just as I was about to slam the front door behind me, he was inside the screen door, pushing against me, begging for one more chance, with crocodile tears rolling down his face. I could hear Ma and Dad in the kitchen talking with Uncle Fred and Aunt Dorothy.

"Grab me a beer while you're in there!"

"Ante up, for Chrissake!"

I stepped back outside and closed the front door, sat on the top step, and lit a cigarette, but my hands were shaking, and it sucked trying to inhale through the wet filter.

Alton handed me his hanky.

"It's clean," he said.

I slapped it out of his hand and wiped my face and blew my nose.

"I'm sorry, I swear," he said. "But I was afraid if you started hanging out with the band, and singing and shit, you wouldn't want to be with me anymore. Please, I beg you. I don't want to lose you. It'll never happen again. I swear. Even if you want to stay in the band. I promise. Please. You've got to believe me."

I felt in control. I pitied him. And I loved him more than I had anyone else in my whole life.

I spelled out the ground rules and gave him another chance, just one. I never told Zach what happened that night, and Zach never asked me to sing in the band again. And Alton never did hit me again, until that night we were eating my favorite dinner in the living room on my 15th birthday: Pork chops, mashed potatoes and gravy, and applesauce.

Ma and Dad and the kids were eating supper in the kitchen, but for this special occasion they allowed Alton and me to eat in the living room at the coffee table, for we were sweethearts and the kitchen would be too crowded. Besides, it was my special day.

Alton carved a bite-sized piece from his pork chop using his fork and a steak knife. But hell, that was no fun. I picked up my pork chop by the ends of the bones and tore off a piece of meat with my teeth. Now that's good eating, getting a little grease on one's fingers, on one's face.

"Don't you have any manners?" he asked.

"Sure, but my daddy's not sitting here watching me so I'll eat however I want."

Alton put down his knife and fork and watched me.

"Eat," I said, slurping and gnawing at the bone.

"You're disgusting! How can I eat looking at you?"

"Then don't look!"

Just as I bit off a piece of grizzle, he slapped the pork chop out of my mouth, twisting his hand, scraping his ring across my cheek.

I hauled off to punch him, but he thrust his forearm into my neck and pinned me against the couch.

"Act like an animal, and I'll treat you like an animal."

I kicked him off me and sprung from the couch.

"You don't have to send me to my room, Daddy. I know the way. And you know your way out the fucking front door."

I jerked from his reach and stomped to my room.

He slammed the front door, and I slammed my bedroom door.

"Isn't Alton staying for cake?" I heard Kali ask.

I leaned against the wall and slumped to the floor.

The next night, Zach's band was hosting a Christmas dance, two blocks away, where they had rented the basement of a church. Alton and I were both there, but not together. Alton flirted and danced with the clique of girls he knew I despised. They all flaunted it in my face. A couple of guys asked me to dance, but I shook my head, left the dance, and went to Zach's apartment across the street. That's where everyone would go after the dance, so I didn't have much time. I scoped out the medicine chest and found a full bottle of pills. I drank down the whole bottle with a couple of beers, put on an album, and sat down to die.

I'm your captain[3] [http://bit.ly/1lsJpV4].

By the time people trickled in from the dance, I was on my own little ship. I sat and rocked as my boat filled with water.

Alton got there first, then Zach. They spoke some mumble-jumble and tried to pull me to my feet, but I was getting closer to my home.

The two of them then stood by the front door, conspiring. When a few others showed up and distracted them, I ran like hell, out the door and down the stairs. But they were right behind me, and Ma was already pulling up in the driveway. I ran around and around the car but they caught me and put me in the back seat. They trapped me like an animal, for god's sake.

"No, of course, I'll never do it again," I promised the doctor who pumped my stomach.

"We're supposed to make a police report, but if you promise. Your mother says you've never tried anything like this before. But I have to ask. Why did you do it?"

Because I've fallen in love with my fucking father, fucking dumb ass!

14
the trooper

From the Halls of Montezuma
To the Shores of Tripoli,
We will fight our nation's battles
In the air, on land, and sea.
First to fight for right and freedom,
And to keep our honor clean . . .

And if the Army or the Navy
Ever look on heaven's scenes,
They will find the streets are guarded
By United States Marines.[1]

"The U.S. Marine Corps Hymn"
[http://bit.ly/1NKhNRE]
Unknown

1971

Being the stupid idiot that my father always said I was, I let Alton back under my skin. Every afternoon after school, every evening, everywhere I went, Alton had called me on the phone or hunted me down, and he begged and he cried.

"I swear on my grandfather's grave. My father's father! I'll never put a hand on you again. May God strike me dead if I do."

Something about swearing on sacred ground got to me. After all, Indians are very spiritual, and they would never swear on someone's grave unless they meant it.

"You ever touch me again, I'll call the police."

I was skeptical for months, but one night in late fall, I was convinced. Alton would never hit me again. And he proved it.

That night, we were leaning up against the kitchen counter, kissing and grinding.

"It's ten o'clock. Let's say goodnight," Ma called out from the living room, as we creamed in our jeans.

About a half hour later, when I was getting ready for bed, the phone rang. I ran for it.

"Gabby, thank god. It's you."

"What's the matter?"

"Meet me outside. I'll be there in a few minutes."

He sounded excited and scared. I slipped on my robe and went downstairs to kiss Ma and Dad goodnight.

"Who was that calling so late?" Dad asked.

"Alton. He just called to say he was sorry. We had an argument before he left."

"You're damn lucky the phone didn't wake up any of the kids, or we'd be having an argument," Dad said.

Yeah. Yeah. You're bad.

"Plus, I wanted to remind you that I need an extra quarter with my lunch money tomorrow for the school bake sale."

Not to mention, I just want to ascertain your exact whereabouts and your level of interest in whatever's on TV.

"Give her an extra dollar," Ma said. "She can buy us a dozen. It's for a good cause."

"Oh, sure. Why don't I just give her my fucking wallet?"

"Fine," Ma and I both said.

"Ha ha ha. Now do you mind? The show's back on."

I kissed them goodnight, went back upstairs to my room, pulled on my sweatshirt and jeans and gobies, and crept down the backstairs, grabbed my coat, and slipped out the back door.

"Here! I'm over here," Alton whispered at the top of his lungs.

"Shhhh. I hear ya. I just can't freakin' see ya."

Alton stepped out into the moonlight, grabbed my arm, and yanked me into the bushes.

"Damn! It's colder than a witch's tit out here."

"I hate that saying—ouch! Freakin' pricker bushes!"

"Shh!" he said. "I gotta book, or my ol' man's gonna kill me."

"Why? What happened?"

"He was so drunk, going off on my ol' lady, that he didn't even hear me come in. She was trying to talk him down to go to bed. But she no sooner turned her back when he picked up the high chair and threw it at her. I didn't have time to think. I just flew right by her and blocked it. Fuck! They both jumped. Like they saw a ghost. But once my ol' man realized it was me, he came after me. Ma blocked him though till I got out the door. But I could hear him cussing me out halfway down the block. Said he was gonna rip me a new asshole. Said if I ever stepped foot back in that house, he'd kill me."

"I hope she's okay. He was probably more pissed off at her after you left."

"I already called her from the same pay phone before I called you. She's fine."

"What'd she say?"

"She said after I beat-feet outta there, he ran around the kitchen banging chairs and throwing shit off the table. Then he staggered into the bedroom and passed out. Said he was already snoring."

"What'd she say about you blocking the high chair?"

"She said I shouldn't have got in the way. She said she could take care of herself. Yeah, sure she could."

"I'm sure she was just trying to protect her little Don Juan, who always knows how to make her laugh, boost her morale," I said, mimicking her, and laughing, though no one could laugh like her.

She loved to tell the story of how she named Alton after a young debonair character in a romance novel, a charming lover boy, who knew how to pick up the spirits—of even the dead—she laughed, a laugh so steeped in love and life, that everyone touched by her smile, including me, got caught up by it, and felt compelled to laugh back with her vigor—and I laughed and I laughed, even if it didn't strike me as funny!

"I'm proud of you," I said, smiling in the dark. "Sticking up for your mother like that. Especially knowing how you and your brothers are all so afraid of him, even Angus."

That night erased any lingering doubt I had. I knew after seeing the pain his father had put his mother through, and how Alton tried to protect her, that Alton would never hit me again.

"What are you going to do now? You can't go home."

"I already called Angus. And, well, you know I been thinking about it a while now. But this leaves me no choice. I'm shipping off to the Marines."

Angus took Alton to the recruiting office the next day, and that was that. Before Alton left, he gave me a stack of different sized iron-on decals of the Marine Corps emblem, a Marine Corps pin, a cigarette lighter, and a sterling silver ring, all of which had the Marine Corps emblem on them, the eagle atop the world with an anchor driven through its heart.

"So you don't forget me," he said.

"I'll wear them every day," I promised.

After Alton left for boot camp, I went to the Army-Navy store and bought three fatigue jackets and a handful of white T-shirts. Then I went home and dug out Dad's record of the "Marine Corps Hymn." I ironed the large USMC decals on the backs of the jackets and the small decals on the T-shirt pockets and in random spots on my jean. I would start my own fad. As I ironed, I played the record again and again, singing along, memorizing all three verses.

"We will fight our country's battles, in the air, on land and sea," I vowed as if I, too, had joined the Corps.

The guys kept hitting on me, even though they knew about Alton, and I hated hurting their feelings, so I left my khaki jackets on over my T-shirts throughout the school day and braided my thick, long wavy brown hair into a bun. I put away my pocketbooks and my makeup. And I wore only Marine Corps jewelry. My mother hated my new look, my new identity, and every time she looked at me, she complained, said I was hiding my beauty, said I was missing the best years of my life.

She didn't understand, but I would be a faithful trooper. And I would have a baby sooner rather than later.

"I wanna have a baby," had become my mantra earlier that year.

"You have to get married first," Ma said.

"Fine. I'll get married."

"Will you stop talking crazy! You're not even old enough to get married."

"I'll be 16 next year. I'll get married then. You can sign for me."

"I won't sign until you graduate."

"Fine, when I graduate, you'll sign. You promise?"

"You know I don't want you to get married so young. For crying out loud, you're still a baby yourself. But hopefully you'll change your mind by the time you graduate."

But I was on a mission.

I wrote off most dances and most school events—except bowling—but even that was worth a quarter of a credit. And I doubled up on my course load and signed up for night classes and Saturday classes. Between studying and going to school and babysitting, I had no time to play. I vowed to complete the 11th and 12th grades in one school year flat. Period. And then I could get on with my life.

15
the American pie

"This'll be the day that I die."[1]

"American Pie" [http://bit.ly/1OmlWxI].
By Don McLean [http://bit.ly/1LunT6V].

Winter 1971 to Fall 1972

A VAST SNOW CLOUD HUNG OVER SYRACUSE by the time Alton came home on leave, which was when he finally popped the question everyone already knew the answer to. Would I marry him?

"Of course! When?" That was the big question.

"Well, there's one little problem," he said, pulling an envelope out of his back pocket. "Along with a 30-day pass, they gave me orders to ship off to Okinawa for 18 months."

"You've got to be kidding me!"

Through the tears I could see that he held a small box in his other hand. He knelt down, and then he twirled a diamond ring onto my finger, at which time I became left-handed.

"At least we have 30 whole days together before you go," I said.

"Um. Well. I want to talk to you about that, too," he said. "I talked to the ol' lady last night—"

"Don't call her that!"

"Okay. Ma! Anyway, after we talked, I talked to the ol' man and to Angus, too. They said she's not herself. Her headaches get so bad that she's out of it sometimes, and she calls my name. They think it would really cheer her up if I would stop there on my way to Camp Pendleton."

"I knew it! Why did they have to move all the way to Iowa anyway? Now you have to split your time. This is ridiculous." I stomped my feet, kicked the wall, punched the table, and threw myself onto the couch face down. "I give up. Fucking insane. I did all this for nothing."

"It's just temporary. I promise. We'll have our whole lives together once I get out of the Marines."

I had only met Alton's mother a few times. But Juanita was a beautiful lady inside and out, and she'd do anything for Alton. I hadn't seen her since Alton joined the Marine Corps because Larry had moved the family to Council Bluffs, Iowa, where he had been living between runs, so they could be together more. But her laugh rippled through my memories every time I thought about the night she let Alton drive and let me sit in the middle and how she turned up the radio when "Proud Mary" played and how she sat in the back seat with the kids and let us sit in the front seat at the drive-in and bought the popcorn and took us to eat at Denny's afterward.

But, still, everything I have worked so hard for just went poof! I cried some more. After all, what could I say?

"Of course, you have to go. I'm just really going to miss you. You will call me every night, though, right? Because once you get to Okinawa it won't be easy to call. Promise?"

"Every night. I promise."

"Tell your mother I'm praying for her" I said. "I know I don't know her very well, but give her my love."

"Give me your love, baby, before I go," he said, grinning, and reaching for my breasts.

"Not until we're married," I squealed and jumped off the couch. "It's the law!" He chased me, and I let him catch me, and we rolled onto the floor laughing and then holding tight and kissing hard. A whole year and a half, I could not fathom it.

But February made me shiver when Larry brought Juanita and the kids back to Syracuse because the doctors in Omaha couldn't figure out the cause of her headaches. I hadn't seen her yet, but Cecilia, Alton's cousin, said she looked like death warmed over. They were staying with Cecilia and her kids, who lived just a few blocks from my house, where I still lived with Ma and Dad, so that Juanita could see a specialist at Upstate Medical Center, a research hospital, where they could run more tests.

But it was too late. The doctors diagnosed Juanita with cancer and scheduled immediate surgery to remove her breasts. But later, tests revealed that the cancer had metastasized. We would only have her company for a few more months at best, the doctors said when they sent her home to die.

The Red Cross brought Alton back to the States on emergency leave, and he hung out with his mother in the room Cecilia had set up for her. In the days after he returned, I visited when I could between school and homework and babysitting. She didn't seem to be in much pain with all the drugs they had given her.

She'd look up at Alton and smile.

"There's my Alton, my Don Juan," she'd say. Then she'd laugh. We'd joke and laugh with her.

"I'm getting better now," she told Alton. "Now that you're here."

"Of course," Alton said. "You didn't think your Don Juan would let you down, did you?"

She laughed and laughed. "You always did know how to boost my morale."

When she would doze off, we'd go outside for a cigarette, and whisper, because no one had told her she was dying. Not that we know of anyway. No one knows for sure what he said, but one night Juanita's father, who they called Guyapi, got really drunk and went to see her.

Cecilia said she saw Guyapi kneeling by Juanita's bed and crying, and that was the last time that Juanita was coherent. Even though his mother was out of it, Alton stayed with her and talked with her and cheered her on and played her favorite songs on a record player, trying to bring her back for at least one last good-bye.

One night, at about ten o'clock, I was studying while the Martin baby slept, when I heard someone running up the back hallway stairs that led up from the street. I ran to the door and double-checked the locks. The person knocked, and I could hear heavy breathing. My heart pounded.

"Who is it?"

"It's me," Alton whispered.

He knew the Martins didn't allow him to come over. They'd fire me if they found out!

Something must be wrong.

I opened the door.

"She's gone," he said, and he slumped into my arms.

I can't remember if I cried that night, but I had to stifle my urge to yelp when his body crushed mine. But something touched me deep inside, and I could not resist. His mother was dead, and my mother's rule was broken.

Alton grabbed a towel for me from the bathroom afterward, and we dressed and off he went—before the Martins got home. As soon as he left I threw the used towel in my book bag. And when I got home I examined every inch of it.

That's so weird. No cherry? I heard virgins always spot. Maybe all those times I hit my privates on the boy's bicycle bar? What was that story Ma told me? Something about wrecking on a bike and the handlebar went up her vagina. That's how she lost her virginity. That's why she didn't bleed the night the three men gang-raped her at a bar on the edge of town the night that her brother forgot to pick her up from school. She was just 15. I can still see her dashing toward the double doors to escape as the men tossed coins to see who goes first, but the doors were locked, and the drunk men laughed.

It was just a few days before Easter when Juanita died, and that weekend, and in the days that followed her death, countless empty bottles of vodka and whiskey piled up in bins at Alton's relatives, most of whom I had never met until she had passed, so I didn't know if they always drank in the morning. I was an outsider looking in, and it was really hard, but I resisted the urge to look under the sheets that hung over the mirrors.

A priest wouldn't marry us on such short notice, so a random Protestant minister conducted the small candlelight ceremony at midnight three weeks later, with a few close relatives attending. Alton wore his service uniform, and Ma whipped me up a white wedding dress, with a detachable bottom, in case I wanted to wear it again. Talk about oxymorons, she made herself a new dress for the occasion, too, which she cut from a cotton fabric of great big black-eyed Susans, against a black background, adding long black sheer sleeves to it. And three white horse heads peered over our shoulders as we posed for pictures and cut the five-tiered cake at the reception the next afternoon at Barry and Sherry's, Ma and Dad's friends who lived downstairs.

Ma signed the paper against her better judgment, but what could she say? I told her I lost my virginity, and that we needed to get married in case I was pregnant. She said, herself, it only takes once. Besides, with my graduation from high school just two months away, hadn't I already proven myself? It seemed Juanita's death knocked the wind out of everyone, even Dad. After all, Juanita was just a few years older than them, and she left behind small kids without a mother. Malcolm, Angus, and Alton were on their own. But Juanita hadn't finished raising 12-year-old Damian, 7-year-old Kyle, and 2-year-old Olivia.

That was up to Larry, now. But he had been a trucker for the last 25 years. He didn't know anything else. He was more or less a visitor when he rolled in and out of town, and he got antsy off the road for more than a few days at a time.

Malcolm pondered taking the kids, but he understood the huge responsibility, and he was struggling as it was to keep his young family together. And Angus couldn't do it. He had followed in his Dad's trucking tracks. Of course, Alton had a stint to finish in the Marine Corps so he couldn't do it.

Cecilia took care of the kids for a few months, but that summer Larry and Angus took the kids back to their trailer home in Council Bluffs. They would alternate runs of beef and pork from the slaughterhouses of Omaha, and Tim and Tammy Tyler, their friends and neighbors, would babysit the kids when their runs overlapped.

But that was no way for the kids to live, especially after just losing their mother, so Alton requested a hardship discharge so we could move to Council Bluffs to take care of the kids. And as an English major, I wrote a very sentimental letter that was sure to melt their hearts. In the meantime, the Corps had stationed Alton in Rome, New York, so that he was within commuting distance. While we waited for the review board to respond, Alton's relatives began dropping like flies, many of them a great aunt or uncle or a third cousin, which took us to funerals in Ogdensburg every two or three weeks.

But the shocker was the phone call the family received just three months after they buried Juanita. In the wee hours of the morning, Guyapi got hit by a truck on a highway just outside of town. He was dead. He was drunk, no one doubted. He had not been sober since his daughter had died. But was it an accident? Or did he walk out into the truck's path? We would never know. And we would never know what he said to Juanita that night. Did he tell her she was dying, or was it something else that zapped her will to live?

Shortly after Guyapi's funeral, Alton got a letter from the Corps, denying him the discharge.

"Fuck them. I'll go AWOL!" Alton said.

"Don't be asinine," I told him. "You'll just hurt yourself."

I had been mulling it over, but now it seemed like the only option.

"I'll go to Iowa to take care of the kids as soon as I graduate. Short a quarter of a credit, my ass."

"Fuck that," Alton said. "What do you need a degree for anyway? I'm your ol' man now. I'll take care of you."

He scooted closer to me on the bench.

"Come on, little girl. What do ya say you skip school today? We can hang out in my room at Cecilia's, ooh-la-la," he said, raising his eyebrows.

"I can't. I promised. But as soon as my summer class is over, I'll go to Iowa to take care of the kids. Then you can join us when you get out."

Everyone thought it was a wonderful idea, except my mother.

"You're just a kid yourself. How're you gonna raise kids out there all by yourself?"

"I'm not gonna be alone. Angus said he's doing short hauls. Plus he said anything I need, he or his father will take care of it. Money, groceries, you name it, even shopping money. Plus, between the two of them on different runs, every few days one of them will be there in case I have a problem."

"That scares me to death, you halfway across the country living with a couple of lonely truck drivers who drink too much."

"Look, I'll have my own money with my allotment check, now that I'm married. Plus, Angus said if I change my mind at anytime, if I don't like it there or if I get homesick, to just let him know. He promised to drive me home the same week for a visit or to stay. Whatever I wanted. Please, Ma, just trust me."

"It's not you I don't trust! I'm sorry, but I can't let you go."

"Ma, listen, please, for the kids. They need someone. And I'm an adult now. I'm married. I don't need your permission to go."

By the time my degree came in the mail, it was like an afterthought. Not even a cake for dessert. As soon as Ma finished eating, she left for her meeting, leaving Dad sitting at the table twirling his spaghetti. I grabbed the broom and headed for the living room to get a jump on my weekend chores so I could spend the whole weekend with Alton at Malcolm and Katrina's house, where we would have privacy in their guest room.

As I swept the cobwebs from the ceiling and walls—reveling in the idea that this was the very last time I will ever have to do chores at my parents' house—Mariah stormed into the living room.

"I need the broom to sweep the kitchen," she said.

"Wait your turn."

"I ain't waiting. You can do your weekend chores on the weekend. Misty will be here any minute."

"Tough."

She grabbed my arm and pinched me as she reached for the broom.

"Ow," I said, pinching her back.

She ran screaming for Daddy.

A minute later Dad charged into the living room.

"Who do you think you are, pinching her?" he demanded.

"She started it."

"She's younger than you. You're supposed to know better."

"What am I supposed to do, just stand here while she pinches me?"

"No, idiot. Just give her the fuckin' broom."

"I'll give it to her when I'm done."

"No, asshole, you'll give it to her now," he said, as he reached out to knuckle me in the head.

"I'm an adult now. If you hit me, I'll hit you back, I swear," I said, waving the broom at him.

With one eye over my shoulder, I finished sweeping. When I returned to the kitchen, they were both gone. I put the broom in the closet and packed my bags.

That weekend, Alton and I said our good-byes at his brother's house, not knowing when we'd see each other again. The Marines were shipping him off to Camp Lejeune on Monday. And a few days later, Angus and I would head for Iowa. I liked Angus. I thought we got along fine. But I didn't realize how much Alton carried the conversation until Angus and I sat speechless for 18 hours in his 18-wheeler. I feigned sleep just to relieve the awkward silence.

When we arrived at their trailer, Angus showed me to my bedroom, a room about the size of a coffin, which was fine. I'm not complaining. The only reason I mention the room size is because—and I'm serious—that night, and many nights that followed, when it seemed I had dozed off, I found myself floating around the room, paralyzed, unable to get down, like when I was 12 and my mother performed the exorcism on me.

Was it something I ate—or had the devil repossessed me?

The next morning, Angus introduced me to Tim and Tammy, and showed me his motorcycle, which he stored in Tim's shed. He promised to teach me how to ride it one day. Then he took me and the kids grocery shopping. I filled the cart with chocolate and peanut butter and pork chops and bacon and maple syrup and orange juice and cantaloupe. And the kids threw anything they wanted in the cart, too.

Once Angus and I stocked the cupboards and freezer, he handed me a hundred dollar bill—wow.

"The ol' man will probably be in Thursday, and he'll set you up with anything you want. Just don't be afraid to ask. He always made sure Ma had whatever she needed. Plus, like I promised, anytime you change your mind, you just let me know. I'll drive you back home as soon as I can."

That first night alone, while the three kids sat in a row on the couch and watched TV, I killed flies.

Every now and then I caught them sneaking a peek at me, and I would try to strike up a conversation, but they weren't interested. On the commercial, without any prompting, Damian changed Olivia into her nightgown, washed her up, and tucked her in. Then when I wasn't looking, Damian and Kyle had slipped off to bed, too. At about midnight, I ran out of flies to kill, and sat down and looked around.

What have I gotten myself into?

It took another two hours to clean up all the dead flies and scrub their blood and guts from the walls and floor.

By the next morning, a new batch of flies swarmed the kitchen. In the daylight, I realized that the trash cans were lined up under the kitchen window, right beneath the torn screens. I tacked plastic wrap over the screens and moved the trashcans to the back of the trailer. And then I killed some more flies while the kids ate their Franken Berry and Count Chocula.

A month had passed, but I never did see my new father-in-law, whom I had only met a few times. Angus said his ol' man got stuck on a long haul to the East Coast and was then sent to Louisiana, or somewhere or another. But Angus called every night to talk with the kids and ask me how I was doing. The kids would chatter away and giggle on the phone, but as soon as they hung up, the curtain of gloom dropped back down around them.

Angus would return every three or four days, but his absence seemed longer as I tried to warm up to three kids who looked at me like I was Medusa. When Olivia fell down and bumped her knee or wanted a cup of juice, I tried to be the first responder, but she shied away from me and clung to her brothers.

One afternoon, I sent Damian and Kyle over to see if Tammy had any butter. How could I forget to buy butter! Wink. Wink.

While they were gone, I tried to coax Olivia into playing patty-cake with me, but she pulled away. I swallowed the lump in my throat and retreated to the kitchen to make a cup of tea.

"Ma-a-a-ma. Ma-a-a-ma," she called out in an eerie voice that reminded me of the nights I listened outside Mrs. Dixon's back door as she called forth spirits from beyond. I wanted so badly to cheer up Olivia, but she seemed content in a sad kind of way, kneeling by the couch playing with her dollies.

"Son of a bitch," I cried out, burning my arm on the steam seeping from the whistler and dropping my mug on the floor. I stomped on the already broken china before throwing myself into a kitchen chair, kicking the adjacent chair.

What in the hell am I doing here? These kids need a real mother. Not someone trying to play house with their lives.

As I tried to blink away the tears, I realized that Olivia was looking at me. I guessed my little tantrum startled her. But she didn't look scared. Instead, she stood up and patted her dollies on their heads, and walked toward me. She looked at me with her big brown eyes, with her featherweight bangs hanging loosely on her brows and her black wavy hair curled around her face. Olivia would turn three in January, but her eyes hinted that she was an old soul. She came closer and put her hands on my arm. For the first time since I had arrived, she let me lift her up onto my lap.

By the time the boys returned with the butter, Olivia was sitting on my lap playing patty-cake. Damian and Kyle lit up like trees on Christmas morning. It was as if they had been waiting for Olivia's approval before they could let me in.

"Let's go to Tim's and ride Angus's bike," Damian said.

"You can't ride a motorcycle!" I said.

"Sure I can. Angus taught me. Come on, I'll show you."

"Come on, Gabby," Kyle said. "It's fun. Will you ride me, too, Damian?"

"Sure. Plus I'll teach Gabby how to ride."

"But Tim's probably not home from work yet," I said.

"He's home. Please? Come on."

Olivia tugged on my wrist.

Tim and Tammy's eyes crinkled when Tim opened the door, and they saw all us Lazores standing on their steps.

"I want to show Gabby how to ride," Damian said.

"Well, what we waitin' for?" Tim said, retrieving a key off a hook.

They pulled the bike out of the shed and, after Tim gassed it up, Damian hopped on, turned the key, and revved the engine. He popped the clutch and peeled out.

Damian rode up and down the dirt road, hitting a few mud puddles along the way.

"Yippee," he screamed as he rode circles around us. I managed not to gasp until he popped a wheelie.

"Oh, my God," I cried out, and everyone laughed.

"Come on, Gabby," Tim said. "You take a spin."

"Not me."

"It's easy. I'll show you," he said.

"Yeah, yeah," Kyle and Olivia squealed.

"Damian!" Kyle screamed over the roar of the bike. "Gabby's going to drive now!"

Damian pulled up to a smooth stop in front of us.

"Here you go, Gabby," Damian said. "Turn this for gas and this to slow down and stop. That's all there is to it."

After three or four stalls I sped off with a jerk, trying to steer around the mud puddles because I was afraid I would hit a pothole.

"Yay!" The boys screamed, and Olivia jumped up and down clapping as I drove off.

As I neared the corner, my mind said to circle back around toward my cheering fans. But every time I tilted the handles it felt like the bike was going to tip over.

"How the heck do you stop this thing?" I screamed, as I careened into the cornfield, whacking a new path until the bike stalled and crashed.

"I'm okay, I'm okay," I yelled, as I sat on the ground laughing too hard to get up.

Tim, Kyle, and Damian came running to my rescue. By the time Tim pulled the bike out of the cornfield, we were all laughing. Olivia saw us emerge from the field and began running toward us. Tammy walked a few paces behind her. Olivia ran up to me and jumped in my arms. As I carried her back to the trailer, she twisted my hair around her fingers.

That Saturday, Tammy and I put a meatloaf in the oven as Tim headed over to the truck stop to pick up Angus. We had just taken the meatloaf out of the oven when a horn beeped.

"Is that them?" I asked Tammy. "Why don't they just come in?"

When we stepped outside to look, there was Alton, walking up the dirt path.

"What the hell?"

"Hey, is that any way to greet your ol' man?"

We hugged and kissed.

"They let you out," I asked, all excited.

"I'll explain later," he said, as Damian, Kyle, and Olivia ran from the trailer screaming.

"Alton! Alton! Alton!" they jumped on him and wrestled him to the ground.

"I missed you," he told me that night as I made up the bed for us in the bigger bedroom in the back. "I missed the kids. I just couldn't stand the thought of you being out here by yourself. And the kids need me too."

"What good you gonna be to any of us when the MPs come knockin' and cart you off to the brig?"

"That ain't gonna happen. I'll go back in a couple weeks and turn myself in. The worst they can do is throw me in the brig for 30 days. Besides, they'll be lenient given my circumstances."

"What do you think you're accomplishing? One way or the other the kids and I will eventually be on our own. You're just putting off the inevitable."

As a couple of weeks turned into a month, I bit my tongue.

Milk. Bread. Um. Comet. Windex. Butter. Let's see. What should we have for dinner tomorrow night? Spaghetti? Hmm. Get some hamburger and bread crumbs. Need eggs too.

Alton rolled over limp.

I strained to breathe. I wanted to get up and go to the kitchen to start my list, but Alton expected me to sleep when he slept, wake up when he woke up, eat when he ate. Shower when he did.

"I'm just trying to make up for lost time," he said when I groaned. But the more I gave him the more he wanted, and I just couldn't seem to get through to him.

"Just another week, honey, I promise."

"I can't take it anymore," I yelled, finally giving him an ultimatum. "Either you go back with Angus tomorrow or I will."

"No, Gabby. Please stay," Alton begged. "I promise, I'm going back. Just give me one more week."

I knew Alton wouldn't go, and I knew he wasn't about to let me go either. So that night I waited until he fell asleep, then I rolled off the bed onto the floor, where my clothes sat in a heap. My military garb retired, I yanked my brown turtleneck over my head, shimmied into my brown tights, and slipped my gold-checkered jersey over my head. Scooping my hair back with one hand, I reached under the bed and pulled out the small bag and my pocketbook, both of which I had packed with haste and stashed under my side of the bed when Alton was tucking the kids in the night before.

I took one last look at Alton, then I slipped out the back door. There was just enough moonlight to see my way along the side of the trailer. But I didn't even make it to the front walk before Alton's hand clamped down on my shoulder.

"Where do you think you're going?"

"I thought you were sleeping," I said, twirling around.

"I don't sleep until you sleep."

"I told you, I'm leaving. And if you don't turn yourself in and make things right, I'm leaving for good. I'm giving you 30 days, then I'm either going to turn you in myself or file for a divorce. Your choice."

"What are you, crazy? What do you think you're gonna do, walk all the way home?"

"No, I'm not stupid, asshole."

"Then how the hell were you going to get all the way back to Syracuse?"

"I was going to walk up to the phone booth on the main road and call a cab to the truck stop. Then I was going to ask around until I found someone going east."

"Damn! You don't even have a coat, Gabby."

"I'm leaving somehow or another. And you can't babysit me every minute of the fucking day."

"Fine. Go back with Angus tomorrow then. But I have to stay. My Dad needs me. I can't let him down."

"You're ruining your life. You're ruining our lives. The longer you wait to go back the worse it's going to be. And if they have to pick you up, they'll have no mercy. Then who's going to take care of the kids?"

"A man's gotta do what a man's gotta do."

"Yep, you're a real man. Just remember, you've got 30 days to make your final decision. I can't live like this, with my heart pounding every time someone knocks on the door. And I don't want to be married to someone who's going to spend half our lives in some brig somewhere."

We stayed up all night, and I packed my things. At daybreak, Alton drove Angus and I to the truck stop, and I slept in the sleeper the entire drive back home.

Two weeks later, on a Friday night, Larry rolled into town with Alton, who promised to turn himself in on Monday morning.

We spent that weekend at Malcolm's house, with his cheery wife, Katrina, and son and daughter. It was a nice middle-class home, and I felt like I was sneaking a glimpse of our future life once Alton straightened out his mess with the military. We all had hopes that they'd show leniency given his mother had died and Alton had three underage siblings. But the more he procrastinated about turning himself in, the more that hope faded. But new hope arose, now that Alton would turn himself in Monday morning. So we might as well enjoy what would be our last weekend together for a long time.

That Saturday night we lay in the guest bed, whispering and giggling like two little kids, hoping that Malcolm wouldn't come in and yell at us for making too much noise. But we laughed harder at the thought of it.

"No! Don't tickle me," I shrieked. "Really, stop! I hate that!"

"Say uncle."

"Uncle!"

"Alton!" Malcolm yelled, knocking on the door.

"See? Now you've done it," I whispered.

Alton climbed into his pants and opened the door.

"Finish dressing, quick. We've gotta go. Dad had an accident."

"Where? How bad?"

"Middletown. Really bad. He went off a bridge. He's at Horton Memorial. Here's the directions. I'll drive. Hurry up and get dressed, man. I'll tell you more on the way."

I tied the belt on my robe and Alton threw on his shirt and snatched up his socks and shoes, as we followed Malcolm out to the living room.

"Middletown's two hours away," Alton yelled. "Let's go, man. I'll put my shoes on in the car."

Katrina and I sat up and drank coffee waiting for the phone to ring. It was inconceivable to me that God would take the kids' father just six months after taking their mother. But God did. Larry's heart stopped just a few minutes before Alton and Malcolm arrived, the doctor had said.

The trailer hung halfway over the side of the bridge, but the cab had plunged face down into a swamp below, where Larry's skull was crushed, his face bashed in, and one of his ears was cut off. Newspaper articles described the scene in detail, including the looters who stole the pig carcasses that littered the roadway. The cause of the accident, though, was a mystery.

Two hundred people filed into the wake, each with their own opinion.

"I think he sensed he was going to die," Billy said. "That's why he made his rounds to all the bars before he left."

"Maybe," said Marley, the bartender from the Dew Drop Inn. "Harry said he saw him that day at the American Legion, too."

"He never did that," said Flo. "He made it a point to say goodbye to every single person at the VFW before he left the bar that afternoon."

"He stopped by our house, too, on his way out," said Auntie, his sister who lived upstairs from their mother. "That was a first!"

But he didn't drink a drop of alcohol, according to everyone he saw that day.

"Malcolm said the truck dragged against the guard rail for a 120 feet before the weight of the swinging meat tipped the truck," said Geraldine.

"But no skid marks," Marley said. "Don't figure."

"Maybe he just couldn't face life without Juanita," Bernice suggested. "You don't suppose he—"

"No, of course not. We all know he's been depressed since Juanita passed but, no, that's not him," said Wayne, one of Larry's good buddies. "Maybe he fell asleep."

"I don't know. That doesn't fit either. I think not having anyone to take care of the kids. That's what pushed him over the edge," said Martin.

Martin's right. First you left. Then you forced Alton to leave. Larry died almost exactly 24 hours after dropping off Alton, his last hope of someone to take care of the kids.

No one said it out loud, but I could see the accusatory fingers pointing from everyone's eyes. I could hear what they were thinking.

Why didn't you stay in Council Bluffs? Why did you strand poor Larry, abandon those poor kids? What will come of them now?

That week, the family met several times to discuss the kids' future. Everyone agreed they wanted them to stay together. But who was mature enough, strong enough, financially fit enough to raise three more kids? After a lot of soul searching, Larry's brother and sister-in-law, who lived in Syracuse, took in Damian, Kyle, and Olivia.

After they buried Larry, Alton turned himself in. The Corps sentenced him to the brig for 60 days, and life went on. But every time someone mentioned the curse of death on the Lazore family, guilt rose up from my bowels.

I still hadn't gotten an allotment check, first just because the government was plain slow at processing it, and then, of course, Alton went AWOL, and now, of course, Alton is in the brig. So I took a job at Carrols, a fast food joint downtown. There I was, a grown woman—16 years old—a high school graduate and married and everything, but stuck moving back home with Mommy and Daddy.

I felt as if the bitter wind just blew me from one snow drift to another. Everything was frozen, it seemed, even time. And I waited. Waited for Alton to get out of the brig. Waited for my first allotment check. Waited for the day that Alton and I would have our own place. But first things first, I waited for the snow to melt. But it would not melt soon enough.

16
the rape
(well, not a real one)

Winter 1972 to Spring 1975

MA AND DAD TOOK ME OUT TO THE HAPPY HOUR, their usual hangout, for my 17th birthday. Dad bought me a beer, and I was relieved no one bothered to ask for my ID. Sitting at a table in front of the window, we chatted, keeping an eye on the heavy snowflakes as they swirled about the neon light in the window, eventually gathering on the window ledge and creeping up the smoke-stained glass. Dad sang along with the words to "Happy Birthday," which he had played on the jukebox. Just as I was getting into the holiday spirit, the phone behind the bar rang.

"It's for you, Zach or Rose," the bartender called over. "They said it's an emergency."

Ma rushed to the phone and Dad and I stood up and tried to hear what she was saying. When she said, "Oh, my God," we put on our coats and buttoned up.

"Give me the keys, Dad," I said. "I'll start brushing the car."

"It's Mariah. Some maniac raped Mariah. Right in our backyard," Ma said as she backed the car out of the parking space.

"Oh, my God. Oh, my God." That's all Dad and I could think to say as Ma filled us in on the few details she knew.

"Who called you?" I asked.

"Barry, downstairs. That's where she ran when she got away. They're upstairs now."

As soon as we got home, Mariah ran up to Dad, who uttered assurances to her, while Ma called the police.

It was too horrible for me to imagine, being raped, especially a child, a virgin who had just turned 15 years old a few weeks ago, and in a foot of snow in her own backyard, wearing the beautiful white fur coat that looked like Cruella de Vil's coat, spotted like a Dalmatian, which we often fought over after Zach's wife had given it to us.

"'You're a virgin?' he asked, like he couldn't believe it," Mariah told the two policemen. "That was the only thing he said. Then he ran off."

The police took the report and then went outside to investigate, but they never did turn up anything.

A month later, I was walking home from work at dusk. The cold wind snapped at my bare legs, but at least it wasn't snowing. Just four blocks from our house, a car pulled up alongside me and slowed and turned into the driveway I was about to cross. As the electric window on the passenger side hummed downward, I thought he was going to ask for directions. But instead I saw a bulge protruding from the left side of his jacket, which concealed his right hand.

"Get in," he said, patting his vest pocket.

He drove within a half a block of my house and kept going. He drove out to the Indian Reservation and parked. Something about the back seat of the car. Something about a penis. Something about red hair.

Somehow two or three hours had passed by the time he dropped me off two blocks from my house in front of the convenience store on the corner of W. Onondaga and Dudley streets, just caddy-corner from Grandma Lazore and Auntie's house, which was dark. Grandma Lazore was almost always home but, of all times, they went up North for a week.

I stood there in the dark in shock.

Should I run home or run into the store?

"What if he changes his mind and comes back for me?"

I ran into the store, which was empty but for the clerk, an older guy who ran the store. I walked up to the counter trying to think what to say, if I should ask him to call the police or what.

"You know, you don't belong here. You belong with your ol' man," he said. "Run along, and you won't get hurt."

Stunned at his words, I dashed from the store, leaped down the steps, and ran home as fast as I could. Breathless, weak, my legs burning, I ran up the stairs and through the house to the kitchen. I collapsed on a kitchen chair, not at the table, but in the extra chair in the far corner of the room, where the glare of the light couldn't quite reach.

"What the hell's the matter with you," Dad asked, looking up from his newspaper.

"She looks like she saw a ghost," Ma said. "What's the matter, Gabrielle? Where've you been?"

"Someone raped me," I sputtered.

"Oh, bullshit," Dad said, flipping his hand and smacking the newspaper.

"Jesus, Zach. Why would she make up such a thing?"

"She's sick in the head. She saw how much attention Mariah got."

"Tell us what happened, Gab," Ma said. "What did he look like?"

I shrugged.

Red hair. Light skin. Freckles.

"How did it happen?" Ma asked. "Where?"

I didn't answer.

You didn't even put up a struggle like Mariah did. Chicken shit.

"She can't tell you what happened," Dad yelled. "She can't tell you because she made up the whole thing. She decided to go gallivanting after work. And now she's making up this cockamamie story."

Mariah was thrown in a foot of snow and hit in the face. You were in a plush warm car. You weren't really raped. Not like she was.

"I think we should call the police," Ma said.

"Don't be ridiculous. And tell them what? She won't even tell us what happened. Besides, what are we going to do? Call the police every month and tell them another one of our daughters was raped? They'll think we're fruitcakes."

"Gabrielle, please. Tell us what happened."

"I'll tell you what happened. She's jealous of Mariah. And you're doing exactly what she wants. Even if she was raped, she was probably asking for it. Look at the way she's dressed for crying out loud. What do you expect to happen when you wear a skirt up to your ass?"

Dad stormed off to the living room to watch TV, and Ma didn't say she didn't believe me, but she didn't call the police either.

It wasn't a real rape. Not like Mariah's.

I went into the bathroom and locked the door. I avoided the mirror as I undressed. I stood under the shower and closed my eyes.

I wasn't a virgin. Not like Mariah.

The first body part I washed was my vagina. As I lathered up the soap, my fingers fumbled through my pubic hair, then crawled up my vagina. I stroked vigorously, violently, raping myself with the soap, until my vagina was burned raw.

There! Now that's rape.

I sunk to the floor of the shower.

But I didn't sit on his lap. He came after me. Yes, but you were wearing a mini-skirt.

The next morning, I buttoned up my old pea coat from high school over my black corduroy pants and a black long-sleeved baggy sweater over a turtleneck. With my Carroll's uniform in a bag, I tried walking another route to work. I crossed the street every six or eight houses, on the lookout every minute. I had to stop and verify that every male walking or driving by didn't have red hair. My own parents did nothing, didn't even believe me. And the red-haired guy would know that. He'd know he could get away with it again. About three blocks from my house, I saw a guy with red hair drive by. I turned and ran all the way back home.

I called my boss and told him my parents kicked me out so I had to move to my brother's on the other side of town. And since I didn't have a car, I had no way to get there. Then I took a bus to the other side of town to the K-Mart near Zach's house. They needed an inventory clerk. I told them the same story, and they talked to my boss at Carroll's, then hired me on the spot.

That afternoon, I hid behind a tree down the street from Zach's house, on the lookout still, until I saw him pull up in front of their house.

"I have to get out of Dad's," I told him. "Please. I just got hired at K-Mart right up the street. I'll pay you room and board, and babysit whenever you want. I'll do the dishes. I'll help with the—"

"Whoa. It's okay. Trust me. I know how you feel. Remember? I used to live there, too. I don't know how you've survived this long in that house. You can move in as soon as you want, if you don't mind sharing the baby's bedroom."

"Oh, thank you," I said, hugging him. Then I dragged out my bags from behind the tree.

That night, as we sat at the dinner table, Zach told me it was in the works still, but they were thinking about moving down to Virginia.

"Maybe the Tidewater area, near Norfolk," he said. "Maybe you'd be interested? You'd get a lot closer to Alton's base."

"I'd love it. I'd be willing to up and go tomorrow."

"Well, I don't know about tomorrow, but we were thinking about driving down there for a long weekend next month. You can go with us if you want. Maybe Alton can meet us there for a visit."

There is a God.

"Well, you know I love Mom and Dad. I just don't want to live with them," Zach explained when he invited them to go with us to Tidewater, hoping to convince them to move out of Syracuse. Other than the military, Dad had never been out of New York. Of course, Mom would leave Syracuse in a heartbeat if she could, so she stayed home to get the kids off to school, hoping we could do the convincing.

The night we arrived, while Zach and his family stayed in military housing, it was as if Dad and I had entered a time capsule, and only that time existed. We had adjoining rooms at this strange little hotel run by Joan Crawford. As she led us up this winding staircase, she explained the rules, ending every sentence with a cock of her head as she bugged her eyes, grinned, and flexed her neck muscles.

It was dark by then so we couldn't see anything out our windows, but we could hear the waves walloping the shore. I talked Dad into sneaking out two chairs from the kitchenette while I packed a six-pack of beer in a cooler. The light of the moon hung over us as we dragged our chairs toward the water— the first time either of us had ever seen an ocean up close and personal. We talked for hours, every now and then ending a sentence by cocking our heads, bugging our eyes, and flexing our neck muscles. And we laughed. We laughed until our chairs tipped over. And then we laughed some more.

As to moving, Dad would not be persuaded. But Zach's family and I moved to Tidewater in March, and a month later I moved to Jacksonville, where Alton and I moved into a trailer park 10 miles from the base. I didn't tell him what had happened. I didn't know how he'd react. He might think I'm too dirty to touch now that I'm not his little virgin anymore. Besides, he might ask me questions. He might ask if I fought back.

I thought he had a gun. But, no, I never saw it.

Or, if he found out, he might even go AWOL again, this time to hunt down the guy with red hair.

It wasn't like it was a real rape anyway.
A few weeks later, my morning sickness began.
What if the baby's born with red hair and freckles?
Throughout the pregnancy, I puked everything I ate, including the vitamins and iron pills. I was anemic, and the doctor warned me that the baby would be born anemic too.
The baby can't be a redhead because I had a period before I got the morning sickness. It can't be a redhead because my due date would be sooner. Do the math.
But no matter how hard I tried, my body refused to believe me. It repulsed almost everything.
What if the due date is wrong? What if—
A few months later, it was weird, but Alton got busted for a couple of pot seeds in the pocket of his fatigues. He said they set him up. He said it wasn't enough pot to charge him. He said they were just trying to make an example of him. For all I knew, he could have put the pot in his own pocket and set himself up as a way to get out of the military. I was so homesick, I didn't care one way or the other. When they offered him six months in the brig or an Undesirable Discharge, he didn't hesitate.
We are going home!
When we returned to Syracuse, I felt like I had just returned to civilization. I didn't get out much in Jacksonville, other than playing pinball at the Laundromat a mile from our trailer on Saturdays. Alton said he didn't like to take me out because it was a military town, and the guys might gawk at me, might want a piece of me.
Once we were back in Syracuse with our family and friends, I decided to tell Alton, just in case. Or he might think I cheated on him. We were lying in bed in the dark late one night talking about things that happened to us when we were little kids.
"I don't know how to tell you this," I started. "But something terrible happened back in January. Was it the 21st or 22nd?" I trailed off as it occurred to me that I could not remember much about the incident at all.
It wasn't the reservation in Nedrow, that I know for sure. It was an Indian reservation I wasn't too familiar with. I think the Oneida Reservation?
"Anyway," I started again.

But Alton had rolled over on his elbow, and when I began to speak, he pursed my lips with the fingers of his other hand.

"I know," he said. "Angus told me months ago about some red-haired trucker bragging to some of the other truckers about raping a Lazore chick. They said the guy drove one of those Red Star trucks. The guy said he did it out on the reservation to make a point. Fucking racist said Indians are always complaining about white people screwing them out of their land, and then they turn around and marry our women. He decided he'd screw one of their women too, a white one, right on their own land. He bragged about it. But then he never showed his face again. Angus and his buddies will fucking kill him if they ever find him."

"What made you think it was me?"

"You and Katrina are the only white Lazore chicks that we know of. Angus asked Katrina, and she said it wasn't her, so we knew it had to be you."

"Why didn't you tell me you knew?"

"I was really pissed off at first that you didn't tell me. But Angus made me swear not to say anything. He said a lot of women don't like to talk about it. Anyway, that's the past. I'm here now, and I don't care if the baby's born with red hair or green hair, I'll be here to protect you from now on."

I snuggled up safe in his arms. At last, I felt liberated from my father and had found someone who believed me, someone who loved me, someone who will protect me.

The morning sickness gave way to a backache, and a few weeks later I gave birth to a magnificent little half-breed boy, the baby I had been aching for it seemed all my life. I weighed in at 107 pounds the day after delivery, but fat little Alton weighed 8 pounds, 13 ounces, with not an anemic cell in his body.

At little Alton's checkups, though, I would ask the doctor about his trembling hands, but the doctor said not to worry. He'd outgrow it. He said I was the one he was concerned about, that I needed to rebuild the strength and muscle tone I had lost during that draining nine months. But I wasn't worried about it. What I had lost, little Alton made up for.

In the next year, though, it became apparent that I would need to rebuild my strength if little Alton and I were going to survive big Alton's anger, which would pounce out of nowhere, like a cat on a mouse. Alton's nightmares about his mother and father intensified. And as if the nightmares and drinking were related, the more bizarre the dreams became, the drunker he got when we went out on Friday nights. And the drunker he got, the more jealous he became, the more possessive he became, the easier it was to trigger his anger. As the anger grew, he became more and more slaphappy, then punchy.

"Come on you little hussy," he yelled, staggering about 10 feet behind me. "I saw the way that pimple face was looking at you."

"I don't know what you're talking about."

"The fuck you don't. Like you weren't looking his way every chance you got."

"Shhhh. It's 2:30 in the morning. Someone's going to call the police."

"Let them call the fucking cops," he yelled louder. "I'll tell them too! You're a hussy. I saw the way you looked at him when you walked by his table."

"Stay out here while I go in and get little Alton. I don't want my mother to see you like this."

"Sure. We got to impress the Hayes's. The perfect little Walton family. Hah!"

"Just shut up! I'll be right back."

As Ma helped me put on the baby's snowsuit and wrap him in his baby bunting, we could hear Alton still hollering outside.

"Why don't you stay here tonight with the baby," Ma said. "Let him go home and sober up."

"That'll just make things worse," I said. "We'll be all right."

I scooped up little Alton and left.

As we rounded the corner, Alton continued yelling.

"That's all you ever wanted me for, isn't it? You wanted a baby. Now you got your precious little baby and you don't need me. Hey, let me carry the precious little baby."

"No, Alton, come on. You know you're drunk. And it's slippery out here."

In one fell swoop, he grabbed the baby and pushed me down in the snow.

"Give me the baby, Alton." I yelled, slipping a few times as I scrambled to my feet.

"I've got him. He's fine. Aren't you, you little pervert. See, he's fine." He held him up in the air, holding the baby bunting with one fist.

I kept trying to approach them, but Alton would sway as he tried to push me back.

"Alton, stop! You're going to drop him. Oh, my God, Alton, stop it!" I screamed.

Then I saw Ma running up the street toward us in her bare feet in the snow. Before Alton knew she was even behind him, she whisked the baby from him.

"I can't believe you two," she said, crying and screaming. "My God, risking this innocent baby's life. Drunk and fighting. You two should be ashamed of yourselves. No wonder this baby shakes."

She stalked off with Alton in her arms.

"Awww. Did your Mommy come to the rescue?" he said. "She didn't rescue you, though, did she? Like I said, you're mine," he said, pushing me back into the snow.

"You mother fucking asshole," I screamed, as I scrambled to my feet again. But I was no match for him. He threw me to the ground again and jumped on me.

"When I get done with you, no one will want you," he said, pinning me to the ground as he bit me all over my face with his strong straight white teeth, none of which had ever had a cavity.

"Look, Mom. No face. Go show that to your mother!" he said, as he stood up and staggered toward home.

"I'm calling the police," Ma said. "Look what he's done to you, and to the baby. Somebody could have been killed out there. The baby could have been killed if I hadn't followed you two."

"No, don't call the police, Ma. He's gone."

"I don't understand you," she said. "How can you put up with this kind of abuse?"

"It's not that bad, Ma. He was just drunk. Everything will be okay in the morning."

"One of these days it's not going to be okay. I'm scared to death for you and that baby. Maybe you can protect yourself, but who's going to protect him? Maybe you think you've got it under control, but go look in the mirror. See who's got it under control."

"Shut the fuck up," I screamed, as I ran to the bathroom, slammed the door shut, and looked in the mirror. My face was so bloody I didn't recognize myself.

"Gabrielle? I'm sorry," Ma said, knocking on the door. "Please open the door. Come on. I've got a wet towel and a cold pack. Let me clean you up."

I opened the door and collapsed in her arms. She held me for several minutes, then led me back to the dining room, where she sat me down. She dipped the towel in a bowl of warm water and began dabbing my face with it, her soft gentle fingers stroking the sticky hair from my face.

For the next three days, Alton called on the phone begging me to come home. He pounded on the front door, but we pretended not to hear. He'd knock on the windows, and we'd pull the shades. Then one morning I was coming back from the bathroom, and there he was, on his knees, his hands cupped in prayer, his eyes full of crocodile tears. He began begging me through the glass of the front door.

"Please come back home. I beg you. You're all I've got. I was drunk and stupid. I'm sorry! I swear it'll never happen again. I swear. I beg you. Please give me one more chance. I don't know what's got into me. I think now that we're back in Syracuse. It's like I'm just beginning to realize that both my parents are dead. I know it's no excuse. And it'll never happen again. I'll never drink again."

I can't abandon him like I did Damian, Kyle, and Olivia.

"Go home," I told him. "I'll come by later so we can talk."

As the scabs and bruises on my face healed, I stayed at home trying to appease him. I was all he had, I understood that, and he didn't want to share me with anyone. But in the months that followed, it got to the point that he forbid me to go by myself to the store or to the Laundromat across the street or to my mother's, two blocks away. He would even make me wake and dress little Alton at 9:30 or 9:45 at night because he had run out of cigarettes or beer, and he would not leave us alone for even five minutes to run downstairs to the Delaware Groceteria. Even though I tried to do everything to please him, he still got drunk, and we fought. But no one needed to know, that is, until one sunny afternoon in October, just weeks before Alton's first birthday.

Big Alton was still at work when an urge to take a walk to the park overwhelmed me. I strapped little Alton in his stroller and walked up the hill to the Tot Lot, where Val and Michelle and I used to hang out after dark as teenagers, gazing out at the lit city below us, making grand plans for our futures.

As I pushed little Alton in the baby swing, one dream in particular crossed my mind: to hitchhike to New York City, where we would take the elevator to the top of the Empire State Building, the tallest building in the world!

I sighed.

Well it used to be.

I gazed at the city below from the hilltop playground.

This is about as high as you'll ever get.

I looked at my watch.

I am like totally screwed!

I would be lucky to get home before Alton, much less cook dinner, for not only had my dreams slipped away, so had the time.

"Why couldn't you just wait until I got home to go to the park?" Alton yelled at me. "You know I don't like you walking the streets alone. What are you doing, trying to get raped again?"

"It's broad daylight, for crying out loud. Who do you think is going to get me?"

"It was broad daylight when Bozo the Clown got you, wasn't it? Is that what you want to happen again? Look, if you're going to be out gallivanting all day every day, you might as well get a job."

"Fine, I'll get a job. I want a job."

"Over my dead body," he said, pushing me toward the bedroom.

I knew what he was up to. He had done it before. But there was no way I was ever going to let him lock me in the bedroom again.

I pulled a steak knife from the silverware drawer.

"I dare you. Touch me again, and I'll cut your fucking heart out."

He laughed, his beautiful Don Juan laugh, and then he dove for the knife.

As I drew the knife back, it slit him across his left arm.

He stopped in his tracks.

"Look what you did to me," he said. He ran to the sink, wet a dishtowel, and pressed it to his arm.

"A few inches over and you could have stabbed me in the heart."

"I didn't do it you fucking idiot. You did it. You jumped into it, you idiot. Why didn't you stay where the fuck you were?"

"I'm sorry, honey," he said. "I don't know what the fuck's the matter with me. I'm sorry. Let's just pretend this never happened. Put the knife down, and let's talk."

He sat at the kitchen table and caressed his wound.

I put the knife down and sat across from him.

He looked up, a sad gentle look on his face, and then he flew up in a rage and flipped the table over on me, knocking me backward in my chair. We struggled on the floor. I managed to crawl out from under him and run toward the counter. He was right at my heels and swept everything from the counter onto the floor. He grabbed me by my hair and began twisting it. I screamed and swung and kicked and spit.

Then someone knocked on the door.

"Open up. It's the police."

I leaped toward the door and unlocked it.

"Look what she did to me, officer."

After the officers took our statements, they arrested Alton.

"Why the hell are you arresting me? I'm the one bleeding. She doesn't have a mark on her."

"You haven't seen the bruises on her back or the bumps on her head? And stop whining. That's nothing but a superficial scrape on your arm. You're lucky she didn't cut your heart out. She probably could have gotten away with it."

The two cops laughed.

"She's got plenty of neighbors around here who are willing to testify on her behalf. They're the ones who called us. So if I were you, I'd keep my mouth shut before you get yourself in even deeper."

The court granted me an order of protection that forbid Alton from coming to the apartment, or anywhere else I might be. The court order provided me the time I needed to build up my defenses, to harden my shell—and my heart—so that by the time Don Juan got the opportunity to wallow his way into my guilt and pity, I had buried the emotional bones in a tomb deep within my soul. No one could exhume them, not even me.

Earlier that year, Zach and his family had moved to Biloxi, Mississippi, where they had gotten saved in a fundamental Baptist church. He had called Ma and Dad to spread the Word. He told them about a sister church in Syracuse, and he pleaded for us all to go there, to save our souls. But we couldn't find that church to save our asses. At last, that December, when Zach came home to visit for the holidays, he led us straight to it.

He stood by beaming as our whole family marched into the pew like in a parade. But the service was much like the ones at the other churches we attended by mistake. I had no idea what Zach was expecting, but I prayed that we wouldn't disappoint him. And at the closing of the sermon, God answered my prayer.

"Let us close our eyes and bow our heads," the pastor said.

After a moment, he continued.

"Do you know beyond a shadow of a doubt that if you died today, your soul would go to heaven? If not, raise your hand. Are you absolutely positive that God has forgiven all of your sins? If not, raise your hand. Do you know beyond all doubt that your name is written in the Book of Life? If not, raise your hand."

He paused again.

"I'd like everyone to keep their heads bowed as the choir leads us in the next hymn. When the music begins, I'd like anyone who raised their hand to come forward. Even if you're in the middle of a pew, don't hesitate. Your brothers and sisters will gladly step aside to clear you a path. Come. Come forward now."

"Just as I am" http://bit.ly/21WDVCm], the congregation began to sing.

As I excused myself, and found my way to the end of the pew, I kept my head bowed. Once I arrived at the aisle, a woman took my hand and squeezed it as she led me to the steps at the foot of the altar.

"Let us pray," she said, sitting me on the step and putting her arms around me. She began whispering, telling me to repeat after her, "I believe."

After several minutes the pastor began to speak from the pulpit again, all excited because so many had been saved that morning. I was confused. I was just answering the preacher's questions. Then he told me to come forward if I had raised my hand. So I did. But somehow that meant I got saved. By walking the aisle, he said, in front of the whole congregation, we had confessed our belief that Jesus Christ died on the cross to redeem us, an act in itself worthy of redemption.

I felt tricked somehow but, as I looked around, I realized my entire family, even Dad, had walked the aisle. After the service, everyone cried and sang praises to the Lord. It was like a family reunion, with all 10 members of the Hayes family in church together. Maybe the energy of being together moved us, maybe it was the Christmas spirit, maybe God fired us up, I don't know, but we were drunk on Spirit.

"I once was lost, but now am found" http://bit.ly/1OnauQ7], I was chanting from the depths of my soul, when Zach pulled me aside and pleaded with me to stop the divorce filing.

"It's too late" [http://bit.ly/1OXA2Yx], I told him, resisting the urge to break out in song. "Something has died, and I just can't fake it."

"It's never too late," he said, opening to Matthew, Chapter 19, from the King James version. He began to read.

"Whosoever shall put away his wife, except it be for fornication, and shall marry another, committeth adultery: and whoso marrieth her which is put away doth commit adultery" [http://bit.ly/1jUpooy]. He looked up from his Bible.

"Do you understand," he asked. "If you divorce, any man who goes out with you for the rest of your life will be committing adultery. And you're only 18."

"I'll be 19 in a couple of weeks," I said.

"Okay, 19. But you're bound to want to get married again. Now do you want to take on that responsibility? Do you want to condemn your own future husband to hell as an adulterer?"

He paused to look at me.

"I know it looks hopeless to you right now, Gab," he continued. "But God can work miracles, you know, if we trust Him. If Alton gets saved, you can both start your lives over again, the right way. You know how different you feel, how joyful you felt after getting saved? Well, Alton will be a new person, too, if he accepts Christ into his life, you'll see."

"I don't know," I said. "I can't picture him walking the aisle."

"You don't know that. Only God knows that. Call him. Invite him to church next Sunday. It may save his soul. It may save your marriage. It's too late to save his mother and father. They're already dead. But maybe you can help lead him to Christ, lead his brothers and sister to Christ. Maybe you can help save their eternal lives. It's the right thing to do."

Alton jumped at the chance to meet us at church the next Sunday.

"Just as I am—"

"Do you know—" the pastor began.

Alton slipped out of the pew to be first in line.

"Wait outside while I go downstairs to the nursery to get little Alton," I told Alton after the service. "We'll surprise him. But it'll be better if everybody's not standing there."

"Come on, Alton, let's get your coat on. Hurry, Mommy's got a surprise."

They hadn't seen each other in a couple of months, and I was sure it would be a delightful reunion.

"Look, look! Who's that," I asked, as we approached Alton, who was leaning against the rusted out Volkswagen Bug he bought the week before.

As soon as little Alton saw big Alton, he began to shake, and it dawned on me his hands had not trembled since big Alton had moved out. But we had set the wheel in motion and had to give it a whirl. Besides, now that we were both saved, we would live happily ever after, and Alton would soon realize that he need not be afraid anymore.

Alton and I were baptized in the same pool at the same time the following Sunday, where we made a commitment to quit drinking and smoking. And instead of going to the bar, we attended church three times a week. But something didn't click. Something was missing. We needed a smoke, needed a drink, needed to get out. We hung in there, though, and kept trying, until March, that is, three months later.

I had just finished folding a load of laundry in the basement and had scuffled up the stairs in my slippers, when I saw it: Big Alton stood in the kitchen towering over little Alton, who sat in his high chair. Before I could scream out, big Alton swung his clenched fist into little Alton's face, stopping just a split hair from his nose. I saw the terror in little Alton's eyes. He flinched and his whole body trembled. God or no God, I had to protect my son.

I looked down at the floor and cleared my throat. Big Alton swung around, and I looked up like I hadn't seen anything.

"Tell Mommy how you and I are playing," Alton said.

"You know what, honey? I've got a real craving for ice cream. What do you say? Want to make a store run?"

"Sure. We can all go," he said, unsnapping the high chair tray. "What do you say, squirt? Wanna go get ice cream with your ol' man?"

"Actually, I'd rather he didn't today. It's cold out, and he's got a runny nose."

"Oh. Okay."

I could see his wheels turning, but he didn't say anything.

"Give your ol' man a kiss," he said to me. "I'll be right back."

In five minutes flat I emptied the contents of his dresser in garbage bags and threw them out on the porch and bolted the locks that could only be opened from the inside. I put Alton in his crib with a bottle and turned up the stereo full blast. By the time Alton returned, I had taped a note to the door window. I stood by the door but out of sight.

"Alton: I saw what you did to little Alton. No wonder the poor baby is shaking all the time. Go quietly, or I'll call the police. The order of protection is technically still in effect."

"Damn it! The ice cream's melting," he screamed, after pounding on the door for 10 minutes. Then he picked up the bags, flung them over his shoulder, and walked off.

To keep from visiting my sins upon an innocent man, I vowed to never remarry, and nurtured instead my relationship with God. I went to church every Wednesday, and twice on Sunday, wishing services were more often. It seemed like such a long time, especially from Wednesdays to Sundays. Like an addict, I needed my church fix more often.

I had begun to see my purpose in life, just like Uncle Ben said I would years before. I began teaching the message of Salvation, trying to convert everyone I knew. I decided that one day I'd like to be a Sunday school teacher, but I had so much more to learn. I began asking questions at every opportunity.

One evening after Bible Study, after Brother Martin left the pastor's office, I tapped on the pastor's open door.

"Hi, pastor. I have some questions if you have time?"

"Gabrielle, I see, uh, well. I think it's best, that is, I'm rather busy. I'm sure my wife can answer any questions you have. Why don't you set up an appointment with her?"

"Well, I just want to ask you. I've noticed that when I raise my hand during Bible Study, you never call on me. I know the Bible says women ought to keep quiet in the church. But I thought Bible Study was different. It's not like I'm questioning what you say in the middle of a service. It's just I don't under—"

As the pastor's phone rang, he held up his hand.

"Hello? Yes. Just a moment," he said to the caller, then looked back at me. "Do you mind closing the door behind you?"

I had noticed other doors closing, too, like the bus ministry, which paired a female to a male to witness door to door Thursday nights. I was running out of people to preach to, and it seemed like a good way to get my church fix. So I joined. I didn't have any friends, not anymore, not since Alton and I had married. So I didn't have anyone to invite as my bus ministry partner, especially not a male.

Three weeks in a row, they said they didn't have anyone to partner with me, so I volunteered to sit in the nursery, instead. But no one ever called me. When I asked how to become a Sunday school teacher, and no one seemed to know, I began to realize that the doors of the church were closed to me even when I was on the inside. They didn't shut the church doors in my face, but they could shut the doors of their hearts when a divorced woman knocked.

I believed in God, but I retreated from the church. With my soul's source of food cut off, I began going through withdrawals, yearning for something, but I didn't know what.

PART IV

"If a mother does not want the baby . . . People come into analysis at forty, fifty, sixty, however old, those patterns are still there. The child was not wanted. This image of being huddled in the uterus, trying to stay alive, trying not to be dumped out, particularly if the mother tried to have an abortion. Even in dreams deep, deep, deep in the psyche— now they won't appear at the beginning of analysis because these dreams are so painful they are not endurable to a weak ego. So the psyche is very kind. It doesn't put up these dreams until the ego is strong enough to take it. And sometimes the ego is barely strong enough. But the dreams just start to come in. And eventually it has to be dealt with. I was not wanted. I was not loved.

"I think that's what a lot of addictions are about, the fat body that acts as protection for the terrified soul is both an armor against the world and it's a protection for what's inside.

"The dreams that we dream are our healing images or our destructive images, whichever way. And the one results in miscarriage and the other in delivery."[1]

Marion Woodman [http://bit.ly/1PoTLrw]
Sitting by the Well [http://bit.ly/1OagpMK]

17
the secret delivery

Fall 1975

"Y̲OU SET YOUR STANDARDS WAY TOO HIGH," Ma said, after yet another guy hit on me and walked away from our table, like a naughty puppy with his tail between his legs. Ma hadn't seen all the different guys I had dated in the month after I broke from the church. Dinner. Party. Sex. The morning after. Sex. Breakfast. A night at the bar. Necking. One guy after another. It wasn't what one might think, that is, not for pleasure or to get high. Not like Theresa Dunn. No. I was on a mission. But none of them could pass my test, a test they didn't know they were taking, a test they failed again and again. Two, three days, and I was done with them. Just one misspoken word could do it, could put them on the reject list. Because I damned sure wasn't going to marry my father again.

I sipped my beer between drags until Dad sunk the eight ball in the corner pocket.

"The usual?" the loser asked, shaking his head and stumbling up to the bar. Dad nodded as he walked back to our table, with just a little gloat on his face, the rich royal blue fabric of his suit glistening as he passed under a barroom lamp.

"You need a man to take care of you," Ma said. "And you're never going to find one with that attitude because no man can live up to your expectations."

"I'm in no hurry. I'm only 19, you know. It's not like I'm on the verge of becoming an old maid."

"But you have a baby. How many men are you going to turn down who are willing to take on that responsibility before the well runs dry?"

"Don't worry. I can take care of myself and little Alton. I'm making almost $500 a week."

"Yeah. But you're working two jobs and paying a sitter for more than 80 hours a week. How much is left over? Plus, little Alton hardly ever sees his mother."

"It's just temporary, until I get on my feet," I said.

"You have a short memory, Rose." Dad said. "We've lived through tougher times than that. I remember when we had several kids, and I couldn't find a job. At least she's not stuck in the welfare rut."

Dad pinched a nerve.

With mixed feelings, I remembered the day I went to the Bureau of Vital Statistics to get a copy of my birth certificate so I could prove who I was to somebody. Dad wouldn't give me my birth certificate out of his locked filing cabinet because I might lose it, he said. So I had to take the bus downtown.

The deputy registrar asked me if I wanted the regular certificate or the detailed version. I chose one of each.

The regular certificate verified that someone named Gabrielle Elizabeth Hayes was born on December 17, 1955, in the County of Onondaga, Syracuse, New York. That was it. Nothing more to say.

But this detailed certificate, what secrets will it reveal?

As I unfolded the second document, my hands shook and the butterflies in my stomach took nosedives as if I were opening a top-secret file. As I read it, I felt as if someone had dropped little breadcrumbs on my path, and at last I had a few morsels to chew on, morsels some may turn their nose up at, but to me they were a feast.

> The father's age at the time of this child's birth: 22
> Color or Race: White
> His usual occupation: Factory Worker
> Kind of business or industry: Un-Employed
> The mother's age at the time of this child's birth: 21
> Color or Race: White
> Length of pregnancy: 40 weeks
> Weight of child at birth: 7 pounds, 6 ounces
>
> Was the blood of this child's mother tested for syphilis?: Yes. 7-8-55.
> What preventive for ophthalmia neonatorum did you use?: Silver Nitrate 1%
>
> And Charles O. Rose, M.D., hereby certified that he attended the birth of this child who was born *alive* on December 17, 1955, at 3:24 a.m.

"Yeah, but she's working at a pocketbook factory all day," Ma said, shivering, then huddling under her pink sweater. "And at a bar all night. She's never going to meet anyone decent in those places."

"Or here," I added, deciding not to mention my train of thought. I had come running in all excited telling them that day what my birth certificate said. But Dad was pissed, insulted that they had listed him as "Un-Employed." Not that it wasn't true. It just wasn't anybody's business. And Ma didn't like it one bit either.

"Look! It even states the length of your pregnancy, my weight, and my time of birth! I was a night owl—3:24 a.m.!"

They were not impressed.

"They always say 40 weeks," Ma said. "That's standard. But who really knows."

Ma and Dad's attitude baffled me, sickened me, really. Nonetheless, I read my birth certificate over and over again for weeks as if it were a best-selling novel. I savored the few crumbs on my plate for they were the only connection I had to the day I was born *alive*. Sometimes, it was the only proof I had that I existed.

"Good game," the loser said, handing Dad a Black Velvet and ginger. "Rematch?"

"Maybe later," Dad said. And I knew he was about to launch into one of his stories about the good old days. I knew by rote the stories he told, but I enjoyed listening and encouraged him to continue during the next couple of hours as Ma interjected her memories whenever he paused. Somehow, perhaps due to a little alcohol influence, they regressed deeper and deeper into their memories beyond the rehearsed stories and revealed a story they had spent my whole lifetime hiding, the story of my conception and birth.

"We'll take another on my tab," I told the waitress, who had stopped by to empty our ashtrays. I recognized the uncharted territory and wanted to avoid any distractions.

"Your father was in Korea for 18 months, and by the time he came home, Zach was already a year and a half old. They were strangers."

"Hell, we were strangers, Rose. Back then, making a long distance call overseas was out of the question. Plus, neither of us wrote letters."

"I tried to write. But I'd break down crying. And I didn't want to worry you, so I'd tear them up."

"For the entire 18 months, we never exchanged a single word," Dad said. "We had only been married for six months before I left. Think about it. We had been apart longer than we had been together at that point."

"I know. And here I had waited for a whole year and a half, living for the day your father would come home. But when he finally did, he wouldn't have anything to do with me. He spent every night at the bar."

"Yeah. That wasn't too nice of me."

"But finally one night, I got his attention. I think it was the first day of spring, as a matter of fact, and I had just finished making my Easter dress, which I was trying on when I heard him come in. I pinned a flower right here," she said, pushing her hair back over her right ear.

"She floated into the living room, where I was sitting in my recliner, and began doing the hula, singing our song."

"I'm yours," they both sang.

"I saw her in that dress, her cheeks as pink as the flower in her hair."

"Almost nine months later to the day, you were born. But I'll tell you what. It was the toughest nine months of my life. Once the rabbit died all hell broke loose."

"Yeah. We'll take one more," Dad said, as the waitress walked by eyeing our glasses.

"We're not ready for another baby, your father argued. Zach doesn't even know who I am yet, much less—"

"Oh, it was crazy. Just home from Korea. No education. I was depressed. I couldn't figure out where to even begin to find a job, and here she was telling me she was pregnant."

"So your Aunt Velma gave me some pills to take to abort the fetus."

"It was crazy," Dad said.

"Neither of us believed in abortion," Ma said. "But she made it seem so innocent. If I took the pills she gave me while I was only in my sixth week, I would bleed, but not much more than a regular period. She said the fetus would look like any other blood clot ever flushed down the toilet. Your father and I talked about it and agreed. I went to the bathroom to take the pills. I cried for a long time, until he knocked on the door asking me what was taking so long. I couldn't do it. I flushed the pills down the toilet. Boy was he mad when I told him."

"I was young and immature," Dad said. "I'm sure glad she didn't listen to me though. Or we wouldn't have you today."

"He wouldn't have anything to do with me for the rest of the pregnancy."

"She would be sitting up crying when I'd get home," Dad said. "But I was nasty. I was so angry all the time. I wanted everything perfect. She'd clean the house spick and span, but if I saw one spot she missed, I'd start cussing her out."

"You got it from your mother, Zach, your perfectionism. And Gabrielle's just like you."

My skin crawled.

"Yeah, my mother always was a perfectionist."

"I'll never forget one night," Ma said. "I had cleaned that house inside out, upside down and backwards. I was determined that he wouldn't have a single thing to complain about when he got home. That night, he went to hang up his jacket in the closet and found jelly on the inside of the closet doorknob, and he went into a rage. That was the one and only time your father ever raised his hand to me. Well, you know me. I'm always cutting out something or another. And I had had enough. I held up those scissors, looked him straight in the eye, and I dared him."

"Yeah," Dad said, shaking his head. "I don't know why I was such an ornery little devil."

"Hell, if he couldn't think of a reason to criticize me, he'd yell at me because he went to the bar! It made no sense. I couldn't figure him out. Anyway, I cried myself to sleep just about every night the whole time I was pregnant for you. Then the night I went into labor, he said I was on my own. He said it was my fault. I should have taken the pills. Did I realize that I had flushed $20 down the toilet? Besides, it was Friday, and he wasn't about to let it interfere with his night out, as if he didn't go out every other night of the week. I never felt so alone in my whole life when he slammed the front door on his way out."

"I've always regretted that night," Dad said, cleaning his eyeglasses with his hanky.

"I called Grandma Williams to see if I could borrow her car. Told her I was in labor. Said your father wasn't home. But she said no. She said she had promised my brother, precious little Gilbert, the car for a Christmas dance. She was weird. She and Grandpa Williams never wanted me to marry your father. So whenever we needed anything, she wouldn't help. Like they were teaching me a lesson for marrying beneath my station."

"Yeah, and now look," Dad said. "We're the ones who host all the holidays. And we're the ones who gave them most of their grandchildren, all but three."

"I had no one else to turn to at the time," Ma said. "The contractions were getting closer together, and I was scared. So I asked Mrs. Bertram to watch Zach, and I walked up the street to the bus stop. I just remember standing there crying on Salina Street in front of Woolworth's waiting for the transfer bus to the hospital. It was snowing and the cold wind was stinging my face and legs. Women didn't wear pants in those days."

"Just think," Dad said. "If you had waited one more week, you could have been born on Christmas Eve, on my birthday."

He chuckled, and hit the table with his knuckle.

"But it was weird," Dad said. "As if you sensed it. From the first day your mother brought you home from the hospital, you screamed if I as much as touched you. Whenever I tried to pick you up, you'd start gasping like you couldn't breathe. If your mother had to go somewhere, you'd scream and cry and kick and fuss the whole time she was gone, like you were angry, even when you were only a few months old."

"That's how you got that scar on your wrist," Ma said. "I went to buy groceries while you were sleeping one afternoon. When I got home your father was in the living room watching basketball. He had the TV blaring to drown out your screaming. But mother's instinct, you know. I knew at once something was wrong. That was not your ordinary cry. I went running upstairs screaming at him, 'Can't you tell there's something wrong with that baby?' When I got upstairs I saw that your wrist was lodged between the mattress and the crib bar. I panicked and yanked out your arm without even thinking to pull back the mattress or letting down the bar first. It left a nasty burn mark on your wrist. Gee whiz, I realized afterwards. I could have broken your arm!"

"I didn't realize it," Dad said, shaking his head. "I thought you were just having your usual temper tantrum because you woke up and somehow sensed your mother wasn't home. I often think about it. Wishing I could go back and change the way it was, that whole year you were born, so it would be better for you and for your mother."

"Last call!" the bartender yelled.

"Let's pay up and go to the Little Gem for breakfast." I said.

"Sounds good to me. I'm starved," said Ma.

"I haven't eaten in say, oh, eight hours," Dad said, counting the hours back on his watch to when he ate his fish and fries at Big Jim's.

I knew it! I somehow always knew it, but now I have images and words to attach to my feelings. I wasn't crazy after all!

As every cell in my body cradled the knowledge of my birth, I shook off "Pig-Pen's" dust like a gust of wind shakes down a field of dandelions, scattering the seeds of its blowballs to greener pastures.

PART V

"Once the door is opened, the bird who has lived in a cage all of its life shrinks back from freedom and the terrors of the unknown. It is the Self, the ordering center of the personality, that presents the ego with the challenge to move to a new level of consciousness. If the ego is afraid to make the passover, preferring to clutch to what it has always known, then psychological and physiological symptoms break out. These the ego has to deal with, for learning the meaning of these symptoms and situations is what leads to the new level of awareness and a new harmonious balance between consciousness and the unconscious. So long as consciousness is afraid to open itself to "the otherness" of the unconscious, it experiences itself as the victim. Once it is able to open itself to the new life flowing through, it becomes the beloved. To be a victim is to be raped; to be the beloved is to be ravished...

"Paradoxically, that point can only be reached when the ego is strong enough to be vulnerable enough to surrender. That, for the woman, is the point where her own feminine ego is so firmly planted in her biological roots that she is free to take on her own biological and spiritual identity."[1]

Marion Woodman [http://bit.ly/1PoTLrw]
Addiction to Perfection [http://bit.ly/1X6OqTQ]

18
the golden dream

The "Wedding of the Century" took place on July 29th, 1981, when Lady Diana Spencer married Prince Charles and became Diana, Princess of Wales. The wedding was watched on television by 750 million people worldwide.

Bio.
[http://bit.ly/1IA9D1G]

In 1981, more Americans watched Luke and Laura's wedding on *General Hospital* than Prince Charles and Lady Diana's televised nuptials. The daytime soap opera was a cultural phenomenon, and the headstrong Laura, played by Genie Francis, was the role model for millions of young women.

Bio.
[http://bit.ly/1IA9D1G]

Winter 1975 to the Early 1980s

MY BIRTHDAY HAD NEW MEANING TO ME. And I planned to celebrate my 20th that coming Friday like a thousand shooting stars. But before the potential meteors could even gain altitude in my atmosphere, that is, before I could even pop my first beer, I lost one and a half jobs.

Mrs. Geppetto invited me to have lunch with her that Friday at her bar, which, you know, was like weird, till it all made sense when she said that they had to cut my hours in half.

And at 5 p.m., when they pulled the plug on the assembly lines at the pocketbook factory, the manager announced that we would all be paid for work not performed in the coming two weeks. It took me a minute to realize that the layoff included the company's one and only pocketbook inventory clerk, you know, me.

This guy Teddy was tending bar that night, and he tried to cheer me up.

"Here, taste this. On the house," he said, setting a Pink Lady on the "G" of an embossed napkin.

"Yummy," I said, licking the froth.

He smiled and winked at me.

Sure, I'd seen Teddy around. But me and his thick, sable-colored mustache had not yet become acquainted—until that very second. I peered over my cocktail glass, observing him, as he strained a martini for Rita, topped off the head of Chico's draft beer, and then lit my cigarette, all with a graceful gait, as if he had choreographed it.

As if part of the show, shades of brown shimmied across his shirt as two bolts of cream slashed through each other diagonally. Meanwhile, his jeweled belt buckle glistened like a crown above the flair of his brown slacks, all of which professed that he was no slouch.

I stole glances at the gold rings flashing on his fingers, one with a diamond setting! Not one of the spate of guys who tried to wheedle their way into my heart after Alton and I had split up had a moustache, much less rings, except for Alton, of course, with his peach fuzz and a wedding band.

The mirror behind the bar reflected the light from green and red bulbs as they pulsed to the beat of "Blue Christmas," which was playing on the jukebox, as a group of us regulars sat on one end of the bar, trying to instigate some merriment.

Between serving other customers, Teddy would throw in his two cents, while setting before me one fancy concoction after another.

"Mmmm! What's this one called?"

"Golden Dream," he said, and in that moment, when I looked into his eyes, I could see in them the warm tones of a spotted tiger's-eye. I could see in them a golden dream.

Mrs. Geppetto, who said she'd give me a ride home that night, joined me at the bar at last call.

"Teddy likes you," she said. "He wants to know if you'll go to breakfast with us after we close."

"Really? Hmmm. I don't even know him."

"Aw, you know Teddy Franklin. He's harmless. A real teddy bear. I've known him for years. Come on, it'll be fun."

Mrs. Geppetto and her husband were an old Italian couple who had become like my guardians over the last few months or so that I worked their bar. One or the other always came in at closing time to help me clean up and lock up, and then drive me to my aunt's house to pick up little Alton, and then drop us off home. Like Ma, Mrs. Geppetto was concerned about my love life, or my lack thereof.

"Okay, sure. He knows I don't drive, though, right?"

"He'll drive you home. Don't worry. He drives that brown Monte Carlo, parks it right out there on the side," she pointed toward the window, though you couldn't see anything out it.

"Yeah, I've seen it."

"Great! It's settled then."

It wasn't until a few months later as I recounted our first "date" to a friend at Geppetto's that we realized Mrs. Geppetto had succeeded at her matchmaking.

"You're kidding," Teddy said. "She told me that it was you who liked me and wanted me to take you out to breakfast."

"Wait till I see her," we both said, grinning from ear to ear.

Of course, I left out the fact that we necked that night in his car until our toes froze off, and then I invited him to come over for Sunday dinner, well, you know, pizza.

That Sunday, the minute Teddy saw little Alton, he knelt down, and stretched open his arms.

"Come to Daddy," he said.

"I don't know if that's a good—"

Little Alton, who had been doing a spectacular job of making the expression, "the terrible twos," sound like the understatement of the century, leaped right into Teddy's arms.

"See, he knows," Teddy said, and the two of them sat on the floor and began to build a tower with alphabet blocks.

As Dickens said, it was the best of times and the worst of times. All in just a matter of a few weeks, I lost one and a half jobs, fell in love, and got evicted. I probably could have stayed, but Alton had to go. The landlord usually just tabulated in Alton's damage with the monthly rent, but this day he yelled at me, as if he thought Alton were cursed.

"Take your bambino and go. No money. Vai! Diavolo! Non voglio soldi. Vai!"

The morning before, Alton's urgent cries for Mommy had snatched me out of a dream. Alarmed, I shot out of bed and landed in cold water, I swear, a foot deep. I sloshed out to the kitchen, where Alton hung from the kitchen cupboard above the sink, afraid to let go, the Lucky Charms box just outside his reach.

Thank God Alton held on. Thank my lucky stars the landlord and his wife are out of town this weekend.

I spent most of the day filling and dumping buckets, then pans, then bowls of water until they wouldn't cut it anymore. Then I used every towel and blanket in the apartment, as well as every piece of clothing we didn't need to wear, to sop up the rest of the water. Before the landlord pulled into the driveway the next day, my floors were dry. How was I supposed to know that water would seep into the flooring, into the wiring through their ceiling, and drip onto their bedroom set, ruining their carpet and their brand new mattress!

I didn't know what to do, so I called my cousin Shirley to come over and babysit, and I went to the bar, where Teddy was setting up for happy hour. I explained the situation, assuring him that I had everything under control.

He dropped a quarter in the jukebox.

"I can help" [http://bit.ly/1Hyynav], his lips synced to the words as he shifted his weight from side to side, flexing his biceps, like he had just gulped down a can of spinach.

I burst out laughing.

He pointed at the shiny dimes pinched between the fingers of his left hand, then he drew back his right index finger, and ducked into the phone booth, where he talked and hung up, and talked and hung up, between incoming calls.

When Teddy emerged several minutes later, he eyed my empty beer bottle, strolled behind the bar, flipped off the cap of a Miller, and began to pour.

"Rita says they're hiring at Syracuse China. That's right on Court Street," he said. "They pay $300 a week. Plus, it's piecework so you can earn bonuses. She said she's sure she can get you in if you want."

"Really? Cool!" I said, raising my beer.

"Oh, I haven't served desert yet," he said. "Chico said there's a two-bedroom flat for rent right next door to him, and he's friends with the owner. We can see it tomorrow night, if you like."

"That's Washington Square, right around the corner. That would be perfect!"

"Only $250 a month," he said, crinkling his eyes, knowing that's what I was already paying for my tiny pad, where little Alton was technically sleeping in a large walk-in closet.

The next night as I walked through the flat, Teddy and the owner and Chico studied my reaction.

"What do you think?" Teddy asked, when they left us alone in the master bedroom.

"Well I don't know," I whispered. "How much does he want for the security deposit? What if I don't have enough after I put them through all this trouble?"

"Don't worry about that. Just tell me if you like the place."

"It's great. I just—"

"Then it's settled."

I followed him to the living room, where he pulled out a gold-plated money clip from his front pocket.

"This'll cover the first month's rent and the security deposit," Teddy said. "But write the lease up in her name."

Then he chuckled.

"But you don't mind if she invites me over, do you?"

"Of course not," the owner said. "As much as she likes."

"I don't feel right about this," I said to Teddy later.

"Hey, it's for us," he said. "And I plan to spend as much time there as you'll let me. We're in this together, okay? We're a team, right?"

Teddy visited every other night after dinner, and we'd watch television. I often sat straight-faced, but Teddy would fall off the couch, clutching his chest, laughing.

"What? What's so funny?" I'd ask, laughing at him laughing, feeling foolish sitting right next to him and viewing the same scene, yet getting nothing out of it.

Then, like Maureen, who used to explain the Bazooka bubble gum comics to me, he would explain it to me. In the beginning it was as if he had to train my sense of humor. But after a while, I began to recognize the humor myself, and began to laugh without a cue from him. I began to see humor that he didn't see, and had the pleasure of sharing my little jokes with him. And he'd laugh. He hadn't thought of it that way, he'd say.

Teddy taught me rhythm, too, lots of rhythm, in lots of places.

In that first year, he whirled me around in my liquid gold dresses and sequined-studded spiked heels on sheer sheets of plastic embedded with flashing colored lights as silver cubes danced on our skin.

Then when business picked up, the Geppetto's hired a live band for Friday and Saturday nights. They paired Teddy and I behind the bar, and between serving 300 customers—and earning $500 a night—Teddy taught me the bump, then the double bump.

And sometimes, when little Alton would spend the night with his cousins, Teddy would pick me up on his way home from work. I'd see his mother peeking out from her front-room window in anticipation of his arrival. I would focus on my feet until we climbed the stairs, out of view, to his private entrance.

He'd draw the drapes while I curled up in the chair in the corner of his living room. I'd study the crinkled foil behind the painted glass of a Bengal tiger, which hung on an adjacent wall, and tell him the latest news about David Hamilton and Laura Webber. He'd fluff the throw pillows, buff the marble-topped coffee table with a chamois cloth, and rinse off his small dinette set.

But not for a minute did either of us forget that his mother was waiting for him downstairs, keeping a plate of roast beef and potatoes warm for him. His dad waited too. Not to eat, but to ask Teddy to run up to the corner store to buy him a case of Schlitz.

Teddy knew the routine well, had been following it for the last five years since he had divorced Gina after he caught her naked with another man in the backseat of a Buick on a summer night along the parkway, in the backseat of the Buick that Teddy had bought her because she said she needed more freedom.

"I'll be back in a flash," he'd say, winking and tapping my nose.

He would return with two plates of food, which he sat on placemats on the table in the kitchen. Then he'd wipe down some silverware and two wine glasses, stack some albums on his stereo, light several candles, and dim the lamps. After eating, we'd sit on his royal blue crushed-velvet sofa sipping wine until midnight, chatting. Then he would lead me to his bedroom and unbutton my blouse and unsnap my bra. He would caress me and guide my hands, showing me what he liked. I'd start to rush or push or grab, but he'd soothe me, stroke my shoulder blades.

"Listen," he'd whisper.

"Me and Mrs. Jones" [http://bit.ly/1Hyynav] gushed into my soul, and I heard it like never before. When every muscle in our bodies quivered, we'd fall asleep in one another's arms, the blues still weaving beautiful patterns in and out of my dreams.

Those were the days.[1]

"What will the neighbors think?" his mother would spew through her false teeth the next morning.

"Mom! Don't busy yourself about the neighbors. I'm a big boy. What's it to them?"

Teddy always held my hand as we walked through his mother's minefield toward the kitchen, where his dad sat in wait to heal the wounded. Dad would squeeze my shoulder on his way to the stove to stir the food.

"I hope you're hungry," he'd say. "I'm cooking rats and snails and puppy dog tails."

As he loaded up our plates with linked sausage, scrambled eggs, hash browns, and biscuits from scratch, he'd ask how's the monkey. That was always his first question.

"Alton's doing great," I said, one morning. "Except for that little joke you taught him last Saturday."

He laughed, and coughed, and laughed again.

"Oh, I'm sorry. Did that cause a problem?"

"I thought he had forgotten all about it," I said, and Teddy and I began laughing our butts off thinking about it.

His mother scowled.

"We were in the middle of dinner at my parents' house last Sunday," I said, "along with about 20 relatives. Suddenly, right when everyone was in the middle of slurping it up. I'm telling you, it was as if he understood exactly what you meant about timing. He demanded to know, loud and clear, why there were horse balls in his spaghetti."

Teddy and his dad and I broke out laughing all over again. Teddy's mother tried to look at the ceiling, but she couldn't help it. Her lips curled. As much as she tried to dislike me and the monkey, I sensed she was beginning to accept us.

"It was so gross, Dad," I said, when I caught my breath. "Just like you said. People were spitting out their food, and everyone groaned and pushed back their plates."

"But Gab's the one you got into trouble," Teddy said. "Little Alton kept a straight face, kept on eating. But I thought Gab was going to wet her pants. Something about laughing hysterically while you're apologizing loses all credibility."

Those were the days.

Teddy not only taught me how to laugh and how to dance and how to make love, he taught me how to drive, a motor vehicle, that is, but, uh, not so fast.

It was just a silly dream of mine, anyway, to one day drive a metallic green Mustang, like the one I had seen at a car lot on Geddes Street when I was 12 years old. I must have mentioned it to Teddy, because one day he surprised me with a 1965 Mustang.

"It needs some bodywork and a paint job," he said. "But it only cost $200. And after I prime it, Chico said he'll paint it."

"But I don't even know how to drive."

"Take your permit test, and I'll teach you."

But teaching me to drive was more like a travesty than a tryst, like a Ricky and Lucy marathon but, no doubt, the process only amused onlookers.

After months of wear and tear on each other's nerves, something clicked into gear for me. My shoulders back and my chin up, I waved good-bye out the opened window. I was ready to take on the highway.

But as I peeled out of his sister's driveway, Teddy yelled at me, like Ricky yelling at Lucy, saying I was driving too fast, that I was showing off.

Halfway down their hill, I jammed the car into park.

As Teddy's Monte Carlo screeched out in agony, he punched my arm, not hard, not on purpose, more like a kneejerk, as if I had hit him in the gut.

Then he growled at me like I had just attacked his cubs, something about stripping gears and blowing a transmission, like I knew the first thing about cars.

"Switch! Now, dammit," he ordered, opening the passenger door.

"No. I'm driving," I yelled back, gripping the steering wheel.

But when I saw the distress in every line on his face, I recoiled like a turtle's head withdrawing back into its shell.

"I'm sorry," I cried. "I promise. I won't do that again. Please!"

"Check your mirrors," he said, shuddering, then straightening himself in the passenger seat, and shutting his car door.

I smeared the beads of tears on my cheeks and checked both mirrors. And then gently, ever so gently, I shifted the car back into gear.

Teddy never yelled at me again when I was driving. And I never threw the car into park again, while moving, of course.

By the time I got my driver's license, Teddy had fiber-glassed my car and had primed it, and Chico had ordered the metallic green paint. But I couldn't wait. I had discovered some very cool seat covers that were green and had dream catcher designs in them. And I would need floor mats and a steering wheel cover. So I kissed Teddy and Alton good-bye and drove to Northern Lights.

I drove straight to the mall with no problem. But by the time I finished shopping, the clouds had darkened and big fat raindrops were splattering on my windshield. I circled the entire parking lot, I swear, six times, but I couldn't find a left exit to save my life.

My leg was weak and trembling as I held down the brake pedal and surveyed the area, my teeth clenched, my fingernails brushing my cheeks raw.

"Beep-beep!"

I flipped the car behind me the finger.

Fuck it!

I pulled out and turned right with the flow of traffic, terrified I was going to get lost. Just seconds later I spotted it to my left, a sign that read "SYRACUSE," with an arrow pointing toward a left ramp. I veered from the right lane toward the sign.

"Bam!"

A car in my blind spot—not that I looked—slammed into me, shattering the driver's-side window and the windshield. And like a William Tell arrow shot from a high-powered cross-bow, my car nailed that sign right between the poles, and knocked it down.

Freaky deaky!

The driver who chucked my car into the median pulled off to the shoulder and sprinted toward me as I scampered from my car toward him.

"Are you okay?" he asked.

"I'm fine. You?"

"We're fine," he said, pointing to small children in the back of his station wagon.

"Thank god!"

He searched my eyes as I stood there shivering at dusk in the rain in my shorts and halter-top. Then his eyes wandered, and I followed them, looking at myself, realizing that my flesh sparkled with slivers of glass.

"You're probably okay," he said, as we exchanged insurance information. "But just the same, you should get checked."

He ran back to his kids, and I ran across the highway to a pay phone.

"I'm fine," I told Teddy, my teeth chattering.

He left Alton next door with Chico and drove to meet me.

"Everything's going to be fine," he repeated every 30 seconds or so as he rigged up a rope from the engine and fed it through the busted windshield to maneuver the car back home. Then he handed me his keys and told me to follow him.

"Are you tripping? The car's too dangerous to drive like that. I can't let you. Get it towed!"

"I've got this," he said. "I'll be right in front of you. We'll drive very slowly with the flashers on. It's a straight shot, not even five miles. We can do this."

"I can't drive! I just had an accident! I can't stop shaking. And I think I'm going to throw up. I'm never going to drive again!"

"You will," he said. "You have to. It's like being thrown from a horse. Unless you get right back in the saddle, you'll be afraid of it for the rest of your life."

"Okay, well, I got thrown from a horse, and I never rode a horse again. And I'm fine with that!"

"Come on," he said. "You can do this. I know you can."

"You're mad at me, aren't you?"

"Of course not. Why would you even think that? Accidents happen. I'm just grateful no one was hurt. Now, come, on, Gab. Take the keys. Please. We'll be fine."

I smacked the keys out of his hands and followed him out to the road, promising myself that if anything happened to him driving the car with a rope in the dark in the rain, I'd never forgive myself.

But just as Teddy promised, we made it home in 20 minutes, without a hitch. After he carried Alton into bed without waking him, he sat me in a facing chair in the kitchen. All I could think about was the game Operation as he surgically removed each sliver of glass with a pair of tweezers. As I cocked my head and marveled at the intense kindness in his eyes, my emotions splashed all over the kitchen, like someone had shaken up a bottle of Dr Pepper.

"Love will keep us together" [http://bit.ly/1IAbZoK], I sang my heart out to him.

Those were the days.

"I know you said you have a son, but—"

The doctor who did my exploratory laparoscopy scratched his head as he turned the pages of my chart.

"But considering the chronic infections and dysplasia you've exhibited since you were a preteen," he said, "and the lesions and layers of scar tissue built up on your tubes and ovaries. Hmm. Did you mean to say that you adopted?"

I assured him that I pushed for four hours prior to giving birth to little Alton just three weeks before my 18th birthday, and he assured me that if I hadn't, I might have regretted not ever having children, because my reproductive organs were beyond repair.

After my first hysterectomy, I woke up every four to six hours, so they said, only long enough to scream out in pain, at which time a nurse would come running with a shot of morphine and stick it in one of my hips to knock me back out.

I say first hysterectomy because once the doctor cut me open, he decided that reconstructive surgery was worth a try, considering my age. The routine procedure turned into a mini-series, and I was strapped on my back to an operating table for eight hours.

Three days later, when I regained consciousness, the doctor patted himself on the back as he told me about the miracle he had performed.

"I never consented to that," I wailed. "I just wanted to be rid of the pain. And I know my body. The pain will come back, and I'll have to have another surgery."

"Well, if you hadn't been sleeping around, you wouldn't be having these kinds of problems," the doctor said, backhanding the air as he turned on his heel and left.

Sure enough, a few years later, I had to have a second hysterectomy. But something was still wrong. Another few years later, I was stuck, literally. My spine froze at a 30-degree angle. I was unable to stand erect or touch my toes for a year and a half before one of the best neurosurgeons in Syracuse, New York, Dr. William Stewart, spotted a shadow in my CT myelogram and diagnosed me with a rare birth defect of the spine.

And they said it was all in my head.

Two days after my back surgery, they admitted Teddy into the same hospital—after my brother-in-law found him unconscious on the floor of our new flat, next to the marble-topped table smeared with blood. He had a ruptured spleen, which they had to remove.

We theorized that it had ruptured two days before when he had hit his stomach against the sink when he had climbed through the kitchen window headfirst because I forgot to leave the front door unlocked before I left for the hospital. We figured driving around in a utility truck all morning to visit different job sites probably exacerbated the internal bleeding.

Of course, I felt guilty, but Teddy said it was worth every stitch as the nurses took turns pushing my wheelchair down to his room on the third floor, where we took turns feeding each other ice-cream.

Those were the days.

As Teddy's mother put it, he and I were living in sin, dating for two years, then living together for two years. But to her that was better than the alternative: marriage.

"I want to get married," became my new mantra, although I really didn't know why, anymore than I understood my drive to go to school at age 3 or to have a child at age 15.

Perhaps, I thought it would please my parents and grandparents, that is, by doing the 'right' thing, the Christian thing. But it would have pleased them if I would go to church, too, but that wasn't happening. Besides, Jesus and I talked every day. And I didn't get any kind of vibe from Him that He was condemning me.

Perhaps I thought we should get married for the sake of our two sons, both from broken homes from our previous marriages? Hmm. Or was it the principle, the idea that Teddy refused to make that kind of commitment to me, denied me the greatest intimacy of all between a man and a woman?

I think that's it, you know?

In the winter of 1978, we chattered apart in the cold between rage and passion for nearly six weeks, with the ultimatum of marriage or nothing, hanging over Teddy's head.

Then one afternoon, I shucked my cloak of pride and trudged through a foot of snow. I knocked, then stood at the door, waiting, though I had the key. When Teddy opened the door and saw me, my hair white with snow, my cheeks red, my nose running, he took me in his arms.

Neither of us said a word.

On St. Patrick's Day, March 17, 1979, a J.P. married us, and Ma and Dad and Lizbet and her husband witnessed the occasion. When Teddy's mother and his sister and his ex-wife figured out that we were married—six months later—it was as if they waved the white flag. Up to then, Teddy had tried to do the impossible: He tried to appease us all.

"Anything to keep the peace," was his motto.

But that fall, as we began to wear our wedding rings in public, Teddy's mother stopped calling me Gina. And she gave up inviting Teddy's exes over the same day as she invited me. Gina stopped dragging Teddy into court every other month to increase Charlie's child support. As a matter of fact, she gave up Charlie all together, demanding that we raise him or she would put him in a home for delinquent boys.

Teddy's mother, who now insisted I call her Mabel (though I never could quite bring myself to call her by any name), began calling me two and three times a week when the kids were in school to take her somewhere or another. Sometimes we went to Denny's for lunch after her doctor appointment, and then to the drug store. And after her surgery, I drove down to her house every day to help her bathe and eat and run her errands.

When she recovered, we would drive around town on trash day, stopping to pick through other people's bins. Other days we roved cemeteries, reading tombstones and picking mushrooms. She taught me the difference between the edibles and non-edibles, the poisonous from those that were not. When we returned to her house, she would clean the mushrooms while she watched her soaps, explaining to me the latest plots, while I washed her dishes or waxed her furniture or mopped her floors.

Those were the days.

"You're like joking, right." I said, searching his face.

But Teddy wasn't smiling.

"But like that's not fair!" I moaned. "Like when do we ever have time for us? You work two jobs as it is. And now you're like telling me you want to work our vacation, too? That's like insane."

"It'll be an extra $1,000 on top of my vacation pay," he said.

"Like big deal. You keep working and working. But when do we ever get to like enjoy the benefits?"

"Well, I was hoping to surprise you," he said. "But I've been saving for a down payment on a house."

"Oh?" Now he had my attention.

"Besides," he said. "It's not like work at all. We'll spend lots of time together. You'll love it. You'll see. I used to work it every year. It's a blast."

Own our own home?

"I just don't get it," I said. "Rides and cotton candy? There's like other stuff I'd rather do."

"I know," he said, and I recognized that look, his look of surrender.

"Oh, never mind!" I said. "But next year I get to choose where we spend our vacation."

"Fair enough," he said, and we both chuckled.

"Now that that's settled," he said. "I want to point out that we can still have a little mini vacation without the kids the week before the fair. Charlie can spend the week with his mother and maybe Lizbet will take Alton for the week?"

Oh, my. Like total freedom all week with no kids. It was like we were dating all over again when Teddy picked me up each night after work and drove us to the fairgrounds. He picked up his free entrance pass and stickers and drove right up the midway, showing me the way around.

Every few minutes he'd pull off to chat and introduce me, and we'd never decline a draft beer or a Coney hotdog or a gyro or a sausage hoagie. We watched carnies erect roller coasters and Ferris wheels and merry-go-rounds and tents and temporary buildings as Clydesdale horses and goats and roosters trotted through the streets. And by the time the gates opened for the public, I felt like part of the State Fair family.

As I drove through the gate onto the fairgrounds on opening day, I tooted at the vendors and the carnies I had met.

"People probably think we're big shots," said Dad, who sat in the back seat with Charlie and Alton.

"It's a good thing we don't have to walk," Ma said, as she looked out the passenger-side window. "I'd never make it through this crowd."

"Look! Look!" The boys shouted every few minutes. "I want to go on that. Can we go there?"

"They'll be plenty of time to do everything," I said. "We're going to be here every day for 10 days."

I pulled up to the Ice House where Teddy worked, and he motioned me into a small lot to park. And the party began. For the first hour we ate soft pretzels and mustard and nachos and drank beers while the kids ate funnel cake and cotton candy.

"It's time to make my runs," Teddy said, when we finished eating. "Where would you like to begin?"

"Let's start at the buildings and like work our way up to the midway to the rides," I said, and the kids groaned.

"I'll be right back," Teddy said.

We stood there looking around for a few minutes, when someone pulled up alongside us.

"Your chariot awaits," Teddy said, and I burst out laughing at the sight of him, a 240-pound grown man sitting on a little ice scooter.

"Hop in," he said, pointing to the back of the scooter, which had just enough room to seat two. "Ladies first."

He dropped Ma and I off in front of the Dairy Building and went back for Dad and the boys. As Teddy helped the kids and Dad out of the ice scooter, we all laughed. I could see Dad felt a little silly, but that he loved every minute of it. Ma had been to plenty of county fairs in Weedsport when she was a kid, but she and Dad had never been to the New York State Fair.

"I'll meet you guys at the Haddock Paddock at six o'clock," Teddy said.

But we saw him sooner than that. Every hour or so he'd pull up and toot, and hand us coupons for free sodas or tickets to go on rides or free game tokens. And every time he took off again, we laughed at the sight of him on that scooter.

"I have never seen anyone so happy to be working in my whole life," Dad said.

"I've never seen anyone who loved life like him," Ma said. "He's always on the go, living every minute to the fullest. Does he ever take a day off?"

"No he never does," I said, looking at Teddy as he glanced over his shoulder and smiled at me before disappearing around the corner.

Those were the days.

At sunup on Saturday mornings, Teddy and the boys would take off. They'd stop first at Teddy's mom and dad's house to mow the lawn or rake the leaves. Then they'd stop and buy pastries or sticks of pepperoni or lobster. Other times they stopped at Carmen's, who gave them fresh vegetables from his garden, or Mario's, who gave them homemade sausage, or Billy's, who gave them venison. When I'd wake up around 10:30, Teddy and the kids would be downstairs waiting for me with some delicacy or another. As I approached the kitchen, I could hear the kids and Teddy chatting and giggling. As soon as Teddy spotted me coming through the living room, he'd lead the kids in a song that was written the year I was born.

"Here she comes, Miss America" [http://bit.ly/1OUuX1w].

I'd smile as I sat on my throne at the kitchen table, likening myself to Vanessa, tee-hee, still wearing my bathrobe, my hair spiked, my eyes not yet adjusted to the light.

Teddy would cook breakfast while the boys recounted riding a horse or a tractor or witnessing the birth of a new litter of puppies, one of which we later named Lucky, because Alton was lucky I would let him have a dog, considering I still hadn't overcome my fear of dogs, which my mother says stems from the time a bulldog got in my face when I was a toddler in a stroller.

Teddy would take naps between kung fu movies while I chauffeured the boys to a birthday party at Chuck E. Cheese's or a bowling alley or a roller-skating rink. On Saturday nights we designed our own pizzas and drank beer while they baked. We played penny poker until four in the morning with Ma and Dad, and with whoever else felt like dropping by. And on Sundays we hosted an open house, with Teddy and I taking turns each week cooking our specialties. Throughout those years, Dad and I would look at each other, bug our eyes, grin, and flex our neck muscles.

But we never got stuck in a routine with Teddy, who was always off seeking one venture or another to make a few bucks, whether he called G-52 at the bingo hall or ran the blackjack tables on casino nights at Geppettos' or ran around a clambake selling raffle tickets. I don't think he ever made much money though, because he always invited Ma, Dad, and me. And by the time he paid our way in and treated us all to beers or sodas and popcorn or burgers and raffle tickets or bingo sheets, or whatever else the event called for, he must have been lucky to break even.

But he always had that look on his face when he was working, that look I saw in his face on opening day at the New York State Fair, that look like he was in his glory.

"Even if I win a million bucks," Teddy told the storeowner every day when he played 3-1-7 in the lottery. "Save me a job."

As I revived my dream to become a writer, Teddy dreamed of the day he'd retire and work at Balduzzi's Big-M as a box boy.

Those were the days.

19
the blockage

Early 1980s to Fall 1985

"I HAVE WRITER'S BLOCK, MA" I complained, puffed up, like the expression in and of itself proved I must be a writer.

"I feel like I've run into a brick wall, myself," she said. "You realize I earned my LPN over five years ago, but I'm still working as a home health aide!"

"I know! And I've been blathering about my correspondence course—you know, all their great feedback—but I just don't know how to apply their advice to my writing outside the assignments. Sometimes I think they just stroke my ego because they want my next installment."

I had been trying to write the true story of how Zach and I (a month after my divorce) had abducted Lizbet at age 15—at my parents' request because they were afraid she was going to get knocked up—and drove her 1,600 miles from Syracuse, New York, to Cheyenne, Wyoming, hoping to save her soul. I didn't just sell seven rooms of furniture for $1,000 on a moment's notice, I sold out my favorite little sister, because back then I sensed that something crucial deep inside me was missing, and even though I didn't know what, I was sure I would find it in Cheyenne.

I would lie in bed with Teddy, our legs entwined as we watched *Knot's Landing* or *Hart to Hart*. But my writing was always in the back of my mind. Once Teddy dozed off, I'd bobble out of our waterbed and tiptoe down the stairs. I would sit at my roll-top desk in my office off the dining room, and swivel back and forth in my matching oak chair, and admire my Commodore 64, which I had just upgraded from the Commodore 32. I would appraise all of the accessories on my desk, from the paperclips to the stapler, as the fresh mountain-grown aroma of Folgers filled the air. Then I would push back the computer, and open my notebook.

At first, tidal waves of words ripped ashore, flooding page after page and notebook after notebook, as I spilled my guts into the margins, as pen after pen dried up. But day after day as I reread my work, my ideas seemed to sink deeper and deeper until the narrative evolved into a very messy, complicated story about religion and philosophy and psychology, and I realized I was in way over my head.

Scrawling and scratching as I sipped from my coffee mug, with its skyline of New York City fading, I would rip out one page after another, but it felt more like I was ripping out my own heart.

When we got custody of Charlie, Teddy had said he preferred I stayed at home because he was gone all the time, anyway, and he made enough money, anyway, and—

"Hey! No objections here," I had said. "That'll give me more time and flexibility. You know I've always wanted to be a writer!"

That was two years ago, and I really didn't have anything to show for it.

"What if, what if!" I said, reaching across the table and lighting Ma's cigarette. "What if we take night classes together? You can go for your RN and, um, I guess writers get like English degrees. Anyway, we could take some of the prerequisites together, like freshman English and math, until we branch off into our own fields. It would be like freakin' awesome!"

"Get me the phonebook," Ma said. And we were on our way.

Teddy thought it was a great idea, especially taking classes together so we wouldn't have to drive through downtown alone at night. But Dad complained that she never used her first degree—even though he knew damn well that the Visiting Nurse Association passed the new RN requirement just a few weeks after Ma graduated.

"What am I supposed to do when you're at school?" he asked her.

"You can come over here and hang out with the boys, you know," I said, wishing he would, but, you know.

Just as Dad's arguments repeated themselves, Ma's determination to answer her inner voice did not vacillate.

But that first semester in English 101, I was mortified. I had written a spectacular interpretation of "The Artificial Nigger." As one who had been lost much of her life, I was quite familiar with the expression, "Oh Gawd I'm lost! Oh hep me Gawd I'm lost!"

"Fuck Therasia 101!" I screamed through my tears at the "C" on my essay, which she had taken a bloody scythe to. "Fuck her! What does she know? Everyone knows I'm a great writer. Everyone asks me to write for them, even my mother, who got a B!"

Then when I wrote an essay after reading Émile Durkheim's *Suicide*, having firsthand experiences with wanting to die, Professor Doppelgänger, who looked just like my father (who had a theory that his father, who he caught a glimpse of once kneeling at his bedside like a child, was secretly Jewish—that's why he would never speak of his religious beliefs or the past)—anyhow, he gave me a great big fat "D," said he couldn't even tell if I had read the book.

Dickweed!

Once I swallowed my anger—which then wedged itself in my gut like a rotten peanut still in its shell—I saw the dumpster, and a new urge arose: to be sucked down a sewer.

"No rush," Ma said, when she arrived a half hour early to pick me up for class one night. "We've got time for a cup of coffee. Your father was just getting on my nerves."

Teddy had been in the bathroom for half an hour, but when he heard Ma talking in the kitchen, he finally emerged.

"Hi, Ma," he said. "Can I ask you a question, as a nurse?"

"Of course," she said.

"It's kind of weird, I'm warning you, but my bowel movements look like beef jerky."

"Teddy! Like, that's gross, you know!" I said.

"I'm serious," he said.

"Have you tried taking a laxative?" Ma asked.

"I think I'll go put my makeup on upstairs—while you two talk some shit," I said. "Ha ha."

First, Teddy tried laxatives, then Pepto-Bismol for the cramping, then prune juice. But nothing worked.

"Still like beef jerky," he told Ma.

"I think you should see a doctor," she said.

Teddy wasn't the kind of guy who would go to a doctor, but he trusted Ma. So he set an appointment with the factory doctor, who then sent him to a specialist, who sent him to another specialist. But it wasn't until he missed two days of work in one month that I realized the problem was serious.

"I think they're giving you the runaround," I said. "Make another appointment. But this time I'm going with you."

"I don't know what good you think you're going to do," he said. "They've done every test imaginable. The doctors think it's all in my head. And maybe it is."

That day, the damn doctor kept us waiting for two hours past our scheduled appointment, and I was steaming by the time a nurse led us into the examination room.

"You're taking up my valuable time every other week complaining about constipation," Dr. Ventura said, shaking her head. "But all the tests are negative. I don't know what you want me to do for you."

"Look," I said, but she wouldn't look at me.

"I've been with him for almost eight years, and he's never once complained about pain. And up until recently, he hadn't missed a day of work in 16 years. Something is wrong, and I'm not leaving this office until you figure it out."

"Well, what exactly would you like me to do?"

"You could at least do like an exploratory surgery to see if something's constricting his bowels, you know? I once had a cyst like the size of an orange, but the doctor couldn't find it until they went in through my belly-button and looked around. You could at least do something like that. And if you still don't find anything. Then, like fine, we'll get out of your hair."

"If you want to put your husband through unnecessary surgery, then fine. We'll set it up. If that's what you want, Mr. Franklin?"

Teddy nodded.

Ma, Dad, Zach, and I took turns pacing the floor in the waiting room the morning of Teddy's exploratory surgery. The scheduled 40 minutes stretched into three hours before Dr. Ventura graced us with her presence.

"I'm sorry, Mrs. Franklin," Dr. Ventura said, looking at her clipboard. "We found a tumor the size of a grapefruit constricting your husband's lower intestines. We removed as much of it as we could. And I can't say until the results come back from pathology, but it looks malignant."

The results of the biopsies confirmed it three weeks later. The oncology specialist delivered the diagnosis: Teddy had non-Hodgkin's lymphoma, cancer of the lymph nodes, and it had metastasized.

The first round of chemo shrunk the tumor to the size of a pea. But it was not enough. In the next two years, through several rounds of chemo, Teddy lost his hair—and about 100 pounds.

He eventually became too weak to work, so I took a temp job at Diebold, where Zach worked. I felt guilty leaving Teddy at home while I went to work, but I found comfort knowing that between Lucky and Uncle Gilbert, Teddy was never alone during the day. Of course, everyone knew Lucky's credentials: a mutt Teddy had adopted for Alton, a mutt who loved and was loved unconditionally. And Uncle Gilbert was a certified public accountant—and a certifiable health nut and germ fanatic—who had been living in Troy, New York, for the past 20 years, where he roller skated almost every night and traveled on weekends to skate in competitions and exhibitions.

But it was an unfortunate fact that children had begun to dominate the rinks, and mothers and fathers were uncomfortable with a grown man hanging around the rinks, striking up conversations with their little girls.

"I have spent $6,000 a year at those rinks," he said. "How dare they ban me after I supported them all these years!"

By moving to Syracuse, Uncle Gilbert would have a clean slate at the area rinks, plus a handful of his great nieces and nephews who loved to roller skate to provide a great cover for him.

We brushed under the carpet the story that Grandma Williams told us years ago when she caught him doing something inappropriate with the three-year-old daughter of one of her neighbors. We thought it possible that Grandma Williams misinterpreted whatever she saw that day. Or maybe we just turned a blind eye because Uncle Gilbert was like a godsend, who not only took care of Teddy during the day but also took the kids skating several nights a week—and paid for it.

Still, there was no denying. Uncle Gilbert was a little weird.

"Do you know the speed by which a germ can travel from the toilet bowl to your toothbrush," Uncle Gilbert asked Alton, when Alton left the toilet seat up.

"That's kind of sick when you think about it," I said. "I love this house, but why would they build the bathroom off the kitchen?"

"Plumbing logistics," he said. "I know you leave the door shut, but flushing the toilet with the lid up sprays bacteria instantly up to 20 feet away."

"Gross!" Alton said, as he went back into the bathroom to put the seat down.

"Anyway, I have enough savings to get by for about a year," he said. "So you don't need to worry about Teddy when you're at work. I'll be here."

And he came to the house everyday to drive Teddy to chemo or to the store or to get lunch or to get ice-cream or to go to a movie or to play hands of gin rummy.

At night, after work, I cooked dinner, then we would chat or play a game or watch a show. Then Teddy and Alton would kiss me goodnight at eight or nine. Teddy tired easily, and Alton had school the next day. But I would still be wired. Uncle Gilbert would run up to the store and pick us up a six-pack of beer. Then we'd sit at the kitchen table until midnight, while I picked his brain, then argued with him over our differing views about God, about the meaning of life, about lifestyle preferences among gays, about abortion, about life in general.

By the fall of 1985, Teddy had lost another 20 pounds, and he was self-conscious about being bald, or so I thought, because he kept making jokes about it. I suggested we buy him a wig, and he went along with the idea. But it didn't look natural, the way he lifted it up off his head, like it was a top hat, nodded to his friends, and then plopped it back down. I realized then that it was me who felt self-conscious about his hair loss.

"Your baseball cap's like totally fine, you nut," I said, the next time we were getting ready to go out.

But wig or no wig, Teddy's buddies backed off it seemed when we entered the bar.

"Hey, man! How you doin'? Good to see ya," they'd say, then pat his back or shake his hand.

"Sorry, we were just heading out," they would add, though they still had half a beer in front of them.

"It's nothing personal," Ma assured me. "People just don't know what to say or do. They feel helpless. So they avoid him, not him, per se, anyone who is sick, especially if they are terminal."

"That probably explains why Charlie moved back to his mother's right after Teddy was diagnosed," I said.

"Yeah, he probably just doesn't know how to deal with it. And then there's some people who have this crazy idea that cancer is contagious. So I don't know. People are weird."

Teddy didn't seem to notice. Or maybe he understood better than the rest of us. But when he started talking crazy about maybe going with the guys to New York City, a trip sponsored by Geppetto's Athletic Club, I was afraid for him.

I, myself, had passed on the last two women's bus trips to Atlantic City because I felt uncomfortable. And Teddy had been too sick the last two years to go on the men's trips. So it seemed weird to me that Teddy would want to go considering we had lost touch with most of the old Geppetto crowd since he had been diagnosed.

"Maybe you should talk to Ma," I said. "See what she thinks."

Teddy adored my mother, whose eyes would sparkle whenever she imagined that she had found Teddy before I did.

"I would have dumped your father to snag him if I found him first," she would tease me.

"Hey! Maybe we got our soulmate wires crossed somehow," I would answer. "Considering you two are closer in age than we are."

The story never got old, the story of the night that it occurred to me to ask Teddy how old he was. I was sitting on one end of the bar talking to the girls, most of whom were in their early 30s. Granted I had just turned 20 a few months before, but I was mature for my age.

"Hey, how old are you, anyway?" I hollered down to Teddy, after his friend Rita happened to bring up the subject of age.

"What?" he cupped his hand around his ear.

Two hours later, after I had forgotten all about it, Teddy flashed the inside of a matchbook cover before my eyes, with a number written on it.

What? 3-8?

Then it hit me!

I fell off my barstool, literally.

But shocked as I was, age made no difference between us. In the years to come Teddy and I and Ma and Dad became the best of friends.

"Hello, Dad? Can I talk to Ma," Teddy asked.

"Hi, Ma. I got a question. You know how I used to go to New York City with the guys every year? Well, the trip's coming up next month, and well, you know I'm on crutches to get around sometimes. But I've been feeling better lately, since that last round of drugs."

Teddy paused.

"Yeah, I really want to go. But, you know, Gab's not so sure it's a good idea."

He listened.

"Yeah, okay," he said. "I guess that's true. Really? You think?"

Teddy looked at me and smiled.

"So how are you? Good for you, Ma! We'll see ya later."

I waved to him not to forget.

"Oh, yeah, Gab says hi. Love you, too, Ma."

"What, what?" I asked.

"Ma says I should clear it with my doctor first. But if he doesn't see a problem, then, hey, she thinks I should go for it."

"But what if you have a relapse? And how are you going to keep up with the guys on crutches?"

Teddy shrugged and grinned, and his eyes lit up.

"Ma says they have doctors in New York City, too, just like here. Plus, she could see no reason my doctor wouldn't prescribe me a wheelchair. Or rent one if I have to. What the heck!"

"That is wicked cool!"

"By the way, she got an 'A' on her art project."

"She is freaking wicked cool."

Ma was the coolest, smartest person in the world. And I loved her beyond capacity. But I still had some tiny reservations in my heart when I drove Teddy to Geppetto's that morning.

As we sat in the parking lot waiting for everyone to arrive, I recalled our vacation with his sister and brother-in-law. They had all been to New York City before but, of course, I had not. Like adults taking a child to the circus for the first time, they hung back and beamed at me while I swooned over every sight and sound.

They winked at each other from the street corner when I jumped on the back of a 6-foot tall stranger—much like I had jumped on Zach's back when a dog barked—to catch a glimpse of Elizabeth Taylor and Richard Burton leaving the Broadway theater. And I left them sitting on a bench feeding pigeons while I struck out on my own to climb the spiral staircase to the crown of the Statue of Liberty.

Then we laughed at Rodney Dangerfield, live, at Dangerfield's in Manhattan. And stood eyeball to eyeball with the Rockettes at Radio City Music Hall and the hookers in Times Square and the garbage that lined the streets. Then smooching with Teddy in the horse-drawn carriage, that turned around at the entrance to Central Park. And clinking glasses in the bars and clubs, whose lights only dimmed at daybreak. Then risking our lives to hail a yellow checker taxi. And it was just like in the movies, the graffiti and the dark hooded figures that lurked in the underground subway. I thought my lungs were going to burst as I ran like hell back up the stairs to street level, where the three of them waited.

But my most breathless experience transpired on the observation deck more than a hundred flights up as I remembered a fantasy I longed to fulfill while swinging at the Tot Lot years before. It didn't matter that the Empire State Building wasn't the tallest building in the world anymore, or even the tallest building in New York City, for that matter. I had made it to the top in my mind.

Of course, the Empire State Building was the furthest thought from the minds of the men who were boarding the tour bus that morning. They were hyped up over a drinking binge away from the civilized world where they could moon each other and toilet paper the walls and put lipstick on the first guy to pass out. As the guys took turns fighting over who was going to push Teddy's wheelchair, Teddy caught my eye and winked at me.

I nodded and smiled.

One of my girlfriends spent that weekend with me, and we went out on the town on Saturday night. When we got home at two in the morning the kids were still up, that is, the babysitter and Alton and her son and daughter. As we fumbled with the key in the lock, giggling like two schoolgirls, the kids opened the door. They were in a frenzy over some psycho movie they had just watched, and they barricaded us in front of the door as they recapped the gory scenes they had just seen.

"You know you shouldn't be watching scary movies," I said. "You know you'll have nightmares."

No one noticed that the storm door on the enclosed porch didn't shut and latch behind us.

The next morning as I held my head together on my way down the stairs, Alton came running to the bottom of the stairs.

"Mommy! Mommy! Something's wrong with Lucky. Hurry. She's in the driveway. I touched her, and she's hard."

"Oh, my god," I cried, as I ran after Alton out the back door.

Lucky lay at the head of the driveway, in front of the shed. A bloody trail told us how she spent her last moments. A single trail of blood led up to the gate that we kept locked so she couldn't get out. When she couldn't get in, she turned around and nudged the shed door, which we also kept locked. Then she turned to head back down the driveway, but she must have sensed her plight. The trail of blood ran around and around in a circle, and then stopped where she had collapsed. I touched her. But like Alton said, her body had stiffened like as if she had been stuffed by a taxidermist. I ran back into the house screaming. Like Alton, I needed another opinion.

"Dawn! Something's wrong with Lucky. Please! Come quick. She's in the driveway."

Dawn followed me out the back door, and confirmed it for Alton and me: Lucky was dead.

She called animal control, and once they removed the body, I hosed down the driveway. That Sunday night, the night Teddy was arriving back from New York City, I offered to tend bar at our neighborhood tavern just two blocks away, because I didn't want Teddy to walk into our house and wonder why Lucky didn't come running. I thought it would be better if I told him first.

That night as Teddy told us all about the crazy stunts the men pulled on each other, I forced a smile.

Crap.

I wanted him to enjoy the moment. But he might wonder later how I could laugh at a time like this.

Damn. This was like totally a bad idea.

Our friends vacated the bar one by one, not wanting to leave, but not wanting to stay either. When Teddy and I were alone, I told him that Lucky had somehow gotten out the night before, that she got hit by a car, we presumed.

For the next several moments, Teddy's wails echoed off the walls. I had never seen a grown man cry out loud.

The next day, I called in sick for myself and Alton. While Alton drew a picture of Lucky, Teddy carved a cross out of wood. And I gathered stones. We didn't have her body, but we felt her spirit as we built a little burial site in a corner of the backyard.

I hate you, God!

That night, I sat at the kitchen table with my eyes glazed over, sipping a beer and smoking a cigarette.

"Cheer up," Teddy said, handing me a souvenir.

I unwrapped a Little Orphan Annie coffee mug, and he read the caption, "The sun'll come out tomorrow."

20
the praying hands

"Yesterday, December 7, 1941—a date which will go down in infamy—United States of America was suddenly and deliberately attacked by naval and air forces of the Empire of Japan.... I ask that Congress declare that since the unprovoked and dastardly attack by Japan on Sunday, December 7, 1941, a state of war has existed between the United States and the Japanese Empire."[1]

Franklin D. Roosevelt
"The Infamy Speech" [http://bit.ly/21cfYqi]
December 8, 1941

"**Dec 30.** "Palestinian terrorists staged coordinated attacks [on December 27, 1985] on check-out counters of the El Al Israeli Airlines in the Rome and Vienna airports, hurling grenades and firing submachine guns into crowds of holiday shoppers. Fourteen persons, including four Americans were killed and more than 110 wounded in the two attacks that left the two terminals strewn with bloodied bodies."[2]

Newspaper Clip
"Terror strikes Rome, Venice airports"

Chronicle of the 20th Century
[http://amzn.to/1NKQu9z]

December 1985

TEN DAYS BEFORE FINAL EXAMS BEGAN, the day before the anniversary of Pearl Harbor Day, another day began that would go down in my personal history as a day of infamy.

The whole family had met that morning at the Greyhound bus station to see Patrick off to Fort Bragg. As the bus pulled out of the parking lot, Ma blew her nose and cleared her throat.

"Why don't we all go to lunch?"

"I'd like to, Ma," Zach said. "But I've got a meeting in 20 minutes."

"Sorry, Ma," I said, wincing as a knife twisted through my gut instinct. But Zach had gotten me the job, and we had driven to the station together, so if he had to go, I had to go. One by one, each of the other five kids said they had to go, too.

We all hugged good-bye, of course not knowing that our lives would be forever changed by dinner time.

I was supposed to clock out at 5 p.m., but at 5:20 I was still answering the phone.

"This is Gabrielle. How can I help you?"

"Gabby! It's me, Lizbet. We're at St. Mary's. Dad and I, in the emergency room. It's Ma. We don't know if she'll make it. Get Zach and hurry!"

My muscles shook like Jell-O as Zach drove the couple miles to the hospital, where we found Dad and Lizbet standing in a hallway.

"They took her that way," Dad said, his face ashen.

"What happened?" Zach asked.

"I don't know. I mean, your mother had a dizzy spell in the parking lot at the station this morning. She stopped and held onto the car for a minute. But then she said she was okay, and I forgot all about it."

"Did you go to lunch," I asked. "How was she then?"

"No. She decided to skip lunch and drove me straight to work. Then about 4:00, she called me and said she felt weird so she was coming here. I told her to pick me up on the way. As soon as we got here, they took the insurance information and told us to take a seat. But your mother couldn't sit. She kept pacing, saying something's wrong. I went up to the desk twice but they were busy, said we had to wait our turn."

"Did they even take her vitals?" I asked.

"They never touched her. She was pacing and mumbling and, all of a sudden, she stopped and looked at me for a split second. Then, with her last breath, she whispered, 'Help,' as she began to faint. I managed to reach her just in time to break her fall. But by the time she hit the floor, she was already turning blue. Then everyone came running—nurses, doctors, everybody. They got her on a gurney and rushed off. Told me to wait here."

"Hayes family?" a doctor asked. "Please, this way."

We followed him to the hallway outside Ma's room in intensive care. I could see glimpses of her when someone went in or out. As the doctor tried to explain, the door opened again, and just like in the movies, I heard someone yell, "Clear!" Then I saw someone else pounce on her heart with a machine to jolt her back to life.

After failing to stabilize her for an hour and 20 minutes, they injected a saline solution into the main artery of her left leg to jumpstart her heart, which stabilized her at last. The doctor sent us to a waiting room where we held a vigil for her. Meanwhile, Grandma and Grandpa Williams started a prayer chain that spread across the country within hours. But on Monday morning, her doctor painted a hopeless picture.

"She's stable for now," he said. "But we can't tell how much oxygen was getting to her brain during resuscitation. Even if she survives, she will most certainly have brain damage. She'll likely be on life support, perhaps in a vegetative state, for the rest of her life. Plus the saline injection caused massive tissue damage, partly because of her weight. Gangrene has set in. We'll probably have to amputate. And if we have to resuscitate again, we might have to inject the solution in her right leg, and that's prone to gangrene, too. So I highly recommend that you sign a DNR."

"I'm not signing anything," Dad said. "She's only 49 years old for god's sake. You keep her alive, whatever it takes."

"I'm so sorry, but it gets worse. We got her lab work back. Even if she lives, she has terminal lung cancer. She has about three months to live regardless. We're only prolonging her suffering without any regard for the quality of her life."

"You do what you've got to do," Dad said. "But no one's pulling the plug."

"I don't know what you expect from us, a miracle? She's been a heavy smoker for 30 years and her weight," the doctor said. "We're not gods, you know."

"Exactly. You're not God," I said.

Then I took Dad aside.

"Have faith, Dad. Don't leave it up to the doctors. Put her in God's hands. If it's her time, God will take her, whether they intervene or not. If it's not, she won't need resuscitation."

"I asked God to give me a sign yesterday," Dad said. "And then last night I dreamed that your mother was sitting up in a chair in her hospital room, when she suddenly looked up at me and asked me, 'How are we doing financially?'"

"There's your answer," I said.

Dad signed the paper not to resuscitate, and we all prayed.

That afternoon, I drove Teddy to his chemo therapy, a new concoction not yet approved by the FDA. But it showed promise.

"I'm really sorry," I said. "Being gone all weekend."

"Hey, we're the ones who are sorry that we couldn't be with you when you really needed us. But we said our prayers, and she's going to make it."

I nodded and smiled.

As he sat in the recliner under the skylight in the midst of green plants and mellow music, the medicine dripping into his arm through the intravenous needle, Teddy began to itch and turn red. Instant hives appeared all over his body as the technician came running and snapped off the intravenous. But it was too late. The reaction was severe, and they admitted Teddy to the hospital next door.

That night Teddy's doctor pulled me aside and told me the words I had dreaded to hear for more than two years, the very words Mom's doctor had said that morning.

"You do realize that your husband only has a matter of months?"

I called Lizbet and asked her to take Alton for the night so I could spend the night with Teddy. After visiting hours, the hospital lights dimmed, and the nurses made their last rounds before the shift change. As the evening lull settled in, I curled up with Teddy in his hospital bed and chatted. Unlike the robust man who once held me, he trembled with weakness as I caressed the fragile bones in his rib cage, his wrinkly neck, his sunken jaw line, his hollow cheeks and eye sockets, his fuzzy head. I asked him the question I had been mulling over for months but couldn't figure out how to ask.

"If you knew you were dying," I said. "Not saying that you are, of course. Just curious. If you knew you were dying, and a magic genie said he would grant you one last wish, what would it be?"

"That Ma gets better," he said, hands down, like nothing else mattered.

"Um, well," I don't know what answer I expected but he caught me off guard. "Well, what if the genie doesn't have power over life and death? Then what would your last wish be?"

"To take Alton to Disney World," he said, again without hesitation.

"Oh, my gosh. That would be so awesome. Remember that summer? We were still newlyweds. Real class, in your brand new fully loaded Monte Carlo—with a sunroof!"

"Our Monte Carlo," he said. "And how could I forget the best time of my life?"

"Remember the Tunnel of Love?" I asked, giving him the wink, wink.

"No one saw us. I swear," he said, and we smiled.

"And on the way home," I said. "Just when I thought the best times were over, you took that little detour to Myrtle Beach?"

Teddy stretched out length-wise, pulling his hands behind his head.

"Can you feel the sand between your toes?" I asked.

Teddy wiggled his toes and smiled.

"Can you hear the sound of the waves thrashing against the shore? Can you smell the ocean breeze filled with salt and fish and seashells?"

Teddy took a deep breath, sighed, and then dozed off.

In the weeks that followed, Teddy found comfort in a particular ornament, a gift to him from Grandma and Grandpa Williams. In the middle of the night or in the middle of the day, anyone passing through the living room could escape his attention as he focused on the white glow of the ceramic praying hands. Even in broad daylight, even when you couldn't see the hands glowing, Teddy wouldn't let anyone turn off the nightlight.

Day by day, he watched less and less television, and instead occupied long hours alone just staring at those praying hands.

I couldn't understand it. I kept wanting to turn on the television so he wouldn't be bored. But he said no, he was fine. I worried that he might be depressed, giving up, but he said, no. He was content. I took sly glances at him each time I found an excuse to walk through the living room. And each time I was amazed at how peaceful he seemed, the flecks of topaz still glowing in his brown eyes, the only feature that hadn't changed since the cancer attacked his body.

Unlike Teddy, I had a war raging within. One minute I was grateful that at least for now they were both alive. But the next minute I was cursing God for robbing me of both my husband and my mother at the same time. When I wasn't using all of my energy to hide my anger, I was feeling guilty, guilty when I was with Teddy because my mother needed me, and guilty when I visited my mother because Teddy needed me. And no matter which one I was with, I felt guilty about little Alton. He had just turned 12 years old a week before his grandmother's seizure, and I couldn't imagine what it must be like for him. It seemed all of our worlds were caving in around us and, quite possibly, coming to an end.

Alton felt her absence, but he couldn't see his Grandma lying motionless in a critical care unit, hooked up to a half a dozen machines. He couldn't see his Grandpa, who had become a permanent fixture in her room. But he could see his daddy, who once roused him on Saturday mornings for adventures. He could see him lying on the couch, too weak to get a glass of water at times, too weak to even make his way to the bedroom, that had once been my office. I would go to check on Teddy, and find Alton already sitting on the floor next to him on the couch, messaging his back and whispering to him. We'd sit with Teddy until he dozed back off.

Every day at lunch and after dinner, I drove up to the hospital to see Ma. Day after day, no good news. No bad news. All we could do was wait and pray.

"Teddy says, hi, Ma. Sends you his love. And Alton, too. They want to come see you, but Teddy's been really weak since that last round of chemo. And Alton's too young. They won't let him in. But they send their love. You're in their prayers."

Ma would stare through me, like as if she were the one alive, and I was just an apparition. I knew she probably didn't know who I was even if she could see me. She did nothing to indicate that there was any life left in her. But the pulsing green light on her heart monitor confirmed she was alive. The rhythmic beeping of the various monitors and the rising and collapsing whooshes of the machine that pumped oxygen into her lungs had become comforting sounds. Like a symphony orchestrated by Bach, the various instruments integrated to create a magical melody of peace and solitude and life. She looked serene in her own little world.

In the middle of January, one of my professors called to say that the registrar could wait no longer.

"I hate to do this to you. I can only imagine what you are going through. But if it helps, I would be happy to come to your house to administer your makeup exams myself," he said.

Of course, I felt guilty for not going to the hospital that day. But I had to study. I consoled myself with the fact that I had never missed a visiting hour yet.

Besides, Ma would never know the difference.

The next afternoon, when I walked into her room, I could not hear the calming music of her machines. I could not hear the heart monitor or the whooshing of oxygen pumping. And I could not see the blank stare in Ma's eyes. At the very instant I stepped into her room, she lifted her head from her pillow, pointed her accusatory finger at me, and gurgled hoarsely through her tracheotomy.

"You come every day!"

Shock and guilt and awe raised goose bumps on my arms and neck as I rushed to her. A quick glance at Dad, who had jumped up when she spoke, told me he was as confused as I was.

What does this mean? What are the implications?

Dad and I stood there for a minute, wanting to be in two places at once. We didn't want to leave Ma's side. But at the same time we were itching to charge from that room and call her doctor.

I pushed the call button, and a nurse appeared.

"My mother just spoke," I squealed at her. "A whole sentence. Please page her doctor right away. Tell him the Hayes family would like to hold an emergency meeting as soon as he can get here." The nurse didn't hesitate. Anything we wanted, whenever we wanted a meeting, or any special privilege, the hospital staff bent over backwards to accommodate the family of a woman who collapsed and turned blue on their emergency room floor six weeks earlier, the woman whose vital signs they overlooked taking that December afternoon, the woman who refused to die against all odds.

"Do you realize what this means," I asked Dr. Thomason. "If she knew I missed a day, then she recognizes the passing of time. She's aware of the sun setting and rising. Do you know what I mean? She recognizes my face. She can speak. But now, ever since she spoke, she's lapsed back into her trance state. I don't understand."

"Well, we've had to keep her heavily sedated, you know. Ever since that day she ripped out her heart catheter. Then there's that time she yanked out her tracheotomy tube."

"I know, but that's why you strapped down her wrists. Why did you need to sedate her, too?"

"Well, we didn't want to keep her strapped up all the time. It seemed inhumane. So we increased her morphine."

"I didn't know she was even on morphine! Did you, Dad?"

"I thought she was in a coma," he said.

"Well, no wonder she's lying there like a zombie," I said. "I want her off the morphine, now."

"The morphine's highly addictive. We'll have to decrease gradually."

"Do what it takes," I said. "But don't restrain her. If she rips off her heart catheter or her trachea tube, leave them off. If she's ripping them off then she either doesn't need them or she doesn't want them."

Dad's eyes widened and he clenched his jaw. But he didn't say anything. Ever since Ma had been admitted, I was once again his "Little Toughie." And the stuffed tiger that had "My Little Toughie" written on its T-shirt, which Dad had brought me when I was in the hospital for my first hysterectomy, proved it.

He looked at the doctor and nodded.

Within a few days, Ma ripped out two of her tubes again, so the doctors left out the tube that led from the hole in her neck to the machine. But they left in the tubes that led into her lungs just in case. And they removed the heart catheter from the little pocket they had sewn up in her chest. Her face squished with determination, like a child demonstrating her independence for the first time, as she fumbled with the levers on the bed, shooing away our helpful hands, and raising the head of her bed to a sitting position. After shimmying to a comfortable position, she reached out to touch us, to look at us, as if she had been blind and could see us for the first time.

A pulmonary specialist began intensive respiratory therapy, teaching her how to breathe all over again. And a speech specialist brought her markers and an erasable board, alphabet stencils, tablets on an easel, and pencils so that she wouldn't strain her newfound voice. Soon Ma was writing, shakily, with misspelled words. The vast vocabulary she had built filling in crossword puzzles and playing Scrabble had been erased from her mind. But she was doing more than we ever thought she would. She was communicating.

Two weeks later the doctors had her up and sitting in a chair. And Dad and I were floored when we walked into her room one afternoon, and she asked, "How are we doing financially?"

She wanted to know how Dad was able to pay the bills when he was at the hospital every day all day. She wanted to know about his job. Did he get fired?

"Nope," he said. "The doctors knew I couldn't live without you so they signed the papers saying I needed time off. Now look at me. I'm here with you every day, and my paychecks are still coming in, paying the bills." He chuckled.

He began to tell her about their house, modest as it was, and she listened in awe.

"The bills are all paid?" she asked. "A phone in every room? A television set in every room? A stereo system? A dishwasher! And wall-to-wall carpeting! We must be rich," she said, her eyes glazing over.

"But the kitchen's not pink anymore? Hmmm. How long have I been sleeping?"

That semester, I got a 'B' in history and interpersonal communications, and I got my mother back, well, physically, anyway.

21
the athlete

> Now you will not swell the rout
> Of lads that wore their honours out,
> Runners whom renown outran
> And the name died before the man.[1]
>
> Excerpt from "To An Athlete Dying Young" [http://bit.ly/1I9aFMD]
> By A. E. Housman [http://bit.ly/1YovwF2]

"**Jan. 31.** The [space shuttle] Challenger exploded in a ball of fire shortly after it left the launching pad at Cape Canaveral on January 28, [1986,] in the worst accident in the history of the U.S. space program. The disaster was witnessed by thousands of spectators in Florida and by millions of television viewers."[2]

> Newspaper Clip
> "Challenger explodes as horrified nation watches"

"**April 2.** A bomb exploded aboard a TWA jetliner today on its flight from Rome to Athens, killing four passengers as they were sucked out of the hole blasted in the airplane's side. ... A group called the Arab Revolutionary Cells later issued a statement saying that the bombing was in retaliation for 'American arrogance' and last week's clashes with Libya in the Gulf of Sidra."³

Newspaper Clip
"Four killed as plane is bombed in Athens"

"**April 5.** La Belle Club, a discotheque in West Berlin, rocked to a different beat last night when a bomb tore a hole in the floor and collapsed the ceiling, killing two and wounding 155.... Located near U.S. Army housing, the club is popular with American G.I.s, one of whom was killed.... West German officials think the Libyan Government of Col. Khadafy may have been responsible."⁴

Newspaper Clip
"Terrorists bomb Berlin G.I. hangout"

"**April 30.** The Soviet Union has acknowledged that a major accident occurred four days ago at a nuclear generating plant at Chernobyl in the Ukraine. West German and Swedish experts say the Soviets have asked them for help in handling the accident, believed to be the worst in the history of nuclear power."⁵

Newspaper Clip
"Chernobyl accident releases deadly atom radiation"

Newspaper clips from
Chronicle of the 20th Century: The Ultimate Record of Our Times
[http://amzn.to/1NKQu9z]

Spring 1986

"WHAT A CRAZY WORLD WE LIVE IN," Dad said at the close of every news broadcast. From our little world in one hospital ward or another, we watched the tragedies of the world flicker by us on the television suspended from the ceiling and newspapers from the gift shops.

"The sun'll come out tomorrow," Teddy reminded me on those days it rained heaviest in my soul. And the sun did come out on Valentine's Day, the day the doctors moved Ma out of intensive care and into a private room.

The nurses granted us unheard of permission to plug in colored lights and a small Christmas tree in her room. We strung up the pictures her grandchildren had colored for her during the months she was unconscious—pictures of Rudolph, and Santa, and Jesus in the manger—and the cards that wished her a merry Christmas, a happy new year, a happy anniversary, and a happy valentine's day.

That Friday evening, as couples lingered over dinner, sniffing rosy bouquets, clicking their glasses of wine, and feeding each other chocolate strawberries, Ma's family—her husband and children and their spouses, her brothers and sister, her Mom and Dad, and her grandchildren, too—gathered in her room and sang Christmas carols and exchanged the presents that had been stacked in closets since the bagging of dried up Christmas trees. Ma and Dad's cheeks both had a rosy glow when she opened his gift, a huge clock with roses for hands that moved from hour to hour.

Throughout that evening, I should have been ever so grateful. But something was missing.

Like 15 fucking years of my mother's memory!

I just couldn't stand it that she thought her favorite ice cream was strawberry, now, not Nutty Buddies. I made the mistake of telling her so. And Dad told her, too. He told her that, no, she's mixed up, silly thing, that strawberry ice cream was his favorite flavor, not hers. But she would not concede.

"No. Strawberry has always been my favorite," she had said through her tears.

So rather than make her cry, I bit back the tears. The close friendship we had developed during the last 10 years had been erased from her memory. And I fought back the urge to rebel like a teenager when she looked at me like I was 15 years old again, pointing her finger at me, making demands, her hands on her hips. I tried not to cringe when she recalled the good old days, not the days when us kids were small, as she used to recall, but her own childhood memories, which were much more vivid to her now, for some odd reason.

Just as she had forgotten, I tried to forget, too. I tried to forget that her grandchildren seemed somewhat familiar to her, and I tried to forget that the sight of Teddy only rang a distant bell. I tried to forget about her cancer, too. But the doctors didn't forget.

In March, her doctor scheduled a biopsy to determine what stage her cancer was in since they first diagnosed it.

"Nope," Dad said, holding up his hand. "When she's strong enough, I'll take her to Roswell. I'm not letting you treat her. You know that."

"Of course," her doctor said. "But it may be a while before she can travel. So let us just take a look, see what's going on."

"Fine," Dad said. "But I don't care what you find. You're not treating her."

The day before Ma's release, Dr. Thomason stood before us, hemming and hawing.

"The biopsy came back negative," he said. "The cancer is, uh, gone."

"Or it never was," Dad said.

That day we rejoiced. But for years we speculated. Was it Grandma and Grandpa Williams's nationwide prayer chain that healed her? Or did the lab technicians mix up her test results with someone else's? Or was it something far more sinister, as Dad suspected?

"The doctors planned to shoot her up with cancer like they did Oswald," Dad said. "If we sue, their liability might be lessened if she were dying of cancer anyway. But to cover their butts, they just had to have one last look at your mother's lungs before they discharged her, so I wouldn't take her to Roswell. Tricky dicks."

That was Dad's theory. And when my faith in miracles teetered, I agreed with him.

The doctors discharged Ma on March 15, and two weeks later, the day before Easter, Teddy was re-admitted into the hospital.

Lizbet and I were heading out the door to take the kids bowling, but Teddy objected as I paused by the couch to give him a peck on the forehead.

I sent Lizbet and the kids ahead and sat beside him on the couch.

"What's the matter?" I asked. "You were fine a few minutes ago."

"My shirt. Can't get it on," he whispered.

I tried to feed his arm into the pajama sleeve. But his arm was heavy. It flopped to his side.

"Are you just doing this right now because you don't want me to go?"

He didn't answer.

I draped the shirt over his shoulder and tried to pull his other arm through the sleeve but it, too, went limp.

"Are you okay?"

He tried to speak but his words slurred, his eyes rolled.

I dialed 9-1-1, and in seconds the sirens ripped through the air as the rescue squad drove the two blocks from their driveway to ours. The paramedics, who had known Teddy for years, rearranged the living room furniture to clear a path as one of them took his vital signs.

"His pulse was so weak. We almost lost him," he said, after the others heaved Teddy's stretcher into the ambulance. "Good thing you called when you did."

Late that afternoon I stood alone at the window in the smoking area and watched as the sunset painted streaks of golden light over the tops of buses and cars as they went about business as usual.

Teddy's doctor cleared his throat, and I butted my cigarette.

"I just reviewed the sonogram," he said, as I followed him down the hallway. "The tumors are putting pressure on his lungs and his heart. I'm sorry. He doesn't have as much time as we thought. With chemo he might live three more months. But without it, it's just a matter of weeks."

I called my mother. When she said she would pray, my heart crumpled like she had just wadded it up like a piece of scrap paper and tossed it in the trash.

We don't need fucking prayer. We need you!

"Mrs. Franklin. You can see your husband now," the nurse said. "A room upstairs will be ready shortly."

I followed her to Teddy's temporary room, and I marveled at the sight of him, lying there as if lounging on a faraway beach, his eyes closed, his right ankle propped up on his bent left knee, his hands folded behind his neck, a light smile on his lips.

"I'm thirsty," he said.

"What would you like, sir?" I asked. "A Pink Lady? Or perhaps, a Golden Dream?"

"A Golden Dream would be nice," he said.

I walked over to the sink and poured a little water in a paper cup.

"Here you go," I said, guiding the cup to his mouth.

The look of relief on Teddy's face turned to panic as he began to choke. I screamed for a nurse.

"Don't you know he can't have anything to eat or drink? He's on morphine! His muscles are too relaxed to swallow," the nurse said, sitting him forward and patting his back. "You could have drowned him," she said.

"How was I supposed to know? How come no one told me?"

That's when I knew it was all my fault. Teddy almost dying. Ma almost dying. I was causing it all myself, maybe unwittingly, but just the same.

Zach arrived a short while later with the preacher from his new church. Pastor Davis shooed me from the room so he could ask Teddy if he knew where he'd go this night should he take his last breath. I had known all along, and so had Teddy, of course, to be with his Father in heaven. But somehow the pastor took credit, as if he, himself, saved Teddy, which seemed a little premature to me anyway, praying over Teddy, like a priest delivering last rites, as if Teddy were going to die that night.

As Pastor Davis, Zach, and I stood by, the doctor came in and explained to Teddy the prognosis.

"I know this is difficult. We'll honor your wishes."

"I'm ready," Teddy said. "No more chemo."

We each paraphrased the doctor to ensure Teddy understood. But he didn't budge.

"I'm ready when the Lord is ready," he said. "No more chemo."

That night when I got home, I sat at the kitchen table drinking beers and chain smoking. I couldn't stop thinking and hoping that Teddy hadn't heard me on the phone with the bill collectors, promising that they'd get their damn money when Teddy's life insurance paid off, assholes.

I hope he isn't letting go just so I can pay the bills! What kind of fucking monster am I, anyway?

The chocolate Easter bunnies and peanut butter and coconut eggs and bags of jelly beans and yellow marshmallow peeps still hid in the closet among the purple straw baskets and pink and yellow grass, though it was almost three in the morning on Easter Sunday.

I need to fill the baskets before Lizbet brings Alton home in the morning. What will he think if the Easter bunny hasn't come yet?

But I couldn't move. So I sat there watching my life with Teddy pass before my eyes, remembering everything between he has two strong arms—he can help—to the ruptured spleen that I was convinced caused his cancer cells to go awry—to the helplessness he felt when he couldn't put his shirt on that afternoon.

It was a quarter to 4 in the morning when I called the hospital.

"Hi. This is Teddy Franklin's wife," I almost whispered. "Sorry to bother you, but I just wanted to check on Teddy. I hope he's sleeping well?"

Before she could answer, I heard a buzzer go off in the background, a sound I knew well. I could see the red light flashing over the doorway of Teddy's room.

"I have to call you back," she said.

As the dial tone buzzed in my ear, I began to chant.

"Please, God. Please don't let him be in pain. And please, please, don't let him be afraid."

As I looked at the clock at 4 a.m., a stillness filled my soul. No tears could be shed. No words could be thought. No joy. No grief. I blew my nose and then waited for the phone to ring.

That was the end of the story. Some unknown woman occupied my mother's body, and Teddy's body was void of soul, both of them gone from me, gone so far away from me, I thought as I scanned the vast sky in the months that followed.

I tried to maintain the strength that I had pretended for so long. But something in me had died. Anger filled the drunken gaps in my memory, anger at God, anger at the world. The branch of faith that I had clung to throughout my 20s snapped. I felt like the little kid standing next to the dumpster in the school courtyard long ago.

At my request, the monument place etched praying hands onto Teddy's tombstone, but I didn't have much to say to God after he took Teddy from me on March 30, 1986. I didn't have much to say to Uncle Gilbert, either, after that night he crashed on my couch a few weeks after Teddy died. I awoke before dawn, my jeans around my ankles, my top up, my thighs wet, the matchbook I had put in my bedroom doorjamb on the floor.

22
the vulture

My love in other veins, your heart I maimed;
It bulged from your eyes red with intellect.

With smart drops filing down your face, you framed
love's art with reasons no logic should select.

My heart thrashed yours; it shared not your desire.
It chafed your brain; broke blisters scabs can't mend.

Your love, small facts, stripped mine, as if for hire,
But more than friends, I could not comprehend.

Your passion smashed its fists and swore its rest;
Refused, you loved no reason we should live.

You stalked my withheld breath, your last request.
Perhaps guilt clogged your educated sieve.

To be God's guest wants sad rape repented;
You left me bonds, your hair, both blood-clotted.

Gabrielle Hayes Franklin, 1988

June 1986

SOMEHOW UNCLE GILBERT CONSTRUED our late night debates as lovers' quarrels. He thought once Teddy died, I'd be a free woman, free to marry him. I loved him, of course. He was my uncle. Maybe I did mislead him. Maybe I did clamor for his attention in my time of need. Maybe I was asking for trouble.

But I didn't sit on his lap!

The thought of marrying him, having an affair with him, with anyone, for that matter, repulsed me. And I told him so.

"Besides, that's incest for god's sake," I said. "You're my mother's brother!"

"The taboo against incest only arose because they claimed genes from the same pool deformed the offspring," he said in his calm, intellectual voice. "But for eons people accepted it as natural. Royalty required it. They had to marry a distant cousin or uncle to keep the royal blood in the family. And the practice dates back to time immemorial. How do you think Adam and Eve's children procreated?"

"I don't care. And it wouldn't matter if we weren't related. Teddy just died two weeks ago. Give me a fucking break. You mean all this time that you've helped us, kept us company, helped me with Teddy and Alton, you were really just a vulture waiting for Teddy to die so you could swoop in and take his family? You're sick!"

It was true, and I knew it. Uncle Gilbert was sick. He had been seeing a psychiatrist for years. The men in white coats wrested the gun he held to his own head and strapped him in a straight jacket more than once when he went crazy at his home. His only son, Gilbert, Jr., was there. He witnessed his father's suicide attempts, called 9-1-1, once when he was 10, and later when he was 14. Grandma Williams had relayed the stories to us a long time ago, but they were vague memories now. I thought he was better. He said his depression had been cured, though he still mourned Gilbert, Jr., who hanged himself at age 19 in a vacant lot a year ago, the morning before the court martial that was to hear the case against him after MPs busted him and his friends with a couple of reefers.

It was tragic. But I could never fill his void. And I could never allow him the opportunity to take advantage of me while I was sleeping again. I barred him from my house. I refused his phone calls, and I avoided going anywhere where I might run into him.

Time after time, he'd hunt me down, beg and rationalize and implore me to reconsider. I would cup my ears, tell him to stop. I couldn't bear to hear any more. I couldn't take the pressure, the stress, the shame. But he wouldn't give up. He left dozens of incoherent messages on my answering machine, something about love and suicide and lonely and a gun and a note and please and I beg you, words that tingled my scalp, words that disrupted the rhythm of my beating heart, words that sickened me.

I listened to the last message he left, gulped the last of my beer and pressed delete. Wallowing in alcohol, I couldn't think what to do. I need Teddy. I need my mommy. I can't cope with my own needs or tend to Alton's needs, how can I cope with him?

He's been threatening suicide for as long as I can remember. Surely I won't be his last straw.

Fully dressed, I crawled into the bed in the guest room, where I often slept after Teddy died, and pulled the sheet and blanket over my head. I had just dozed off when the phone rang. My eyes opened but I did not budge. It only rang twice. I stared into the darkness, waiting.

"Mommy. It's Grandma," Alton said, nudging me and handing me the phone. "She said it's important."

"Ma?" I snapped on the lamp and sat on the edge of the bed.

"Gabrielle. It's your Uncle Gilbert. I don't know. I have a feeling something's wrong."

"Did he call you?"

"No. I haven't talked to him all week. It's just a feeling. Something's wrong. Please, can you send someone to his apartment to check on him?"

"Mother. I can't do that. It's past midnight."

"I'm worried sick. Please, there must be something you can do."

I sighed. I can't tell her about his advances, his demands, his threats. She wouldn't understand.

"You don't understand, Gabrielle. I'm serious. I'm afraid something terrible is gonna happen. I can't explain it. I just feel it. Please call the police."

"Ma! What am I supposed to say? My mother has a feeling?"

"Yes. Tell them your mother is concerned about him. Tell them to just go to his apartment and check on him. If everything's okay, then great. But at least they can check."

Her voice sounded so rational, so familiar, the words she used, the way she said them, like as if my old mother was back, the remarkable woman with just the right mix of common sense and intuition. Then I caught myself, reminded myself that ever since the hospital discharged her two months ago she had a tendency to overreact to everything.

"Ma, why don't you just get some sleep? We'll talk in the morning."

"Gabrielle, I'm telling you. It might be too late in the morning. Please call the police. Please?"

"All right, Ma. I'll call."

I hung up and collapsed back into the bed.

How will I explain such a weird request to the police?

Before I could think it through I dozed off. I had drunk enough beer to knock me out until at least noon the next day. But something awoke me, a dream, a feeling, I don't know. I sat up. The red numbers on the digital clock glowed in the dark.

Only 4 a.m. But I was wide awake.

Something is terribly wrong. I can feel it.

I went downstairs to the kitchen, but when I turned up the dimmer switch the bad feeling intensified. I turned the light back down and, in the semi-light, I set up Mr. Coffee. As the machine began to gurgle, I sat at the kitchen table and lit a cigarette and a scented candle. In seconds, the flames raged from the wick, flaring, it seemed in warning.

Somebody is watching me. I can feel it.

My eyes scrambled to search the kitchen window, but I could only see the reflection of the flames. I jumped up and pulled the string, crashing the blinds to the windowsill. I butted the cigarette in the ashtray, then crept into the dining room, then the living room, pulling shades and blinds and closing drapes until I was satisfied that no one could see in.

Back in the kitchen I poured a cup of coffee. Sat down. Lit another cigarette. The flame in the candle relaxed. I meditated on it while I waited for day to break.

If only Teddy were here. If only my mother—that's right! She called me last night! Oh, my god! What if she was right?

I remembered what happened just two weeks after Teddy died, when Uncle Gilbert, my sister Lizbet, and I flew to Texas for Peter's wedding. I was happy for my brother but a wedding so soon after I lost Teddy, that would tear me up. I couldn't even bear to walk through a lingerie department. But everyone said it would be good for me to get a change of scenery. Against my better judgment I went, and it was even worse than I had imagined. Physically, I sat in the pew at the church, but my mind was screwed up, my heart torn apart. I didn't even realize how bad I looked until I saw the wedding pictures.

We were grateful when Mariah's in-laws invited Uncle Gilbert to stay with them. Their history went way back to when our mother and Mariah's mother-in-law were kids, and they had some catching up to do. Meanwhile, Lizbet and I rented a hotel room so we could do our own thing, since most of the family in Texas didn't drink or smoke. We had just checked into Room 112, got our luggage unloaded and unpacked, when the phone rang.

"Gab. It's Mariah. I don't mean to alarm you. But I think you should know. It was just so strange. Uncle Gilbert just called here. I didn't answer the phone, Rick did. But Rick thinks it's weird, too."

"Oh, my god. What?"

"Rick said he sounded weird, like he was drugged or something. But he recognized his voice."

"What did he say?"

"Well, like I said. Don't be alarmed. He said, well. I'll just spit it out. He said Room 112 won't need a wakeup call tomorrow morning."

"Oh, my god! How did he even know what room we're in?"

"I don't know, but Rick thinks he might have had our number and the hotel number written on the same piece of paper and dialed our number by mistake."

"That's it. We're out of here. I'll call you when we find somewhere else to land."

When I relayed Mariah's message to Lizbet, she required no explanation. She repacked the bags while I called the front desk to request security. The hotel manager arrived at our door in 30 seconds flat. He stood watch while we waited for security. Then he helped us carry our bags to our rent-a-car while security surveyed the area. He even refunded our money on the spot.

It was well past midnight, but Lizbet and I were both wired. She drove all night stopping for coffee at various convenience stores along the way. We talked and shared theories and questioned motives, both of us too afraid to stay in one spot for too long, afraid we would miss our wakeup call.

When we called Mariah the next day, she said Uncle Gilbert had arrived with her in-laws for Saturday brunch that morning, like nothing had happened.

Maybe nothing would have happened. We'll never know. But how could I tell my mother about that night? Maybe she was right. Maybe I should have called the police last night.

I looked at the clock. Almost seven.

"Rrrrrrinng!"

The phone damned near threw me against the wall.

"Hello?"

"Gabrielle! You're okay. Thank God! Did you call the police?"

"Ma! I was just going to call you, but I didn't think you'd be up yet."

"I never went to bed. I've been sitting here by the phone praying all night."

"I'm so sorry, Ma. I've been sitting here myself since four o'clock this morning, thinking about what you said. You're right, something is wrong. I'll call the police right now. I'll call you right back."

I dialed 9-1-1.

At 8:30 that morning, the doorbell rang.

The police! They said they'd go to his house. Not my house.

"Mrs. Franklin? You placed the call to check on a Mr. Gilbert Williams?"

"Yes."

"What's your relationship to Mr. Williams?"

"He's my uncle, my mother's brother. She's the one who wanted me to call," I said, getting defensive. Either I was in trouble for wasting their time, or I was a prime suspect in his death.

"I'm sorry to say, Mrs. Franklin, but Mr. Williams expired at about five this morning."

I listened in a daze.

A gunshot wound to the head. Something about rigging the trigger of a rifle with a broom handle. At about five this morning the couple in the next apartment. A poker game. A night cap. They heard him stomp up the stairs. Breathless. How odd. So late. His car never left the driveway. Must've taken a walk. An engine backfiring. Something about a note. Not a suicide note. Nothing to explain it. But he left a note declaring his executrix, a certain Gabrielle Elizabeth Franklin.

"It's not your fault, Gabrielle," Ma said, when I called her. "Even if you had called the police at midnight. They would have checked on him, and he would have been fine at that hour. I can't explain it, but I was more worried about you, and Lizbet, too. I didn't want to scare you, but I think he was sick."

She's remembering something.

"Where is Lizbet, anyway? Have you heard from her?"

"Knock, knock," Lizbet hollered, letting herself in.

"She's coming in the front door as we speak."

"I don't know about you," Lizbet said. "But I've had the most freakin' weird night. The kids have been up half the night. Do you mind if they take a nap in the guest room?"

"Sure. I got Ma on the phone. What happened?"

"I don't know. Call me a fruitcake if you want," she said, after she sent the kids upstairs. "But I woke up out of a sound sleep at four this morning with the worst case of the heebie-jeebies I've ever had in my life. I was so nervous, I couldn't sit still. So I bundled up the kids, and loaded the car. We've been driving around all night. It felt like that night that Uncle Gilbert said we wouldn't need a wakeup call. So what's up with you guys?"

"This just gets like weirder and weirder," I said. "You're not going to believe this."

Ma had it all figured out by the time she walked in the front door 10 minutes later.

"I don't know exactly what he was planning to do. But look at the timeframe," she said, sounding a lot like the mother I used to know. "He's outside your house Lizbet. As he works up the nerve to carry out his plan, you suddenly rush the kids to the car and peel out of the driveway. I know you peel, Lizbet."

We snickered.

"This confuses him. He wonders. Is someone onto him? He walks the four blocks to your house," she said, looking at me. "He stands in the shadows for a few minutes. Before he can make his move, the lights go on at four o'clock in the morning. You're suddenly running through the house pulling all the drapes and blinds. Something's amiss. He senses it. He wonders. How could they know? Maybe the cops are onto him, too. He becomes paranoid. He walks the 10 blocks to Onondaga Ave. Rushes into his apartment at 4:30. Maybe my prayers screwed up his plan. Maybe he had a change of heart. Maybe he felt guilty. I don't know. But thank God you both are okay. I would have never forgiven myself if my brother did something to hurt either of you."

Ma meant well. But she had it all turned around. If I hadn't misled him, if I had only given in to him, this would have never happened. He loved me. But in his hour of need I shut him out, scoffed at his suicide threats when I should have been helping him to get help. After all he did for us!

By the time Lizbet and I went to Uncle Gilbert's apartment later that week, the maintenance crew had already ripped up the blood soaked carpet and scraped away the particles of his brains that had splattered on the walls. The owner seemed to think it was important to share the details with me. But, he pointed out, the crew could not scrub clean the blood that had penetrated through the carpet and stained the wood floor underneath.

"Let me know what it costs for the wood and labor to replace that section. I'll cover it," I told him.

"Oh, no. I didn't mean that. Don't worry about a thing. I just want to express my sympathies for your loss."

"Thank you."

I avoided looking at the bloodstained floor as Lizbet and I fingered through all his belongings, sorting out items for his sisters and mother and the Salvation Army. I felt like a traitor, an intruder. I felt dirty. As executrix of his estate, I would do my duty to clear up any of his outstanding debts and see to it that all monies or properties were distributed according to his Last Will and Testament. But not now. I choked back the acid that had spurted up to the back of my throat. I dumped the contents of his filing cabinet into a trash bag and threw it in the backseat of my car. I would sort through his life at home, later, after the memorial service, over a few drinks, maybe a lot of drinks.

Six weeks almost to the day since we buried Teddy, we congregated for yet another funeral. But Uncle Gilbert's passing was quick. No funeral parlor or church service. No digging a grave or purchasing a tombstone. No chilling blasts from military bugles. With a few short words in a room that looked like an ordinary conference room, where only a few pictures of Uncle Gilbert hinted to the occasion, we said our good-byes in 10 minutes, and went on our way. That's the way he wanted it. Aunt Sylvia asked for the urn. She'd sprinkle his ashes over the sites he requested, she promised, even if it was illegal.

Later that week, Lizbet helped me sort through his personal papers. I had already read his Last Will, which left all of his worldly possessions to Gabrielle Elizabeth Hayes to dispose of as she saw fit. Done. Cremate him and dispose of his ashes, some near his son's grave, the rest over the Atlantic Ocean. Done.

But as I read through his papers, his life insurance policies, his pension plan, his bank statements, his savings plans, everything, I became nauseous. The man who had killed himself over me, left me every dollar to his name.

"The life insurance companies will never pay the benefits on those policies, though," Lizbet said. "Not in the case of suicide. They have clauses you know."

We read the fine print to confirm it, but both policies had clauses promising to pay the benefits even in the event of suicide. So I was rich. Between what Teddy's insurance paid and Uncle Gilbert's insurance I had nearly a half a million dollars. But I didn't want Uncle Gilbert's money. The sooner I could wash my hands of it the better. In the days that followed, I spent the money right and left, buying anyone and everyone in my path anything they wanted, dropping thousands of dollars at a time.

All the money in the world couldn't fill the gaping hole that Teddy's death had left in my life, as well as lots of little holes around the house, considering that we no sooner buried him when his mother demanded back everything she had ever given us.

Not only did Teddy's mother and sister disown me, but they forbid Charlie to visit me—after I gave him all of Teddy's clothing and jewelry. Poor Teddy. If he were in his coffin I know he would have turned over. At first, I went shopping and bought new stuff to fill all the little holes. But still unable to fill the void, I remodeled the kitchen, and added on a new master bedroom and bath, and put blue siding on the house. But I still could not bear the emptiness. And I couldn't bear the burden of my parents, who leaned on me when I needed them the most. So I sold the house for twice what we paid for it and moved 500 miles away to Virginia Beach, where I bought a new house, one that had no memories in it, and registered full-time for college, where I would meet Emily Dickinson, who understood exactly how I felt.

> I lost a World—the other day!
> Has Anybody found?
> You'll know it by the Rows of Stars
> Around its forehead bound.
>
> A Rich man—might not notice it—
> Yet—to my frugal Eye,
> Of more Esteem than Ducats—
> Oh find it—Sir—for me!¹

I lost a World—the other day!" [http://bit.ly/1NgRXso]
By Emily Dickinson [http://bit.ly/1NKcGkb]

This work is licensed under the Creative Commons Attribution-ShareAlike 3.0 Unported License. [http://bit.ly/1NgRXso].

To view a copy of this license, visit http://creativecommons.org/licenses/by-sa/3.0/. [http://bit.ly/1Olbl8c]

Or send a letter to Creative Commons, PO Box 1866, Mountain View, CA 94042, USA.

PART VI

"Four is an age-old symbol, probably going back as early as the Old Stone Age. It occurs in the image of the 'four rivers' of Paradise, the cradle of mankind. The four cardinal points of the horizon, the four phases of the moon, the four seasons, the four primary colors, etc., are fundamental elements in our experience of the world. Probably the structure and cell division of all organic matter are also based on this primordial law of fourness; it forms a natural pattern of order within all created matter. The quaternity of the elements as the basic substances of the world in the old natural philosophy, the four humors and temperaments in ancient medicine....According to Gnostic view, the quaternity was the soul itself.... For Pythagoras the square was the symbol of the soul... .

"Jung has found the quaternity to be the archetypal foundation of the human psyche.... Mandalas, those remarkable images for meditation found in oriental religions and also occurring frequently in the psychic development of the modern occidental, are based on the quaternity principle and may be regarded as symbols of the 'primordial order' of the psyche... .

"The important place assumed by the quaternity in our dream suggests its decisive significance for the dreamer's psyche. According to Jung, the appearance of four in a dream always symbolizes something very important that concerns the dreamer personally; it is, as it were, the creative background of a religious experience that has been vouchsafed to man in endless variations throughout his history."¹

> Jolande Jacobi [http://bit.ly/1I5eBmU]
> *Complex Archetype Symbol*
> *in the Psychology of Carl G. Jung*

23
the dead babies awaken

DEAD BABY

I'm holding a dead baby, which I recognize as a newborn, even though it's the size of a toddler. The baby is very heavy and hard. I feel both appalled and immensely sad.

Dream Journal Entry
January 1990

BABIES DROWNING

Small children between two and four years of age keep falling in the water. Two or three babies have already drowned and are floating on top of the water. I'm devastated but no one else seems to notice.

Dream Journal Entry
January 1990

FREDDIE KRUGER WANTS MY NEGATIVES

I had dropped off some pictures of Teddy at a photo processing place to have duplicates made. The person who was to develop the photographs calls me on the telephone to question me about the pictures. He demands that I turn over the negatives. Suddenly we are at a wedding, and he is chasing me. I run and hide. He finds me. I run and hide again and again, but he keeps finding me. I am terrified for I recognize him as Freddie Kruger.

Dream Journal Entry
January 1990

BABY, DEAD OR ALIVE?

An infant is lying on the floor. I realize the baby isn't breathing or moving. A rectangular little box-like contraption that has four circles of numbers indicates that the baby is alive. But then the numbers go blank. I run around screaming, trying to get help. I want someone to help save the baby. The baby makes a noise and moves, and I think that babies couldn't do that if they were dead. I realize this baby MUST be alive. Yet I have trouble believing it.

Dream Journal Entry
March 1990

THE BABY I LOVE VERSUS THE MESSY BABY

I am taking care of these two little babies who I had given nicknames to. One baby I know quite well and therefore love him more. But so that neither baby would be jealous, I put a great deal of time into getting to know and love the other baby, who isn't as attractive and has something spilling from it a lot.

Dream Journal Entry
April 1990

1990

NIGHTMARES OF DEAD BABIES startled me awake night after night in the years after Teddy's death. But I didn't have time to think about them upon awakening for I had classes to attend, stacks of textbooks to read, a library to digest, homework to finish, term papers to write, exams to study for, meetings to attend, a GPA to top.

Driven to achieve—or to forget—I joined lots of campus clubs and organizations. By my senior year, I was elected president of Omicron Delta Kappa Society, The National Leadership Honor Society; and inducted into Sigma Tau Delta, the International English Honor Society. I served as writer for the campus yearbook, editor-in-chief for the campus newspaper, editor-in-chief for the campus magazine, tutor for freshman English, tutor in the computer lab, peer advisor to freshman students, volunteer for an adult literacy program, representative for the student body at monthly town hall meetings, member of an ad hoc committee to rewrite the campus honor code, blah, blah, blah.

Somewhere between classes in geology, ethics, history, mythology, and French, I learned to appreciate Shakespeare—and Jesus—from a feminist's point of view, delved the depths with Moby Dick, bumped heads with Plato, walked medieval forests with the Green Knight, romanticized the plights of the English poets, mourned with Emily Dickinson, got lost in Milton's paradise, sat by Walden Pond, and rocked endlessly out of Walt Whitman's cradle.

"I'll give you the OK, but be warned, Whitman was an atheist," said Dr. Hermann, my English professor and advisor.

On that note, I set out to prove that "Out of the Cradle Endlessly Rocking" was an allegory for Adam and Eve in the Garden of Eden, an allegory for the rise and fall of man, an allegory for the birth, life, and death of Christ, and an allegory for the Bible as a whole. The paper was due in just a few hours, but I was still skimming through stacks of books from the library.

I found it! Oh, my, God!

I was not alone. Several scholars had pointed out that "Out of the Cradle" was analogous to Eastern religions as well as Western religions.

That's it! Whitman didn't believe in a particular religion. "Out of the Cradle" was illustrating Whitman's belief that all religions are one!

I ran from room to room as megalomania spun a magnificent pattern in my brain. As I ran into the living room, the screen on the television had paused with the words "Saved by the Bell."

I gotta get a grip.

Dr. Hermann didn't seem too convinced. He marked a few question marks in the margins and wrote "A-" in the corner. It was like the line in one of my short fiction stories, where one of my characters "answered the telephone," to which he commented: "Actually answered someone <u>over</u> the telephone?"

Fuddy-duddy!

For the last two years, I had attended just about every campus picnic, campus dance, and campus fundraiser, all the while running round and round Keats's Grecian urn.

"Run! Run! Run!" I had screamed as little Alton, not so little now as a teenager, sprinted past Dean Buckingham and went on to break the ribbon at the finish line at the annual Campus Olympics. Alton had become a familiar face on campus, and he fit right in considering he was closer in age to most of the students than I was, including Liam, who I flirted with like a schoolgirl behind the bleachers, but more like Keats's "unravish'd bride," I would not be caught.

But I was running from more than Liam. I was running from this: "Then one morning, when a brisk wind was shaking down crisp leaves from a young, but dying, chestnut tree..."

I filed my 10 short fiction stories face down in my bottom desk drawer and promised to one day rewrite and publish them. Just one more semester hung over me before I could get on with my life.

"The Symbolic Life: Creating a Synthesis," I read the course title.

"Sounds interesting," my friend Kathy said. "I took a philosophy class with him my junior year. He's a wonderful teacher—and I got an A. You definitely don't want to take that religion class with Dr. Jordan. Remember, he's the one who screwed up my GPA."

That January, the first day of spring semester, I entered Dr. Sturm's classroom with trepidation. I didn't know him. But to my surprise, he knew me. He threw out the red carpet, and I began a journey that would change my life.

We started the semester by reading "The Symbolic Quest" by Edward C. Whitmont, which introduced me to Carl Gustav Jung. Intrigued, I read that symbols have the power to describe the unknown.

"In Jung's terms, Whitmont says that a genuine symbol is not a chosen abstract designated to specify certain objects (such as a negative or plus sign before or after a number—which are merely signs)," I wrote in my first assignment. "But rather, a symbol 'is the expression of a spontaneous experience which points beyond itself to a meaning not conveyed by a rational term.'"[1]

The grayish-whitish sphere that I had forgotten about appeared out of nowhere. Could my secret image be a symbol of some unknown phenomenon? At last, someone to ask, someone to confide in.

Dr. Sturm!

"It's spherical, but not a circle or a flat disk. It's colorless. Well, grayish-whitish, but it's not transparent. It seems smooth, but it is not shiny or dull. It has a desirable substance with dimension, something I would like to touch but can't. Nor can I see its backside. It doesn't move or speak. It just hangs there," I said pointing to the back left side of my head. "Ha ha. Please don't tell me it's all in my head."

Dr. Sturm grinned.

"Not at all. You've described what Jung called a spontaneous image."

"Yes! That's right! I didn't create it. It was just there since I could remember."

"And no need to worry. Spontaneous images are not the masks or products of pathological minds, as Freud theorized, but a powerful source of information and guidance, which projects an individual's inner truth."

"Very interesting."

"I suggest you research the mandala. I suspect your sphere may very well be a symbol of your higher Self."

"Mandala?"

"Yes," he said, pointing to the jacket of *Man and His Symbols*, a book I had just bought for his class. "We won't get to it until the second half of the semester but you can look ahead."

Somebody believes me!

"Another thing. Try drawing your image. See how it looks on paper."

Imagine, a picture of my soul.

I scribbled ever so lightly spiral after spiral. I turned the pencil on its side and shaded circle after circle. I drew it large. I drew it small. I sat back and studied it. But it was useless. No matter how hard I tried, the image on paper looked like a stupid hairball.

I thumbed through the index of Jung's book.

Mandala, p. 161.

As I flipped to that page, I was overawed to see the image of my soul, the very image I was trying to draw.

I'm not crazy.

"The psyche can be compared to a sphere with a bright field on its surface, representing consciousness. The ego is the field's center....The Self is at once the nucleus and the whole sphere; its internal regulating processes produce dreams."[2]

"This is what my image looks like," I told Dr. Sturm, opening my book to that page. "But when I tried drawing it, it just looked like a hairball."

"A hairball is a powerful image," he said. "Form associations to that. What is a hairball? How do you feel about it? What is it made of? How does it form?"

That night I drew lines and circles leading from one thought to another...hairball ... tangles ... pain ... hairball ... disgusting...soap scum ... residue ...hairball ... spider ... spinning ... web ... cocoon ... hairball."

"In this particular pattern," Dr. Sturm said when I showed him, "you feel very negative about the image. Can you define those negative feelings?"

As I contemplated my experiences relating to hair, I remembered my mother ripping the snarls out of my hair when I was a child. Images of tumbleweeds wisped across a desert. Images of walking blindly to the kitchen each morning as a child, my eyelashes stuck together with green and yellow gook, which my mother pried open after soaking my lids with tea bags. Images of my hair as a frizz ball after my mother gave me home perms. My mother's long hair—so snarled after she rejected all care when she lost baby Bobby that it had to be cut off. Biblical passages from Corinthians, Chapter 11, crossed my mind. If a woman has long hair it is a glory to her. Then some myth, I can't recall, when a hero's power is zapped after his hair was shaven.

Back to the drawing board: "Hairball...clogged drain...water stops flowing ... water, the sustenance of spiritual and physical life ... ocean ... body of water ... body of Christ ... emergence ... dedication of baby ... baptism ... rebirth ... matrix ... mother ... moon ... image of soul ... hairball."

I came full circle.

"Look at all the imagery focusing on creative feminine power in this pattern," Dr. Sturm said. "Moon. Water. Mother. Baby. Hmmm. Baby. I suspect—especially considering how often you dream about babies—that the baby may be your Self-image. It's something worth exploring."

That night, I sat at the dining room table with my pencil and composition notebook at hand and began a dialogue—what Jung referred to as an active imagination—that is, a dialogue between one's conscious and unconscious.

"What part of me do you represent," I asked the mystery sphere.

It's response was spontaneous, like it had a mind of its own.
Your oversoul.
"What are you?"
Peace. The ideal.
"What is your function?"
No response.
"Are you trying to give me a message?"
No response.

Images of decapitations and hangings flitted through my mind. Then I saw a rope yanked around a neck and an object slit its throat. Frightened that I was capable in that moment of committing suicide, I backed out, took a deep breath, and then tried a different approach.

"Is my ego too weak to handle communication with you right now?"

Yes, it is.

"What do I need to do to make it stronger?"

Approach the hairball.

I took another deep breath and then summoned forth the hairball, which hopped right into my line of sight.

"What's your name?" I asked.

Mike.

"Mike?"

I was taken aback because I expected a feminine name, a feminine voice, or at least a name more mystical—but Mike?

Mike, he repeated. *Short for microphone.*

"Ha, ha. Who do you speak for?" I asked.

Your unconscious.

"Oh! You know, several times in the past I've had conversations with you. But the second I become aware of it, I can't remember it."

You're not supposed to.

"Why?"

It would hurt you [pause]. *Mystery* [pause]. *Body waste* [pause]. *The trinity* [pause]. *Unsnarling. Unraveling.*

Images of hair blowing in the wind and tumbleweeds blowing through a desert wisped through my mind.

Hair is beautiful, though it is dead matter.

"Are you trying to tell me that the dead matter in my life is beautiful?"

Yes. Savor them. Keep them alive. Teddy. Mother. Love. Innocence.

"I thought I should let them die."

They can never die. But your heart is dying. You let your feelings die. A certain sensitivity is lacking. Comb out the tangles in your life and your hair will grow long and beautiful.

"What are the tangles in my life?"

You know what they are.

"Marriage?"

Yes, as soon as possible.

"Can we talk about something else?" I asked, thinking about how Quentin had proposed to me, but I wasn't ready for marriage.

That's it. You're always trying to run away.

"I don't see what marriage has to do with the oversoul."

It's the inner peace.

"Are you saying if I get married I'll have inner peace?"
You know it.
"But—"
It'll all work out.

Mike stopped talking, and a knife-like object cut the hairball in half. Again and again, the hairball split in half then rejoined, while Mike jumped over it unscathed. I tried to get Mike's attention, but he ignored me.

Get on with the project, he finally said. *Take it easy.*

"If I get married I'll have inner peace," I announced to Dr. Sturm. "My boyfriend asked me to marry him. But I said I wasn't ready. But maybe my unconscious is trying to tell me to go ahead. If I do, I'll have inner peace."

"Before you make any major decisions," he said, "try thinking of marriage in symbolic terms. Jung would say marriage in dreams often symbolizes the union of opposites, the union of the male and female aspects of the psyche, that is, the Self. Think about the wedding dream you had. It may be inviting you to a symbolic marriage. But you keep avoiding it."

That night, Dr. Sturm's words hit me over the head as I read a footnote in *Psyche and Symbol*,[3] which defined the syzygy as a joining together or conjunction, which reminded me of the word conjugal, relating to marriage.

Aha.

"If one wants to bring off the trick not only intellectually but realize the feeling value as well, one must for better or worse come to grips with the anima-animus problem in order to open the way for a higher union, a conjunctio oppositorium. This is an indispensable prerequisite for wholeness. Although wholeness seems at first sight to be nothing but an abstract idea (like anima and animus), it is nevertheless empirical in so far as it is anticipated by the psyche in the form of spontaneous or autonomous symbols. These are the quaternity or mandala symbols"[4]

Wow.

I ran a backward dialogue[5] of everything Mike said. "Inner peace. Marriage. Untangle my hair. Savor the dead matter in my life. And then, trinity? That makes no sense. Body waste. Mystery. The mystery of the body waste is in the trinity? Like the temptation to use a word other than 'savor,' when recording my dialogue—for dead matter hardly seemed appetizing—I also had an urge to strike the word 'trinity' from the dialogue because it just didn't make any sense to me. After all, it was not surprising that a hairball might use terms such as 'unsnarling' and 'body waste.' But I couldn't imagine what the trinity had to do with a hairball, so I researched Jung's view on the trinity.

I found that Jung questioned why Christians reverted to the triad to "construct its Trinitarian God-image" in spite of the special need of quaternity symbolism. After investigating several cases of the 'rather rare' trinitarian symbols, Jung said that in such cases he noticed high degrees of unconsciousness and primitivity.

I couldn't read fast enough.

"The saving symbol is then a triad in which the fourth is lacking because it has to be unconditionally rejected."[6]

All the little duckies were lining up.

It is the consciousness of my yin, my feminine aspect relegated to unconsciousness since I was a child struggling to survive in a patriarchal world. It is the denial or belittling of dreams, of intuition, of creativity, aspects patriarchy often deems pathological, even evil. That fourth thing was the dark side of God, the dark side of me, the Shadow, that part of me that awaits integration to make me whole.

I began to understand the necessity of the joining of opposites to make me whole, the need to readapt my yin and to rediscover my yang so that a marriage could take place—not between Quentin and I—but a symbolic union within my own psyche. I understood that the sphere on the left side of my mental horizon indicated unconsciousness. That to find balance, to make things right, my symbol of Self, the disk on my mental horizon, would need to move from my unconscious left side, where it had appeared to me as a child, to my conscious right side in order to be integrated.

As I made one exciting connection after another, I wrote a 33-page research paper, which I titled, "My Symbolic Quest," which I concluded—mightily and joyously—with the following paragraphs.

"Though this paper draws to a close, my symbolic quest has just begun....In spite of the interwoven complexities of my psychic condition manifested through the images of the hairball, the dead infants in my dreams—who by the way have started kicking and sucking their thumbs over the course of this semester—and the grayish-white sphere looming on the left side of my mental horizon, I have only begun to unravel and unsnarl the many strands of the magic circle, the mandala....

"The magic circle, in its many forms, seems to promise the eventual inner peace, which Mike said I would experience if I stopped running away, and allowed my yin and yang to merge.

As von Franz said, 'The contemplation of the mandala is meant to bring an inner peace, a feeling that life has again found its meaning and order' (*Man and His Symbols* [http://bit.ly/1I9CmFb], p. 213).[7] I know that it will be a lifelong process of 'becoming,' and I know that between peaceful feelings will be trying times of anger, chaos, fear, and pain. But at least now, I hope I will not forget my potential for inner peace."

I concluded my paper with a handwritten note.

"Dr. Sturm: Please see the attached picture of the fetus which I photocopied from *The Power of Myth*, page 124.[8] Interesting how the caption reads, 'Otto Rank declares that everyone is a hero in birth, where he undergoes a tremendous transformation, from the condition of a little water creature living in a realm of amniotic fluid, into an air-breathing mammal which ultimately will be standing.'

"The amniotic pouch looks just like the sphere in my head," I continued writing, "except I can't see the fetus in it. Perhaps the hairball blocks the baby. Also notice that the infant is not sucking its thumb. My Self-image sucks its thumb, just as I had throughout my childhood. But perhaps my insecurities can be reckoned with. Perhaps someday I will not suck my psychic thumb. For now I can only hope that I will never forget my potential for inner peace."

I would read the last sentence of my paper many years later and cringe at just how—poof—like forgetting your wish once you blow out the birthday candles, I forgot about "My Symbolic Quest." I forgot about God, too. It baffled me, considering that I had never stepped foot inside the campus chapel, that the reverend asked me to deliver the opening prayer at the commencement service.

You're a hypocrite. No I'm not! Yes you are.

"Out of the Cradle" enabled me to write a prayer based on my memory of being a Christian rather than based on my belief that religions are man's interpretation of what they think god is, a prayer that Mom and Dad and Zach, who would be in the pews that day, would approve of.

But once I returned to the 'real' world, the godless world, and couldn't find a job, once my house went into foreclosure because Social Security had cut off our benefits when it ruled it had overpaid Alton and me now that Charlie claimed to be legally blind and would recoup his share of the benefits paid to us for the previous four years, once Alton and I lost our home and moved in with Zach and his family in Northern Virginia, once my research journals were packed away in boxes along with my yearbooks and other remnants of my life, once all that happened, I forgot the healing power of those fantastic revelations. They shriveled up like an umbilical cord that was severed a long time ago.

PART VII

"The usual way in which the anima or animus is experienced is in projection upon a person of the opposite sex. Unlike the projection of the shadow, such projection of the anima or animus lends a quality of fascination to the person who 'carries' them in projected form.

"'Falling in love' is a classic instance of mutual anima and animus projection between a man and a woman. During such a mutual projection one's sense of personal worth is enhanced in the presence of the person who represents the soul image in projected form, but a corresponding loss of soul and emptiness may result if the connection is not maintained.

"This projective phase, the unconscious identification of another person with the soul image of one's own psyche, is always limited in time; it inevitably ends, with varying degrees of animosity, because no actual person can live up to the fantastic expectations that accompany a projected soul image.

"And with the end of projection comes the task of establishing a genuine relationship with the reality of another person. . . . .If the projected anima or animus is not integrated when the projection is withdrawn, the process is likely to occur again with someone else."[1]

James A. Hall
Jungian Dream Interpretation [http://bit.ly/1NlTnDH]

"Some people have yearning for the archetypal reunion so they may get into a compulsive relationship, where they project the God onto the partner, or whoever it is they happen to choose and then project their soul out on someone else and of course then they are tied into the other person. And even if the other person is abusing them they cannot get out of the projection.

"If there's no understanding, no conscious understanding of the difference between the human and the divine, by the age of 25 or 30 you're in trouble. By the age of 40 you're in BIG trouble. Everyone you fall in love with is supposed to be God. So you keep projecting God, women onto men. And then you wonder why they disappoint you. And men wonder why they're married to a witch... . There's no way a man can be a God. Similarly there's no way a woman can be a Goddess."[2]

Marion Woodman [http://bit.ly/1PoTLrw]
Sitting by the Well [http://bit.ly/1OagpMK]

24
the crack in everything

> "There is a crack in everything.
> That's how the light gets in."[1]

Leonard Cohen (http://bit.ly/1YoxF3x)
Leonard Cohen: Selected Poems , 1956–1968 (http://bit.ly/1I5fTOS)

Also listen to Cohen's beautiful song, inspired by these words,
"Anthem" (http://bit.ly/1N7bI5s)

VEHICLE OUT OF CONTROL/TODDLERS DROWNING

I'm at a party—in a house?—with Bert. I go to the car to get something. The car starts to roll, and I can only operate it with my hand on the break and gear. I'm half in and half out of the car, trying to keep it under control. I end up at a health spa where there's a swimming pool. The vehicle is now a motorcycle, and later becomes a pogo stick.

Small children between the ages of two and four keep falling in the water. I can see two or three children who had already drowned and are floating on top of the water. No one else seems to notice. One girl is sitting on the bottom without breathing, but she appears to be alive. Another small child falls in (about 12 feet deep), but now there is no water in the pool. I think the child would have to be dead after that fall, but she recovers without apparent injury.

The floor under my feet keeps moving forward bringing me to the edge of the pool. I am petrified of falling in. I stand in line by the door to get help, but the lady there is sarcastic toward me.

Undated Dream Journal Entry
Early 1990s

Early 1990s

YOU ONLY MEET YOUR SOULMATE ONCE IN A LIFETIME—if you are lucky—so I was told. So I didn't waste my time. I had one boyfriend after Teddy died, named Quentin, who taught me the art of fishing and how to play chess and Scotland Yard and Mille Borne—and how to appreciate basketball. Let's go, Orange!

He was witty and smart, and we had a lot of fun. But guilt-ridden, I kept trying to dump him like the Styrofoam container that we tossed after packing up the tackle box. And just like the fish he taught me to catch, I would bait him, catch him, and he would ask me to marry him, then yank, off with the hook, I would toss him back in. In a month or two I would miss him, and I'd fish him back out—until one day I tried to lure him in with the prettiest bucktail jig I could find, but he refused to nibble, and from then on I was on my own.

I ignored the drowning babies in my dreams. I'd rather hang out at the Corner Lounge and plan my next chess move against my fellow patrons over beers—and shots of Grand Marnier, courtesy of the loser.

"It's your turn, Gabrielle," Bert said, eyeing the board through his thick lenses.

"I know. I know," I said, clutching my queen by her crown as Norton, Moe, and Virginia studied the board over my shoulder.

"I'll have another beer, Shelly," I called down to the curly redhead. "When you have a minute."

Bert's going to think I'm an idiot if I move into checkmate.

I'd win some and lose some when I strategized against Norton, the insurance guy, or Moe, the taxicab driver, or Virginia, the ballerina-anorexic. But for some reason, Bert intimidated me.

Bert and Norton were both about 15 years older than I was and, at age 35, I wasn't attracted to their skinniness or pocked faces or pasty-white skin or graying hair or balding heads. But, hey, they were harmless. They didn't push me for sex like the younger guys did. We could talk for hours, and we did just that, talked through many a nights, one night with Bert, another night with Norton.

I told them off the bat that romance and sex didn't interest me. I just wanted to be friends. After all, my soulmate had died in 1986, and I would carry a torch for him for the rest of my life, and for all the other heroes who had died in their prime.

In the months that followed, it seemed the more Bert made me laugh, the more serious Norton became, and the more Norton began to distance himself. I didn't ask because it might be awkward if he wanted to take our relationship to another level.

One night—I didn't know where Norton was—a brawl broke out among a bunch of the young guys over some girl. As the table flipped over, Bert leaped up in front of me with his arms outstretched to block the debris. Yes. He played the bit of a drama queen, and he looked a little silly. But it was pretty cool when he hustled me down a hallway, like a secret passageway, that low and behold led into the restaurant next door, where we sat and had a late dinner on the house. Bert had friends everywhere we went—and they all spoke of him like he was a god.

When one of the younger guys would hit on me, Bert would set him straight, and set him to marching. As I reflected on his instinct to protect me, I began to realize how much he loved me and how safe I felt when I was with him. Of course, he wasn't my soulmate, but I had a terrible yearning for the intimacy that Teddy and I had shared, especially our ability to anticipate each other's needs. Bert seemed to have that. And he made me laugh like only Teddy (and Maureen) could.

Within six months, we were exclusive. So the night Bert told me that Orville, his housemate of 10 years, no longer wanted to share his bachelor pad now that he was starting to get serious with his girl, too, it only seemed natural that Bert would move in with me, since we were always together anyway. And being old-fashioned as he was, it only seemed natural to Bert, since he was moving in with me, that he ask me to marry him. That night, after several celebratory drinks, we made love for the first time—well, we tried anyway.

When I reached into his underpants—ick! I don't know if I gasped out loud or if I just thought it, but I extracted my hand as if I had touched a squishy worm instead. But he was so tall and his feet were big! We peeled off each other's clothing and pressed our skin together, licking each other's lips. Breathless, he guided my hand back down there, but it was still squishy. So we gyrated a lot with the penis between us, massaging my belly button.

I don't know if either of us climaxed, or if we just wore out. And I don't know if it was the booze or if he was impotent or if he was just smaller than most men, not that I had been with most men. But I had read somewhere that the average was six inches, not that I ever measured anyone either. Anyway, it was before the popularity of Viagra, so I don't know, maybe he just needed a little help. Or maybe I just didn't turn him on. I would never know because we never discussed it—and we never attempted that sex thing again. And that was fine with me. I was content to have someone to hold me, protect me, work the crossword puzzles with me, and share expenses, too, of course.

Not that I needed financial help, but I liked the idea of a safety net in case of an emergency, like what happened when Social Security cut us off without warning. I still received Teddy's pension each month, and I had just gotten a $2,000 a year raise from my job as deputy supervisor and proofreader at NASA in Washington, D.C.

Plus, I got really lucky finding a split-level ranch on a corner lot for rent right around the corner from Zach's house for only $725 a month, and it had a basement apartment that the owner allowed me to sublet, which paid $250 toward my rent each month. But Bert had something I didn't. He owned 10 acres on Paris Mountain, which he had bought years before so that he and his buddies would have their own private hunting ground. Once we were married, it would be like having our own Poconos.

Shelly and I used to love driving up to the mountain on her weekends off to party with the guys. Well, Shelly loved to because she was in love with one of Bert's best buds. Bert wasn't even there half the time, but even if he was, we didn't see much of him because he spent the day in the woods building a tree stand or clearing some debris after a storm. When he came in from the woods, he would shoot the shit while he guzzled down a six-pack of beer, ate his steak or burger or sausage hoagie, and then off he'd go to bed in his little camper—even if it was still daylight. He was used to it, he said, given that his alarm clock had been ringing at 4 a.m. for the last 20 years for his shifts at United Airlines, where he worked as a flight attendant supervisor.

The rest of us partied on, drinking and playing poker in the pavilion, lit only by kerosene lanterns, until almost daylight. With no electricity—or a bathroom—Shelly and I would hold it until we were about burst, then we would take turns shaking a path with a stick and holding the flashlight for each other. Then we'd prop up our lawn chairs under the stars. I would close my eyes and listen to Bert tinker with the gas stove and coffee pot.

But it would be different now, now that Bert and I would be married, now that I would join Bert's exclusive club. As soon as his pals found out about a wedding on the mountain, they went up every weekend to cut down trees and shrub to clear a patch that would hold 200 people plus parking. They built an archway for the ceremony—and even an outhouse, which they painted mauve to match my dress and Bert's tie and cummerbund. As a finishing touch, they carved a vent in the outhouse door in the shape of a crescent moon and stars.

The day before the wedding, one of Bert's friends, who owned a florist shop, drove up the mountain with a truckload of vases and flowers and ribbons and crepe paper and table cloths, with which she decorated the archway and the large screened-in tent where we would cut the cake.

That night, for the first time ever, Bert invited me into the camper, which until then had only sheltered him and his closest buddies.

What a pigsty!

We would sleep fully clothed, and it would be dark, so we would not see that a couple of his buddies were sleeping in the bunks on the other end. As the sunlight streamed in through the screened vent, I tried to convince myself that it was okay.

At least I won't have a hangover on my wedding day. At least I won't have a hangover on my wedding day. At least I won't have a hangover on my wedding day. At least...

But I couldn't get to sleep to save my ass, listening to all my friends out there partying. As 50 voices trailed off as this one and that one said goodnight, Shelly and Norton's drunk talking filled the darkness. They knew something I didn't, and they agreed that I was making the biggest mistake of my life.

Stupid bitches. They're just jealous!

Glad that I had found true love again, my mother and father drove down from New York, as did several of my brothers and sisters and cousins and their families—and even Grandma Williams—some of whom even wore bib overalls, as the invitation suggested as appropriate attire for a mountain wedding. Bert's son and daughter and granddaughter were there, too, of course, as well as about 150 of his friends, each of whom went out of their way to tell me how lucky I was to marry such a loving and generous man, and I assured each of them that I was grateful.

It was a sunny day in mid-May in the mid-70s, and nothing could top that day on Paris Mountain, nothing except the honeymoon trip the next day to Paris, France! The flight attendants, as a wedding gift to their boss, ushered us into first class and plied us with caviar and Dom Pérignon. I was no connoisseur, and not much of a champagne or fish person, but, oh my, it was to die for.

The next two days we walked the streets of Paris, where men and women sat at tables on the sidewalks with their poodles and Yorkies in chairs next to them or their bull terriers or Jack Russells tethered to the legs of their chairs. We would take a table now and then to sample the breads and cheeses and beers at various brasseries.

Then we strolled up the Avenue des Champs-Élysées, from la Place de la Concorde to le Arc de Triomphe, through les jardins, as I admired the statues along the way of the Marly Horses, Napoleon, and Cupid. As I read in awe each plaque, Bert feigned patience. Thing is, while the guys were cutting down brush to make a path to the outhouse, I was brushing up on my two years of French so that I could buy postage stamps and order breakfast. Dr. LaPierre told our class that if you at least try to speak French the natives would be more hospitable. But the clerk at *La Poste* made me repeat my request six times before turning around and speaking English, plain as dirt. And the server at the café the next morning outright laughed at my attempt to request ice in my water.

Bert must think I'm an idiot.

Our last day in Paris, big raindrops fell on us one at a time as we paused a couple of blocks from La Tour Eiffel, its height overshadowed by my view of it as just a lattice of bed frames.

"What does it do?" Bert asked.

"Nothing. Just a monument," I said.

"Then not worth getting caught in the rain," he said.

But the honeymoon was truly over when we returned from Paris, and I discovered that there was one person who flat out disliked Bert—my own son, Alton. He had attended the wedding, had driven his 1973 black Beetle Bug, with its snazzy sideboards, up Paris Mountain, which I misinterpreted as his approval. No, he said later, he just did it to honor my wishes—and he wanted to see his cousins. We no sooner returned from Paris when it occurred to him that he was an adult, he had finished school, and he didn't need parental guidance anymore, especially from a stepfather. He packed his stuff and moved back to Virginia Beach to reclaim his past life, the one he had before Social Security ripped it out from underneath him.

I cleaned out a dresser for Bert, and before he could unpack his suitcase, Alton had moved out, as did my sublet girl downstairs, which was weird.

"We could use the privacy anyway," Bert had said. "And don't worry. I'll make up the difference in the rent."

My shoes felt like they were on the wrong feet as Bert and I tried to become better acquainted. As Flag Day and the Fourth of July approached, Bert seemed preoccupied with the flag that once draped Teddy's casket. Still folded in a triangle in its protective case on the hutch, the flag had not been unfurled since the day the Navy officers had presented it to me after firing three shots into the air, their 21-gun salute ripping out my heart.

"If you really want to honor Teddy," Bert said, "we should raise the flag on a pole. I think he would like that."

I had no idea the proper protocol, but what Bert said made sense. So when I said okay, he happened to have everything he needed to install a flagpole and a flag. I didn't say anything to Bert, who seemed so pleased with himself, but every time I looked at Teddy's huge flag on that short post, my heart sank and my guts tossed and turned. When a heavy rain splashed mud up on it, I hung my head. And when the rain turned to ice, the flag hung its head. It would be our only winter together, Bert and I, and it would be brutal.

Bert never did chip in on the rent. And I wasn't privy to his checkbook or his other financials, but he cried poverty and sold five acres of his Paris Mountain lot. That was just the beginning of the end. The Corner Lounge shut down. The chess games ceased. The taxicab driver died of a massive heart attack. The ballerina-anorexic looked like she was going to die any day now, her face gaunt and her teeth rotting out. And Norton wouldn't even look at me.

Week in and week out, Bert said it was too hot or too cold or too rainy to drive up to the mountain. As the parties on the mountain became distant memories so did the days that Shelly used to pop in for a few beers on her nights off or drag me out to a yard sale or a flea market at the crack of dawn on Saturday mornings.

When we walked into what Bert called "my" bar, where we went on weekends, everyone—even Norton—fled to the other side of the room like cock roaches scatter when you turn on the light. It was a different scene at "Bert's" bar, that is, the daytime bar where all his buddies hung out and drank all afternoon, the bar where he would be half in the bag by the time I got off work. I had just landed my new dream job that fall, a job as the editor of a monthly newsletter for a local trade association, where I served as reporter and photographer for hearings on Capitol Hill—with a $10,000 a year raise—and the title of Communications Associate.

"The usual," I said, smiling, no, bubbling over, with so much to share about my day.

Bert would look at the clock.

"I have to get up at 4 a.m., so drink up."

Bert preferred that I go home when he did, went to bed when he did, and got up when he did. So we compromised: I don't have to go to bed or get up when he does as long as I go home when he does. I just don't need to be hanging out with my friends at the bar, like he does every night after work. Just because he drinks every day, doesn't mean I could or should.

Fuck you!

For much of that winter, as I focused on my new job, the chill in the words and gestures between Bert and I were enough to induce frostbite, making the modern Ice Age outside look warm and inviting as three-inch thick glaciers swept over houses, yards, trees, driveways, roads, and power lines. Whole neighborhoods, towns, cities, and vehicles were paralyzed—except for Bert, who managed to drive his Chevy truck right out of our subdivision to get to work, and to the bars, every day.

Still stranded at home, I slit the sides of a trash bag and spread it on the porch outside the front door, sat on it, and propelled myself down the porch and stairs, onto the lawn, and down the embankment. Then I crawled the rest of the way to my black Firebird (with its cool orange racing stripes). Determined to go to work and maybe even for a drink afterward, I blasted the heat while I chipped away at the ice. At last, I swerved out of my street and revved up enough power to drive up the side street. But the tires spun out as I tried to climb the never-before-noticed incline.

Forced to retreat until the next thaw, I pulled out the short stories I had filed away in my desk back in college and began to rework them. As I researched potential publishers, the gestures began flailing. Bert didn't actually hit me—he was adamant about that. But he would slam me against the kitchen wall, or rip off my blouse, or talk with his hands, which accidentally gave me a bloody nose. Don't blame him. It was me who stuck my big fat nose into his knuckles.

But just as the thaw came that spring and crews worked 24/7 to repair the damage and restore the electricity to hundreds of thousands, our hearts began to melt, too, as we tried to repair the damage to our relationship. Just when I began to feel warm and fuzzy, Bert jumped up off his barstool and stormed out of the bar, stranding me without a ride home. I was flabbergasted. No one had ever done that to me before.

"What got into him?" Ed asked.

"I have no idea, but I'm sure he'll be eager to tell me what I did wrong when I get home. So anyway, you were living in West Virginia for the past year? I wondered what happened to you. How bad were the ice storms there?"

As Ed proceeded to describe that winter in West Virginia and how he nearly died of the flu, my mind wandered back to Bert.

No doubt he thought Ed was flirting with me or I was flirting with Ed. Or both! For god's sake, we were just having a conversation.

I drank a couple more beers, said thanks to Ed, who paid my tab, and then started to walk home. But it was getting dark. I had walked a couple of blocks, watching my back every step of the way, when I noticed another bar across the street had several vehicles parked out front, a bar I had only been to a few times before I met Bert.

I stopped to see if I knew anyone there who could give me a lift home. I recognized several people, but they may as well have put up their forefingers in a cross as I approached them, even Norton. I explained to the bartender how my car broke down and how I needed a ride home. It was just a mile or two. The bartender gave me a beer on the house and apologized, but he couldn't leave the bar unattended. After Norton heard our conversation, he walked over.

"I let my daughter take my car tonight," he said. "But when you're ready, I'll walk you home if you want."

We chatted like it was old times until the top of my roof came into view.

"This is as far as I go," he said, sticking up his palms.

"What is your problem?!"

"You really don't get it do you? If Bert finds out I walked you home, he'll send his ghouls after me."

"That's ridiculous!"

Without another word, Norton turned on his heels and hauled ass back toward the bar.

What the fuck!

I ran around the corner, from the back to the front of my house, up the front lawn and onto the porch. Grateful to have arrived unscathed, I turned the knob on the front door.

It's locked!

I knocked on the door and rang the bell, but when Bert didn't come, I pounded harder and then knocked on the living room window.

I waited a couple of minutes, but Bert still didn't open the front door.

"Let me in, you son of a bitch!" I screamed, pounding once more on the door and punching the doorbell.

"What the fuck?"

I picked up the snow shovel that was propped up by the front door and smashed it through one of the living room windows. I cleared the glass, climbed in, and charged through the living room and up the six steps to the bedroom, screaming my brains out.

"How dare you? How dare you strand me with no money and no keys! And now you have the audacity to lock me out of my own house. You stupid bastard!"

Bert lunged from the bed, tackled me, and tightened his bony fingers around my neck. Kicking my feet and thrashing my arms, I squirmed and pushed and pulled. But this ornery, wiry bastard had me pinned to the bedroom floor.

"Say uncle," he demanded. "Say uncle!"

"Help me. Help me," was all I could eke out, as I thought about the little man caught in the spider web as he cried out in the movie, *The Fly*.

My spirit departed. My body went limp.

Quick like a bunny, Bert hopped off me and back into bed.

I scrambled to my feet and fled down the stairs. I ran around the kitchen for a minute.

I can't stay here. But I can't leave either.

Shaking, my heart pounding, I plucked the wireless phone from its base and sat at the kitchen table and stared at it as I tried to think what to do.

"Fucking shit," I gasped, when someone began pounding on the front door.

"It's the police."

Red lights were flashing in the living room windows as I opened the door and whispered to them.

"You can't do this. My husband has guns. He has a gun in his night stand."

"Everything's going to be okay, ma'am. May we come in?"

"Okay," I said, backing up all the way to the kitchen doorway.

"Where is he now, ma'am?" he asked.

I pointed up the stairway.

The two male officers walked to the bottom of the stairs.

"Sir, you need to come downstairs."

Silence.

"Sir, it will be better for you if we don't have to come up there to get you."

Something thumped, and as we looked at one another, Bert appeared at the top of the stairs wearing only his tighty-whities.

"What," he asked, rubbing his eyes. "What's going on officers?"

"Your neighbors called. Said they heard screaming and glass breaking. You didn't hear your window break, sir?"

"I didn't hear anything. I came home at 7:30 and went straight to bed. I work at the airport, and I have to be there by 5 a.m."

"Tell you what. How about we get your pants for you, sir, and then we can talk."

"Sure. They're on the back of the bedroom door."

"Why don't we give them some space," the female officer said to me, motioning me through the kitchen and into the dining area.

She asked me to tell her everything that had happened that night, which I did, though my voice was raspy and squeaky and it hurt to talk, much less swallow.

When I finished, she examined my neck.

"It takes a lot to bruise the neck," she said. "But he clearly did. You might not be so lucky next time. You can stop him, you know. Just say the word, and we will take him with us right now."

"I can't! He'll kill me. He'll kill you!"

"I don't think you realize how close he came to killing you tonight. We can protect you, but only if you press charges. Can you do that?"

"I might as well. He's going to kill me either way."

"I'll be right back," she said.

I twisted the lock in the doorknob, tiptoed out the back door, darted to the end of the yard, and burrowed myself in a thicket of grapevines. Panting, I studied the back of the house looking for anything that moved.

"Miss. Miss," the female officer called to me from the back door.

"You can come back in now. Your husband has been arrested. He's in the patrol car and handcuffed."

But Bert was out by the next morning.

Granted, the judge issued a temporary order of protection forbidding him to come near me until our court date. But a stupid little piece of paper won't stop Bert. So I looked up a battered women's hotline in the phonebook and called to see if there were any other options other than waiting around for Bert to come and finish the job. The lady on the phone described the beautiful view from a large home on a hill in a remote area.

"It has a large paved driveway and plenty of parking once you are able to safely get your car. You will be provided a private room, but you will share the kitchen and bath with other women and their children. Of course, no cigarettes or alcohol are allowed on the premises, but do pack—"

As she talked I imagined a stranger driving me to this place, with Bert hot on our tail and jumping out and shooting us upon our arrival.

To be truly safe from Bert I will have to give up everything, even my freedom, and start over somewhere else.

"Thank you very much," I said. "But I'm afraid I might as well take my chances on the outside. I would, however, like to take you up on your offer to set me up with free legal counsel."

I felt confident in an attorney that was recommended by a women's shelter. After all, if services for abused women recommended an attorney, they must know who the best lawyers are for matters of domestic violence, you know?

As the court date approached, Alton called me.

"I'm telling you, Mom, I don't trust him. I never did!"

"I know, but—"

"Just to be on the safe side, get some boxes and pack up everything. I'll get a couple friends, and we'll drive up there, get a truck, and load up everything by Tuesday morning."

"I don't know. I don't think a judge would actually let him come back. I mean the police witnessed the bruises on my neck."

"But he's devious. And he has a ton of friends in all kinds of places. I'm telling you, you can't risk it."

"No, I know, but it seems a little over the top. Plus, all the way from Virginia Beach?"

"Just humor me, okay? I'll do everything, if you just pack the boxes. You can call me from the courthouse. If the judge says he can go back to your house, I'll drive off with the truck. If the judge orders him not to return to the house, we'll unload the truck right back into the house."

"Okay," I said. "Either way, I might want to go into hiding anyway."

After Alton and I hung up, I called Shelly. Within the hour she was at my door wielding an industrial-sized tape dispenser, half a dozen rolls of tape and paper, and several rolls of bubble wrap.

"I got boxes in the truck," she said. "All flavors."

"Why didn't you tell me?" I asked her, as we wrapped and packed. "Why did you wait until the night before the wedding to say a word? And even that was behind my back."

"You wouldn't have listened, Gabby. Besides, by then Bert had you hook, line, and sinker."

"Still, why did you end our friendship just 'cause I got married!"

"I didn't! I called you about a hundred times. But no matter what time I called I got your answering machine or him. And every time he said you were in the shower or sleeping or sick."

"That's so weird. How did I not hear the phone ring?"

"I don't know, but one day he flat out told me not to call you anymore. Couldn't I take a hint? Gabby obviously doesn't want you in her business anymore."

"What the hell? Shelly! I would never say that to you."

"I know that. But it didn't matter. He said he'd file harassment on me if I called you one more time. He threatened Norton, too. Said he had ways to take care of him if he kept hanging around you."

"How could I be so blind?"

"You don't know the half of it. Do you remember their last hunting trip on Thanksgiving weekend? All the guys went up, except Norton, of course, cause he doesn't hunt. Well, Bert was so afraid that Norton might hang out with you while they were gone that he convinced his cronies to invite Norton over, and then they 'accidentally' locked him in the man cave before they left. Norton was stuck for two days in Daryl's basement! That's how far he was willing to go. So everybody backed off after that."

"Damn. I remember that Saturday night. I was sitting by myself at the Corner until closing, watching the door all night, hoping Norton would come in any minute. I had no idea of any of this! I was pissed and hurt that everyone wrote me off just because I got married."

"Nope. That was all Bert controlling everyone who got anywhere near you. I did try to tell you in the beginning. Remember? That Bert was very possessive. But you said no. You couldn't see it."

"Mother fucker! I can see it now!"

But it was too late.

Bert took the stand that Tuesday morning, and his lawyer directed his line of questioning to demonstrate to the judge that I had shown a pattern of domestic violence, even from a teenager, when I stabbed my first husband. That Bert was home in bed sleeping like a good boy when I got home at nearly 10 p.m., drunk and violent, at which time I broke the front window. That I was accustomed to hanging out in bars for all hours of the night. By the time Bert and his attorney were done, the judge deemed Bert harmless, and she granted him his request to rescind the order of protection, allowing him to return to his home.

"If you perceive Mr. Stuart as a threat," the judge said, "I suggest you find someplace else to go. Case dismissed."

I called Alton from the courthouse lobby.

"Drive off!" I said. "And thank you. You are the best son ever!"

"Your lawyer let them railroad you," said Zach, who was sitting in the third row and witnessed the whole charade. "And why weren't the arresting officers even there?"

"I know! And I don't understand why we have two court dates anyway. Maybe the police don't appear in domestic court, only criminal court? That's not until next week. But what good is that if he's already living back at my house?"

Bert called me at work that Friday.

"I'm sorry," he said. "You know, the alcohol. We really have to take it easy for a while. How about if I come by the house tomorrow so we can work things out?"

"Are you insane?"

I slammed down the receiver, grateful that my office door was closed.

"Mother fucker is crazy," I whispered. "And he doesn't even know I'm gone yet!"

When I hung up on him, he called Zach to talk some sense into me.

"It's the Christian thing to do," Bert told Zach. "She's a mess. You heard the whole story in the courtroom. But I still love her. She's still my wife. Talk to her. She'll listen to you."

Zack chuckled at his audacity.

"The Christian thing to do is to honor your wife, not choke her half to death," Zach said.

My boss suggested I take the next week off—with pay—so that I could focus on my personal life. Meanwhile, I had rented a room at a cheap motel until I could figure out what to do next.

"The first thing you should do is fire your attorney," said Gretchen, who I had run into at lunch after not seeing her for the past year. "I'm telling you, go see Jerry Johnson. He's the best lawyer in Leesburg. He has helped me and my kids out of lots of jams."

"He does require a 2,000-dollar retainer fee up front, though" said Shelly, who joined us from the bar.

"There's no way I can come up with that kind of money!"

"You'd be surprised," Gretchen said. "Have you talked to your company about it?"

"Well, it was embarrassing, but I did tell my boss. I could have just said I had swollen glands, but I had to explain why I needed some time off for the court dates. I've only been there six months, you know, so I don't want to push my luck."

"I'm telling you," Gretchen said. "Companies are more understanding about these things than they used to be. I'll bet if you asked for an advance on your salary, they would give it to you in a heartbeat. You just pay it back like $50 a month or whatever arrangement they make."

"Even if they would, it's too late, now," I said. "Court is tomorrow morning."

"Go to your office right now and ask for the advance," Gretchen said. "I'll call Jerry and tell him how you got bamboozled and see what he can come up with. I swear, there's no way it should take your lawyer three months to write up your separation agreement anyway!"

"You might as well try," said Shelly. "The worst they can say is no."

By rush hour that afternoon, I was sitting in Jerry's office with a check for $2,000. I started to tell him what was going on but he already knew the story, and his wheels were already in motion.

"I'll have your separation agreement drawn up tonight along with a petition for an order of protection. He will either sign them or risk jail time. It's that simple. Be in the courtyard by 9 a.m. If I'm not there, just wait. I'll find you."

But the next morning the prosecutor sought me out with the bad news.

"It's the same judge who presided over your case in domestic court. And she refuses to hear the case again unless we have new evidence."

"As a matter of fact, we do," said Jerry, appearing out of nowhere. "The arresting officer is here to testify to the bruises she witnessed that night on my client's neck. She will also share other vital details of the case, which will corroborate my client's account of that night."

"The judge agreed to hear the case again," the prosecutor reported back, but Jerry was gone again.

I was pacing in the courtyard, chain-smoking, waiting for my case to come back up on the docket, when I saw Jerry loping across the courtyard toward me.

"I gave your husband an ultimatum," he said, handing me an envelope. "Either sign the separation agreement and agree to abide by the order of protection I drew up or take your chances in criminal court. I told him by the time I was done, he would be a convicted felon, even if he managed to avoid actual jail time as a first-time offender. He fired his attorney, but he signed both documents, which I gave to the bailiff, who turned them in to the judge, who signed off on both."

Everything happened so fast that Jerry gave me back the bulk of the retainer fee to repay my company, and I was free. I marveled at the amazing turn of events as I ordered an ice tea at the bar the next afternoon. I didn't tell Zach yet, but I would be sleeping in my car that night if I didn't find a place to live that afternoon. As I sipped my tea, I noticed another woman at the other end of the bar, also drinking an ice tea. Except for the bartender, the bar was otherwise empty, considering it was halfway between lunch and happy hour.

There is a reason the Universe put us together in this spot at this time on this day, both of us drinking tea, both alone. What are the odds?

"Excuse me," I said, clearing my sore throat.

She glanced up from the soap opera.

"You don't happen to know anyone who has a room for rent, do you?"

"Actually, I just might. But let me make a call," she said, giving me the once over as she walked past me and dropped a quarter in the pay phone.

"I'm Vera," she said, when she hung up. "Let me explain the situation."

"Gabrielle. Please, thank you."

It's two female housemates," she said, drawing a map on a napkin. "It was three, but last week they got ditched by one. They're good people. I've known them for years. The rent's $250 a month, but it's a nice home on a cul-de-sac. You'd have your own room, already furnished, plus full access to the kitchen and laundry."

"Oh, my, god. That's awesome."

"If I were you, I'd go over there right now, because one of them has to be at work by 4," she said, and I realized she must have overheard my discussion with the bartender.

I drove straight there, and Flo, Leona, and I hit it off. New friends and new adventures were on my horizon as I dozed off in my new bedroom that night.

It took weeks for my vocal chords to heal. But my faith in men was beyond repair. I resigned myself to a life of being single. All the good men had died young.

25
the repeat offender

Summer 1994

"ALL MEN THESE DAYS ARE ASSHOLES ANYWAY," I said, my new mantra. And every now and then, I'd meet a guy who would confirm it, like this guy Griffin. I was filling in for Gretchen at the bar one night, when he walked in and ordered a beer, and I mean ordered a beer. As I searched the coolers, he rolled his eyes.

"Can I get a bottle of Bud today, or should I call ahead next time?"

Fuck you, Bud!

I handed him his beer, my look colder than the bottle.

All men these days are assholes anyway.

I would not waste any more of my life on them. Instead, on weekends, I ran around the yard chucking a tennis ball into the sky, higher and higher each time, then running to catch it, experiencing me, my breath, and the grass between my toes.

Meanwhile, the kiddy pool that Flo had bought for her grandchildren would be filling up with water from the hose that I had propped up. When it was almost full, I would drench myself in suntan oil, lie on an inflatable raft, and work on an acrostic puzzle—my new favorite thing—and tip a few sea-breezes, tanning and sweating and dunking.

I also cried most of the summer, but good cries, good long cries with me and Michael Bolton, alone in my car, my long lost love, Teddy, on my mind, in my heart. And then I'd turn up the volume for Richard Marx.

"Right here waiting" [http://bit.ly/1PUwbuR], I sang, as I listened to the distant laughter and tasted the tears, trying to catch my breath as the ocean waves washed across my face.[1]

26
the lie

Female writers are particularly prone to the demon lover: Emily Brontë, Emily Dickinson, Virginia Woolf, Sylvia Plath. Women can still fall in love with Heathcliff and love him most when he stands with the dead Catherine in his arms rejoicing that now she is his. They do not see that it is a death-marriage. Women who sentimentalize over Emily Dickinson's love poems tend to overlook the poems of raw agony that were written in an heroic attempt to stay sane and alive.[1]

Marion Woodman [http://bit.ly/1PoTLrw]
Addiction to Perfection [http://bit.ly/1X6OqTQ]

Psychologically, the most pernicious aspect of the demon lover is his trickster quality. He often appears as the perfect bridegroom, but for all his godlike perfection he is still a little boy looking for a mother, and continually demanding his victim's motherliness. Loneliness meets loneliness and they cling together in a symbiotic bond ... In the vacuum left by her loss of feeling, the negative animus attacks, telling her she is unlovable, unworthy, ugly, and forever his prisoner. So long as she falls under the spell of that voice and projects that animus onto the outer man, the rejection she fears will begin to happen because by projecting her negative animus she instantly constellates the man's negative mother.[2]

Marion Woodman [http://bit.ly/1PoTLrw]
Addiction to Perfection [http://bit.ly/1X6OqTQ]

End of Summer 1994 to Winter 1997

I SWEAR TEDDY HEARD ME BECAUSE HE SENT ME AN ANGEL the night that I met Gretchen at the bar to celebrate her 49th birthday. Between sips of champagne, she read our astrology scrolls, then she marveled over how her numbers added up to great success in her love life and finances in the coming year. When she gave up trying to convince me that the Chaldean system was more accurate than the Pythagorean system, she asked me my date of birth.

"It's going to be a bloody exciting year for you," she said. "It's all about new beginnings—a good time to start a new job or a new relationship."

Gretchen ogled Griffin, who was pulling his darts from the dartboard.

"He's bloody good looking," she said. "That dimple, those long blond curls, those green eyes—and that cute butt. He's got that one funky tooth, but other than that. Hey. Ask him his date of birth."

Griffin mumbled a date as his dart landed in the bulls eye.

"Blimey. The next year for him is all about laying new foundations. You guys are totally simpatico."

"Well, doesn't matter. He won't ask me out because I've made it clear to him and every other guy in here that I'm not interested."

"It's the '90s, for Pete's sake," she said. "Ask him out, or I will!"

It was against my better judgment, but the next time he walked by, I asked him if he wanted to go out sometime, the icy exchange over a bottle of beer a few months earlier chalked up to a bad day at the office.

I didn't think he heard me until he walked up to me when Gretchen was in the restroom.

"You serious?"

When I said yes, it was all over. In that moment, we fell in love at first sight.

When we came up for air, we scoped each other out.

"What do you do?" he asked.

"I'm a writer at a trade association, just got promoted from communications associate last month. And you?"

"I'm an implementation manager at Sprint," he said. "Been there five years."

"What's that? An implementation manager?"

"I coordinate the installation of new data systems."

That was good enough for me.

"Do you mind if I ask you how much you make?" he asked.

"Sure, 35 a year, plus my deceased husband's pension. You?"

"Forty-five" he said. "Sorry about your husband."

I told him about Teddy and Bert. He told me about his ex and his military days. I told him about my college days.

"That's cool," he said, that I had a bachelor's degree. "I put my ex-wife through all kinds of schools but she never did anything with any of them."

"Like what?"

"Well she was in the Army for starters. That's where I met her. She learned all these administrative skills. But after her discharge, she wanted to go to real estate school. Then paralegal school. Then—after I paid for it all—she sat back on her butt and watched soaps. She used to call me 'corporate man,' like it was a dirty word. At least you work for a living."

"I love my job! I'm telling you, I promised myself when I was a kid that I would never work a job that I hated like my father did, bitching every night, quitting or getting fired, and going on and off welfare. I love to write. And I'm a writer. So my job's not like work at all."

The lakes in Griffin's eyes filled to the brim with love for me with each word I spoke, and adoration sparkled as if I had just sung the National Anthem, he with his hand to his chest, me with my white blouse flapping in the wind like a flag, surrendering to his charm.

"I have to warn you," he said. "My feet are ugly."

"Bet mine are uglier—bunions and hammer toes!"

Ugly feet? Who cares! We felt comfortable in each other's shoes.

"Said I loved you but I lied"[3] [http://bit.ly/1PIVYI6], he sang, and I swooned, surprised that he knew every word.

"Get a room," the other patrons whined.

"You're just jealous," I teased back, as we paid our tabs.

I followed Griffin to his house, where we sat in lawn chairs in his backyard, gazing at the moonlit silhouettes of trees as we drank beers and compared our life stories.

Griffin cut hay and milked cows as a kid? Whoa! He seemed so citified, his career, his quick wit, and his travels around the world, living in places like Greece and Australia and Germany.

"I've been on my own ever since I can remember," he said. "My mother always acted like she did us a big favor bringing us into the world. She loafed around watching soaps, demanding we fetch for her, like we were dogs. We did all the cooking—dishes—cleaning—you name it."

"I never thought of it that way. I mean, my parents had us fetch for them too, but I thought it was like a natural dynamic between parents and kids. I mean, I hated chores. But when I was in charge of the house and my younger sisters and brothers, I was in my glory. Hmm. Maybe they just let me think that so I would work even harder to please them? Maybe it was all a façade to have more control over me?"

"Yeah. It's all about control. My mother always had to be the big cheese. Then when my brothers and I got jobs, she acted like we owed her our paychecks, too. At first I gave her money. But one day I needed to borrow from her. She called me every other day to remind me. I paid her back two weeks later with interest and never borrowed from her again. But I never gave her another cent after that, either. I stopped calling her years ago because every time I did, she would just try to put this big guilt trip on me. Really? She never so much as made me a birthday cake!"

"Damn, man. That's terrible," I said. "My parents always celebrated our birthdays. It was the best day of the year no matter how broke they were. My mother always baked a cake. And my father lit the candles. And the whole family would sing. And we would take turns scooping ice cream. And they always had at least a couple of presents for the birthday kid, even if it was just comic books or paper dolls or a board game. Not just birthdays, but they treated every holiday as special. Hey. I mean, it was a hand-me-down, but I was frigging thrilled when my dad gave me his old stereo for my twelfth birthday-slash-Christmas present!"

"Hey, I was lucky if one of my brothers happened to say happy birthday when we passed in the hallway." He paused a moment then chuckled. "Anyway, that's the past. It's no big deal. I just wouldn't want to treat anyone the way my mother treated me growing up."

"I hear ya," I said. "Hey. What religion are you?"

"I grew up Catholic. Went to Catholic school as a kid."

"Wow! That's just crazy. Me, too!" I said.

Our belief systems had changed since those days. Each in our own way had abandoned the white-haired man in the sky for an amorphous, non-gender being somewhere, somehow, with no beginning and no end, but not anything any words could capture.

"Church is a crock," he said. "Like a quote I read in an e-mail the other day. Going to church doesn't make you a Christian any more than going to a garage makes you a mechanic."

"Amen to that."

He took my hand, and we tiptoed up to his room, careful not to wake his housemates. And then we climbed into each other's bodies. Exhausted inside and out, I curled up on Griffin's shoulder and ran my fingers through the patch of curly hair on his chest, trying not to move so his arm around my shoulder—so his fingers resting on my breast—would not drop from me. I craned my neck to look at him, at his curly eyelashes and the soft shiny bristles that cast a shadow on the slight cleft in his chin. His cheeks and forehead glowed in the light streaming through the window from a nearby street lamp. I could almost see his halo. I gazed at my little cherub, the sweet taste of heaven on my lips as I drifted off to la-la land.

"Said I loved you but I lied," Griffin and I sang along to Michael Bolton—live in concert—our first 'real' date a few weeks later, as Michael Bolton just happened to be on tour in the D.C. area. We sat in the VIP lounge, courtesy of Sprint, and delved into hors' d oeuvres and raised our glasses so a server could refill our choice of cocktails.

Un-freaking real!

Several months later we rented a house together, the month after a rough March, when tempers flared as we mourned our lack of privacy at the bar every night. At last, our own place, with no housemates telling us to smoke outside or jumping in the shower ahead of us or telling us to turn down our music.

At our housewarming party, we opened all sorts of Raphaels—which I had requested—for I wanted to celebrate the angel in my life. I decorated the house with the vintage Renaissance art: sets of pictures in gold frames with matching plaques and candles, refrigerator magnets and coffee cups and pot holders and cookie tins, journals and stickers and pens and pencils, sets of bath towels and shower curtains and matching soap dish and dispenser, and throw rugs and gold-framed posters.

After work, Griffin would stack CDs, and we would take turns singing as he concocted recipes for dinner, and I sorted the mail, folded a load of laundry, and set the table for dinner. While the masterpieces baked or stewed, we chatted about our day and figured out a five-letter word for Aphrodite's lover. Griffin would feed me one of his olives from his vodka martini, and I would lick the salt from his fingers as an extra bonus.

One Saturday at noontime, still dressed in our sweats and robes, Griffin took me by the hand and led me into the living room. We sat on the thick ivory-colored carpet and basked in the radiance of a slow-burning fire in the fireplace, everything clean and airy in our new home. April showers tapped on the bay window, but it felt like Christmas morning as we sipped hot coffee spiked with Kahlua.

As Griffin turned up the volume, a baby cried and a helicopter warbled overhead as I nibbled on a bagel.

"Listen," he said, and I stopped chewing.

"We don't need no education. We don't need no thought control."[4]

Then he opened a little box that contained a pipe and a baggie.

Munching on left-over bacon, we talked about our first day of kindergarten, our first cigarette, our first beer, the first time we left home, the first time we had sex. We talked about the day JFK was assassinated, or at least I did since Griffin hadn't been born yet. But still his point of view amazed me. I was 40, but in comparison he seemed so mature for only 31, and so educated for someone who never went to college.

It was a dumb question, and I already knew the answer. But I wanted to hear Griffin say that he loved me so much, that no matter what, our love could endure anything. I needed him to allay my biggest fear, my fear of losing him.

"Boredom. I wouldn't stay in a relationship if I was bored," he said.

Griffin looked at me with sad puppy-dog eyes.

"Hey, you. Don't look like that," he said, tapping my nose with his forefinger. "I'm just being realistic. You wouldn't want to stay in a relationship no matter what. Anything could happen. Don't worry about what may never be. Come what may and live for today. That's my motto. If and when something happens, then we'll deal with it."

"I know," I said. "I guess I'm just being a romantic."

"Good-bye, blue sky (http://binged.it/1N7sjpP),"[4] Griffin sang.

In the next year I learned that Griffin lacked motivation, which he was the first to admit. He liked to sleep in. I liked to get up early, play tennis, and work out. Not him. He had a bum knee from a bike wreck. I loved the outdoors. He didn't like to stray too far from the television or stereo. I liked to read and play games. He liked drama and action movies on HBO, and sex on television was neither here nor there. Nudity made me uncomfortable. I liked sitcoms. He was trusting. I doubted it. I feared. He was undaunted, except for confrontations. He hated to see the boat rock. I didn't like to lose. He gloated when he won. I got embarrassed. I was trying to impress everyone. But he didn't care what others thought.

He liked to cook and eat. I hadn't cooked much since Teddy died. Besides I was on a diet. He looked on the bright side. He didn't get hung up. Not me. If it didn't go my way, I couldn't get over it, no matter how hard I tried, sometimes for hours or days. "Anxiety" was my middle name. His middle name was "Whatever." I was uptight. I screamed. He bit his tongue. I was too sensitive. He shrugged a lot. He listened to Howard Stern. I liked Jack Diamond. But opposites attract, after all, right?

I called my parents every few weeks, and we would talk for hours. But Griffin had no desire to talk to his father, and he refused to call his mother, even after one of his brothers told him she had breast cancer. Not that he hated her, he said. He was just indifferent when it came to her.

"The way a man treats his mother is a good indication of how he will treat his wife," my mother always said.

No. Griffin would never treat me like that, terminate our relationship as he did with his mother, refuse to even return my calls. I just can't imagine that.

In the next year we not only celebrated our promotions and our pay raises, we celebrated buying the house that we had rented. Plus another trade association offered me a position as a communications manager—in a building adjacent to Griffin's office—which was just a mile from the house. So we went home for lunch most days, eating leftovers and playing gin rummy and having sex half undressed in our suits and skirts.

We had our bowling nights, our dart nights, our leagues and tournaments and trophies, and our poker nights, and cookouts and vacations. Every Saturday we cranked up the stereo and cleaned. I dusted and washed windows and scrubbed toilets while he vacuumed and shampooed the carpet and waxed the hardwood floors. And on Sunday mornings, we would lie in bed, taking turns getting each other's coffee, eating breakfast in bed, watching movies and filling in the blanks of that day's crossword puzzle. Then we'd shower and head to the golf club.

"Hey, babe," Griffin said one afternoon, patting my knee, as we drove toward the club. "You know, you're good for me. If it weren't for you, I'd still be in bed watching TV."

"If it weren't for you," I said, "I'd still be wading alone in Flo's kiddy pool."

With both of our divorces finalized at last, we decided to get married before the end of the year for a tax break, as Vera suggested. Not really. That's just how I presented it to Griffin. I just wanted to get married as soon as possible and it happened to be winter. I created the most beautiful wedding that my mind could imagine, planning every detail from the dress and tux and cake and rings, from the vows to the flowers, from the number of logs in the fireplace to the placement of the candles on the tables, down to the order that the deejay would play our songs and who would dance with whom and when.

"I finally found someone (http://bit.ly/21cfuR5),"[5] we sang our wedding song cheek to cheek.

When I awoke the next day, my eyes were swollen shut.

"Just allergies," I lied. "More like mid-May than late December. Fucking shit."

27
the banana peels

CRUSHING THE BABY DREAM

Griffin insists on getting custody of a baby, but once it is given to him, he leaves me with the baby and disappears. I hold the baby and play with it, thinking how beautiful it is and how much I love it. But then the baby's appearance begins to change. Something is wrong with it. The baby makes all these messes with a flour and water mixture in these puddles around a picture it is painting.

Then the baby hops on a car of an electric toy train set and rides around on the tracks in circles. Suddenly, some kind of evil creature wallops the baby in the head bashing its skull. I'm very mad at myself for not grabbing the baby off the train because I knew that the creature was going to crush it. It was like part of the game.

Now the baby looks much bigger and, as it suffers from the blow, its shell breaks open and out of it emerges my dog Tasia. I feel just terrible about this, and I'm explaining it to my dad, who is suddenly standing there. But he is indifferent to me, like he knew, and I should have known, that this was going to happen.

Dream Journal Entry
October 22, 1996

Late 1998 to Early 1999

"BUT JAMIE AND PAUL ARE NOT REAL," Griffin cried out in his defense. "It's a TV show!"

"But it feels like *they* are real, and *we* are the TV show, the way they are doing stuff and we are the ones just sitting here watching them."

Griffin rolled his eyes.

"I mean, look at us. We play Mario Carts every night and watch TV. You drink your vodka martinis while baking chicken in a pre-seasoned packet and boiling water for instant rice. I pop a Coors Light and open the mail, fold the laundry, and clear the table for dinner. We should do something different tonight!"

"I gotta go, babe. We'll talk about it tonight," he said, pecking me on the lips and walking down the hall.

He opened the foyer closet and pulled out his overcoat.

"Who was that calling so early?" he asked, looking down as he buttoned up.

"It was Alton. He wanted to be the first to wish me happy birthday."

Griffin turned to look at me, his face stricken.

"I'm in trouble again," he said.

"How could you forget my birthday? We've talked about it several times this week."

"I know. I'm sorry. But you know we don't have much money."

"Oh, bullshit. We make $100,000 a year, and you can't afford a card? And even if we were broke, how much does it cost to say happy birthday?"

"I didn't think."

"You never think when it comes to me."

"I've got to go. Early meeting. See you tonight. Happy birthday."

"Yeah. Thanks a lot."

Ten days later, on our anniversary, nothing.

Two months later, we had the same argument.

"If it's so damned important to you not to get in trouble, then why would you ignore Valentine's Day when you know how upset I was when you missed my birthday and anniversary?"

"All the holidays are important to you!"

"Yes, that's true. So what?"

"That wasn't the way I was raised. We never celebrated holidays when I was growing up. It's just not a big deal."

"That's funny. You didn't seem to mind the birthday party I threw for you last month."

"I told you then my birthday's not a big deal. I told you not to do it."

"Fuck you! I won't ever celebrate your birthday again. Or buy you a valentine."

"Fine with me," he said.

Forget the holidays, Griffin began to forget to hold the door for me, too.

"What the hell's the matter with you?" I asked.

"Nothing. Why?"

"You just walked out in front of me and let the door slam in my face—and left me standing there—in front of everyone."

"I just wasn't thinking,' he said. "You take everything so personally!"

"What's there to think about? You don't think about it when you're going in or out of a store and someone's approaching at the same time. You didn't think twice about it earlier when you almost cut in front of the bartender when you were heading to the restroom. You paused and motioned her to go first. I think you do think about it when you let the door shut in my face. To hold it open would be the natural reaction."

"Why do you always have to make such a big deal out of everything," he asked. "Have you been taking your hormone pills?"

"You're such a fuck wad," I said. "You're rude to me. And then instead of apologizing, you want to know what's wrong with me?"

"One of My Turns" [http://bit.ly/1lda5bp]," the voice announced. "Pink Floyd."

Griffin turned up the volume.

When we got home, he took out the dogs, then slung his coat over the kitchen chair. I hung up his coat and slammed the closet door. He shrugged and went to the bedroom, kicked off his shoes in front of the television, and turned on Nick at Nite. I picked up his shoes and shot them into his side of the closet.

"All of this over a stupid door," he said.

"Can't you see it's more than that? It's respect. It's knowing the things that hurt me and avoiding them. But I swear when I tell you something bothers me, it becomes your purpose in life. It's gotten so I can't even ask you to vacuum anymore without an argument. Everything I say now is nagging. I can't even say let's go golfing because now that's nagging."

"Look! I've been under a lot of stress at work, putting out one fire after another, working to seven o'clock or later every night. When I get off work, I just want chill."

"Bullshit! You wouldn't have to work that late if you went in earlier in the morning like I do, like you used to. You work the same fucking number of hours as you always have. Whether you work 7:30 to 5:30 or 9 a.m. to 7 p.m., that's still 10 hours a day not counting the two-hour lunches you take just about every other day."

Griffin grunted and turned up the volume on the TV, and I stormed back to the kitchen. I was beside myself. I wrote all of my angry thoughts in my journal until I was able to calm down. Then I pledged to myself that I would not lose my temper again, no matter what. I managed to get by 10 days without screaming until one night, when Griffin was working late as usual, I sat at the table, deep in thought, trying to remember a dream image from the night before, focused, and concentrating, I could almost see—

"Arf! Arf!" Tasia barked out the window like a maniac, like someone was skinning her alive.

"Mother fuck. Son of a bitch!"

Tasia and Dakota hung their heads and headed for the bedroom.

Damn! What the hell's wrong with me? I had been doing so well. But there I go, right off the deep end without a second's notice.

"I'm sorry, guys," I said, as I walked to the fridge to grab another beer. But they retreated anyway.

Words I had just read that week crossed my mind.

"Cultivate the art of awareness; catch yourself in the act without judgment and without excuse to enable the old patterns to begin to fall away.... The next time you lose your temper, stop what you're doing and think about everything you feel, your pulse, your heart, your stomach."[2]

I decided not to follow the dogs to the bedroom to sweet talk them just yet. Instead, I sat back down at the kitchen table and replayed the scene in my mind.

Tasia's barking. My chest tightening. My breath catching. My head jerking. My stomach lurching. My voice lashing back. All in one fell swoop. Then it hit me. Those were the same feelings I had as a kid when Dad knuckled me out of a daydream.

So that's what I'm really responding to!

After coaxing Tasia and Dakota back into the kitchen with treats, I sat back down and reread a paragraph I had highlighted in *Women Who Run With the Wolves* a few days before.

"In some ways, old emotions are more like a set of piano strings in the psyche. A rumble from topside can cause a tremendous vibration of those strings in the mind. In Jungian psychology, this eruption of great feeling tone is called constellation of a complex. Unlike Freud, who branded such behavior as neurotic, Jung considered it a cohesive response, similar to that made by animals who have been previously harassed, tortured, frightened, or injured. The animal tends to react to smells, motions, instruments, sounds which are similar to the original injuring ones. Humans have the same recognition and response pattern."[3]

As I finished reading, I heard Griffin's key in the front door.

I couldn't wait to tell him about my major breakthrough in understanding my anger, the first step in resolving it. But Griffin looked indifferent as he nodded and shrugged obligatory responses as he guzzled down a couple of Jacks.

"A rough day at the office," he said. "It's so late. I don't feel like cooking. What do you think? Order pizza? Chinese? Italian subs?"

Then he looked at Tasia.

"What good are you? You still don't know how to fetch the cable guide."

Night after night, weekend after weekend, when Griffin couldn't find anything on TV that we could both agree on, we would drop banana peels in each other's paths, squashing each other with lightning bolts, and bashing in each other's heads.

"Mother fucker!" I screamed, as Griffin ran Mario right over me, flattening Donkey Kong like a pancake. As I waited for the system to pop me up with new energy, I knew something must shake our stagnant world, or I would surely die.

28
the little rag doll

Now when I say mother complex, I'm talking about corporations. You work for the corporation. You twist yourself to suit into the corporation's ways....And these systems that we get into, they just twist us out of the reality of our own soul. So that when we get to be 40 or 45, all of a sudden we think, if this is what life is, what's the use? I'm not living.[1]

Marion Woodman [http://bit.ly/1PoTLrw]
Sitting by the Well [http://bit.ly/1OagpMK]

GRIFFIN IS KILLING ME
Griffin is killing me with a weapon of some kind that I couldn't recall upon awakening. In the dream it seemed so real, and I couldn't believe it. [The shock woke me up.]

BASEMENT/ELEVATOR
Griffin and I run in the back door of a building, but to exit we must go out the entrance. Two men in business suits are behind us, and one keeps offering to help Griffin to get out, although he ignores me. Someone refuses to let us leave, but the helper guy tells Griffin to follow him, and I tag along. But the guy stops at the elevator, like he doesn't know what floor to push. Then he pushes "F"—the Fax Floor. I gasp, "Oh my God! Not the basement!" [The shock woke me up.] [Uncut dream journal entry available at http://bit.ly/1ZyhNMA]

Dream Journal Entries
September 17, 1998

Summer 1999

"SHE EMBARRASSES ME IN FRONT OF EVERYONE," I yelled at Griffin. "Today, right in front of Tam, she asked me why the website wasn't ready to launch. Then when I tried to explain, she said she didn't want to hear it. Stupid bitch. She doesn't know shit about writing and testing cgi scripts and setting up fields in pdf forms and writing html coding and cleaning up and importing graphics. Besides, I am almost done with the website. I just have some links to verify. But even when I tried to tell her that, she cut me off. She just wants to see it live even if it means I have to work till midnight every night. But god forbid if I'm five minutes late."

"I know what you mean," Griffin said. "Remember when I went through that crap with Randall? Every morning when I got in he would look at his watch. Hah! I pointed out—"

"And then to top it off, I'm sitting there writing the capital gains press release when she comes into my office at 4:30 demanding that I finish the capital gains press release. No shit! It's not like anyone was even there to review it, anyway. The whole legislative affairs department was on the Hill all day. But, no, she had to go on for half an hour about how I need to prioritize my work. I don't know what the fuck she's talking about. It's not like I ever miss my deadlines."

"That's what you're telling me, but what did you say to her?"

"I told her I was working on the press release. She said sure. She's just anal. And it's the fact that it's the last minute. Stupid bitch."

"You need to go over her head again."

"Why? It didn't do any good the first time."

"What did you say to her when she criticized you in front of Tam?"

"Nothing," I sighed. I knew what Griffin was going to say next.

See! You need to speak up for yourself. You always let everyone walk all over you.

"But every time I speak up for myself, I get accused of overreacting or being defensive. You say so yourself."

"It's the way you handle yourself. If that had been me, I would have said right to her face, right then in front of Tam, that it was inappropriate for her to criticize me in front of a coworker. And then I would have offered to summon Janet for a meeting."

"I couldn't say that."

"Why not? It would have shut her right up. You would have pointed out the fact that she was criticizing you in front of Tam. That would have embarrassed her, put her on the defensive. She'd have been the one apologizing. And she wouldn't want you to call Janet because she doesn't want Janet to think she can't handle her own staff. You have to learn how to use a pinch of sarcasm with a smile to put people in their places."

"I know. I know. But she pisses me off so much, I'm afraid I'm going to blow up one day and end up getting fired."

"They're not going to fire you for speaking your mind. I have to put up with three mouthy subordinates every day. And I can't just fire them if they disagree with me. If I did, they'd all be out of jobs, including me."

"I guess. Maybe I'll talk to Janet tomorrow."

"Like I said a hundred times, you need to get out of the whole trade association mentality, and start looking for a real job. More money, and less nonsense. Anyway, you want to order pizza and play Mario Carts until Leno comes on?"

"Pizza's fine, but classes start soon, and I need to brush up on my algebra and statistics. It'll be a lot of work, but I'm sick of writing fluff—and kissing Aleisha's ass."

Before the alarm went off the next morning, I was at my computer typing up my dreams. I happened to scroll back to a dream I had had a year ago to the date, a dream I would never forget because this particular dream sickened me.

BATHING MY DIRTY MOTHER

My mother sits naked on a chair. She's fat and very dirty, and a substance like thick rust exudes from her. I'm appalled because it seems I'm required to give her a bath. She's sitting with her back to me, and I try to wash her. We are in a public place, I think at work because I can see Tam at a distance watching us. I'm embarrassed because of how my mother looks, how dirty she is, and how this must be humiliating to her to need someone else to bathe her.

She is also able to remove her head, which she does several times. She removes her head and bends forward to put it on the floor, then uses her arms to lift her back and chest back to the sitting position. Then she bends forward, picks up her head, and puts it back on.

I pull a curtain around us, but it keeps slipping away, exposing her. I try to scrub her back with a sponge that's not very moist, nor does it have soap on it. I scrub very hard getting some of the rust off, but I'm worried that I may be hurting her.

She asks me why I didn't use the washcloth, why I wasn't prepared. Then I lather lots of soap and water on my hands and wash her armpits. But that's as far as I can go. I can't even begin to fathom washing her private parts.

Dream Journal Entry
August 19, 1998

In a note to myself at the time, as I recalled the images of my mother taking her head off and putting it back on, it seemed that her face shifted back and forth with Aleisha's, and I wondered if my mind was playing tricks on me. Either way, the image disgusted me, and I shook it off as I showered and got ready for work.

When I was ready to go, I went to the bedroom to say bye to Griffin, who was straightening his tie, making sure the arrow pointed to his penis.

"Have a nice day," I said.

"Oh, I will," he said. "I'm getting off at noon today. We have a golf tournament, Sprint against MCI."

"Must be nice, having a 'real' job and all," I said, rolling my eyes.

By the time I got to work, I had managed to shake off yesterday's confrontation with Aleisha.

"Good morning," I said, as I walked past her office.

"Good morning," she said. "You look sunny in that yellow suit."

I laughed.

"Hey, thanks. I would have never thought to buy a yellow suit, but it was on sale. Your hair looks nice. What did you do?"

"My hair dresser colored it last night. A little lighter than usual. But I'll get used to it. Are you ready for this morning's meeting?" she asked.

"I'm ready."

Tam, Libby, and Janet joined Courtney, Aleisha, and I in the small conference room. We chatted and sipped coffee while Aleisha sorted her papers.

"Let's see," she said, turning her scarf a little to the left and then a little to the right.

"The scripts are due for review by 9/1," she said. "The handbooks are due to the in-house printer by 9/1. The online newsletter is supposed to go live by 9/1. The traditional print newsletter's due to the mail house by 9/1. The in-house ads by 9/1, and the list goes on, due 9/1, due 9/1, due 9/1. It's beginning to sound like 9-1-1. Who developed this schedule anyway?"

She paused, and we all laughed and cleared our throats and took another sip of our coffee. She did of course.

"Considering most of these projects are on your plate, Gabrielle, why don't you start us off?"

"Actually, all of them are on my plate, in total, 17 projects," I said, glancing around the room, wondering if anyone but me suspected that Aleisha had set me up to fail by making the schedule so tight.

"Let's see. I'm up to date with what's been turned in on the scripts so far. You know how that goes. But they'll be ready for review by 9/1. As far as the handbook guts go, I gave the in-house printer my pieces for copying on Tuesday. And once the meeting department turns in their stuff, Tam will coordinate the stuffing."

Aleisha looked at Tam, and Tam nodded.

"As for the online newsletter, I e-mailed you a link to review the site earlier. Once you approve it, I just need to upload it live."

"Nice job, Gabrielle," Janet said.

"Thank you. Of course, the admin council approved the hard copy of the newsletter, and the printer picked up the job this morning. I should have a blue-line by next Tuesday. And if all goes according to schedule, the mail house should receive the newsletter by the 27th, five days ahead of schedule."

"Well, we can't have them mailed that early," Aleisha said.

"I know," I said, glaring at her.

"Why not," Janet asked. "What's wrong with the members actually receiving the newsletter on the first?"

"They won't be expecting it yet," Aleisha said. "We need to be consistent."

"I say let it go as soon as it's ready," Janet said.

"Well, okay. So long as the blue-line looks good," I said. "Tam can change the time slot for the newsletter with the mail house."

"Okay. Tam, did you make a note of that?"

"Yes," Tam said, glaring at her.

"Okay. Let's move on," Janet said.

"I finished the in-house ads for the magazine, which are ready for review. Since everyone liked the fliers so much, especially the design of the Elevator Speech and homepage flier, I just modified the sizes and tweaked them."

"I loved them," Libby said. "And those sponsorship fliers and media kit materials you did have been really pulling in some bucks."

"Great!" everyone said.

"Alright, let's speed it up," Aleisha said.

"I finished the marketing brochure design and gave it to Libby to input the text. The Information Center has the homepage brochure and flier for review. As you know, I finished The Outstanding Service Award brochure back in July. Next, the admin council is reviewing my magazine article and, last but not least, here's the first draft of the notebook covers, front and back. I whipped them up this morning."

Each person gave their updates and the meeting wrapped up at 11 a.m.

I no sooner sat at my desk—feeling pretty good about myself—when Aleisha tapped on my door, walked in, and halfway shut the door behind her.

"Gabrielle, I don't know what you were thinking, but these notebook covers look unprofessional."

"But you told me to leave the covers in the same format as last year. Just change the dates and this year's conference slogan. See?" I said, as I pulled out last year's notebook to show her.

"Oh, come on, you could still do better than this."

"Oh, come on! You specifically told me not to go off on one of my creative tangents for something that doesn't generate revenue."

"Why do you always have to get so defensive? Just see what you can do to spiff it up."

I froze like the blue screen of death.

"An error has occurred."

Control-Alt-Del.

"Any unsaved information will be lost."

The next thing I remember, I was looking at the sunshine pouring through my office window, but in my yellow tweed, I was invisible.

It's a great big world out there—Griffin's probably getting ready to go out golfing in it—and you're stuck in here, feeling like someone stuffed a rag in your mouth.

I spun my plush, ergonomic executive chair around to face my desk.

I didn't go to college so I could write puffery for some stupid trade association. I had envisioned being an author sitting in a loft writing from my soul. I could hear Marion Woodman's voice echoing in my head.

"If this is what life is, what's the use? I'm not living."

My spacious office and my state-of-the-art office equipment, which I had boasted about, now meant nothing.

I stood up to run down the hall screaming. But a wave of nausea slapped me back into my chair. Like a violent protest in the 1960s, thoughts of quitting assailed my mind, and no other thought had the strength to endure the outrage. I sat like a little rag doll, my legs dangling, as I directed my human-sized body to type a letter. I shoved it in Aleisha's mailbox and walked out the mail room door in a giddy daze.

I quit! I quit!

Griffin might be worried about paying the bills at first. But I'll find another job.

It's not like it was a real job anyway.

Griffin said so himself.

29
the brick in the head

> But the agony of coming to consciousness comes through some immense suffering....Now usually there's some brick in the head that comes along about that point. Now the brick in the head may be the loss of a relationship....an illness...an addiction....so whatever that brick in the head is, it will be the wedge that starts the differentiation process that will take you towards your own femininity and your own masculinity.[1]
>
> Marion Woodman [http://bit.ly/1PoTLrw]
Sitting by the Well [http://bit.ly/1OagpMK]

MY NOTEBOOK ENTRIES WHILE READING *THE ENNEAGRAM*

I am amazed at how closely the characteristics of the Type Eight, the Challenger, which is my personality type based on the Enneagram test, describe me. About Eights, the Enneagram book refers to the Instinctive Triad of Rage, Aggression, and Repression Problems:

- Eights try to control their environments, constantly putting out energy so no one can get close enough to hurt them. This aggressive energy often emerges as rage.
- Eights tend to act out rage. Because of their fear of being rejected, divorced, humiliated, criticized, fired, or harmed, Eights attempt to defend themselves by rejecting others first.
- As a result, Eights become blocked in their ability to connect with other people or to love, since that would

give the other power over them, which is their basic fear.
- The more Eights build up their egos to protect themselves, the more sensitive they become to any real or imagined slight to their self-respect, authority, or preeminence.
- The more they shut down to avoid physical or emotional pain, the more hardened they become.[2]

The Wisdom of the Enneagram [http://bit.ly/1OaQMLz]
Don Richard Riso [http://amzn.to/1On8fPl]
Russ Hudson [http://amzn.to/1QZ7YEM]

If a person is not able to trust, for example, he or she will interpret erroneously the words and actions of others. If a husband tells his wife that he must attend a business meeting, although he would like to be with her, and if his wife is unable to trust, she may take his meaning as a rejection, or as a signal that his work is more important than she is. This misunderstanding results from her inability to accept what her husband has told her, from her inability to trust him. As the husband continually experiences his wife's misunderstandings, they generate within him feelings of surprise, sorrow, frustration, anger, resentment, and, eventually, the rejection that his wife mistakenly perceived. Thus, the wife, through the dynamic of distrust, creates her most significant fear....

An angry personality, for example, will create unpleasant, even tragic situations, until its anger is faced and removed as a block to its compassion and love, to the energy of its soul.[3]

Gary Zukav [http://bit.ly/1PJaBez]
Seat of the Soul [http://bit.ly/21cicpI]

Crossing the Bridge

I'm sitting up high, driving our new Dodge Durango. As I speed down the road, the road turns into a bridge of metal grates rising up over a body of water. I don't recognize where I am. As I cross the bridge, I'm in a regular car, I think my Mercury Topaz. I try to find some landmark that will assure me I'm on the right road. But in the strange lighting from the overcast sky, nothing looks familiar with only darkness and fog ahead. I am scared to death because I can't see where I'm going. Afraid I might get lost, I do a u-turn and head back the way I came. But in the darkness, I can't tell if I'm driving into a one-way or two-way highway.

But then a few cars pull up out of the darkness, and I ask the drivers if it is two-way, and they wave me through. I drive on, but I still can't see anything. Out of nowhere, a huge train or truck almost slams into the back of us—now there's another woman driving instead of me—which would have caused certain death.

Just as we say, "Whew!" Bam! We smash through huge iron vertical beams in a meridian. We chop right through them and then crash into concrete poles that look like pillars, like what hold up bridges. [I woke up shaken and certain that the last collision was fatal. Also, 20 years ago to the date, Teddy and I were married.]

Dream Journal Entry
March 17, 1999

Fall 1999

IT KILLED ME TO DO IT, BUT I URGED Griffin to take a few extra days to visit his family after his business trip to Kansas City. A few years ago his dad had sent him his regrets, along with the blue plaque with a bedtime prayer on it that had hung on Griffin's wall when he was a boy. Then last summer, Griffin took me to the farm where he grew up, where his father was raising a new family after Griffin's mother had left his dad.

What a blast, driving a tractor and baling hay.

"Are you sure?" Griffin asked. Then as if he suspected that it might be a trap, he said, "No. I can't go without you."

"Go ahead. I'll be fine."

"Oh, no. Remember when I flew to Ohio last year for training? You ended up costing us $300 to have a security system installed. And then you thought the guy installing the security system was out to get you."

"Oh, come on," I said, laughing. "He was a little weird. You said so yourself. It was supposed to take three hours. But it took him till one in the morning. Plus he took it upon himself to take the dogs out for a walk! Who does that?"

"Come here, you," he said, smiling, as he pulled me in.

As the date of his flight neared, I smiled a lot, but every cell in my body was sending out distress signals. Nothing I could pinpoint, but when I stubbed my toe, I grabbed the hurricane lamp off my nightstand and smashed it against the wall. Griffin seemed to understand. He cleaned up the mess, then we made love.

I dropped Griffin off at the airport and drove the five miles back home, all the while feeling like I had lost my best friend.

You're so silly!

As I unlocked the front door, a plane passed overhead.

That could be him.

As I looked at the sky, I felt Griffin's presence slipping away from me, so very far away from me.

Griffin's going to die!

"Stop it!"

You create your own reality.

The voice in my head repeated the phrase that I had read in book after book. But I didn't get it. I mean, I don't create reality. It just happens, and then I have to deal with it.

Griffin will land safely in Kansas City.

I sat by the phone.

It's not like him not to call.

Imagining the worst, I kept calling his cell and his room. By the time he answered, it was two in the morning. He was drunk, and I was livid.

"I don't want to go through that again," he said the next day. "I'll call you as soon as I get to Dad's. The farm's about four hours south of here, so probably around nine."

"I love you," I said.

"I love you, too."

"Be careful."

"I will. You, too."

I met Della for happy hour that night, my journal in hand. I didn't tell her about my death intuition. But I did read to her my dream journal entry from a few days earlier.

SOULMATES AND THE ALTERNATE UNIVERSE

Griffin and I are in some other dimension, like an alternate universe. We had just watched someone forced to go through an ordeal to be reincarnated so that he could be with his soulmate because the soulmate's parents had died.

Griffin and I move on to the next scene, where we see a woman with light hair, who is rather plain looking. She is unaware of our presence as we hover above her. We understand that when Griffin is reincarnated this will be his new wife, his soulmate. I'm indifferent about this. But as the scene unfolds, the woman's parents, who appear very old, are about to die. Griffin is upset, complaining that now he will have to go through the same ordeal as the person we observed earlier, since he must ask them for her hand, but there will be many obstacles to doing this if they have already passed. But then it occurs to me that Griffin should not be reincarnated to be another's husband. He and I are soulmates.

"We're already married," I blurted out, startling myself awake.

"Interesting," Della said. "I think we have many soulmates. If that were my dream, I'd think that unconsciously you know that. But consciously you deny it. That's why you woke yourself up."

"I don't know," I said. "I've always thought we only had one soulmate. Otherwise, what would be special about it? But then again, I don't know. I always thought Teddy was my soulmate. And then there was Griffin."

"There are many reasons people come in and out of our lives," Della said. "Not every person we fall in love with is necessarily our soulmate."

"Hmm. That reminds me of what a psychic said years ago, when my sister and I had a palm reading. She said we were twin souls. I wonder what the difference is between twin souls and soulmates."

Della and I pondered soulmates and twin souls for another round of beers, then we meandered across the parking lot to Awakenings, a New Age shop, to see if anything new had come in. That's when I saw the book. The cover, not the title, caught my eye: an unborn infant, pink and translucent, a close-up image of the fetus I had seen years ago in Joseph Campbell's *The Power of Myth*.

I had to have that book—no matter what it's about.

"*Wheels of a Soul*." Written by a Rabbi!

The subtitle was "Reincarnation," a subject I had shied away from for I was tainted with my mother's notion about the subject. She ranked reincarnation somewhere between witchcraft and space aliens, that is, somewhere between utter evil and pure nonsense.

I checked my voicemail when I got home, but Griffin hadn't called yet.

He should be there by now!

I called his cell, but the prerecorded operator said his phone was outside the calling area. Images of Griffin sitting dead in a wrecked car crossed my mind.

Stop it! You create your own reality.

To divert my attention, I popped a beer, sat at the kitchen table, and called Ma and Dad. We talked about the tornado warnings, about the $200 Ma won at Bingo last week, and about the movie they saw Friday night.

"I see dead people," Dad whispered.

"I swear, you're going to see a dead person in that theater one of these days," Ma said. "I've been telling you for months, the air in there is poison. I don't know what it is, but I can't breathe in there."

"Oh, for crying out loud, silly. It's the same air we breathe everywhere else. I'm the one with the lung problem. Don't you think I'd notice?"

"There's no use arguing with you," Ma said. Then she inhaled and exhaled a deep breath to prove that the air at home was just fine.

Their bickering was a good diversion for almost two hours while I stood on standby hoping a call would beep in any minute. But it never did.

When we hung up, I called Griffin's cell again.

Still out of range!

To block out images of blood and body bags, I began thumbing through my new book. In addition to discussing reincarnation, the book described how to determine if you are married to your soulmate.

Talk about synchronicities!

At first, based on Rabbi Berg's theory, it appeared that Griffin and I were soulmates. I felt comforted. But in the very last chapter, the very last page of the book, in the last entry, the book said Capricorns and Sagittarians cannot possibly be soulmates. Griffin, a Capricorn, was a feminine earth sign, and I was a Sagittarian, a masculine fire sign; therefore, we detested one another.[1]

I read it in my books. I saw it in our day-to-day living. I saw it with my own eyes in my own dreams, and rut or not, I still couldn't imagine my life without Griffin in it. I sat there staring at the phone, pleading for it to ring. But it stared back at me in silence. I tried to imagine what could have held him up. I saw his rent-a-car hitting a semi head on. I saw him slumped over in the front seat, the truck on fire. I saw the ambulances and people running to help him. I saw our house, our bed, empty.

I tortured myself until almost midnight.

"Where are you?" I asked, when he finally answered. "I've been worried sick."

"I'm fine. I'm at Old Grady's, you know, where we had beers and subs when we went out that night with my sister. I would have called, but as soon as I got to town, they were all ready to roll."

"Who?"

"Everybody. My sister and all my brothers, those in town anyway, and their spouses."

"Why didn't you at least call me so I didn't have to worry all night?"

"I didn't think it was a big deal."

"You don't think it's a big deal not to call your wife when you say you will," I screeched so loud the dogs moped into the bedroom.

"Hey, let me talk to her," I heard one of Griffin's brothers say.

"How are you?" he asked me.

"Fine," I said.

"So glad Griffin could make it out this way. Some of us haven't seen him in five years."

"Yeah." I had nothing to say. I could hear Griffin and the others laughing in the background.

"Well, sorry you can't be here."

Pause.

"Well you take care," he said, and handed the phone back to Griffin.

"Yeah?" Griffin said, like he wanted to know what else I could possibly want.

I hung up on him. I called him back. I screamed. I hung up on him again. I called him again.

"Why didn't you call me?"

"I don't know. I didn't think you'd even be home."

"Even if I weren't home, you could have left a voicemail so I'd know you got there okay."

"Well, I didn't. There's nothing I can do to change that now."

"You fucking bastard," I said, slamming the phone down on him again.

By the time I called him back again, he was on his way back to his dad's farm.

"How could you do that to me? You promised you'd call when you got there."

"I didn't think it was a big deal."

"If it's not a big deal, then why not take a minute to call me? Especially after our argument last night!"

"Look, Gabby, get over it. You think I have to account to you every minute of the day. Well, I can't take it anymore. As a matter of fact, I'm so sick of it that I'm just going to end it now. Faster. Faster. I'm doing 70 now, faster, 80, down the road, around the bend. I see the bridge ahead. Here I go. 90. I'm almost to the bridge, five-four-three-"

"What are you doing?" I screamed.

"Two-one......sh-k-k-sh-k." The phone went dead.

No! No! No!

Screaming and crying I dialed his cell number again and again. But only the prerecorded operator answered.

I called his dad's number, but there was no answer.

For the next two hours, I called and cried and screamed and called. But nothing.

Beside myself, I called his dad's number again. Finally, Griffin's little half-sister answered.

"He's not here," she said.

"Are you sure? I'm really worried. If he got in an accident how would anyone know?"

"I'll go look again," she said.

"Yep, I found him" she said. "He's sleeping on the couch in the backroom."

I stood up, sat down, and stood up. I paced from the kitchen to the dining room to the living room and back. I slammed chairs to the floor, the unfinished floor that Griffin insisted he could lay himself. I kicked over the hassock in the living room. I knocked our wedding picture off the mantel and stomped on it.

The next morning Griffin called and said he was sorry. But it didn't mean anything to me. It felt like I had been hit in the head with a brick, and I felt dizzy and nauseated. After we hung up I took the dogs out for a walk, like the walking dead, my face bloated, my eyelids almost swollen shut.

I looked up at the sky, and it seemed so very far away from me, far away like Teddy, and now like Griffin. I lost them both. And I realized God was preparing me for death, just not in the way that I had imagined. We would both survive, perhaps, but I felt like a peanut shell that had been cracked open only to discover that an insect had already devoured the insides.

PART VIII

"The return to the Garden is about coming full circle. It's about returning to a place with knowing, bringing to it a consciousness that was not there before. It's a new vision of the Garden because we have changed. Understanding the meaning of the Garden makes us a part of the whole of life.

"Blake talks about the child's world of innocence. Then we go out into "generation," as he calls it, or the world of experience. We live in that world until we return to the Garden, bringing to it our knowledge of experience and consciousness so that we see it as if for the first time.

"That conscious seeing is the higher innocence, Blake's Jerusalem. Now we can see, and we can hear, and we can smell, and we can touch with a totally different perception. I really feel that we human beings have to go through some near-death experience in order to value the Garden."[1]

Marion Woodman [http://bit.ly/1I8tNua]
"Abandoned Soul, Abandoned Planet" [http://bit.ly/1Xl7UyI]

"There is a saying, 'You can't go home again.' It is not true. While you cannot crawl back into the uterus again, you can return to the soul-home. It is not only possible, it is requisite."[2]

Clarissa Pinkola Estés [http://on.fb.me/21cfBMo]
Women Who Run With the Wolves [http://bit.ly/1Sd2y7B]

"What is it, then, that inexorably tips the scales in favor of the extra-ordinary? It is what is commonly called vocation: an irrational factor that destines a man to emancipate himself from the herd and from its well-worn paths. True personality is always a vocation and puts its trust in it as in God, despite its being, as the ordinary man would say, only a personal feeling. But vocation acts like a law of God from which there is no escape. The fact that many a man who goes his own way ends in ruin means nothing to one who has a vocation. He must obey his own law, as if it were a daemon whispering to him of new and wonderful paths. Anyone with a vocation hears the voice of the inner man: he is called."[3]

Carl G. Jung [http://bit.ly/1SdQJhc]
"The Development of Personality" [http://bit.ly/1MM8ctq]
in the *Collected Works* [http://bit.ly/1Xl9hgX],
vol. 17, pp. 180–181, ¶s 308–309.

30
the magical smile

"During the darkest times the feminine unconscious, the uterine unconscious, Nature, feeds a woman's soul. Women describe that in the midst of their descent they are in the darkest dark and are touched by the brush of a wing tip and feel lightened. They feel an inner nourishing taking place, a spring of blessed water bursting forth over parched ground ... from where they do not know.

"This spring does not solve suffering, but rather nourishes when nothing else is forthcoming. It is manna in the desert. It is water from stones. It is food out of thin air. It quells the hunger so we can go on. And that is the whole point ... to go on. To go on toward our knowing destiny."[1]

Clarissa Pinkola Estés [http://on.fb.me/21cfBMo]
Women Who Run With the Wolves [http://bit.ly/1Sd2y7B]

"Many a woman is feeling precisely that: she never lived. Now she is determined to find herself. But in her desire to sacrifice the old attitudes, she is experiencing a very real death. What begins with an attempt to change her relationships, may end with no husband, no home, no friends, even no children ... .

"Suddenly life becomes a vacuum. Fate seems to turn against her. The woman she was is dead; the new woman is not yet born. She is in a cocoon. Instead of being terrorized by her aloneness and her feelings of abandonment and rejection, she can use this time to work on herself.

One of the things she will surely face is her own inner killer—the overdeveloped masculine in herself that kills her femininity."²

Marion Woodman [http://bit.ly/1PoTLrw]
Addiction to Perfection [http://bit.ly/1X6OqTQ]

"It may sound odd at first, but frankly, people converse with their soul all the time .... Because it is considered such an untoward thing, we have learned to camouflage this interval of soulful communication by naming it in very mundane terms. So, it has been named thusly: 'talking to oneself,' being 'lost in thought,' 'staring off into space,' or 'daydreaming.'"³

Clarissa Pinkola Estés [http://on.fb.me/21cfBMo]
Women Who Run With the Wolves [http://bit.ly/1Sd2y7B]

"The dialogue between the ego and the Self creates the soul. The crystals and the snowflakes and the teardrops, all manifestations of spirit in concrete form, are gradually woven into the rainbow's threads of heaven. And the gossamer garment falling on the shoulders of Dumbellina becomes the blessing of the Goddess. It is delicate as rain, but it changes life from a meaningless puzzle into an awesome journey."⁴

Marion Woodman [http://bit.ly/1PoTLrw]
Addiction to Perfection [http://bit.ly/1X6OqTQ]

"A neurosis is by no means merely a negative thing, it is also something positive. Only a soulless rationalism reinforced by a narrow materialistic outlook could possibly have overlooked this fact. In reality the neurosis contains the patient's psyche, or at least an essential part of it; and if, as the rationalist pretends, the neurosis could be plucked from him like a bad tooth, he would have gained nothing but would have lost something very essential to him.

"That is to say, he would have lost as much as the thinker deprived of his doubt, or the moralist deprived of his temptation, or the brave man deprived of his fear. To lose a neurosis is to find oneself without an object; life loses its point and hence its meaning. This would not be a cure, it would be a regular amputation."[5]

Carl G. Jung [http://bit.ly/1SdQJhc]
"Civilization in Transition" [http://bit.ly/1HhSWaW]

Spring 2000, Part 1

AS THE PLANE RUMBLED DOWN THE RUNWAY I FELT LIKE LESS—husband-less, home-less, dog-less, car-less, key-less, hopeless.

Hey, what's the worst that can happen? The plane crashes and we all die?

"Hah! At least then no one can blame me."

What is wrong with you!

The plane's piercing shrill after liftoff intensified to the point where it felt like it might blow up—or I might crack up—and it reminded me of the day Marcy became possessed when she was in her 40s, how I witnessed the loss of her mind. And later I saw the effects of her exorcism, too, that left her like an empty shell, the nut inside eaten by drugs and machines, her blood drained, her vitality sucked away clean. Her puffy eyes somehow moved closer together.

As I stared out the window, I wondered if Marcy's experience foreshadowed my own disentombing. A cloud crossed the sun's path, and I saw my reflection in the window, my eyes swollen and displaced. I wondered if Marcy felt like her brain was slipping on a banana peel, too, just before she gouged out the potatoes' eyes.

Your focus creates your reality.

As the plane settled in its flight path, I studied the other passengers. One woman, a row up, fidgeted through her purse. A yuppie-looking guy folded his newspaper in half on his lap and closed his eyes. Somewhere up in the middle of the plane a baby began to cry. My eyes paused with pity at the sight of a heavyset woman across the aisle wearing a yellow floral-print dress, who was so large she filled two seats. I remembered how I kicked ass the day the boy up the street, who they called 'Tuffy,' ha ha, called my mother fat.

What happened to you? Now you're more like flight than fight!

The woman sensed my gaze, perhaps, for she looked at me. And she smiled.

In her smile I felt the collision of two worlds. How could I feel as if I'm descending into hell, yet the plane is lifting me up toward the heavens? How could it be that pain groped blindly in the smoke-filled forest of my heart while sunshine danced in the eyes of a woman bearing such weight? Sitting there with my frozen lips and eyes incapable of smiling, how could it be that a stranger could smile—at me—of all people?

Jung's voice spoke to me out of the blue.

"Bidden or not bidden, God is always present."

"I've never left you," another voice said.

I sat up straight and listened.

I felt Teddy's energy, his warm brown eyes, his quiet smile, his soft moustache. It dawned on me. God did answer my prayer that night. Ma and Dad's phone call was God answering. I just didn't make the connection. I couldn't look away from the window, away from Teddy, away from the Divine. The awesome view filled my heart.

In a strange telepathic way, the Divine spoke through Teddy, and we talked a hundred miles a minute. Soaring through the sky, I felt like a bird, no, a plane, no, superwoman.

"You are an orphan—and the whole world is your orphanage," I heard Marion Woodman's voice.[6]

My fear of heights forgotten, I urged the plane higher, higher.

"Ladies and Gentlemen," the voice said over the intercom. "According to the control tower, we're heading into a little turbulence. Please fasten your seat belts."

Cool! This is so awesome.

As the wings dipped in and out of rushing black clouds, Teddy said to rest assured.

"The sun'll come out tomorrow."

The storm had passed, or rather we passed through the storm, and for the rest of that flight I celebrated the Divine, the beauty in the sky, the clouds, the Earth, the people around me, who seemed to sense something about me, who smiled at me. I didn't get it. If I had seen someone who looked a mess like me, I would have turned the other way so as not to embarrass them, or I would have looked at them with pity. But it would never have occurred to me to smile.

Amazing, this world.

During my layover in Detroit, I sat at a deli counter sipping a beer, waiting for a cheeseburger. A little old man hobbled in with a walking stick and looked around. I moved my bag off the seat next to me and smiled at him.

He winked at me as he pulled up the stool.

"It's a beautiful day in America," he said.

As he shared delightful stories about his adventures in London, I smiled and laughed and ate my cheeseburger, the whole thing, without gagging at all.

The anxiety that had spun its cocoon in my belly had hatched into the most beautiful yellow butterfly. I felt utter peace and joy, perhaps the sensations I've heard baby-faced preachers talk about when they're drumming up donations, feelings I usually associated to baloney.

Word got out to every cell in my body: Running to and fro, from mind to body to soul, my blood cells rejuvenated, healing the pink veins in my eyes, erasing the blotches and plumping the wrinkles in my face, draining my bloated lids and bags, drawing out the tension that had long been stored in every nerve and muscle of my body, untying the knots in my stomach, flashing beams of light into the darkness of my heart, and watering the parched desert in my soul.

As I returned to my father's house that spring, as the plane began its descent over Dallas, I heard Adrienne Rich's voice:

> I go down . . .
> I came to explore the wreck . . .
> I came to see the damage that was done . . .
>
> And the treasures that prevail.[7]
>
> Excerpt from "Diving into the Wreck" [http://bit.ly/1PI92oa]
> By Adrienne Rich [http://bit.ly/1NKbMUM]

31
the mess I created

THE MAGICAL EYES
A woman appears, and she asks me if I had read a certain book. I say no, that I'd heard of the book, that my mother has the book, but, no, I have not yet read it. She says she can tell by looking at the way my eyes glow green and blue, that I have the power to fully develop all of the magic in the book. She tilts her head up a little, and I see her eyes and say, "Oh my god. Look at your eyes!" They are deep green, and her pupils change into little pictures.

Dream Journal Entry
April 3, 2000

THE ABANDONED CHILD
There is a stack of boxes before me, which I recognize as chapters of the book I'm writing. I associate the large empty box on the bottom as the section of the book that recounts my childhood, which I had abandoned writing because I didn't like the little girl I once was. "You must love this child before you can love your Self," a voice proclaims.

Dream Journal Entry
April 5, 2000

A GLIMPSE INTO THE EYES OF THE PAST
My mother is sitting in a rocking chair in the middle of the room, and my sisters and I are lying down on the floor around

her, going to sleep. I recognize all of my sisters except for one. I scoot over to the child and study her. Upon closer scrutiny, I realize the child is me at about age four. I look deep into her eyes. They look blank, unresponsive. I speak to her, try to comfort her. At the same time, I marvel at how I'm her own future speaking back to her in the past.

Dream Journal Entry
April 7, 2000

Spring 2000, Part 2

FEELING LIKE A LITTLE GIRL AGAIN, like the day I first got my own bedroom, I helped Ma clean out the knick-knacks and wall-hangings from the guest room and integrated them into the living room décor as Dad stood back supervising, excited, yet anxious, keeping close watch, torn between wanting change and wanting everything to stay the same.

Then like children on Christmas morning, Dad, Ma, and I showed each other our new toys, the toys we'd acquired since Griffin and I had last visited them in Texas almost five years ago. Dad's eyes lit up as he turned on his musical merry-go-round and his train clock that went choo-choo on the hour. Then he showed me how cool he was with his brand new wrangler jeans and a shiny new belt buckle with his name engraved on it that Peter bought him for Christmas.

Then it was my turn.

As I sorted through all the little treasures I had packed in my box, I couldn't imagine what must have broken that coated each piece with a sweet-smelling film of sticky glitter. As if the Universe was sending me a message, everything in my box transported without a scratch—except for the musical glitter globe, the only angel I decided to pack, and that's only because it was a gift from Alton.

"Oh, well. I guess that's that," I said, laughing at the irony as I explained to Ma and Dad my dilemma when I was packing the box.

Then I poured my sacks of stones on the table, explaining the various energies of labradorites and amethysts and obsidians and hematites and rose quartzes and tiger eyes.

"When it's a full moon," I said, "I set them outside in a bowl of water so the moonlight can renew their energy."

Dad chuckled, a hint of doubt smiling in his eyes.

"Remember this picture," he asked, pointing to a picture hanging on their living room wall.

"It's hard to believe 14 years have passed already," I said.

"You can hang it in your room if you like," Ma said, when she saw my eyes glaze over the photo of Teddy, me, and the kids.

I hesitated, then lifted the photo from its nail and hung it above the computer in my room, not with sadness of my long ago loss, but with gladness that Teddy and I had reconnected. For the first time I understood what Della meant about her Mamaw, her guardian angel.

Then it was Ma's turn. From the closet, she retrieved her new easel, her unopened tubes of paint, her pastel chalks, her drawing tablets, and her large blank canvases.

"Every time I turn around, she's buying more paint and more brushes," Dad said. "That stuff's expensive, you know. And that's fine. But she never uses any of it."

"I just got a fabulous idea," I said, looking at my mother. "While I'm working on the book, you can paint the jacket cover. It'll be a joint venture."

"Oh, I don't know," Ma said. "I can't paint like I used to."

"Sure you can!" I said, not knowing why, since I had no idea of her skill level.

"I don't know how she'll have time," Dad said. "She never has time to do the normal things, like dusting and vacuuming. Did she show you her new vacuum cleaner? Freaking Kirby dealer came when I was at the store. She never uses that either."

"I don't know exactly how I want the cover yet," I said, tuning Dad out. "But I know I want this as one of the elements," I said, turning my back toward them, pulling up my sleeve, and pointing out the red and green and blue beads, the red rose, and the feathers, which I had had tattooed on the back of my right shoulder the day that Princess Diana died, not that the two had anything to do with each other. But the tattoo symbolized for me my first step toward discovering my identity.

"Wow, I didn't know that you got a tattoo," Ma said, tracing the design with her fingertip.

"Ah. A dream catcher," Dad said, peering over her shoulder. "You got to be careful, nowadays. They say you can get hepatitis from the needles. Or even AIDs."

"I've read that," I said. "You just have to make sure the place is reputable and sanitary. It's not like I had this done in someone's basement. As a matter of fact, I want to get another one. Maybe a ladybug on my ankle. Maybe a bracelet around my wrist or bicep. I don't know yet."

"Remember that bar, the Lone Wolf Pub, where I took you and Griffin to play darts the last time you were here?" Dad asked. "There's a tattoo place right next door to it."

"Cool. I'll have to check it out. But speaking of Griffin. I've called him several times. But he still hasn't called me back. I just want to know if he's going to stay at the house, take care of the dogs. I gave Della a key. She's going over to feed the dogs and let them out if he's not already there. I'm sure he is. But it would be nice of him to at least let me know."

I went to my new room and dialed his number. I was strong enough now to handle whatever he had to say.

"Sprint. Griffin."

"Hey, it's me. I hadn't heard from you, and I just wanted to make sure someone's going to stay at the house."

He didn't answer.

"I don't want it to go into foreclosure or anything. If you're not going to stay there, I'll have to figure out some—"

"Sure, I'll stay at the house if we can make a deal. I'll take care of the house and all the bills," he said. "If I can stay there for the next year, I'll fix it up. Then you can sell it, get what you can out of it. It's your house. I'm not going to screw you."

"That's fine, um." I started to ask something about whether he was going to get a lawyer, or file for a separation, or do something that would at least begin a closure. But I couldn't figure out how to say it. He read something else into my hesitation.

"I don't see us getting back together, Gab," he said. "I know that's not what you want to hear."

He didn't know it, but he told me exactly what I wanted to hear. Sure, I might have felt better at that moment if he had cried crocodile tears, said he missed me, begged me to come home. Such words might have stroked my weak ego, may have sent me packing. But my soul, my higher Self, would have cried out, would have pleaded with me:

No! Remember crossing the bridge in your dream? How you turned back. Remember the collisions? The fatal ending? You cannot turn back now. Or you will surely die.

"Did you hear me, Gabby? I said I don't see us getting back together."

"Oh, yeah, yeah, okay," I said. "I just wanted to make sure the house wasn't abandoned."

"Well, I've gotta go. I'll call you later."

I knew we were doing the right thing, but I sat there stunned.

It's over. He has no intentions of ever calling me again.

With the dial tone still buzzing in my ear, I remembered the first night Griffin and I looked into each other's eyes, love-stricken, as if by cupid's arrows.

What the hell went so wrong?

Then I remembered Marion Woodman's narcissism concept. Perhaps it applied to us. Griffin and I fell in love, yes, but more like Narcissus. We gazed into each other's eyes, merely dark reflecting pools, and fell in love with our own images, images that reflected back our ideals of the perfect mate. We did not fall in love with each other. We fell in love with the creature in the mirror. I fell in love with my reflection. And he fell in love with his reflection. A perfect match.

With twin images of my own reflection staring back at me from Griffin's pupils, I began to understand that I saw myself only through his eyes, that I had lost my identity in his, that I needed to reclaim myself, whoever that self may be.

With that in mind, I opened the binder where I had clipped the first two chapters of my childhood, which I had rewritten over the last few months, and began to read. Page after page, I frowned and groaned. I thought it was so good when I rewrote it. But to look at it now. It lacked life, energy, left me with the feeling of *so what*. Embarrassed, I tossed the pages in the wastebasket and decided to start over, to leave out those early chapters. I would write the book without that stupid little girl.

I booted up Mariah's old computer to check it out. It didn't have any bells or whistles, but it would serve my purpose. I opened a new document in Word and began to type.

"You're a dreamer, for chrissake."

Two weeks later, I ended up back where I started: looking into the eyes of the little girl I once was.

"Perhaps by returning to where I began I could figure out how in the world I had created such a mess of my life," I had typed.

"Ugh!"

I backspaced over that last sentence and went out to the kitchen, where Ma sat watching Oprah.

I popped a beer and sat down.

"We create the messes in our lives," Oprah's guest was saying at that very moment.[1]

"Wow. Who is this guy?" I asked, jumping up from my chair and moving closer to the TV. "I know him! It's Gary Zukav! I have one of his books, *Seat of the Soul*," I squealed at Ma, who seemed to be entertained though she had no idea why I was so excited.

"I had just started reading it a few weeks ago, before everything fell apart," I explained.

The synchronicity boggled my mind. I wrote it down and walked to the kitchen and some man on the TV was saying the exact thing I just wrote—what are the chances? Besides it was just an expression. I hadn't meant it literally. But no doubt, the Universe was trying to send me a message.

Egged on by dreams, by synchronicities, by my very own written words, I began pecking away at the keyboard, something about a Greyhound bus. Before I knew it, the little girl began to breathe, began to speak from her heart about things I may never have recalled otherwise. As she blossomed like wild flowers from the depths of my soul, I began to like her, understand her, appreciate all her magic. She told me many secrets, but what she didn't tell me was that she was preparing me for the unexpected storm.

32
the unexpected storm

"The long-term effect on the Christian psyche is also real and unfortunate. Like an abused child for whom early trauma continues to define later behavior, Christians tended through the ages to bear a sense of aggrievement and victimhood, even long after they came into power. Christians tended in turn to become abusive toward others when they came into power."[1]

Luke Timothy Johnson [http://bit.ly/1QZbzm5]
The History of Christianity [http://bit.ly/1kPhUVi]

"When a woman has trouble letting go of anger or rage, it's often because she is using rage to empower herself....It is a defense that, once the time for needing it for protection is past, costs plenty to keep....So the clearing of residual rage must become a periodic hygienic ritual, one that releases us, for to carry old rage beyond the point of its usefulness is to carry a constant, if unconscious, anxiety....

"Patience is a good thing to apply to fresh or old rage, as is embarking on a quest for its healing....

"So rather than trying to "behave" and not feel our rage or rather than using it to burn down every living thing in a hundred-mile radius, it is better to first ask rage to have a seat with us, have some tea, talk a while so we can find out what summoned this visitor."[2]

Clarissa Pinkola Estés [http://on.fb.me/21cfBMo]
Women Who Run With the Wolves [http://bit.ly/1Sd2y7B]

"Be conscious of what you are feeling. Experience everything you are feeling. Feel despair, pain, jealousy…Underneath anger, for example, which most people can recognize, if you stay with it long enough you will find pain. Pain that is so intense and so deep that you would rather be angry at yourself or someone else or the universe than to feel it… [Feeling the pain is] necessary for the healing and expression of your soul."[3]

Gary Zukav [http://bit.ly/1PJaBez]
Seat of the Soul [http://bit.ly/21cicpI]

"Hitherto the symbol of the Self, the disk, had been largely an intuitive idea on the dreamer's mental horizon…. Now the golden disk suddenly moves to the 'right' side—the side where things become conscious. Among other things 'right' often means, psychologically, the side of consciousness, of adaptation, of being 'right,' while 'left' signifies the sphere of unadapted, unconscious reactions or sometimes of even something sinister…. Roundness (the mandala motif) generally symbolizes a natural wholeness, whereas the quadrangle formation represents the realization of this in consciousness."[4]

M.-L. von Franz [http://nyti.ms/1SUafPU]
Man and His Symbols [http://bit.ly/1I9CmFb]

REPLANT THE DEBRIS

Ma, Dad, and I are listening to the weather report, which predicts that the lightning will bypass our area. But no sooner did he speak when huge lightning streaks light up the sky, and the house we occupy begins shaking. As the storm passes each house or building, we progress along with the storm into another house or building. Though it seems we are indoors, we can somehow always see the sky.

As the storm progresses, long rectangular black clouds unfold and drop debris all over the place. Sometimes we can see the clouds dumping actual garbage. At one point I spot a fishing net whirling by. Like some kind of scene from *The Wizard of Oz*, I can also see tree trunks whipping through the sky.

"The tree trunks must be uprooted so that they can be replanted," a female's voice explains. And I think, what a mess we will have to clean up when the storm passes.

Dream Journal Entry
April 21, 2000

DON'T DROP THE BABY

Ma and Dad and I are running with a baby, which Dad keeps dropping on its head, which upsets me, angers me, especially because Ma acts oblivious to it.

Dream Journal Entry
April 22, 2000

THE MURDER OF MY MOTHER

Ma, Dad, and I are in an ambulance rushing Ma to the hospital. Then Dad pulls out a gun. Ma says, "Oh, good, you brought the gun," like she thinks that will protect her. As soon as she says that, he points the gun at her and blows her head off. I'm totally devastated and angry, thinking how un-fucking fair. We all worked so hard at keeping my mother alive, ever since she had had the seizure, and then Dad just kills her anyway.

    Sadness overcomes my feelings of anger, and I curl up in the fetal position and just lie there. I know I have a funeral to go to. And I know I love my dad. But now I don't want to see him ever again. I loved him once, but now that my mother is dead, all my feelings for my father are dead, too.

Dream Journal Entry
February 16, 1999

Spring 2000, Part 3

"**SHE'S BEEN DEAD FOR 14 YEARS,**" Dad yelled when I checked Ma's pulse, in jest, saying I thought she might be dead, she's been sleeping all day, after all.

"Why would she want to get up?" I screamed back at him. "With you bitching at her the minute she opens her eyes. I wouldn't want to get up either."

"My nebulizer's not working right," she sighed, sitting forward in the living room recliner, pulling out her nasal cunnula, which was attached to her portable oxygen tank.

"There's nothing wrong with your machine, silly. They've checked it a dozen times."

"She's probably just depressed," I said, thinking I'd be depressed, too, if I had someone yelling at me all the time.

"I'm just tired," she said. "I'm not getting enough oxygen at night."

"Oh, here we go again," Dad said, as Ma looked up the number to technical support.

"The tests indicate that the machine is producing the right level of oxygen," the technician said that night.

"A waste of—" Dad began to roll his eyes.

"But the tests can't tell us how much oxygen is actually getting through—good grief, look at this," he said, pulling the blackened filter from one of the machine's compartments.

Ma didn't have to say, "See, I told you so." The expression illuminated from her face as she stood there with one hand on her hip.

That night as I dozed off I could hear them arguing over spilt milk.

"I want to buy some scratch-offs. Give me a five," Ma demanded, as if to say that if she had to go to the store she would get a reward for her efforts.

"But the milk's for you, silly," Dad gasped back through a coughing spell. "You're the one who spilled it. Why do you act like you're doing me a fucking favor? I don't even drink the fucking stuff."

"It could wait until tomorrow, Zach. We don't need milk tonight."

"But the carton's almost empty now," he screamed, his voice suddenly so loud, so close to my door it seemed, for a split second, he might bust through my door screaming some more, blaming me, belt in hand.

The next day, when Dad was at the store, I asked Ma about the argument the night before.

"We didn't argue last night. I didn't think he was angry." She shrugged. "Maybe I've just gotten used to his moods."

Maybe I was just dreaming.

"What were you guys arguing about last night?" I asked Dad, as he put the milk in the refrigerator.

"We weren't arguing, not really. I just didn't feel like going to the store because I felt lightheaded. I was coughing my fool head off."

They're making me crazy, and they can't even fucking hear themselves.

That night, I decided to have a few beers, no, really, a lot of beers. I guzzled them one after another. As I broke open a second six-pack, Ma and I started talking about a book of hers which we had both just finished reading, *Pain and Pretending* by Rich Buhler, which discusses the effects of child abuse. But Dad interrupted us.

"Oh, come on. Just about everybody's been abused," he said. "Even Oprah was abused, wasn't she? Why can't everyone just get over it?"

"Why the hell can't you just get over it, Dad? The abuse in your life that made you so angry. Why don't you just get over it instead of taking all your anger out on us for all these years?"

"Oh, bullshit," he said. "When I was a kid, and when you kids were young, that's the way it was. It wasn't called abuse. It was called discipline. What's wrong with kids today? I'll tell you. Because people nowadays spare the rod and spoil the child. They believe in all this psychobabble. We had violence on television. And we got our asses kicked when we got out of line. We didn't turn out to be murderers or rapists. So what's wrong with kids today? Killing each other in the schools. Killing their parents. Doing drugs. Joining gangs. I'll tell you what's wrong with the kids today. They need a good old-fashioned spanking with the belt."

"What's wrong with the kids today?" I yelled back. "I want to know what's wrong with the adults today, the adults from your generation. What's wrong with the adults who create the violent video games? What's wrong with today's adults who write the scripts for the movies, the adults who can't seem to cram enough violence and sex into just about every scene? Now with cable, six year olds are getting up before their parents on Saturday mornings and watching rapes and murders and naked men humping naked women."

I was on a roll.

"Maybe that's why kids are so angry today, killing in the schools, escaping pain with drugs. They don't even know it, but they're just by-products of all the abuse handed down from generations before them. That's what you did to us. Tell me this. How come it's against the law for adults to hit other adults but not illegal for a grown man or a grown woman to hit a defenseless little child?"

Up to that point Ma acted like she wasn't paying attention. She had bent over and was brushing the dog, assuring Princess that everything was okay. But she had to put in her two cents.

"It's just like we saw in the movie the other night, *The Ten Commandments*," she said. "The people rebelled with all this corruption, bowing to false gods and getting drunk while Moses was up on the mountain. Just like little kids when their father turns his back. They need their father standing over them every minute with a whip."

"For crying out loud, Ma," I said. "Why do you have to brush the dog in the house? You're getting dog hair all over the kitchen."

"Gabby's always saying mean things to me, Princess. But she's always nice to you. Sometimes she says I'm not her mother. But that's okay. I've got thick skin. Come on, Princess, let's go outside."

But before she could stand up, I went into a rage, and Princess crawled out from under my mother's reach on her belly and then ran out of sight.

"You're not my mother," I spat at her. "My mother was strong and confident. She taught us that we could do anything. I know who my mother was. But who the hell are you? You act like the child you speak of so vividly now, the six or seven year old, who tried to buy friends with candy. You're not the mother who raised me. My mother danced circles around all of us since I could remember. She stood up to City Hall. She protected me from neighborhood bullies, from evil spirits. She ran Mothers' Club. She was a leader among her friends. They called her when they needed a cup of sugar, a recipe, a dress hemmed, a haircut, a letter written, a petition drawn up, a shoulder to cry on. But now look at you guys. You just sit there, oblivious. You guys scream at each other but can't even hear yourselves—"

Suddenly, I could hear myself, see myself, see the pain in my mother's face, see my hand holding the smoking gun. All I wanted to do was shrivel up in a little ball and die. I ran to the bathroom, closed the door, and looked at the eyes in the mirror. My tears dismantled Dad's mask and dagger and Ma's armor and shield.

As I watched myself step out from behind the trees into the moonlight, my camouflage heaped in a pile at my feet, I remembered a concept I had read in Jung's *Man and His Symbols* [http://bit.ly/1I9CmFb]. And it made sense for the first time.

The animus, which the father shapes in a woman, can convince the woman that she is not who she really is. When the destructive projection falls away, the woman will realize that she has reacted just the opposite of her real feelings and thoughts.[5]

I'm not me. I'm a mere extension, a composite, of them. I always thought that I was just like her, but she always said I was just like him.

Pointing and gesticulating and mouthing my words at myself in the mirror, I continued the conversation.

We were both right! I was him and I was her. But that's him and that's her. But who am I? I have been robbed! My identity. My individuality. My soul. They demanded it in exchange for their acceptance when I was a little shit! And look where it has gotten me: A life full of anger and confusion and heartache—and parents who can't stand the sight of me because I look just like them!

I know, a cliché with a bad rap for decades, but true. I had begun my quest by asking myself, "Who am I?" Something inexplicable demanded that I find myself. Most people chalked it up as a copout, a coward's escape, an ego trip, a selfish endeavor.

But that night, I felt validated. It was a real thing, a real need, to discover one's true Self. It struck me as cruel that a father could and would creep in like a thief and steal his child's soul without the child realizing it.

However, I found hope in Jung's assurance that once the deceit of the animus enters a woman's consciousness, its creative energy can actually be used to build a bridge to Self.[6]

33
growing pains

"The Enneagram is the bridge between psychology and spirituality....We must realize we are not our personality. To begin to grasp this is to undergo a transformation of our sense of Self. When we begin to understand that we are not our personality, we also begin to realize that we are spiritual beings who have a personality and who are manifesting themselves through that personality. When we stop identifying with our personality and stop defending it, a miracle happens: our Essential nature spontaneously arises and transforms us... .

"Personality is like a cast, the more extensive the injuries, the more extensive the cast has to be; it is necessary to heal but must be removed or it limits full functioning. See the personality as a temporary cast, an utterly necessary aid because it has developed most powerfully around the soul's greatest wounding. It has become strongest, when we are weakest...."[1]

The Wisdom of the Enneagram [http://bit.ly/1OaQMLz]
Don Richard Riso [http://amzn.to/1On8fPl]
Russ Hudson [http://amzn.to/1QZ7YEM]

THE COLOR OF THE SOUL

I see three symbols in front of me that somehow express to me that they represent three layers: the upper and lower, which eludes me upon awakening, but in the center is the soul, which is a pinkish-orangey color disk. I try to make sense of this, thinking that the soul should be a true red color rather than wishy-washy colors that I can't pinpoint. It occurs to me that perhaps the spectrum of the color wheel in my brain is out of kilter.

Dream Journal Entry
April 7, 2000

LIZARDS IN A SPHERE

I'm very excited contemplating a circle formed by two lizards, one black and one white, which I realize form the Yin and Yang symbol. With great awe, I suddenly understand its symbolism of totality, including the mysterious quality of its transcendence.

Dream Journal Entry
May 19, 2000

Spring 2000, Part 4

"**PORK CHOPS, MASHED POTATOES AND GRAVY,** and applesauce," Ma announced when I walked into the kitchen.

"Mmmm. Smells good," I said, grabbing a plate.

"The dogs were beginning to wonder if you were okay in there," Dad said. "Gee, it's been about six hours since we saw you."

"Yep," I said. "I'm on a roll. I wrote 4,000 words already tonight."

"Wow," Ma said. "I couldn't write that many words in a whole year."

"Your mother's been sitting there," he nodded toward her chair. "Playing with little papers and cutting them out. I don't know what the heck she's doing. Me, I've been just sitting here twiddling my thumbs."

"I'm drawing the book cover, Zach. I told you that."

"Yeah, but silly, why would you need to draw it and then cut it out and then paste it on to the paper? Why don't you just draw it on the paper to begin with?"

"Grrrrrr. I don't know," Ma said, wringing her hands. "I just have to draw it so I can get a really good picture of it in my head before I begin to paint."

"Still, why do you have to cut it all up in little pieces and make such a mess?"

I knew what Dad meant. Ever since her seizure, Ma entertains herself for hours with scissors. It irked him to watch a grown woman sitting there for hours cutting out little shapes like a four-year-old concentrates on cutting out paper dolls. But Ma didn't understand the issue, the fact that her cutting fetish served as a constant reminder of the seizure that stole away Dad's wife, my mother, the woman we once knew.

"It ain't hurting nothing," Ma said. "I clean up the mess."

"Hey, Dad," I said, licking the grease from my fingers. "Good pork chops, huh?"

He picked up his fork and his steak knife.

"What do you think," Ma said, holding up the prototype of the book cover.

"Oh! Cool," I said. "I love it."

The book cover didn't interest Dad much. He had a bigger mission on his mind, the springing ahead of clocks one hour, which was no easy feat for a man who collected clocks.

"I'm wore out," he said. "I've been changing clocks all day."

"But the time doesn't change until tomorrow at midnight," I said.

"Yeah, but with all the clocks and watches in this house, I need two days to change them all," Dad said, half sighing, half chuckling. "Your mother's almost as bad as me. She has six watches herself."

As he spoke, he leaned over to put her jewelry case of watches back on her side of the table, and tipped over his glass of orange juice with his elbow.

"Mother fuck. Son of a bitch!" Dad yelled, jumping up in a rage, pushing himself back from the table so none of the juice would spill on him. As the glass crashed to the floor, the dogs ran out of the room.

"I can't fucking believe I did that. Wasting a whole glass of juice. This fucking table's always so fucking cluttered."

"It's all right, Dad, no big deal," I said, already hovered over the mess with a broom and a dustpan. I scooped up the broken glass in the dustpan and trashed it, and sopped up the juice with paper towels and rinsed the floor. Before Dad could stop screaming, I poured another glass of juice, set it on his coaster, and sat back down in my seat. Ma never budged. She sat cutting out another dream-catcher because she said the edges looked crooked on the last one she cut out.

"There, like nothing ever happened," I said. "Eat before your food gets cold. Ma, you too."

Dad shuddered as he tried to shake off an outrage that didn't play out its natural course, kind of like getting robbed of a sneeze, but much more violent. I knew that shudder well.

"I had just smacked Princess," Dad said, reminiscing later that evening, "for jumping around like a nut. Stupid dog gets so excited. I know she was just trying to play, but Pixie's so little, you know. Princess could have hurt her. Princess went berserk. She grabbed a pillow off the couch and snapped it back and forth between the couch and the chair, crying and growling and whimpering and frothing at the mouth like a maniac. I tried to get a hold of her. But it was like she had cracked up. She was acting so crazy she was scaring me. So I never hit her again. You know, you got to be careful with Border Collies. They say you can easily break their spirit—"

"Son of a bitch!" Ma yelled. "Probably has dog hairs all over it."

Dad zipped under the table, picked up Ma's paintbrush, ran it under the faucet, dried it with a paper towel, and sat it back on the table next to her. Then he wiped the paint off the floor, all in the matter of a few seconds.

A few weeks later, Dad surprised me again.

"Gabby-doll," he said, filling a bowl with water. "It's a full moon out tonight. And I can hear your stones crying, 'Energize me. Energize me.'"

That night, while Dad and I sat outside, talking about all the things we regretted, wishing upon the stars that all mean things said and done could be unsaid, undone, Ma painted the sky, not my sky, but some sky that evolved from her own mental landscape.

"Yeah, I see," she had said, when I showed her two samples of skies she could choose from. Then she sat for an hour just studying them, one sky, a swirl of blue and white with a galactic effect; the other kind of a grayish-blue with streaks of gray and pink.

"Either one," I had said. "The main idea is to make it look mystical like in my dream of crossing the bridge."

"I love the blending," she said, when Dad and I returned to the kitchen.

She had set the easel up on the kitchen counter and sat at the table admiring it from across the room. Aghast, I searched for words as I blinked at a fiery sky with black patches.

"Well, actually, you know, I don't remember the sky being any particular color. I guess it was foggy and overcast, really. Maybe your sky better captures the dream than those pictures I showed you."

"Yes, that's what I was thinking," she said, gloating. "I really love that sky. Now what colors do you think for the water? I know you said you wanted the water green but all I have is this shade," she said, holding up a tube of St. Patrick's Day green.

"I think you can get the effect I'm looking for if you mix it with black," I said, pointing to the television set on the kitchen counter. "There. About the color of the television screen when it's turned off, almost colorless. Then you can put the fog over it after the paint dries."

I went to my room to get some writing done, and when I returned to the kitchen a few hours later, she had painted the water beautiful shades of blue and aqua.

"Wow," I said. "But, um. I don't know. I thought we agreed that the water would be dark green, almost colorless."

"I don't know," she said.

"Look," I said, getting annoyed.

I turned on the water faucet.

"See. What color is the water? It's not blue. Water's not blue. It's colorless. When have you ever seen blue water?"

"I don't know," she said, massaging her scalp with her finger tips. "We had blue water in the crick I used to swim in as a child."

"The blue was just a reflection of the sky. Anyway, that was a hundred years ago back before we polluted it. Besides, how can you have such radiant water under an overcast sky?"

"Well, I can paint over it again once it dries," she sighed. "That's enough for tonight."

I sighed.

"No, actually, that's all right, Ma," I said. "Maybe if you can just tone down some of the blue. I really like the effect you've got going on, that dark blue patchy look in the water. So, it's fine. Just tone down the brightest greens and blues and I think it'll be great."

When I went back to my desk, I thought she was going to bed.

But an hour later I could still hear the TV. When I went out to the kitchen, I was horrified. She had repainted the water, every last drop of it, with puke green.

"Ma! What did you do? I told you I liked the dark blue patches. You didn't need to cover the whole thing."

"You wanted green water. There's green water."

"What are you, colorblind? That's not the color of the TV screen. That looks like—"

Don't say puke. Don't say shit.

She grabbed a rag and began scrubbing all the green paint off. I stood by helplessly, feeling guilty about frustrating her. By the time she finished, I couldn't believe my eyes. It looked perfect.

"That'll work! I love it. Now when you add the fog, it'll be exactly what I had in mind."

"I won't add the fog until I finish the bridge cables," Ma said.

"That's a good idea," I said, holding in my sigh until I was out of hearing range.

The next night, after bingo, as she picked up the paintbrush, I couldn't bear to watch. Blocking my peripheral vision with my hands, I honed in on the *Honeymooners* for the next half hour while she struggled to draw the cables in pencil. She used to have such a steady hand, smooth and generous as it graced any canvas or paper before her. But now she struggled. Her hand shook. When she finished, she turned the easel so the painting faced me and smiled.

"Ma! Drawing always came so natural to you. But now you try too hard. Those cables don't even line up right, and the perspective is all wrong. You always try too hard at everything instead of just being yourself, and it comes off phony. Even when we go to the restaurant you think you have to clear the table when we're done eating. Why? The waitresses at the Dunbar already love you for just being you!"

Her eyes welled up, and she stretched the bagging skin under them to stop the tears from dropping.

"Ma, I just want you to be you. You used to be so—"

"I don't know who I am anymore. I think when I had that seizure, I lost my soul."

I didn't know what to say to that.

I wrapped my arms around her shoulders and told her I was sorry, told her how much I loved her.

After she went to bed, I sat at the kitchen table for a long while and studied the cables.

There was nothing wrong with them, I decided. The fault was all in my own perspective.

I made some coffee and took the whole pot out to the table on the back porch, where I sat for the next several hours smoking cigarettes, looking at the patio clock that glowed in the dark, as the hands took me back in time.

"You're so insecure," I could hear my mother's voice condemn me with impatience and disdain. I think I was just three or four years old the first time that she told me I was so pathetic. I didn't know what she meant or what I did that disgusted her. But it hurt worse than when Daddy called me stupid.

And now when I look at her—ever since she had had that seizure and lost 15 years of her memory—she is the one who is so insecure.

Are you angry because she has fallen off the pedestal you had put her on since you were a child? Are you angry because you see in her an aspect of yourself that you don't like? Is it really you who tries too hard to please others and the very act of attempting perfection causes you to fail? And those you try to please reject you because you seem like a phony to them?

I went to the bathroom, heated up another cup of coffee in the microwave, and then returned to the porch.

No matter how hard your mother tries, no matter how hard Griffin tried, neither of them can re-create what you perceive as the perfect image in your mind. They can't even see it much less deliver it. No matter how hard they try, they can't please you.

As I replayed the scene with my mother again and again in my mind, Griffin's hurt expression, as if I had kicked him in the gut, flashed through my mind. All I said was that his red golf shirt clashed with the plum colored pin stripes in his shorts. It wasn't that important, I told him. But he knew better. He changed into a white polo shirt.

Every day after that day, though, he checked with me before he got dressed, asking me if this tie matched that shirt or this shirt matched these slacks. For years I summed it up with a laugh.

"All men are colorblind!"

But as the Texan sunrise streaked the sky with various shades of red and pink and plum, it occurred to me.

What if I'm the one who's colorblind?

This whole new spin shook my perceptions of myself and the whole world. And I could not stop my mind from making one connection to another. Awake all night and then all day, I waited and waited, repeating over and over the point Pastor Buckley made a few weeks ago at Mariah's 25th wedding anniversary celebration.

"How you touch someone does not merely affect that person for just that moment, but for eternity. So be careful how you touch the people in your life and in your passing."

"Mother," I said, stroking her hair. "It's almost three in the afternoon. I was thinking we could take a walk if you get up soon. At the coliseum."

"I've been awake a couple of hours," she said. "I just didn't feel like moving."

She unstrapped her oxygen mask and pulled herself out of bed.

As we walked around the coliseum parking lot, I told her how bad I felt and about the pictures in my head.

"I know what you mean," she said. "I get pictures, too. But the pictures I draw on the paper never look like the ones in my brain. I'm just not very talented, I guess."

"But you are. You draw and paint beautifully. It's not your fault you can't see the pictures in my brain. It's stupid of me to expect you to be a mind reader. You're doing a wonderful job painting the cover. Even Dad's been getting excited about it. Every time someone walks in the door, it's the first thing he wants to show them."

Ma smiled.

"You know," I said. "Sometimes when I watch you paint I get this urge to take the paintbrush from you and paint. Not because I want to take it from you. But because I envy your talent. I can't even draw stick people."

"I've always told you, Gabrielle, you are very creative. You could paint if you wanted to."

"You know, I think maybe I'll take a painting class. I think I'd really like that."

Ma smiled.

"You will paint one day," she said.

That night I didn't feel much like writing. Although Ma seemed to be in good spirits, I couldn't erase in my mind the mean things I had said to her the night before. So I logged onto the Internet to play spades.

I hyped myself up for it, tried to get emotionally ready. This time if someone starts rattling off some nasty comment about a card I discard or a bid I fail to make, I will not get mad. I will be the new me, the one who no longer loses her temper.

Not long into the game, my partner got ticked off at me and blasted me in an IM. Instead of spitting back a scathing IM as I usually would, I typed back, 'sorry.' But it didn't feel right. It didn't feel authentic. I felt like a traitor to myself. It felt like I was weak and sniveling. I hated it. I wanted to rattle off that nastygram. That would have made me feel good. I am what I am. Fuck it.

"Fuck you!" I IM'd my partner back and then logged off.

Venting my anger and feeling good about it reminded me of what I'd read about Eights in the Enneagram book about seeing gentleness as a weakness. I pulled the Enneagram book out and lay on the bed to read some of the passages I had highlighted.

"It is time to remove the cast, to touch the wound, to function fully, to heal," I whispered, as I fell off to sleep.

Ma and I took a walk around the coliseum parking lot the next day, too, and chatted, like we were getting to know each other all over again. But I noticed she didn't attempt to return to painting the book cover. Why would she? Poor thing. What I put her through. I doubt she will ever return to it. And that's okay. It's my own damn fault.

I create the messes in my life.

About one the next morning, I finished writing the frustrating scene of my mother painting the water while it was still fresh in my mind. When I went to the kitchen for a break, I was surprised and relieved to see that Ma had put the easel on the table and was painting.

Give me the strength to love whatever she does. Forget the picture in your head.

I popped a beer and watched the "Honeymooners" for a few minutes with Dad.

From the corner of my eye, it looked like she was dabbing the paintbrush on the sphere.

Oh, no! Not the soul. She had painted it so perfectly to match the soul I saw as a child.

"I think I should paint the cables now. What color do you think?"

"Oh, I don't know."

Be careful. Don't say silver, or she'll paint them her metallic silver. I saw that tube. If she does, the cables will outshine the whole thing.

"Gray, I think would work," I said. "What are you painting now?"

"Oh, I was just fixing the road," she said.

Whew!

"Can I look, or would you rather I didn't?"

"You can look."

I stepped back around behind her and looked, but I couldn't see what she had been painting other than the yellow line down the center of the road, which I had told her I didn't want.

"I also added some blue to the water," she said, her eyes blinking with pride, her lips curled up in a childlike grin.

My mind scrambled through a menagerie of pictures until it paused at the sight of blue and green scribbles taped to an old refrigerator. I couldn't take it anymore. I flipped out. The sounds that emanated from me did not come from my cheeks or my mouth or my throat or my lungs, but from my belly. Not anger, but laughter rocked my soul and erupted through my heart. Ma began laughing, too. So did Dad. We laughed until we coughed, until we cramped.

"I've done my part," Ma said, smiling at me. "Now it's up to you to paint the little car crossing the bridge to Self."

With paint still dripping from my brush, my journey just beginning, I could hear Della's voice.

"Baby steps," she said. "Baby steps."

34
the healing mother

THE NEW HOUSE

I have a large, painful growth on the back of my hand, which my mother removes while I am unaware. I'm amazed when I see that it's gone. Then suddenly I'm standing in a brand new house. It still needs furniture and decorations. But the house is really nice. The walls are white and clean. I'm surprised that I got a house so soon after Griffin and I broke up, and I'm excited about decorating it. The house already has a microwave in it and a few other appliances. I also see some things I'm apparently working on, like puzzles or the book.

Dream Journal Entry
April 9, 2000

Spring 2001

A YEAR LATER ALMOST TO THE DAY after I had waved good-bye to my mother from the window of a Greyhound bus—it was as if she was sending me back out into the world a second time—I sat at my computer filling in some of the details in the chapters about Teddy dying and her seizure. I had even skipped happy hour that Friday night to work, but at about 8:30, as I read and reread the last sentence I wrote, I was overcome with such grief that I couldn't write another word.

"I felt like the little kid standing next to the dumpster in the school courtyard long ago."

What is wrong with you? Surely you've come to grips with this by now.

I went to my bedroom and crawled atop the comforter, curled up in a ball, and listened to the rain.

As I tried to sort my feelings, my cell phone rang, and the digits of Ma and Dad's phone number lit up the caller ID.

I hadn't even given Ma and Dad my cell number yet. How could they be calling me?

I pushed the green button.

"Who died," I asked, hoping we could have a good laugh.

"Well, actually, we would have called you earlier, but we couldn't find your phone number." Mariah said. "But we did finally find your cell number."

"Well, good, I think. Is everything okay?"

"Well, actually, um, at about 7:30 tonight, um, well, Ma passed away. At the movie theater—"

"Noooooooooooooooo!"

I dropped the phone, and ran from room to room, down the stairs. Up the stairs. Back down the stairs.

"Noooo!! God, noooo!"

I can't breathe in that movie theater. The air in there is like poison.

But the last time she said it, Friday, May 18, 2001, her oxygen snuffed out with the pong of popcorn, she collapsed and turned blue. The paramedics didn't arrive in time. There was no time for prayers. No time to even think.

Who are you, Mother?

I had taunted her. And now that I had just gotten to know her again, I've lost her—again! There would not be a third chance.

Who are you, Mother?

"I'm the same person I've always been," she had told Peter's wife one day. "Everyone thinks I've changed since the seizure. But I haven't. This is who I've always been."

I didn't discover that truth until I called her on Mother's Day, five days before she died. Dad had hung up his end to go lie down because he wasn't feeling well—a first in my recollection. As if someone had turned the clock back 20 years, my mother spoke with such clarity and great recall, like the seizure never happened.

"This is amazing, Mother. It's just like you got your memory back."

"No. This is who I've always been," she said. "I just can't get a word in edgewise when your father's around. Besides, he contradicts everything I say, so it's just easier to let him do the talking."

Guilt ripped my heart out as I thought of all those late night talks between Dad and I while she just listened and said a gratuitous "Mm hmmm" now and then.

As I shook at the podium above her casket, I read to her the Mother's Day poem I had written to her back in 1985—before I had forgotten who she was.

MOTHER

Smiles and stars brightened my dreams
Before my lips parted or my eyes blinked
Because heart to heart we spoke unseen.

Songs and winds stirred and moved me
Before air filled my lungs or sounds I heard
Because your soft voice in me whispered.

Paints and rains promised me colors
Before my soul searched for like metaphors
Because your sunshine shaped my rainbows.

Glad odes and sunshine warmed my toes
Before my skin waxed over hardened bones
Because my blood did flow in your warm veins.

Chimes and moons and ocean waves lulled me to sleep
Before my wake
Because in your womb you rocked me deep.

And floral scents filled my head
Before I felt your face your cheeks of rose
Because your passion nurtured me.

Mother, mother.
You fed me before the earth or sea.
You fed me fruits of love and seeds of grief
And showed me God before I learned the creeds.
I smiled for you before my eyes could glow.
I cried for you before my tears could flow.
I felt your pain before I felt my own
Without reasons, without seasons,
I felt your longings before I knew what you desired.
I loved you before I knew of water or fire.

Then one winter day they cut the cord
And I began to die.

Yet in me grows my loving mother yet growing from her own seeds of love yet planted deep within my soul budding always the love of my mother.

The cord they cut but they can never sever
The circle, the cycle, of your love, Mother.

As I stepped down from the podium, I sensed my mother, content in Teddy's presence. I knew she understood now why the experiences she suffered paved the path she chose to evolve her soul, that now she could see the Intent in my heart rather than taste the bitterness of my words. She understood. One day so would I. So would Dad. There was nothing to regret.

Glancing from one white wall to another in the living room and kitchen, I smiled at the assorted pictures of beautiful goddesses that I had framed and hung all around me—even before I perceived Goddess as the feminine side of God.

And I smiled at the photos of me with all my girlfriends, which Angus had taken at my housewarming party. We had been friends for years but it was as if they were seeing me for the first time as they scanned the fountains and fairies and lizards and castles and precious stones.

"This is my favorite," I said, holding a labradorite up to the light for everyone to see the spectral radiating in colors ranging from dusky gold to peacock blue.

"Wow! I didn't know you knew how to decorate, Gabby," Catalina said.

"Me either!" I said.

"Look at this place. This is so you!" Gretchen said.

"I couldn't have done it without you," I said, considering she helped me put my old house on the market and found a buyer, providing me with enough money to start my life over.

Something so obvious, so natural to others, but new to me, a real live identity of my own.

So me!

"Holy cow, Gabrielle, is this you?" Leona asked, as she browsed the photos I had hung in the hallway. I went to look and saw that she was pointing to the picture I used to hide, the one with a little girl clutching a pink purse as she posed with her brothers and sisters on Easter in the courtyard with the housing project in the background.

"That is me," I said, pleased to recognize myself.

Della's husband said it was cool how I decorated my new place, and so did Angus. But most of the husbands and significant others didn't know what to say.

"Let me guess. Your favorite color is green," one of them said, a safe comment considering the green blinds, the green border around the kitchen with yellow suns and stars, the dream catcher pattern in the green fabric of the sofa, and the dining table and matching hutch with a shiny malachite finish.

"Have you thought about joining a witch's coven?" another dared to venture, with a chuckle.

But Angus and Della's husband appreciated the décor for what it was. Not some weird attack on masculinity. Not an evil expression of witchery. But a genuine, creative expression of one's soul, which I had denied myself for so long, had feared, revered, loved, and hated, that is, the masculine side of God now embracing God's feminine side, the ultimate syzygy.

I scooped up Suzy G., the kitten I adopted last week, before she could knock off any of the pieces of my goddess puzzle, and sat down on the sofa.

"Hello, spider," I said.

Not wanting the critter to end up at Suzy G.'s mercy—or lack thereof—I coaxed it up onto the puzzle box, opened the patio door, and set it free.

You should get in the shower.

"You have plenty of time," I heard Della's voice.

I sat back down on the sofa.

You? A stock clerk? At Booked Solid? How fitting!

"A book coordinator," my manager had corrected me.

"Call it what you want. I love this job."

But you barely make enough money to make ends meet.

"I am safe in the arms of the Universe."

But what if you lose your job? What if you die before you finish this book? What if—

"Don't worry about what may never be," Griffin had said. "If and when something happens, then we'll deal with it."

As I shifted my thoughts back to my new job, I remembered a dream I had had the other night.

THE INTRIGUE OF THE NUMBER NINE

I'm at work, and I am appreciating the irony of working at a bookstore as I stack books, like filling in the pieces of a puzzle, which I recognize as the puzzle of my life. I stack and rearrange the books, first building a foundation, then enclosing the foundation with other books in patterns of four, and then eight. As I complete each level, adding more and more books, I am very satisfied with my accomplishment. Just when I think I am finished, a ninth level appears on my stacks of eight books, a luminous outline of an unfinished level that intrigues me. I try to think. Threes and fours have symbolic significance. But nines?

I fed Suzy G. salmon for breakfast, poured a cup of coffee, and sat at the table, thumbing through the pages of my favorite book.
That's when it popped out at me.
"The nine has been a 'magic number' for centuries. According to the traditional symbolism of numbers, it represents the perfect form of the perfected Trinity in its threefold elevation"' [http://bit.ly/1I9CmFb].
So freakin' weird. Did I dream of the significance of nine and then read it? Or did I read it and then dream it?
Right then, in her effort to swat a moth, Suzy G. knocked the atlas off the bookshelf.
Talk about synchronicities!
Just yesterday at work I had met a quirky old guy in a wheelchair who wanted to know if we had any pocket atlases.
"They're over here, sir," I said, curious as to just how far he planned to travel. "It comes as a set, full size and pocket size. But it's a great price."
"Just bring it to me, would you, deary?"
"Sure."
As I handed the atlas set to him, he pointed up the aisle.
"I just didn't want to lose my wife," he said. "Wanted to keep her in my sights."
"Yeah, well, I can help you find anything you want in this store, but if you lose her?" I laughed and shrugged and threw up my hands.
"Can I tell you something?" he asked, leaning forward.
"Sure."
"Clinton heard on the radio that women's clothing was half off at J.C. Penny's. And he was waiting at the door the next morning before it even opened."

He winked, and I smiled, not at the joke but out of love for a man with a sense of humor, who was trying to stay alive, a man a lot like my father.

Speaking of smiling, I couldn't figure out why my coworkers and patrons kept smiling at me as we crossed paths, that is, until I caught my reflection in the mirror in the memorabilia section.

How embarrassing!

I had been walking around with this silly grin on my face for probably weeks and didn't even know it.

Clock is ticking!

"You have plenty of time."

Della's been saying that for years, but I didn't get it until I realized that half the time I lose my temper is because I'm in a hurry. And when I'm in a hurry, I drop things and break things and bump into things. Just thinking about it, I can feel the anxiety telling my body that something's wrong. It's like driving 60 miles an hour down Route 28 and someone cutting in front of me.

"You have plenty of time," I said, taking a deep breath as I studied my mother's picture, which someone had snapped of her and Mariah at the Mother-Daughter Banquet 10 days before she died.

Time. They say timing is everything.

But something about the timing of her death bugged me. Why would she die the week before the movie *Pearl Harbor* was released—in May? It was like the opposite of a synchronicity. And she died right before the movie *Shrek* began, of all movies, a movie she and my dad would have totally related to. I just didn't get it.

After her death, I searched for her for what seemed like hours on end in dream after dream. Finally, last week, as a huge black sore on the back of my hand began spreading, she appeared to me, and the sore vanished. I awoke thinking about how she had nursed the yin and yang tattoo of two lizards between my shoulder blades in Texas last year. And I was comforted knowing that my mother had healed me, and that she and Gaia, my Earth Mother, and my Great Mother, Sophia, will not abandon me.

PART IX

"Women are finding their own 'mother' containers in which to honor their own bodies, emotions, and voices. When this process develops, women start producing their own pictures, articulating their own thoughts through poetry, essays, or whatever vehicle they choose, and begin to come forward. There's another energy that is necessary to give women the strength to take it out into the world or even to take it into a deeper place within herself. This is the moment of reunion of the masculine and the feminine.

"This inner journey and search for the deeper feminine—and ultimately the reconnection of the masculine and feminine—as a profound experience of finding your own soul and finding the world's soul at the core. The great paradox is that the more you find yourself, the more you find the soul of everyone else. Once you have touched into this place within yourself, you cannot see a tree cut down without pain. You're related to everything. I find more and more women are dreaming about this beautiful little boy and of their own inner masculinity being healed."[1]

Marion Woodman [http://bit.ly/1I8tNua]
"Slow Down and Meet Your Sacred Feminine"
[http://bit.ly/1QD1g85]

35
the pond beyond

"The worst terrorist attack in U.S. history scarred the New York skyline and shook the New York Stock Exchange, which remained closed for a week after the attack. When the markets opened the following Monday. the Dow plummeted more than 7 percent, dropping 685 points. Airline stocks saw some of the steepest declines and the Dow Jones transportation average fell 343 points, or 12.8 percent."[1]

Amy Bingham
"ABC World News Tonight"
[http://abcn.ws/1SUcOkZ]

"We count on our urban symbols to be present. They are not supposed to evaporate. When buildings go away, they go almost as slowly as they came, piece by piece. The architect Cesar Pelli estimates that if demolished conventionally it would have taken two years to dismantle. Pelli, who designed the World Financial Center, four squat towers next to the Trade Center, said to me that he thought of his buildings as 'a set of foothills beside the mountain, and now the mountain is gone.'"[2]

Paul Goldberger
"Building Plans"
September 24, 2001
[http://bit.ly/21cfGji]

THE RADIANT BABY BOYS
I'm sitting in a chair picking up one little boy after another, holding them, telling them each how beautiful they are. As I caress their foreheads, they radiate more and more beauty, to the point of surrealism. I love them very much.

Dream Journal Entry
January 8, 2001

TOO BEAUTIFUL TO BE A BOY
I'm walking through a warehouse, and as I'm going through a turnstile, there is a little boy in front of me dressed in colorful pajamas. The boy is very cute with blond hair. I say hi and he says something about it's nice to have the happy family back together again. A few minutes later, he says that I'm the one who said it was nice to have the happy family back together again. And I said, no, all I said was, hi!

Then I'm at another turnstile entering my new place, and there's a black woman on the left and a small boy on the right. I am sitting on something that places me at the boy's eye level. The woman tells the boy to say hi, and he does. He is a very beautiful black boy with beautiful black braids. I smile at him and ask him his name. He tells me, "Lim." But I'm confused because Lim is a boy's name, and he's too beautiful to be a boy. "Linda?" I ask. They both try to explain his name, and I guess, "Lynn?" They enunciate the name with great deliberation and I realize it's a boy and his name is Lim. I ask him how old he is and he says, "Three!"

Dream Journal Entry
February 24, 2001

THE TRAFFIC JAM
I'm driving back from Washington, D.C., to my house in Herndon, Virginia, about 25 miles north of the District, when I suddenly find myself stuck in a huge traffic jam. The guy in front

of me jumps out of his vehicle and yells to me that the traffic is backed up all the way to New York.

He's upset and worried, he says, because his wife and kids are alone, like they are going to need him, but he won't be there for them. At first, I take the statement as a chauvinistic remark, as if he is implying that women aren't capable of taking care of themselves, that women need men to fend for them, keep them safe.

But I realize I'm wrong. This is no ordinary traffic jam. Something much bigger has happened, some catastrophe, like a war or a bomb exploding.

Dream Journal Entry
December 10, 1998

THE VERY TALL BUILDING

I'm following a lady up the stairs of a very tall building. I follow her at a distance so she doesn't know I'm behind her. I think I know which way she turns at one point, but I make a wrong turn and end up on the rooftop, where I can see other buildings in shambles. It occurs to me that the building I am in could crumble at any moment as well, although there is no bomb threat or anything that I know of. Just the same, I feel an urgency to get out of the building. I have difficulty finding my way down at first, and had to slide down one flight of stairs that was covered in moss.

Dream Journal Entry
February 24, 1999

BODY BAGS

There's a mound of dead bodies in body bags. I open the bags and look at them. They have bewildered expressions. Several of them are small children. I feel sad that they died so young. One at a time, a person pulls a body out of its bag. Another person dresses and preps the body and seats it in a chair. I then perform my responsibility, which is to tie each one's shoes.

Dream Journal Entry
February 17, 2000

THE POND BEYOND THE MOUNTAIN

I'm at Della's house drinking beer with her and her husband at a large round wooden table. Suddenly everything seems to slant, especially the table, and I can't tell if it's really slanted or if my eyes are playing tricks on me. I ask them if they notice it, too. Just as I speak, the table tips over and everything slides. We think it must be an earthquake. A few minutes later, we're looking out a bay window and we can see mountainous terrain (that had never been there before) that peaks then levels off at various increments, each level distinct in colors ranging from a light sandy color to dark brown. As we watch, suddenly the whole mountain crumbles and comes crashing toward us. It is earth shattering, but no one seems too distressed over it.

As I sat there troubled about this, a prophetic sounding voice seems to encompass the Earth as it says, "The pond beyond the mountain is no more."

Dream Journal Entry
September 16, 2001

WORKING THE EVIL BOOKS

I'm at work, and I have four faces of books, maybe stacks which, although I recognize as evil, I'm required to work them into the book run, which has five shelves, not four. I tried to work them into a vertical line, but they didn't look right, so I ran them across horizontally, instead. I have a bad feeling about the books, but I do as I'm required, reminding myself that even evil has the right to the freedom of expression—

It's the Fourth of July, and I have dyed my hair red, white, and blue. There are fireworks, and I'm driving an airplane. I have a co-pilot who is advising me because I have never driven a plane before. I'm amazed how I fly it without crashing it even though several times it seems I should have hit one of the buildings, which I manage to miss by a hair.

Dream Journal Entry
September 25, 2001

Fall 2001

I WAS SITTING ON THE CURB SMOKING A CIGARETTE on the evening of September 10, 2001, watching the airplanes ascend and descend from nearby Dulles International Airport. As I watched one plane, its lights blinking in the moonlit sky, it headed toward the huge silhouette of an office building. I thought for a minute, it came so close, that it might slam into the side of the building. What a horrific yet magnificent sight that would be.

Where the hell do these thoughts come from?

I shook my head.

As the lights of the plane vanished into thin air, I stood up, butted my cigarette, and went back inside.

The next morning at work, I slit the tape with my box cutter and ripped open box after box, each marked with a red and white warning seal, "Strict on sale date: September 11, 2001." One of the stock clerks, Carlos, kept trying to tell me something in his broken English, something about the television in the break room, something about a plane crashing into a building.

"I'll come see in a bit," I assured him. "I have to get this display set up before the store opens. Give me a hand would you?"

Carlos looked stressed. But he helped me pull off the backing of the vinyl poster and hang it on the display case.

"It's true, I don't know Jack," I amused myself as I scraped the air bubbles out of the poster that heralded the new release of *Straight from the Gut* by some guy named Jack.

"Gabby," Carlos said, urging me every way he could short of tugging on my sleeve. "Another plane—at the Pentagon."

"What?"

As I rushed toward the break room, three people brushed past me running toward the exit door.

"They have relatives who work at the Pentagon," someone said.

"Apparent hijackers brandishing knives and box cutters aboard American Airlines Flight 77, which departed from Dulles International Airport at 8:10 this morning bound for Los Angeles, crashed into the Pentagon just moments ago with 64 passengers aboard."

The station replayed the clips of United Airlines Flight 175 careening toward the south tower of the World Trade Center, the otherwise clear blue sky overcast with the smoke of its smoldering sister tower. Someone on the street said 'oh my god,' as the plane dove head-on into the tower, erupting into blazing billows of yellow and orange flames plumed with torrential gusts of gray smoke. I remembered the vision that crossed my mind the night before and the dreams I had had of buildings crumbling.

Was it intuition? Could I have heeded it somehow?

I stood spellbound as the first tower collapsed, as massive billows of smoke and dust gushed up from the earth and chased down pedestrians in the streets of Lower Manhattan.

"The store is now open," a manager announced over the intercom.

Don't they realize that the bones of hundreds upon hundreds of fellow Americans have just crystallized in ash right before our very eyes?

All air travel was grounded but reports of a plane circling Dulles, just a few miles from the bookstore, kept circling around in my head. Another plane just crashed in the fields outside of Somerset, Pennsylvania.

The visage of my mother filled my mind's eye as the physical embodiment of the Great Healing Mother, who, among legions, her large heart, her soft fingers reaching out to the shocked newcomers, the men, the women, the children. Ma barely had time to adjust on the Other Side, not quite four months, the day almost 3,000 human souls, all in a space of moments, crossed over, too.

In the weeks that followed, Della and I rehashed and dissected every detail of the attacks as they became available.

"We have no choice," I proclaimed, "but to go to war."

But Della would not hear of it.

"Two wrongs don't make a right, as my Mamaw always said."

"What are we supposed to do? Turn the other cheek?"

"If we start bombing them, a lot of innocent people will die," Della said. "With all our intelligence and technology, there must be a better way."

"Imagine, though. If we don't retaliate, they will attack again. They will keep attacking until they own us. We won't be able to go out in public or go to work or go to the bar. We'd become the abused and raped women behind veils."

"We need to free those women, not bomb them. If we try to bomb bin Laden, we will end up killing the very people we want to protect. We become the terrorists."

"Well we can't just sit here. Al-Qaeda will take over our whole country, the whole world."

"I know. We do have to defend ourselves and do what we can to prevent further attacks," she said. "But remember what you said just last week. You said yourself, you can't even bring yourself to kill a spider now after all that's happened. Yet now you justify killing human beings?"

Della's words slapped me right across the face, and I remembered something I had read in Gary Zukav's *Seat of the Soul*: "If you strike without compassion against the darkness, you yourself enter the darkness."[3]

Nonetheless, I stood my ground. Declared war. Refused to see Della's point of view, even though a nagging sensation reminded me of something I had read earlier in my journey, that when I denied my femininity, my masculine side would become headstrong, would want to fight, would refuse to listen to anyone else's point of view.

In the days and nights that followed, Della and I became minions to her television set, pondering and fretting over what may or may not occur next.

"How many in a troop?" I wanted to know one night as I lay on her couch propped up on one elbow as she sat in the recliner on the other side of the end table, which we had cluttered with our beer bottles and ashtrays.

"A troop is one soldier," Della said.

"I was a Girl Scout, and we had many troops, each one with a different number of scouts. Troop 246, for example, might have had 362 scouts while Troop 357 might have had 149 scouts."

"A troop is a troop is a troop. One soldier," she insisted.

Our lengthy bantering over how many soldiers in a troop and what countries and oceans were situated where opened books and dictionaries and maps, each leading us to new research questions. The face of the war took on new attributes. We began to contemplate and investigate beyond the mountain, the bearded men and veiled women. We began to realize that the pond beyond the mountain—perhaps a symbol of our ignorance, our supposed innocence—was no more.

Our friends and Della's husband, and their kids, wanted to change the channel, to watch football and the World Series, to get back to normal. But Della and I had to get our news fix, and we did almost every night, all night sometimes, with Della flipping the channels to catch every single broadcast from every conceivable angle.

We learned that whole countries existed that we had never heard of, of cultures and peoples who hated Americans though we didn't even know they shared the same planet. We had heard of Afghanistan, but words like Osama bin Laden and Mahatma Atta and the Taliban, words we didn't even know, couldn't have even pronounced before September 11, rolled off our tongues.

We had no idea that China and India and Russia were in such close proximity to Afghanistan, that many analysts credited Afghanistan with the fall of Russia, that America aided the Taliban with money and arms to drive Russia to their knees, the same weapons and money the Taliban now used in an attempt to drive America to her knees. And we didn't know that bin Laden had declared holy war against America in 1996. We didn't even know what a *fatwa* was. But in a *fatwa* he cosigned in 1998, bin Laden declared that it was the individual duty of every Muslim to kill Americans and their allies, both military and civilians.

> This is in accordance with the words of Almighty Allah, 'and fight the pagans all together as they fight you all together,' and 'fight them until there is no more tumult or oppression, and there prevail justice and faith in Allah.'[4]
>
> [http://bit.ly/1kUKnYI]

In an effort to put the trivial events of my life into perspective in contrast to the wars and tragedies that affected the whole world, I began to examine and challenge my own principles, not just from the narrow scope of my own experiences of love and fear and hate and anger, but from a global view. I remembered how my hatred and anger toward my dad and God and Griffin had consumed me, and I began to realize that the same hatred that created my personal battlegrounds might well be the substance that instigates world wars.

During the sleepless nights following September 11, I played a meditation CD, trying to go back in time, to a time before the womb, to a time when we knew we were all one.

> "You are about to embark on a journey. In the beginning we were one, one with all things, in harmony with the flow of creation. This is a time to return to that flow, a time for you, for finding that healing place and for loving the Self. Adjust your body. Close your eyes. Relax. And breathe. Meditation is the process of focusing inward ... .
>
> "This is a time to recover, to come back to that something you once had, a time for knowing the fullest use of what it is to be human. Dive deeply into the diaphragm. And inhale slowly and fully, awakening the cells and filling the lungs with oxygen, with Life. Surrender into a deeper and healthier level of mind....Know that you are about to be awakened, awakened to a heightened sensibility ... ."[5]
>
> Joanna Cocca
"Light Meditations" [http://apple.co/1SdOv1m]

One night, as the curtain rustled across the floor of 2001, Joanna Cocca's voice created a melody within my dreamscape. There in the dark shadows, I saw Lucy. I reached for her hand and began to run back in time. As the words to the Beatles' song "Lucy in the Sky with Diamonds"[6] [http://bit.ly/1MwQ3lv] flooded my mind, muffled pictures and blurred voices imparted a message I could not hear, could not see, but I understood. Lucy no longer symbolizes a little lost girl crying in a courtyard long ago. No. Lucy no longer embodies fear and abandonment. She is a universal symbol of courage, the courage to take the hand of a stranger and to help them to find their way back home.

THE END
(I mean the beginning.)
:)

In Retrospect

TODAY—THE FIRST DAY OF SPRING 2015—the day I made the electronic version of this memoir available online—is within a matter of days, even hours, of my conception 60 years ago, which is when I began to write this book. Or it began to write me. I think the two are one. But I do know that I could not *not* write it. It was my destiny. My vocation. My calling. And I could not escape it.

Sometimes it was a ray of sunshine, therapeutic, guiding me, teaching me, and inspiring me. But more often than not, as I chiseled away at the rock, trying to exhume my very soul, my memoir hung over me like the dust in "Pig-Pen's" cloud.

It was downright embarrassing.

I was compelled to say I was writing a book. It was like my identity. And I thought it would be done any day now. But after 10, 15, 20 years, people start to look at you a little funny. What's worse—I couldn't even explain it. In hindsight, I can finally say that it's a story of a woman in her 40s trying to climb out of an unconscious life. But with no one to mentor her or to validate her feelings or her quest, she kept falling back into the same pit, especially considering the bits of information she found often conflicted with one another.

For example, in December 2014, her brother Peter surprised her with her kindergarten report card, which he had found when he was sorting through the remnants of their parents' lives. She was excited to see what succulent little morsels would raise her to new heights. But after reading it, she had to scratch her head.

According to Miss Dollard, her kindergarten teacher, her weakest developmental skill—out of Work Habits, Personal Development, Social Development, Number Development, and Language Development—her weakest skill—and ironically the only weakness that Miss Dollard chose to point out—was her inability to make up stories. She just wasn't good at it.

And contradicting Gabrielle's perception of an entire year of her young life, her mother wrote on the back of her report card, "I can't seem to catch Gabrielle's interest in learning. Can you suggest anything?"

And in direct contradiction to her mother's comment, Miss Dollard wrote, "Gabrielle is a very likable little girl. She is interested in school and does well."

It was as if they were all living in alternate universes!

Well, after muddling through the best that I could through many of these types of scenarios, I can finally say that I have found my Self. I have found my way back home. Happiness has extinguished the anger that has always haunted me. Love and gratitude fill my heart and soul. At last, I have tricked the wicked witch into climbing into the oven and have slammed shut the oven door. I am healed!

Ha ha ha ha ha. Ha ha ha.

I must admit that in the early years of writing this book, I thought that by the time I finished it I would be cured, and I would be some kind of guru or something. But now I see it is a lifelong process, a lifelong work, and there are setbacks and complications.

The memoir draws to a close at the end of 2001, but it took me another 15 years to re-member, to re-create, and to analyze the events of the previous 40 years. But upon completion, it was as if the pebble that was lodged in tire treads long ago popped out and rolled to freedom.

Common motifs in the memoir, such as "creating your own reality" and "healing" and a "journey" and "God," were metaphoric and abstract. But upon completion, these motifs came alive with new meaning. The concept of "creating your own reality" is true on more levels than I could have ever imagined. The concept of "healing" has evolved to "integrating." The concept of "journey" is metaphoric. We don't really "go" anywhere, although this is how our brains will likely interpret our experience as we orbit this spiral we call "Self" from one frequency or vibration to another. And "God" has evolved from a static story in a child's catechism, an entity that doles out reward and punishment, to a Divinity which encompasses all energy, which I like to call "Divine Source." Our higher Self cannot be separated from Divine Source anymore than the wave can be separated from the ocean or the flame from the fire.

But these evolutions do not invalidate the initial experiences and perceptions. To the contrary, writing the memoir was just as valuable during the process as it is in hindsight. Now when something pisses me off or hurts me, I don't have to ask why I'm reacting in this way or that way. With my memoir at my finger tips, I can readily evaluate my feelings and validate them. And it is precisely the fact that it took so many years to write this memoir that I am able to see the patterns in my life, and realize that I am not back where I started but, like peeling an onion, I am exploring similar human events but on varying levels of spiritual awareness. I am what I am. I am a Divine being experiencing what it is to be human as I fulfill my small part in the simultaneous expansion of the Universe and the Divine.

Throughout the last 15 years, as the memoir went through various stages of incubation and birth and death and rebirth, I discovered numerous tools (in addition to memoir writing) that were designed to guide Divine souls through the human experience, a continuous cyclical process of self-awareness and transformation, which Carl Jung coined as "the process of individuation."

One of the greatest thinkers and prolific writers of the 20th century, Jung has contributed tomes that will surely be analyzed for ages to come. Jung observed patterns of individuation in his extensive studies of mythology, philosophy, sociology, Gnosticism, Eastern and Western religions, as well as later in his extensive travels and lengthy stays among remote cultures, in which the indigenous inhabitants had not yet paid the price, that is, who had not yet experienced a "loss of soul," which occurs during the process of becoming "civilized."

Add to that, after perusing the bulk of work produced through the ages on the occult and analyzing thousands of dreams—despite his desire to be known first as a scientist—Jung was intrigued by how the progression of dreams and the tenets of alchemy, astrology, the I Ching, numerology, and the tarot all mirror the individuation process, that is, in broader terms, the evolution of the human psyche.

This intrigue laid the foundation for what Jung (as its founding father) would later term "analytical psychology." The syzygy website scratches the surface of Jung's genius with introductions to some of his thoughts on many practices, including dialoguing with your higher Self (what Jung coined "active imaginations"); identifying personality types (the basis of Myers-Briggs Type Indicator); recognizing synchronicities (meaningful but acausal connections between internal and external events), which Jung believed, in turn, activated the so-called archetypes (invisible little patterns embedded in the psyche of the human race as a whole, inherent at birth); bringing to consciousness the contents of your shadow, that is, feelings, thoughts, memories, and experiences we repress, yet we unknowingly project onto others (for example, being repulsed by someone who is too self-absorbed or too headstrong, only to realize it mirrors our own behavior); and analyzing dreams, of course, the bedrock of Jungian analytical psychology.

Please join me on my website, *Syzygy: Crossing the Bridge to Self.com* [http://bit.ly/1HVMSFp] to continue this incredible process of Self-discovery.

The Website

LIVING CONSCIOUSLY THROUGH APPLIED JUNGIAN PSYCHOLOGY

HEEL THE EGO, HEAL HUMANKIND.

AS AN AMATEUR JUNGIAN, I will attempt to fully submit myself—and document on my website—to what Jung termed "individuation," that is, my process of Self-discovery, a process of becoming aware of and integrating the desires of my conscious ego with the repressed characteristics in my unconscious shadow through Self-reflection and Self-analysis so that I may lift the mask of my persona and discover my higher Self.

Self-discovery is not a direct path. It's a process. It's a spiral around the Self. It is our yellow brick road. We may utilize any number of techniques and applications and tools in any combination that appeals to us on any given day, as it is a one-of-a-kind crossing of the bridge to Self. Whether we embark on this journey or not—whether it's conscious or unconscious—we are all on this yellow brick road. We just might call it something else.

This "journey," contrary to common beliefs—particularly religious beliefs—is not about eliminating our dark side or striving for perfection. It is about lifting the mask of our persona and integrating what is unconscious with what is conscious. It is about becoming aware of our emotions, which reflect our higher Self, and honor them and validate them and integrate them. It is about heeling our ego to heal mankind.

As you will see on the syzygy website, some days—as the life I live develops in a dark room of its own making—I cringe at the sight of me. Other days, I marvel. It's both work and play. It is digging and burying, finding and losing, hurting and healing, tearing down and rebuilding. It is love and fear. It is dying and being reborn.

The Sitemap
www.syzygy-crossingthebridgetoself.com
[http://bit.ly/1MMqgUh]

TOP VERTICAL NAVIGATION & MISC.
| Home | Talk to Me | Spotlight | Jung | Dreams | Thought, Theories and Tools | Heel the Ego, Heal Humankind | Out of My Mind | | Structure of the Psyche | My Latest Revelation | Good Deeds |

HORIZONTAL NAVIGATION
| About the Memoir | About the Journey | About the Cover | | About the Author | About Jung | About Jung & Me |

SITE SPECIFIC CONTENT
| Active Imagination | Alchemy | Archetypes | Astrology | | Constellation Theory | Dreams | Dream Analysis | | Dream Symbols | I Ching | Individuation | Mandalas | | Memoir Writing | Numerology | Oracle/Tarot | Psychoanalysis | | Psychological Types | Psychological Types History | | Shadow Work | Synchronicities | | Tools & Techniques |

TAKING CARE OF BUSINESS
| Mission Statement | Terms of Use | Privacy Policy | Disclaimer |

Epilogue

T HAT'S MY MYTH OF Ms. It may not be yours. But if you travel far enough, one day you will recognize yourself coming down the road to meet yourself. And you will say—YES."[1]

"There are countless women of the sixties and seventies who so deeply resented the patriarchy which had destroyed their femininity and that of their mothers that they lashed out against that patriarchy but in doing so they identified with the masculine side of their psyches. In some cases, they turned into the very thing they feared. The witch side of their mothers.

"It is important to remember the witch in 'Hansel and Gretel' who, wicked as she was in keeping them caged, was at the same time forcing them to develop all their ingenuity in order to escape and survive. And it was the feminine principle, Gretel, who never gave up her faith in life, but continuously encouraged her despairing Hansel. When the right moment came, they were alert enough to throw their negativity into the fire and run. But, it was the witch that forced the development of their maturity and their recognition of what was of value to them."[2]

Marion Woodman [http://bit.ly/1PoTLrw]
Excerpts from *Addiction to Perfection* [http://bit.ly/1X6OqTQ]

"Dorothy has completed her Hero's Journey, come to terms with her four survival archetypes, and with courage consolidated her mind, heart, and will. Her most challenging adversary, the Wicked Witch, had proved to be the one who did the most to expand her soul."³

Caroline Myss [http://bit.ly/1N3enbR]
Sacred Contracts: Awakening Your Divine Potential [http://bit.ly/1T9hdBr]

Dedication

I Dedicate My Work to the "Witches" in My Life

Dedications often appear in the front matter, but I find it fitting to include it in the back matter because only through hindsight would I know that the witches in my life are the catalysts to my spiritual growth, without which I may still be stuffing myself on a sugar-coated house.

A parent, a sibling, a boss, a coworker, an in-law, a friend, a neighbor, an acquaintance—anyone who pushes your buttons—is your witch. So rather than struggle with them or resent them or be angry with them, we would best serve our divinity by asking ourselves, "What is Source trying to teach me through this person and/or this experience?"

"Yeah, right. Ha ha."

It's a bitch, but like the witches in "Hansel and Gretel" and the *Wizard of Oz*, our antagonists are fulfilling a sacred contract which—like the painful "growth" on the back of my hand—is intended to help us to progress on our spiritual path, the path of healing, of expanding.

Therefore, I dedicate my Work to the greatest witches in my life—my Mom and Dad. And I no doubt was one of their greatest witches, too, as my memoir does attest. But they were also my king and queen, and I have always loved and appreciated them, whether I was conscious of it or not.

And there were countless other witches in my life, as well. But Griffin, in particular, crossed my mind when I heard Caroline Myss say to a room full of people, who laughed at the irony, "Remember there are just as many people trying to get over having known you as you them."

And then there's Della—duh-ditty-do, Underdog. I swear it's in her DNA, but oftentimes when I look at something from a positive point of view, she points out the negative, and when I look at something from a negative point of view, she points out the positive, which is negative feedback either way from my perspective. But what used to frustrate me most was when I would be telling her about some experience or event, and she would interrupt me before I could finish modifying my sentence with what she perceived as a contradiction to something I may have said in the past.

It wasn't until 2015, when I began my shadow work based on the teachings of Teal Swan and began practicing "The Work" by Byron Katie, that I realized Della was unwittingly pushing the same button that my parents had implanted in my brain, sort of like a computer chip, which had attached to it my anger, my indignation, my hands on my hips—which has been playing on a loop ever since. And like an animal who had been frightened or injured, I realized that I tended to react to smells, sounds, and actions that are similar to my original injuries. Kind of like ringing the bell for Pavlov's dogs.

Now when I think Della is challenging my point of view, I remind myself that it's just an old film clip running in my head, and, in that moment, I can appreciate Della's open-minded vigilance. Nonetheless, the fact that Della can still push that button is Divine Source's way of showing me a shadow aspect of my psyche that still needs healing and validation—which means I still have work to do! (Please join me on my Shadow Work web page [http://bit.ly/1SdQ8Mv] as this process of Self-discovery continues.)

Witches aside, I dedicate my memoir to Doreen (Della) Jane Taylor, the one person on this planet who believed in me, who supported me, who encouraged me, when it seemed—after 20 years in the re-making—that writing this memoir was a pipe dream. She's one of the most generous friends I have ever known. For her, I shall plant a tree.

love you, Dee-Dee
— Barb
☺

Afterword

A N OLD HINDU LEGEND tells of the time when all men were Gods. But they had so abused their divinity that Brahma, the Master of the Gods, decided to take away their divine power and hide it in a place where they couldn't find it. His great problem was finding a hiding place.

When the Gods were called together to solve this problem, they proposed the following: "Let's bury man's divinity in the earth." But Brahma replied, "No, that will not do, because man will dig up the earth and find it."

Then the Gods said, "In that case, let us throw man's divinity into the deepest ocean." But to this Brahma replied, "No, because sooner or later man will explore the depths of all the oceans and it is certain that one day he will find it and bring it to the surface."

So the Brahma said, "Then this is what we will do with man's divinity. We will hide it in the deepest part of man himself, because that is the only place where he will never think to look."

The legend concludes that ever since then, man has circled the earth, has explored, climbed, dived and dug in search of something which is only to be found within himself.

Unknown

Source Notes

The links in the following entries were selected based on added information (and in some cases, reviews) that the sites provide about the author and/or the work. Most biographies are linked to Bio. True Story. And most poets and poems are linked to the Poetry Foundation and/or The Academy of American Poets. When available, a link to the author's website is also provided. Otherwise, most works are available through traditional and online bookstores. For additional publishing information, please see entries in Sources & Resources, p. 409.

Syzygy Defined
1. de Laszlo, Violet S. Ed. *Psyche and Symbol: A Collection of Selected Works from the Writings of C. G. Jung* [http://bit.ly/1Mw72V6], p. 30. (Garden City: Doubleday, 1958.)
2. James A. Hall. *Jungian Dream Interpretation: A Handbook of Theory and Practice* [http://bit.ly/1NlTnDH], pp. 9–10. (Toronto: Inner City Books, 1983.)
3. Ibid., p. 120.
4. Ibid., p. 120.

Disclaimer
1. Emily Dickinson [http://bit.ly/1NKcGkb]. "Tell all the truth but tell it slant—" [http://bit.ly/1PSVJKB]. This work is licensed under the Creative Commons Attribution-ShareAlike 3.0 Unported License [http://bit.ly/1PSVJKB]. To view a copy of this license, visit http://creativecommons.org/licenses/by-sa/3.0/ [http://bit.ly/1Olbl8c]. Or send a letter to Creative Commons, PO Box 1866, Mountain View, CA 94042, USA.

2. Matthew McKay, Ph.D. [http://bit.ly/21bQZn2], and Patrick Fanning [http://bit.ly/1Om9I8h]. Kirk Johnson, ed. *Self-Esteem* [http://bit.ly/1lcGFKI], chap. 9, "Responding to Criticism," subtitled, "The Myth of Reality: A TV Screen in Every Head," p. 187. (Saint Martin's Paperbacks: New Harbinger Publications, 1987.)

PREFACE
1. Gary Goldschneider. *Personology: The Precision Approach to Charting Your Life, Career, and Relationships.* Philadelphia/London: Running Press, 2005.)
2. Based on Hans Christian Andersen's [http://bit.ly/1ML7eox] "Hansel and Gretel" [http://bit.ly/1Lv7NtB].

PART I: INTRODUCTION
1. Marion Woodman [http://bit.ly/1I8tNua]. *Sitting by the Well: Bringing the Feminine to Consciousness Through Language, Dreams, and Metaphor* [http://bit.ly/1Ia3nIr], Session Nine: "Losing Your Life in Order to Find It, Part 1." Audio Series. (Boulder, CO: Sounds True, 1998.)
2. Marion Woodman [http://bit.ly/1I8tNua]. *Addiction to Perfection: The Still Unravished Bride* [http://bit.ly/1X6OqTQ], p. 126. (Toronto: Inner City Books, 1982.)

Dream Journal Entry: "The Black Xs," January 5, 2000.
Dream Journal Entry: "The Frying Pan," February 2, 1999.

CHAPTER 1: THE RED JELL-O
1. Judith Rossner. *Looking for Mr. Goodbar.* (New York: Washington Square Press Publications of Pocket Books, div. of Simon & Schuster Inc., 1975.)
2. Robert Moss [http://bit.ly/1Se2Cnz]. *Conscious Dreaming: A Spiritual Path for Everyday Life*, p. 78. (New York: Three Rivers Press, 1996.)

CHAPTER 2: THE FRYING PAN
Dream Journal Entry: "Circuit Breaker," July 12, 1999.
Dream Journal Entry: "Where Will the Next Bomb Go Off," November 17, 1999.
Dream Journal Entry: "Acquainted with the Dead," December 14, 1999.
Dream Journal Entry: "At the Crossroads," January 30, 2000.
Dream Journal Entry: "Body Bags," February 17, 2000.

CHAPTER 3: THE ART OF DYING

1. Sylvia Plath [http://bit.ly/21cgLHZ]. "Lady Lazarus" [http://bit.ly/1MMwl3c], *Collected Poems*, p. 244. (New York: HarperCollins Publisher Inc., 1981.)
2. Marion Woodman [http://bit.ly/1I8tNua]. *Sitting by the Well: Bringing the Feminine to Consciousness Through Language, Dreams, and Metaphor* [http://bit.ly/1Ia3nIr], Session Three: "Mature Masculine and Feminine Energy."
3. Norman Vincent Peale [http://bit.ly/1OntMXY]. Download a free and updated eBook of *The Power of Positive Thinking* [http://bit.ly/1NmLvSo]. (New York: Prentice-Hall Inc., 1952.)
4. Wally Lamb. *This Much Is True I Know*. (New York: HarperCollins Publishers Inc., 1998.)

CHAPTER 4: THE FIRST DAY OF SPRING

1. Clarissa Pinkola Estés [http://on.fb.me/21cfBMo]. *Women Who Run With the Wolves: Myths and Stories of the Wild Woman Archetype* [http://bit.ly/1Sd2y7B], pp. 190–91, in a discussion on Hans Christian Andersen's *The Ugly Duckling*, 1845. (New York: Ballantine Books, 1992.)
2. Ibid.

Dream Journal Entry: "Packing Stones," January 30, 2000.
Dream Journal Entry: "Gifts," March 1, 2000.

3. Mary Hopkin (http://bit.ly/1N7oSwd) "Those Were the Days" (http://bit.ly/1N7oSMC), 1968.
4. Adrienne Rich [http://bit.ly/1NKbMUM]. "Diving into the Wreck" [http://bit.ly/1kPz2ds], excerpt from *Diving into the Wreck: Poems 1971–1972*. (W. W. Norton & Company Inc., 1973.)

PART II: INTRODUCTION

1. Marion Woodman [http://bit.ly/1I8tNua]. *Sitting by the Well: Bringing the Feminine to Consciousness Through Language, Dreams, and Metaphor* [http://bit.ly/1Ia3nIr], Session Six: "Conscious Femininity, Part 2."

Chapter 5: The Human Bean

1. Edna St. Vincent Millay [http://bit.ly/1Sd3Tv8]. "Childhood Is the Kingdom Where Nobody Dies" [http://bit.ly/1XjheDb]. (Eugene, OR: The Edna St. Vincent Millay Society, 1937.)

Chapter 6: The Dumpster Riddle

1. Emily Dickinson [http://bit.ly/1NKcGkb]. "They shut me up in Prose" [http://bit.ly/1MJsPJ3]. This work is licensed under the Creative Commons Attribution-ShareAlike 3.0 Unported License [http://bit.ly/1PSVJKB]. To view a copy of this license, visit http://creativecommons.org/licenses/by-sa/3.0/ [http://bit.ly/1Olbl8c]. Or send a letter to Creative Commons, PO Box 1866, Mountain View, CA 94042, USA.

Chapter 7: The Storks

1. Hans Christian Andersen [http://bit.ly/1ML7eox]. "The Storks," [http://bit.ly/1YooJs2] *Tales*. Charles W. Eliot, ed. Vol. xvii, pt. 3 of 51. (New York: The Harvard Classics, P. F. Collier & Son, 1909–14.)
2. "Found a Peanut." [http://bit.ly/1YpoGMw]. (However, in the version the leaders taught us at my summer camp, the gates of heaven were not locked.)
3. "Apostle's Creed," a shortened version of "The Nicene Creed" [http://bit.ly/1NKVPxR] (The version I recall is a cross between these two.)

Chapter 8: The Color of Blood

1. Martin Luther King, Jr. [http://bit.ly/1QCneYJ] "I Have a Dream" [http://bit.ly/1XkJCVJ]. (The speech King delivered on the steps of the Lincoln Memorial on August 28, 1963.)

Chapter 9: The String That Broke

1. Excerpts from the "suicide letter" to Martin Luther King, Jr., later proved to have been sent from the FBI, then led by J. Edgar Hoover. Found in the National Archives at College Park, MD, by Beverly Gates, and published in an article in *The New York Times Magazine* on Nov. 11, 2014 [http://nyti.ms/1lCKfy2].

Chapter 10: The First Bite

1. Emily Dickinson [http://bit.ly/1NKcGkb]. "Eden is that old-fashioned House" [http://bit.ly/1Tcgv5J]. This work is licensed under the Creative Commons Attribution-ShareAlike 3.0 Unported License [http://bit.ly/1PSVJKB]. To view a copy of this license, visit http://creativecommons.org/licenses/by-sa/3.0/ [http://bit.ly/1Olbl8c]. Or send a letter to Creative Commons, PO Box 1866, Mountain View, CA 94042, USA.

Chapter 11: The Fine Line

1. Charlotte Brontë [http://bit.ly/1NlgPRs]. *Jane Eyre* [http://bit.ly/1Yo2Ls4]. (New York: A Tom Doherty Associates Book, 1994.)
2. Authorized King James Version Online [http://bit.ly/1N8pODH], Matthew 17:15–18. (The fine line between devils and lunatics.)
3. Authorized King James Version Online [http://bit.ly/1N8pODH], Genesis, Chapters 1 & 2. (The two creation stories.)
4. Authorized King James Version Online [http://bit.ly/1N8pODH], Genesis 2:16–17. (Thou mayest freely eat...)
5. Authorized King James Version Online [http://bit.ly/1N8pODH], Matthew 6:9–13. (The Lord's Prayer)

Chapter 12: The Curse

1. Clarissa Pinkola Estés [http://on.fb.me/21cfBM0]. *Women Who Run With the Wolves: Myths and Stories of the Wild Woman Archetype* [http://bit.ly/1Sd2y7B]. (Different 'thicknesses of skin, different capacities for perceiving pain,' p. 494.) (New York: Ballantine Books, 1992.)
2. Eddie Arnold. "My Daddy Is Only a Picture" [http://bit.ly/1Obf3RH].
3. Margo Smith, "How Far Is Heaven" [http://bit.ly/21chaKt].

Part III: Introduction

1. Marion Woodman [http://bit.ly/1I8tNua]. *Sitting by the Well: Bringing the Feminine to Consciousness Through Language, Dreams, and Metaphor* [http://bit.ly/1Ia3nIr], Session Four: "Leaving the Old Thresholds Behind"

2. Marion Woodman [http://bit.ly/1I8tNua]. *Sitting by the Well: Bringing the Feminine to Consciousness Through Language, Dreams, and Metaphor* [http://bit.ly/1Ia3nIr], Session Six: "Conscious Femininity, Part 2."

CHAPTER 13: THE COLOR OF MY WORLD
1. "In-A-Gadda-Da-Vida," Iron Butterfly, 1968. According to Doug Ingle, Iron Butterfly's vocalist and keyboard player, the title was supposed to be "In the Garden of Eden." But "someone had written 'In-A-Gadda-Da-Vida,' possibly while drunk, on a demo copy. A record company executive saw it and decided to use it as the title, since it sounded mystical and Eastern spirituality was big at the time, with The Beatles going to India and The Rolling Stones experimenting with Indian instruments."
2. "Colour My World," Chicago, 1970.
3. "I'm Your Captain/Closer to My Home," Grand Funk Railroad, 1970.

CHAPTER 14: THE TROOPER
1. "The U.S. Marine Corps Hymn" [http://bit.ly/1NKhNRE], Unknown.

CHAPTER 15: THE AMERICAN PIE
1. "American Pie" [http://bit.ly/1OmlWxI]. By Don McLean [http://bit.ly/1LunT6V]. "America Pie" topped the billboard charts for four weeks in early 1972.

CHAPTER 16: THE RAPE (WELL, NOT A REAL ONE)

PART IV: INTRODUCTION
1. Marion Woodman [http://bit.ly/1I8tNua]. *Sitting by the Well: Bringing the Feminine to Consciousness Through Language, Dreams, and Metaphor* [http://bit.ly/1Ia3nIr], Session Eight: "Losing Your Life in Order to Find It, Part 1."

CHAPTER 17: THE SECRET DELIVERY

Part V: Introduction
1. Marion Woodman [http://bit.ly/1I8tNua]. *Addiction to Perfection: The Still Unravished Bride* [http://bit.ly/1X6OqTQ]. "Once the door is opened, the bird who has lived in a cage...," p. 160. (Toronto: Inner City Books, 1982.)

Chapter 18: The Golden Dream
1. "Those Were the Days" (http://bit.ly/1N7oSMC). Mary Hopkin (http://bit.ly/1N7oSwd), 1968.

Chapter 19: The Blockage

Chapter 20: The Praying Hands
1. Franklin D. Roosevelt, "The Infamy Speech" [http://bit.ly/21cfYqi], December 8, 1941.
2. Newspaper Clip. "Terror strikes Rome, Vienna airports," published December 30, 1985. *Chronicle of the 20th Century, The Ultimate Record of Our Times* [http://amzn.to/1NKQu9z]. Clifton Daniel, ed. Foreword by Arthur M. Schlessinger, Jr. (NY, NY: Dorling Kindersley, 1995.)

Chapter 21: The Athlete
1. "To An Athlete Dying Young," A. E. Housman.
2. Newspaper Clip. "Challenger explodes as horrified nation watches," published January 31, 1986. *Chronicle of the 20th Century, The Ultimate Record of Our Times* [http://amzn.to/1NKQu9z]. Clifton Daniel, ed. Foreword by Arthur M. Schlessinger, Jr. (NY, NY: Dorling Kindersley, 1995.)
3. Newspaper Clip. "Four killed as plane is bombed in Athens," published April 2, 1986. *Chronicle of the 20th Century, The Ultimate Record of Our Times* [http://amzn.to/1NKQu9z]. Clifton Daniel, ed. Foreword by Arthur M. Schlessinger, Jr. (NY, NY: Dorling Kindersley, 1995.)
4. Newspaper Clip. "Terrorists bomb Berlin G.I. hangout," published April 5, 1986. *Chronicle of the 20th Century, The Ultimate Record of Our Times* [http://amzn.to/1NKQu9z]. Clifton Daniel, ed. Foreword by Arthur M. Schlessinger, Jr. (NY, NY: Dorling Kindersley, 1995.)
5. Newspaper Clip. "Chernobyl accident releases deadly atom radiation," published April 30. *Chronicle of the 20th Century*:

The Ultimate Record of Our Times [http://amzn.to/1NKQu9z].
Clifton Daniel, ed. Foreword by Arthur M. Schlessinger, Jr.
(NY, NY: Dorling Kindersley, 1995.)

CHAPTER 22: THE VULTURE

1. Gabrielle Hayes. "My love in other veins, your heart I maimed," 1988.
2. Emily Dickinson [http://bit.ly/1NKcGkb]. "I lost a World—the other day!" [http://bit.ly/1HgXUVw]. This work is licensed under the Creative Commons Attribution-ShareAlike 3.0 Unported License [http://bit.ly/1PSVJKB]. To view a copy of this license, visit http://creativecommons.org/licenses/by-sa/3.0/ [http://bit.ly/1Olbl8c]. Or send a letter to Creative Commons, PO Box 1866, Mountain View, CA 94042, USA.

PART VI: INTRODUCTION

1. Jolande Jacobi [http://bit.ly/1I5eBmU], *Complex Archetype Symbol in the Psychology of C. G. Jung.* Translated by Ralph Manheim. Bollingen Series. (Princeton: New York, 1959.) "Four is an age-old symbol, probably going back as early as the Old Stone Age..." (pp. 166–168).

CHAPTER 23: THE DEAD BABIES AWAKEN

Dream Journal Entry: "Dead Baby," January 1990
Dream Journal Entry: "Babies Drowning," January 1990
Dream Journal Entry: "Freddie Kruger Wants My Negatives," January 1990
Dream Journal Entry: "Baby, Dead or Alive?" March 1990
Dream Journal Entry: "The Baby I Love Versus the Messy Baby," April 1990.

1. Edward C. Whitmont, *The Symbolic Quest,* Princeton UP: New York, 1978. (I am actually quoting Whitmont in an assignment I wrote for class.)
2. Carl G. Jung [http://bit.ly/1SdQJhc], *Man and His Symbols* [http://bit.ly/1I9CmFb], "Part 3: The Process of Individuation," by M.-L. von Franz. (Doubleday: New York, 1964.) "The psyche can be compared to a sphere with a bright field on its surface, representing consciousness. The ego is the field's center....The Self is at once the nucleus and the whole

sphere; its internal regulating processes produce dreams" (caption on p. 161).
3. Violet S. de Laszlo, ed. *Psyche and Symbol: A Selection from the Writings of C. G. Jung* [http://bit.ly/1Mw72V6], p. 9. (Doubleday: New York, 1964.) I finally made the connection after reading the footnote, where the syzygy was defined as a joining together or conjunction, which reminded me of the word conjugal, relating to marriage.
4. Ibid (p. 30).
5. Complete dialogues of four active imaginations are available at [http://bit.ly/1YpSBL9].
6. Carl G. Jung [http://bit.ly/1SdQJhc], *Collected Works of C. G. Jung*, Bollingen Series XX, v. 11, 190–191, "A Psychological Approach to the Trinity," Sir Herbert Read, et al., eds. R. F. C. Hull, trans. (New York: Princeton UP, 1969.)
7. Carl G. Jung [http://bit.ly/1SdQJhc], *Man and His Symbols* [http://bit.ly/1I9CmFb], "Part 3: The Process of Individuation," by M.-L. von Franz, p. 213. (Doubleday: New York, 1964.)
8. Joseph Campbell, *The Power of Myth* (Doubleday Press: New York, 1988.) **Fetus:** "Otto Rank declares that everyone is a hero in birth, where he undergoes a tremendous transformation, from the condition of a little water creature living in a realm of amniotic fluid, into an air-breathing mammal which ultimately will be standing," (p. 124).

PART VII: INTRODUCTION
1. James A. Hall, *Jungian Dream Interpretation: A Handbook of Theory and Practice* [http://bit.ly/1NlTnDH]. "The usual way in which the anima or animus is experienced is in projection upon a person of the opposite sex...,"pp. 16, 17. (Toronto: Inner City Books, 1983.)
2. Marion Woodman [http://bit.ly/1I8tNua]. *Sitting by the Well: Bringing the Feminine to Consciousness Through Language, Dreams, and Metaphor* [http://bit.ly/1Ia3nIr], Session Six: "Conscious Femininity, Part 2."

CHAPTER 24: THE CRACK IN EVERYTHING
1. Leonard Cohen (http://bit.ly/1YoxF3x), "Leonard Cohen: Selected Poems, 1956–1968 (http://bit.ly/1I5fTOS). Also listen

to Cohen's beautiful song "Anthem" (http://bit.ly/1N7bI5s), inspired by these words.

Dream Journal Entry: "Vehicle Out of Control/ Toddlers Drowning," undated from the early 1990s.

CHAPTER 25: THE REPEAT OFFENDER
1. Richard Marx, "Right Here Waiting" (http://bit.ly/1PUwbuR)

CHAPTER 26: THE LIE
1. Marion Woodman [http://bit.ly/1I8tNua]. *Addiction to Perfection: The Still Unravished Bride* [http://bit.ly/1X6OqTQ]. "Female writers prone to the demon lover," p. 136–137. (Toronto: Inner City Books, 1982.)
2. Marion Woodman [http://bit.ly/1I8tNua]. *Addiction to Perfection: The Still Unravished Bride* [http://bit.ly/1X6OqTQ]. "Appears as the perfect bridegroom...but still a boy looking for his mother," p. 137. (Toronto: Inner City Books, 1982.)
3. Michael Bolton, "Said I Loved You But I Lied" (http://bit.ly/1PIVYI6).
4. Pink Floyd, *Another Brick in the Wall*, Part 2. "We don't need no education. We don't need no thought control" (http://bit.ly/1Ida5bp).
5. Pink Floyd, *The Wall*, "Good-bye Blue Sky" (http://binged.it/1N7sjpP).
6. Bryan Adams and Barbra Streisand, "I Finally Found Someone" (http://bit.ly/21cfuR5).

CHAPTER 27: THE BANANA PEELS
1. Pink Floyd, *The Wall*, "One of My Turns" (http://bit.ly/1Ida5bp).

Dream Journal Entry: "Crushing the Baby," October 22, 1996.

2. *The Wisdom of the Enneagram* [http://bit.ly/1OaQMLz], Don Richard Riso [http://amzn.to/1On8fPl] and Russ Hudson [http://amzn.to/1QZ7YEM], p. 36.
3. Clarissa Pinkola Estés [http://on.fb.me/21cfBMo]. *Women Who Run With the Wolves: Myths and Stories of the Wild Woman Archetype* [http://bit.ly/1Sd2y7B]. (New York: Ballantine Books, 1992.) (Note 3 from section in back of book from Chapter 12, "Marking Territory: The Boundaries of Rage and Forgiveness," p. 493.) **NOTE:** There was something very similar in *Controlling Parents* by Dan Neuharth, which is what I was actually reading that day but have been unable to find the exact quote.

CHAPTER 28: THE LITTLE RAG DOLL
1. Marion Woodman [http://bit.ly/1I8tNua]. *Sitting by the Well: Bringing the Feminine to Consciousness Through Language, Dreams, and Metaphor* [http://bit.ly/1Ia3nIr], "Session Three: Mature Masculine and Feminine Energy."

Dream Journal Entry: "Bathing My Dirty Mother," August 19, 1999.

CHAPTER 29: THE BRICK IN THE HEAD
1. Marion Woodman [http://bit.ly/1I8tNua]. *Sitting by the Well: Bringing the Feminine to Consciousness Through Language, Dreams, and Metaphor* [http://bit.ly/1Ia3nIr], "Session Three: Mature Masculine and Feminine Energy."
2. Notebook entries I wrote while reading *The Wisdom of the Enneagram: The Complete Guide to Psychological and Spiritual Growth for the Nine Personality Types* [http://bit.ly/1OaQMLz] by Don Richard Riso [http://amzn.to/1On8fPl] and Russ Hudson [http://amzn.to/1QZ7YEM], which may be paraphrased or direct quotes. **NOTE:** Not sure if this is the book I quoted. I called the book *The Enneagram* throughout, but I cannot find a book by that title only. But the words match very closely to a blog referring to these authors.
3. Gary Zukav [http://bit.ly/1PJaBez], *Seat of the Soul* [http://bit.ly/21cicpI], pp. 78–79. Simon & Schuster, NY, NY (1989). **NOTE:** Zukav used the male as the mistrusting party, but he no doubt used the gender as generic, that is, he is not

differentiating between male and female in this example. I only changed the gender in the quote to a female voice in an effort to correlate the quote to the female narrator of this book.

Dream Journal Entry: "Crossing the Bridge," March 17, 1999.
Dream Journal Entry: "Soulmates and the Alternate Universe," Early 2000.

PART VIII: INTRODUCTION
1. Marion Woodman [http://bit.ly/1I8tNua], "Abandoned Soul, Abandoned Planet" [http://bit.ly/1Xl7UyI]. Excerpt from Nancy Ryley's interview with Marion Woodman, 1998. "The return to the Garden is about coming full circle." Copyright, Quest Books, (800) 669-9425.
2. Clarissa Pinkola Estés [http://on.fb.me/21cfBMo]. *Women Who Run With the Wolves: Myths and Stories of the Wild Woman Archetype* [http://bit.ly/1Sd2y7B], p. 284. (New York: Ballantine Books, 1992.)
3. Carl G. Jung [http://bit.ly/1SdQJhc], "The Development of Personality" [http://bit.ly/1MM8ctq]: "Bidden or not bidden, God is always present." Vocation as a calling. Collected Works, vol. 17, pp. 180–181, ¶s 308–309. "The Development of Personality" is Volume 17 in *The Collected Works of C. G. Jung* [http://bit.ly/1Xl9hgX], a series of books published by Princeton University Press in the U.S. and Routledge & Kegan Paul in the U.K. It contains papers on child psychology, education, and individuation, emphasizing the extreme importance of parents and teachers in the genesis of the intellectual, feeling, and emotional disorders of childhood. A final paper deals with marriage as an aid or obstacle to self-realization.[1] SOURCE: Wikipedia.

CHAPTER 30: THE MAGICAL SMILE
1. Clarissa Pinkola Estés [http://on.fb.me/21cfBMo]. *Women Who Run With the Wolves: Myths and Stories of the Wild Woman Archetype* [http://bit.ly/1Sd2y7B], "During the darkest times...Nature feeds a woman's soul." (New York: Ballantine Books, 1992.)

2. Marion Woodman [http://bit.ly/1I8tNua]. *Addiction to Perfection: The Still Unravished Bride* [http://bit.ly/1X6OqTQ]. "But in her desire to sacrifice the old attitudes, she is experiencing a very real death." (Toronto: Inner City Books, 1982.)
3. Clarissa Pinkola Estés [http://on.fb.me/21cfBM0]. *Women Who Run With the Wolves: Myths and Stories of the Wild Woman Archetype* [http://bit.ly/1Sd2y7B], "People converse with their soul all the time." (New York: Ballantine Books, 1992.)
4. Marion Woodman [http://bit.ly/1I8tNua]. *Addiction to Perfection: The Still Unravished Bride* [http://bit.ly/1X6OqTQ]. "The dialogue between the ego and the Self creates soul," p. 127. (Toronto: Inner City Books, 1982.)
5. Carl G. Jung [http://bit.ly/1SdQJhc], "Civilization in Transition" [http://bit.ly/1HhSWaW] vol. 10, *The Collected Works of C. G. Jung* [http://bit.ly/1NL8GQG], a series of books published by Princeton University Press in the U.S. and Routledge & Kegan Paul in the U.K. The link leads to abstracts of his Collective Works. The work contains essays bearing on the contemporary scene during the 1920s and 1930s, and on the relation of the individual to society. It includes papers focusing on the upheaval in Germany, and two major works of Jung's last years, *The Undiscovered Self* and *Flying Saucers*.[1] and *Flying Saucers*. SOURCE: Wikipedia. (A neurosis is by no means merely a negative thing, it is also something positive.)
6. Marion Woodman [http://bit.ly/1I8tNua]. *Sitting by the Well: Bringing the Feminine to Consciousness Through Language, Dreams, and Metaphor* [http://bit.ly/1Ia3nIr]. "You are an orphan—and the whole world is your orphanage."
7. Adrienne Rich [http://bit.ly/1NKbMUM]. "Diving into the Wreck" [http://bit.ly/1kPz2ds] from *Diving into the Wreck: Poems 1971–1972*. "And the treasures that prevail." (W. W. Norton & Company Inc., 1973.)

CHAPTER 31: THE MESS I CREATED
Dream Journal Entry: "The Magical Eyes," April 3, 2000
Dream Journal Entry: "The Abandoned Child," April 5, 2000
Dream Journal Entry: "A Glimpse of the Past," April 7, 2000.

1. According to my notes, this event occurred on March 31, 2000. But I can't find the show or transcript anywhere.

CHAPTER 32: THE UNEXPECTED STORM
1. Luke Timothy Johnson[http://bit.ly/1QZbzm5], *The History of Christianity: From the Disciples to the Dawn of the Reformation* [http://bit.ly/1kPhUVi], part 1, p. 114. (Chantilly, VA: The Great Courses, 2012.)
2. Clarissa Pinkola Estés [http://on.fb.me/21cfBMo]. *Women Who Run With the Wolves: Myths and Stories of the Wild Woman Archetype* [http://bit.ly/1Sd2y7B], pp. 346–373, "Marking Territory: The Boundaries of Rage and Forgiveness." (New York: Ballantine Books, 1992.)
3. Gary Zukav [http://bit.ly/1PJaBez], *Seat of the Soul* [http://bit.ly/21cicpI].
4. Carl G. Jung [http://bit.ly/1SdQJhc], *Man and His Symbols* [http://bit.ly/1I9CmFb], Part 3, "The Process of Individuation" (p. 215), by M.-L. von Franz.

Dream Journal Entry: "Replant the Debris," April 21, 2000.
Dream Journal Entry: "Don't Drop the Baby," April 22, 2000.
Dream Journal Entry: "The Murder of My Mother," February 16, 1999.

5. Carl G. Jung [http://bit.ly/1SdQJhc], *Man and His Symbols* [http://bit.ly/1I9CmFb], Part 3, "The Process of Individuation" (pp. 189–195), by M.-L. von Franz. Paraphrased: The animus, which the father shapes in a woman, can convince the woman that she is not who she really is. When the destructive projection falls away, the woman will realize that she has reacted just the opposite of her real feelings and thoughts.
6. Ibid. Continuation of preceding quote.

CHAPTER 33: GROWING PAINS
1. *The Wisdom of the Enneagram: The Complete Guide to Psychological and Spiritual Growth for the Nine Personality Types* [http://bit.ly/1OaQMLz], Don Richard Riso [http://amzn.to/1On8fPl] and Russ Hudson [http://amzn.to/1QZ7YEM].

Dream Journal Entry: "The Color of the Soul," April 7, 2000.
Dream Journal Entry: "Lizards in a Sphere," May 19, 2000.

CHAPTER 34: THE HEALING MOTHER
Dream Journal Entry: "The New House," April 9, 2000.

1. Carl G. Jung [http://bit.ly/1SdQJhc], *Man and His Symbols* [http://bit.ly/1I9CmFb], Part 5, "Symbols in an Individual Analysis" (p. 297), by Jolande Jacobi.

PART IX: CONCLUSION
1. Marion Woodman, "Slow Down and Meet Your Sacred Feminine," in an interview with Jane Lister Reis. "The New Times."

CHAPTER 35: THE POND BEYOND
1. "Stock Market History: The 10 Worst Days" by Amy Bingham, *ABC World News Tonight*, referring to September 24, 2001, published August 9, 2011. Full article available at http://abcn.ws/1SUcOkZ.
2. Paul Goldberger. "Building Plans," published in "The New Yorker," September 24, 2001. Full article available at http://bit.ly/21cfGji.

Dream Journal Entry: "The Radiant Baby Boys," January 8, 2001.
Dream Journal Entry: "Too Beautiful to Be a Boy," February 24, 2001.
Dream Journal Entry: "The Traffic Jam," December 10, 1998.
Dream Journal Entry: "The Very Tall Building," February 24, 1999.
Dream Journal Entry: "The Pond Beyond," September 16, 2001.

3. Gary Zukav [http://bit.ly/21cicpI], *Seat of the Soul* [http://bit.ly/21cicpI]. "If you strike without compassion against the darkness, you yourself enter the darkness."
4. "In 1998, bin Laden and Ayman al-Zawahiri (a leader of Egyptian Islamic Jihad) co-signed a fatwa (binding religious edict) in the name of the World Islamic Front for Jihad Against Jews and Crusaders." Wikipedia [http://bit.ly/1kUKnYI].
5. Joanna Cocca, "Light Meditations." Audio CD. "You are about to embark on a journey." I derived great comfort listening to

this CD in 2001, and I still do to this day. [Listen to a preview at http://apple.co/1SdOv1m].
6. The Beatles. "Lucy in the Sky with Diamonds" [http://bit.ly/1Ro2Hgd]

EPILOGUE
1. Marion Woodman [http://bit.ly/1I8tNua]. *Addiction to Perfection: The Still Unravished Bride* [http://bit.ly/1X6OqTQ]. (Toronto: Inner City Books, 1982.)
2. Ibid.
3. Caroline Myss [http://bit.ly/1N3enbR]. *Sacred Contracts: Awakening Your Divine Potential* [http://bit.ly/1T9hdBr].

Sources & Resources

Berg, Rabbi. *Wheels of a Soul: Reincarnation.* New York: The Kabbalah Learning Centre, 1995.

Buhler, Rich. *Pain and Pretending: You Can Be Set Free from the Hurts of the Past.* Nashville: T. Nelson Publishers (acquired by HarperCollins), 1988.

Campbell, Joseph (with Bill Moyers). *The Power of Myth.* New York: Doubleday, 1988.

Conway, Jill Ker. *When Memory Speaks: Reflections on Autobiography.* New York: Alfred A. Knopf, 1998.

Cornell, Judith. *The Mandala Healing Kit.* The Mandala Universe. Boulder, CO: Sounds True, 2005.

Edinger, Edward F. *The Creation of Consciousness: Jung's Myth for Modern Man.* Toronto: Inner City Books, 1984.

Estés, Clarissa Pinkola. *Women Who Run With the Wolves: Myths and Stories of the Wild Woman Archetype.* New York: Ballantine, 1992.

Hall, James A. *Jungian Dream Interpretation: A Handbook of Theory and Practice.* Toronto: Inner City Books, 1983.

Jacobi, Jolande. *Complex Archetype Symbol in the Psychology of C. G. Jung.* Ralph Manheim, trans. Bollingen Series. New York: Princeton UP, 1959.

Jung, Carl G. *Man and His Symbols.* New York: Doubleday, 1964.

Keirsey, David. *Please Understand Me II: Temperament, Character & Intelligence.* Del Mar, CA: Prometheus Nemesis Book Company, 1998.

Keirsey, David, and Marilyn Bates. *Please Understand Me: Character & Temperament Types.* Del Mar, CA: Prometheus Nemesis Books. Copyright © 1978, David Keirsey & Marilyn Bates. Copyright © 1984, Gnosology Books Ltd.

McCants, Glynis. *Glynis Has Your Number: Discover What Life Has in Store for You Through the Power of Numerology!* New York: Hyperion, 2005.

McKay, Matthew and Patrick Fanning. Kirk Johnson, ed. *Self-Esteem*, chap. 9, "Responding to Criticism," subtitle, "The Myth of Reality: A TV Screen in Every Head," p. 187. Saint Martin's Paperbacks: New Harbinger Publications, 1987.

Mellin, Laurel. The Pathway: Follow the Road to Health and Happiness. New York: HarperCollins, 2003.

Moss, Robert. *Conscious Dreaming: A Spiritual Path for Everyday Life.* New York: Random House, 1996.

Myss, Caroline. *Sacred Contracts: Awakening your Divine Potential.* New York: Harmony Books, 2001.

——— . Archetype Cards. Hay House, 2003.

Neuharth, Dan. *If You Had Controlling Parents: How to Make Peace with Your Past and Take Your Place in the World.* New York: HarperCollins, 1999.

Read, Sir Herbert, et al, eds. R. F. C. Hull, trans. *Collected Works of C. G. Jung.* Bollingen Series XX, v, 11. "A Psychological Approach to the Trinity." New York: Princeton UP, 1969.

von Franz, Marie-Louise. *The Classic Jungian and the Classic Jungian Tradition.* Toronto: Inner City Books, 2008.

——— . *C. G. Jung: His Myth in Our Time.* Toronto: Inner City Books, 1998.

Watts, Alan W. *Myth and Ritual in Christianity*. Boston: Beacon Press, 1968.

———. *The Wisdom of Insecurity: A Message for an Age of Anxiety*. New York: Vintage Books, 1951.

Whitmont, Edward C. *The Symbolic Quest*. New York: Princeton UP, 1978.

Wilhelm /Baynes (trans). *The I Ching* (or *Book of Changes*). Bollingen Series XIX, 1950, 1967. New Jersey: Princeton University Press, 1977. Foreword by C. G. Jung.

Woodman, Marion. *Addiction to Perfection: The Still Unravished Bride*. Toronto: Inner City Books, 1982.

———. *Sitting by the Well: Bringing the Feminine to Consciousness Through Language, Dreams, and Metaphor*. Audio Series. Boulder, CO: Sounds True, 1998.

Zukav, Gary. *The Seat of the Soul*. New York: Simon and Schuster, 1995.

Please send questions and comments to
feedback@syzygy-crossingthebridgetoself.com.

1 Magician
6 of Air
18
Overall
17 of Earth